P9-BJC-334

This book
belongs to

Elizabeth George

3-in-1 Collection

A Woman's Walk with God

Beautiful in God's Eyes

Loving God with All Your Mind

HARVEST HOUSE PUBLISHERS

EUGENE, OREGON

Cover photo © Photodisc / Photodisc Blue / Getty Images

Cover by Katie Brady Design and Illustration, Eugene, Oregon

ELIZABETH GEORGE 3-IN-1 COLLECTION

Published by Harvest House Publishers
Eugene, Oregon 97402
www.harvesthousepublishers.com

ISBN-13: 978-0-7369-2185-5
ISBN-10: 0-7369-2185-0

Compilation of:

A Woman's Walk with God
Copyright © 2000 by Elizabeth George
ISBN-13: 978-0-7369-0188-8
ISBN-10: 0-7369-0188-4

Beautiful in God's Eyes
Copyright © 1998 by Elizabeth George
ISBN-13: 978-0-7369-1538-0
ISBN-10: 0-7369-1538-9

Loving God with All Your Mind
Copyright © 1994/2005 by Elizabeth George
ISBN-13: 978-0-7369-1382-9
ISBN-10: 0-7369-1382-3

Printed in the United States of America

07 08 09 10 11 12 13 14 15 / LB-SK / 12 11 10 9 8 7 6 5 4 3 2 1

A Woman's Walk with God

ELIZABETH GEORGE

HARVEST HOUSE PUBLISHERS

EUGENE, OREGON

A WOMAN'S WALK WITH GOD

Eugene, Oregon 97402

Library of Congress Cataloging-in-Publication Data
George, Elizabeth, 1944–
[God's garden of grace]
A woman's walk with God / Elizabeth George
p. cm.
Originally published: God's garden of grace. Eugene, Or.: Harvest House Publishers, ©1996.
Includes bibliographical references.
ISBN-13: 978-7369-0188-8
ISBN-10: 0-7369-0188-4
1. Christian women—Religious life. I. Title
BV4527.G459 2000
248.8'43—dc21 99-059248

For my parents
Henry and Ruth White,
whose home has always been
a rich garden of virtues.

A *Woman's Walk with God*
Growth and Study Guide is available if you'd like
to dig deeper than the Study Guide Questions
included at the end of this book.

Contents

~1~

Preparing for Greater Growth

Several years ago when I spoke at a women's retreat in Bellingham, Washington, I stayed overnight in the home of a warm and gracious couple. After parking the car in the garage behind their house, we walked through their backyard garden and right past an exquisite apple tree. Being from southern California where all we know is orange trees, I commented on how beautiful the tree was. With that, my hostess Jennifer began telling me the story of their apple tree.

Since moving into their home, Jennifer's husband, Tom, has tended this magnificent tree. Wanting to enjoy its Golden Russet apples, Tom has worked hard to improve the tree's production. After doing some research, he even grafted on some branches from their older Gravenstein apple tree as well as several new shoots from a Spartan apple tree. Through the years, Tom has nurtured, fertilized, watered, pruned, trained, sprayed, and protected this tree, and his efforts have paid off as he's seen the tree improve over time.

And that tree's yield is quite incredible. Tom has to prop up the branches to keep them from breaking when they're loaded with apples! Then, when the fruit is ripe, it's Jennifer's turn. She takes the tree's three kinds of apples and cooks, cans, mashes, sauces, dries, stews, slices, dices, and freezes them. Anything you can do with apples, she does! In fact, for dessert the evening I was there, Jennifer served apple crisp, and when I left the next morning she handed me a plastic bag full of dried apples to eat on the plane.

As I think of this couple's apple tree, I can't help but wonder about the fruit of our lives as Christian women. Should you and I as women of God pay any less attention to our own fruitfulness, in our case the spiritual kind, than Jennifer and Tom do to their apple tree? Shouldn't we be actively cultivating the fruit of the Spirit in our lives in order to reflect the glory of God and the beauty of Christ? But what exactly can you and I do to grow these spiritual fruit? What practical steps can we take toward becoming more like Christ as we walk alongside Him day by day?

Understanding the Fruit of the Spirit

Well, my friend, just as Tom studied to learn more about his apple tree and the fruit it bears, you and I need to study God's Word so we can better understand the fruit of the Holy Spirit and how it grows. Throughout the Bible, the word "fruit" refers to evidence of what is within. If what's inside a person is good, then the fruit of that person's life will be good. But if what's inside is rotten, the fruit of that person's life will be bad. Any person who has received Jesus as Savior and Lord and has Christ living within will bear good fruit—

the "fruit of righteousness" (Philippians 1:11)—as God shines forth in his or her life.

The fruit of the Spirit has been described as "those gracious habits which the Holy Spirit produces in the Christian."[1] In Galatians 5:22-23, the apostle Paul lists these "gracious habits": "The fruit of the Spirit is love, joy, peace, patience, kindness, goodness, faithfulness, gentleness, [and] self-control." I'm sure that, like me, you've undoubtedly longed for these noble traits to be characteristic of your life—but how can we make that happen? *Perhaps if I just try harder...* we may find ourselves thinking. But Jesus teaches and models that such individual, do-it-yourself effort isn't the answer. Instead, it's exciting (and comforting!) to realize that the fruit of the Spirit can be produced in our lives in the same way that it was produced in Jesus' life! We will enjoy a harvest of spirituality when we yield to God and allow His Spirit to work in us as we walk through life.

As you and I walk together through God's list of the fruit He deserves in our life, we'll look not only at their beauty and bounty but also at each individual fruit. But we must never forget that all nine fruit stand together: love, joy, peace, patience, kindness, goodness, faithfulness, gentleness, and self-control make up our walk with God. They are like a string of Christmas lights—there is one string with many lights that, when plugged into the electrical socket, all light up at once. However, if one bulb goes out, the entire string goes out. That's how God's fruit is borne in our lives. No one of them can be missing, and all must be evident to be God's fruit.

We also need to remember that because these fruit act as one, they are each borne in our lives in the same way. They are like a watch, which contains many parts. A watch can be taken apart for cleaning and repair, but each piece must be in place for the watch to run. In this book, you and I will carefully take apart each fruit of the Spirit, and then we'll see how they all work together to present a whole.

And as a whole, these characteristics are all produced in the same way. Everything that is said of one characteristic is true of the other eight. They are one and the same fruit, interwoven and related to one another, produced as we look to God.

Walking by the Spirit and cultivating the fruit of the Spirit is what this book is all about. You and I can enjoy a closer walk with God and bear much fruit as we surrender our lives to Him. As we examine each fruit of the Spirit, we'll also be looking at Jesus' life to see its expression in His life. As we follow the real-life example of God's Son, and walk in obedience, we will indeed bear fruit that glorifies our Creator and Lord.

Understanding the Problems

Before we begin learning about our walk with God, we would do well to acknowledge a couple of "stumbling stones" we'll encounter along the path. First, legalism is a problem for us Christians today just as it was for believers in Paul's day. Legalism is the careful keeping of a set of rules which exceeds what is written in Scripture (1 Corinthians 4:6). In fact, Paul wrote to the Galatians because some false teachers (called Judaizers) were teaching that, despite their faith in Christ, they must follow the Old Testament laws. This teaching ran counter to all that Jesus taught and to the fundamental truth that people come to God by faith alone. It also fostered an ugly form of legalism and religion based strictly on works. So Paul called believers to allow the Spirit of God to fulfill the Law for and through them. If they would only "walk by the Spirit" (Galatians 5:16,25), they would be abiding by the Law in a natural and beautiful way.

Another problem you and I have in common with Galatian believers, dear friend, is one we'll face until the day we die, and that is the conflict between the flesh and the Spirit which begins the instant we put our faith in Jesus Christ. Paul writes, "For the flesh sets its desire against the Spirit, and the Spirit against the flesh; for these are in opposition to one another, so that you may not do the things that you please" (Galatians 5:17). These fleshly pursuits result in "deeds of the flesh" (5:19), sins and vices which Paul lists in Galatians 5:19-21—"immorality, impurity, sensuality, idolatry, sorcery, enmities, strife, jealousy, outbursts of anger, disputes, dissensions, factions, envying, drunkenness, carousing, and things like these."

Which weaknesses are evident in your life, beloved? Ask God to help you recognize your fleshly tendencies and deeds by praying David's heartfelt words: "Search me, O God, and know my heart; try me and know my thoughts; and see if there be any wicked way in me" (Psalm 139:23-24 KJV). Then confess anything God reveals to you and submit once again to the transforming power of His Spirit. That's what walking by the Spirit is all about!

Understanding the Call to "Walk by the Spirit"

Aren't you glad that right after the ugly list of sins, Paul moves on to the fruit of the Spirit (Galatians 5:22)? In sharp contrast to the deeds of the flesh, Paul paints a lovely picture of the fruit produced in our lives as we walk by the Spirit. When you and I walk by the Spirit we "will not carry out the desire of the flesh" (5:16) and we can have victory over the flesh. But how exactly do we as Christians walk by the Spirit?

In simple terms, walking by the Spirit means living each moment in submission to God. Walking by the Spirit means seeking to please Him with the thoughts we choose to think, the words we choose to say, and the actions we choose to take. And walking by the Spirit means letting Him guide us each step of the way. It's letting Him work within us so that we can bring glory to God.

Understanding "Abiding in Christ"

Although I'll be giving you many practical suggestions for cultivating the fruit of the Spirit in our lives as we journey through this book, we must never lose sight of the fact that the Bible clearly teaches, "There is none who does good, there is not even one" (Romans 3:12). Paul himself lamented, "For I know that nothing good dwells in me, that is, in my flesh" (Romans 7:18). It is only as we walk by His Spirit that we show forth Christ in our lives. And God gives us the grace to do this as we abide in Christ.

Do you ever wonder what "abiding in Christ" means? In the eloquent allegory of John 15, Jesus says, "I am the true vine" and calls His disciples—then and now—to "abide in Me" (verse 4). Only by abiding in Him can Jesus' followers bear fruit (verses 2,4,5). This call comes as Jesus shares His final words of instruction with His small flock—words concerning His death, words of comfort and warning, words of peace and prayer. He explains that, although He will be gone, they will still have fellowship with Him if they "abide" in Him. The same opportunity exists for you and me today, my friend. To bear fruit for God's kingdom, we must abide in Christ. Such "abiding" has been defined as "continued fellowship with the Lord,"[2] "dwelling in His fellowship and being submissive to His will,"[3] and keeping "contact with Jesus…a constant contact."[4]

I'm sure you join me in wanting to abide in Christ! But what can we *do* to keep our contact with Jesus constant?

What can we *do* to abide in our Lord—to remain close to God and dwell in Him as He dwells in us? What can you and I *do* to share more of His life and experience more fully His presence in our lives? Consider these practical steps for enjoying a closer walk with Him.

Spending time in God's Word is one step we can (and should!) take daily to abide in Christ. Dr. Everett F. Harrison writes, "Abiding cannot be maintained apart from giving the words of Christ a regnant [reigning] position in the heart (cf. Colossians 3:16). He is honored when His Word is honored."[5] So we must be diligent about spending time in God's Word. Do we read, study, and meditate on a regular basis? Frequently enough? Daily? Is our time in God's Word rich and meaningful, or are we merely going through the motions? Because God's Word reveals "the thoughts of his heart to all generations" (Psalm 33:11b KJV), we are able to have sweet communion with Him when we read the Scripture. Besides, there is really no other way to know His thoughts, His ways, or His heart. Oh, pray for God to give you an insatiable appetite for rich fellowship with Him through His Word, an appetite that nothing else can satisfy!

Spending time in prayer is another act of worship that makes it possible for you and me to commune with and abide in Christ. Dr. Harrison points out that Christ "honors His Word when the saints come pleading its promises in prayer,"[6] and a saint of old states simply, "A prayerless life means a life without Christ, without faith, without work, without consistency."[7] As yet another believer has observed, "No blessing of the Christian life becomes continually possessed unless we are men and women of regular, daily, unhurried, secret lingerings in prayer."[8]

Well, dear friend, would an outside observer describe you or me as a person of "regular, daily, unhurried, secret lingerings in prayer"? Is prayer a vital link between us and God—who is our solace and our strength? Do we seek to know more about God, His heart, and His purposes through the holy communion of prayer? If you and I are to abide in Christ and be women who walk with God, we must do all we can to enhance our prayer life.

Obeying God's commands also enhances our abiding in Christ. Therefore, our waking prayer each morning should be to make choices that honor Him and His Word. In John 15:10, Jesus teaches that such obedience was an essential part of His own constant communion with the Father: "If you keep My commandments, you will abide in My love, just as *I* have kept my Father's commandments, and abide in His love" (emphasis added). In keeping His Father's commandments Jesus stayed close to His Father, modeling for us obedience to our heavenly Father.

It's a paradox, beloved. It is *as* we walk by the Spirit—abiding in Christ and obeying God's commands—that the *Holy Spirit* produces *His* fruit in our life. Theologian John F. MacArthur comments on this paradox in the Christian life: "Although we are commanded to exhibit spiritual fruit, it can never be produced except by yielding to the Holy Spirit."[9] You see, the fruit that results in our life *because* of our obedience is evidence of the *Spirit* at work *in* us. We can do nothing strictly on our own to bring about that fruit. But as God's will increasingly becomes our highest aim, our tarnished lives are transformed by the Holy Spirit into a glittering trophy of grace which points the world to Him.

Renewing our commitment to Christ seems appropriate here as we prepare for greater growth. Before anything—or anyone—can grow, it must be alive. Therefore you and I need to ask ourselves a simple question: Am I alive spiritually?

In the Book of Romans, we read that "all have sinned" (3:23); that "the wages of sin is death" (6:23); and that "God demonstrates His own love toward us, in that while we were yet sinners, Christ died for us" (5:8). Jesus took on our sin, dear one, and died in our place. Have you accepted that wondrous truth and named Jesus *your* Savior and the Lord of *your* life? As the Bible instructs us, "If you confess with your mouth Jesus as Lord, and believe in your heart that God raised Him from the dead, you shall be saved" (Romans 10:9). Before you can experience any spiritual growth, this seed of faith in Jesus must take root in your heart and life.

So are you alive? Only three answers are possible—"yes," "no," and "I'm not sure." If you answered "no"—if you have not accepted Jesus as Lord and Savior—you can set foot on the path of walking with God and growing in Him right now by earnestly praying these words:

> Jesus, I know I am a sinner, but I want to repent of my sins and turn and follow You. I believe that You died for my sins and rose again victorious over the power of sin and death, and I want to accept You as my personal Savior. Come into my life, Lord Jesus, and help me obey You from this day forward.

If you aren't sure if the seed of faith has taken root in your heart, you may want to say a prayer of *re*commitment. You could pray these words:

> Jesus, I know that in the past I asked You into my life. I thought at that time that I was Your child, but my life hasn't shown the fruit of my belief. As I again hear Your call, I want to make a real commitment to You as the Lord and Master of my life.

Or perhaps the following prayer better fits your circumstances:

> Dear Lord Jesus, I know that in the past I asked You into my life. I want to be Your child, I think and hope that I am Your child, but I want to know that I am Your child. Lord, give me the reassurance that I have eternal life through You because of Your death on the cross for my sin (1 John 5:13).

Beloved, if you're not sure where you stand with God, let Him know right now in a very personal prayer. After all, God loves you, and He already knows your heart, and He wants to be in close fellowship with you.

Finally, if you answered—or can now answer—"Yes! I know I am alive in Christ now and forever!" take a few moments to thank God and praise Him for all that Jesus has done for you. Commit yourself anew to walking the path of greater growth in God's grace. The following lyrics may help you worship:

> You paid much too high a price for me;
> Your tears, your blood, the pain;
> To have my soul just stirred at times,
> Yet, never truly changed.
> You deserve a fiery love that won't ignore your sacrifice,
> Because you paid much too high a price.[10]

It's the prayer of my heart—for myself and for you—that God would use this book to prompt us to grow in God's grace so that we are "truly changed." May we be moved to give ourselves wholly to Christ. And may we seek nothing other than to follow Him and to exhibit the radiance of the Savior in us as we walk with God. After all, "the world has yet to see what God can do with and for and through and in a man [or woman] who is fully and wholly consecrated to Him."[11]

Section I

Attitudes OF THE *Fruit* OF THE SPIRIT

~ 2 ~

Looking to God for Love

The fruit of the Spirit is love.
GALATIANS 5:22

On June 11, 1994, our younger daughter Courtney was married to Paul Seitz in a lovely ceremony at our home church. As I sat on the front pew, the mother-of-the-bride for the first time, I was awed by the sights and sounds that filled the chapel. They were the product of a whirlwind of busyness on the part of the bride and groom's families and friends. The bouquets of off-white rosebuds and ivy had been arranged by one of Courtney's college friends, and a friend of the family was taking pictures. My fellow choir members were helping with the music—a prelude of hymns on the organ, chimes at precisely two o'clock, and a trumpet to herald Courtney's entrance. Longtime friends had decorated the front platform with green foliage, white blossoms, and trailing ivy from their garden at home. The setting was picture perfect!

One of the greatest pleasures for me that day was having so many family members at the wedding. On the George side of the aisle were my three brothers and their wives, my parents, and my mother-in-law. On the other side of the aisle were Paul's mother and a sister-in-law. Paul stood at the front of the church with his father, two brothers, and brother-in-law. I thanked God for the blessing of a caring family who wanted to share this special event with Courtney and Paul.

All day long I had felt like a cast member in a school play. I had a role to play and I busily went about my duties—until my older daughter Katherine walked down the aisle. She was the last of the bridesmaids, her sister's maid of honor. Suddenly the wedding and its accompanying emotions became very real!

Then I heard the trumpet announce Courtney's arrival. I rose and turned to see standing at the back of the church my wonderful husband Jim with a radiant and confident Courtney on his arm. The moment we'd all been planning for so long was here. Jim's eyes were moist as he escorted his daughter, and Courtney was strong and regal in the classic gown Paul's mother had lovingly made. As the two of them slowly marched down the aisle, I thought about the fact that a whole new life lay before Paul and Courtney.

Now it was time for the ceremony itself, the moment of eternal significance for which all the busyness served only as a humble prelude. As an ordained minister, Jim officiated the wedding and presided over their vows as no one else could have. With the authority of a minister and the love of a father, he summoned the young couple to make a sober commitment, before God and all the people gathered, to love one another for the rest of their days. As I sat sniffling, I heard Jim call upon Courtney and her new husband to love one another with Christ's love.

Yes, I thought, that's what God intends this wedding and all of life to be about—Christian love. His design calls for a bride and groom who love to become a husband and wife who love and, in turn, parents and grandparents who love. He wants His love reflected in brothers and sisters who love, uncles and aunts who love, families who love, and friends who love. I again thanked God for the many evidences of His love that were before my eyes and filling my life that special day.

Learning About Love

We can't read very far in the New Testament without realizing that love is important to God. He calls us as women who love God...

- to walk in love (Ephesians 5:2)
- to love one another (John 15:12)
- to love our husbands and our children (Titus 2:4)
- to love our neighbor (Matthew 22:39)
- to love our enemies (Luke 6:27)

Scripture also teaches that "God *is* love" (1 John 4:8, emphasis added) and that His Son Jesus Christ loved us and "gave Himself up for us [as] an offering" (Ephesians 5:2). We also see love's supremacy when Paul places it first on his list of the fruit of the Spirit (Galatians 5:22).

As children of God, you and I, dear one, are commanded to show forth the kind of love we see modeled by our heavenly Father and His Son. Jesus says very clearly, "This is My commandment, that you love one another; just as I have loved you" (John 15:12). And exactly how has Jesus loved us? And what does the kind of love we're supposed to extend to people look like? We find answers to these questions when we turn to God and His Word. After all, God is love and God is the source of all love, so it makes sense to look to the Scriptures to learn what *He* says about love! Let's look now at five basic principles from God's Word that can help us to understand Christian love.

Principle #1: Love is an act of the will. Every fruit of the Spirit requires decisions, and love is no different. It's hard to love under difficult circumstances, yet that's exactly where most of life is lived, isn't it? I don't know about you, but I especially need love when I'm tired, when I'm suffering in some way, when I'm hurting, or when I'm feeling burdened down. At difficult times like these, I usually don't feel up to loving other people. That's when—I'm learning—it's necessary to activate the will if I am to follow through with actions of love. Commentator William Barclay points out that love "is...a feeling of the mind as much as of the heart; it concerns the will as much as the emotions. It describes the deliberate effort—which we can make only with the help of God...."[1] Christian love, you see, is an act of the will which "needs to be directly cultivated."[2]

Yes, the kind of love Christ modeled calls for deliberate decisions and a conscious effort. His love *in* us is what enables us to give that love when we want to withhold; to reach out to others when we are tired and want to rest; to serve when we want to be served; and to help others when we ourselves are hurting. No wonder Dr. George Sweeting wrote, "Love is work. It demands both conscious and unconscious effort. It demands a continuous, twenty-four-hour-a-day commitment."[3] This kind of love, of course, comes only from God, which is why you and I so desperately need His grace to give it!

For a better understanding of love consider the acts of the will behind the love of God and Jesus revealed in the Bible:

- God so loved the world, that He *gave* His only begotten Son (John 3:16, emphasis added);
- The Son of Man did not come to be served, but *to serve,* and *to give* His life (Matthew 20:28, emphasis added);
- Jesus "*resolutely* set His face to go to Jerusalem" (Luke 9:51, emphasis added) where He would die for us.

Giving, serving, heading for Jerusalem, dying on a cross—these acts of love are acts of the will, not gestures prompted and powered by mere emotion. It is God who gives us the will to love and the ability to act according to our decisions to love in the ways He calls us to love. Will you look to Him to fill you with the kind of love that gave, served, and died to self, the kind of love modeled by our Savior? This, dear one, is one way we walk with God!

Principle #2: Love is action—not just words. Love is also something we *do,* not merely the words that we *say.* Yet acting on our love is not always easy—as a wife knows who pulls into the driveway at 5:30 PM followed closely by her husband! Both of them have put in a long day at the office, so…*who* is going to fix the meal, wash the dishes, and do the laundry? Love means that, even when you and I are exhausted and just want to sit down and do nothing, we cook, serve, and wash. You see, love has work to do, and love does that work—love takes action—even when doing so requires strenuous effort. Our actions—backing up our words—are the proof of our love. That is why we are called to love not with word or with tongue only, but "in deed and truth" (1 John 3:18). I'm sure that Courtney is continuing to discover what the *words* of her marriage vows mean as she daily lives them out through *works* of love performed, with God's help, for Paul. I'm also sure that she's learning she has to look to God to enable her to extend to her husband (and all the other people in her life) this kind of serving love.

And now, my dear friend, where has God placed *you* to show forth love by your actions? Using a phrase from author, wife, mother, homemaker, and grandmother Edith Schaeffer, to whom can *you* demonstrate love "in the day-by-day, mundane circumstances of life"?[4] Every family member provides you with an opportunity to put on the work clothes of love and to serve. If you go daily to a job, love has work to do there as well. If you live with roommates, roll up your sleeves and challenge yourself to do the work of love. In your neighborhood, your volunteer activities, your church, your places of recreation, you are to show forth God's love not only by words and attitudes but by your actions. And God's Spirit, at work in *you,* will cause the glorious fruit of love to blossom in your life as you walk with Him and do His work of love.

Principle #3: Love reaches out to the unlovely. Don't you find it easy to love gracious individuals, mature Christians, and people who say, "Thank you!" when you do something nice? Yes, it's easy to love the lovely, but it's much harder to love the unlovely! I know that people who are cruel, hateful, or unappreciative present a tremendous challenge for me when it comes to loving them.

Yet this is exactly what Jesus calls us to do as women who love Him. In the Sermon on the Mount, He shocked His listeners by saying, "You have heard that it was said, 'You shall love your neighbor, and hate your enemy.' But I say to you, love your enemies, and pray for those who persecute you in order that you may be sons of your Father who is in heaven; for He causes His sun to rise on the evil and the good, and sends rain on the righteous and the unrighteous" (Matthew 5:43-45). Jesus then reminded His hearers that anyone—even those who do not believe in God or follow Christ—can love the lovely: "If you love those who love you," Jesus continued, "what reward have you? Do not even the tax-gatherers do the same? And if you greet your brothers only, what do you do more than others? Do not even the Gentiles do the same?" (verses 46-47). In a parallel account in the Gospel of Luke, Jesus said, "If you love those who love you, what credit is that to you? For even sinners love those who love them. And if you do good to those who do good to you, what credit is that to you? For even sinners do the same" (6:32-33).

Do you see that God's kind of love calls us to love the unlovely just as He Himself does when, for instance, He loves each one of us? God's love is never deserved—it simply *is*. And that's the kind of love you and I are to extend to one another, enemy as well as friend, the unlovely as well as the lovely. Thank God that when the Spirit is at work in our lives, He enables us to do what Jesus commands us to do: "Love your enemies and do good...and you will be sons of the Most High; for He Himself is kind to ungrateful and evil men" (Luke 6:35).

Who in your world falls into the "unlovely" category? Who is irritating, bothersome, ungrateful, or even evil and unrighteous? Who is it that makes your life difficult and brings you misery and heartache? Each one of these people is to be the object of your love. After all, as author Jerry Bridges points out, "To recognize that there is someone I do not love is to say to God, 'I do not love You enough to love that person.' "[5] Through His Spirit, God provides the grace we need to extend His love to the needy people we encounter. Through His

Spirit, God enables us to love just as He loves—everyone…all the time…and without conditions.

Principle #4: We need God to help us love. Just as you and I need God's help for each of the fruits of the Spirit, we rely on God for love. In the Sermon on the Mount, Jesus observed that it is quite natural to love those who love us, but it transcends the laws of nature to love those who hate us. Left only to our natural ways, we would hate our enemies. But Christ calls us to love our enemies by allowing God to love them through us when we can't do it on our own.

William Barclay writes, "[Love] means that no matter what a man may do to us by way of insult or injury or humiliation we will never seek anything else but his highest good…never… seek anything but the best even for those who seek the worst for us."[6] Clearly, we need God to help us love those who hate us! And, when we walk with God and love the unlovely with His love, we become a testimony to what He can do in a person's life. Our life then bears the mark of God because only He can enable us to serve the very person who insults, snubs, or hurts us. In fact, such injury makes us far more dependent on God as we seek to obey His command and love the unlovely.

I recently read about Bishop Whipple of Minnesota, a missionary known as "The Apostle to the Indians." In talking about his life work, he said that for thirty years he simply tried to see the face of Christ in the faces of the Indians he ministered to—to love them for Christ's sake.[7] Do you seek to love the difficult, ungrateful, unkind, unlovely people in your world for Christ's sake? If you can see Jesus in the person who causes you pain, you will—by the power of the Holy Spirit—be able to extend God's love to that person (Romans 5:5). God's love is there for us to give, and we who follow

Christ need to remember that those who are hardest to love are the ones who need it most.

Principle #5: Love expects nothing in return. Isn't it true that when we are nice to someone, we expect that person to be nice to us? And when we are loving toward someone, we expect that same kind of treatment in return? But when Jesus calls us to love our enemies and do good to them, He tells us to do good to them "expecting nothing in return" (Luke 6:35). When we love as God loves and, like Him, are "kind to ungrateful and evil men" (Luke 6:35), we find we need to love without any thought of personal reward.

And, as a question wives often ask me reveals, we may find that ungrateful person in our own home! "Liz," I hear, "I've been serving my husband, but he isn't doing anything in return. I'm doing all I can to show him that I love him, but I feel totally unappreciated and even taken advantage of. Should I stop making an effort to serve him?" Maybe you've had similar feelings. What *does* a wife do in a situation like this?

Even—if not especially!—in our own home, we need God's Spirit to be at work in us if we are to truly love as Christ would have us love. It helps both of us to remember that God is kind to ungrateful men (Luke 6:35). And don't forget—this is the kind of love God offers to us in Jesus (Romans 5:8,10)! So, when you and I serve our husbands (or anyone else), we are to serve simply because God lives in us and wants to extend His love to all people through us (Romans 5:5).

And here's another thought from God's Word to help us: We are to love and serve as if the person before us were Jesus Himself! In John 13:34, Jesus Himself says, "A new commandment I give to you, that you love one another, even as I have loved you." And isn't that what Ephesians 5:22

means—"Wives, be subject to your own husbands, as to the Lord"? The Amplified Bible reads, "Wives, be subject...to your own husbands as [a service] to the Lord."[8] In the same passage, husbands are also called to love their wives "just as Christ also loved the church and gave Himself up for her" (verse 25). You see, the love the Bible tells us to extend in our marriage, our home, our neighborhood, our church, and the world at large is *not* self-seeking. Instead, it expects nothing personal in return. Its only intent is to love as Jesus loved while praying for others to respond to God's message of love through us.

Defining Love

As these five principles of biblical love clearly reveal, love is *the sacrifice of self*. This simple definition seems to crystalize all that the Bible teaches about love. Dr. John MacArthur elaborates: "Love is not an emotion. It is an act of self-sacrifice. It is not necessarily feeling loving toward a particular person. It may not have any emotion connected with it (Romans 5:8). God always defines biblical love in terms of self-sacrifice."[9] It's obvious that since love is the sacrifice of self, it involves effort, not merely emotion. It demands action, not just feelings. It is something we do, not something we only feel or say.

I well remember learning as a young mother that love is sacrifice. Katherine, our first baby, was every mother's dream. She was smiling and responsive. She loved people and she loved being held. Since she was so easy to care for and so much fun to be with, we took her everywhere we went. But Courtney, our second baby, had colic from day one! For the first six months of her little life, she screamed and writhed in pain. Red-faced and uncomfortable, she was completely unresponsive to any acts of love on our part. Some days it wasn't easy to live under the same roof with her!

Courtney was indeed a challenge for me. Yet I kept caring for her, loving her, doing all the acts a loving mother could do—feeding her, holding her, rocking her, and bathing her as she fought and screamed. And not only were our days long, but so were our nights. Sleep came for Courtney—and therefore for us—only as a result of her being exhausted. I certainly didn't *feel* love for her, but—by the grace of God—I *gave* love. It was a time for me to offer the sacrifice of self, to choose to do the works of love and extend love to a not-so-lovely-to-be-with baby without getting anything positive in return. Then, one wonderful day, Courtney relaxed and smiled, and she has been a sweetheart ever since! With the end of colic and Courtney's change of behavior, I continued to love her in a mother's sacrificial way as I had before, but, I have to admit, the sacrifice was then much more rewarding!

And you, dear one? How are you doing when it comes to loving sacrificially? When you and I go before the Lord in prayer, He will help us and show us where we tend to be selfish and where He'd like us to love more sacrificially. He will remind us that we are to obey God as we walk with Him and love one another...even when we don't feel like doing so! And He will help us recognize opportunities to move beyond speaking words of love to doing the actual work of love. As we look to God's Spirit to empower us to give this kind of sacrificial love, may we pray along with St. Francis of Assisi, "O Divine Master, grant that I may not so much seek to be loved...as to love."

Living Out Love

It helps me as a Christian woman who loves God and yearns for a closer walk with Him to see my call to live out love as an assignment from God to love anyone and everyone He chooses to place in my path. Maybe this story about something I do at my house every day will help you to live out love.

Beside my front door at home I've planted some impatiens. This means that the first thing I see every morning when I open my door to go for my walk are these sad, drooping, thirsty flowers slumped over on the porch. In fact, I have to be careful when I open the door or I'll step on them and crush them!

Now I've been trying to grow impatiens for a long time. I've planted them every year with no success—until these few plants, which were leftovers stuck randomly into the ground at the last minute several years ago. Yet they are the only impatiens that have ever made it. Because of where they are—by the doorstep—they don't receive any water from the sprinklers. So every day I must get my watering bucket, go over to the faucet, fill up the bucket, and carry water to these poor little flowers. After all, if they don't get water, they'll die.

Some days I enjoy this little chore and delight in watering my impatiens. On other days, however, I feel irritated: "Why can't you grow and thrive like my other flowers do?" Or, resenting them and the extra effort they demand, I want to yank them up and toss them into the trash can—especially on those mornings when the green barrel is out by the curb and very convenient! In my tiredness, I don't want to take the extra time or put forth the extra energy to water them. I'd rather give up on them and just let them die. On my rebellious, selfish days, I say, "I don't need this! My life would be easier without these flowers!"

But through the years I've kept up my "bucket brigade." I know that if I don't fill my bucket at the faucet and give my impatiens life-giving water, they will die. So I water them every morning before I go on my walk. The only other time

I step out my front door is to get the mail in the afternoon. And, miracle of miracles, as I open the door, these perky, pretty impatiens are smiling up at me! As I look down at them, I'm glad I watered them. No, I didn't necessarily *feel* like doing it, but I did it anyway: I acted on my will, not my feelings. I made the decision and put forth the effort to give the flowers water and keep them alive.

Tending to impatiens has shown me (and I hope you, too!) one way you and I can view the challenge of loving the people God places in our path. We may not necessarily *feel* like loving them, but when you and I allow God to fill us up with *His* life-giving love, we can then carry *His* love to others and pour it out into their lives. The love is not ours—it's God's. But when we present our empty selves to the *Source* of love and are filled by *Him,* then we are able to share *His* love with thirsty people. When we act on our will instead of our feelings, make the decision to love, and put forth the effort to love, God is able to pass on *His* love to others through us.

And if, for example, I am to love my husband the way I want to love him, I need to be filled by God's love every day. I must choose to go to God and present my empty self to Him. Then when He fills me with His love, I am then able to go back to Jim and pour out God's love on Jim. My bucket brigade goes on all day long, for Katherine and Courtney too, and for anyone else God allows to cross my path.

And I confess—I have my hard days! But on the hard days, when I frequently run dry, I go back to God many times so that He can fill me again and again with His love for the people I encounter. When, for instance, I offer a friendly greeting to a woman who doesn't respond, my flesh says, "Well, if that's what I get for being nice, forget it!" But I know that is exactly when I need to run to God and have Him fill me afresh with His love for that woman so I can share it with her. She is someone God wants to show His love to, and I can let Him do so through me. I can let myself be the vessel that carries His love to her.

At times, the love God fills me with in the morning seems bountiful and unlimited, and I can share His love until the sun goes down. But then come those days—those *hard* days!—when I seem to be beating a path back to God minute after minute. Maybe the task is harder, maybe the heart of the person I'm trying to love is harder, maybe my own heart is harder, or maybe I'm not spending enough time with Him to receive what I need to share—I don't know. I do know, though, that only as I keep turning to God can I keep loving the people He places in my path.

Once again, it's God's love, but I'm the empty vessel. It's His "water" that fills me...if I let Him. And, unlike me with my bucket for the impatiens, God *always* wants to fill me. *And* He will do so as many times as I need Him to in the course of a day...and throughout my life. After all, He is the One "who gives to all men generously and without reproach" (James 1:5). He is limitless love, and He is willing and patient as He fills us with His love to share with others. Then, between the two of us, God and I can get the job of loving done!

I hope and pray that this illustration from my daily life helps you, too, dear one, to look to God for His love...and then to live out that love.

Love Lived Out by Ruth

I love looking to the Bible for examples of women who walked with God. And I think that in Ruth we have an example of sacrificial love in the many ways she lived out God's love for a hard-to-love woman, her mother-in-law, Naomi.

Ten years before the story begins, Naomi had moved to Moab from Bethlehem with her husband and two sons. The Bible says, she "went out full" (Ruth 1:21). Then, while they lived in Moab, her sons married and Naomi's family grew to include two daughters-in-law, Orpah and Ruth. But, as Naomi explained to her friends when she returned to Bethlehem after the death of her husband and two sons, "the Lord has brought me back empty" (1:21). Orpah had chosen to stay in Moab, so Naomi returned to Bethlehem alone, except for Ruth. As people welcomed her, she said to them, "Do not call me Naomi [which means "pleasant"]; call me Mara [which means "bitter"]" (verse 20).

Now living in Bethlehem with Naomi, Ruth had the opportunity to live out God's love for her mother-in-law. She rolled up the sleeves of her robe and went to work loving this hurting, dried-up, bitter woman. During harvest season, she served Naomi by gleaning in the barley fields (2:23). Ruth provided for her mother-in-law and herself through the back-breaking labor of the "barley brigade." Every morning as the sun rose, Ruth went out into the fields to glean the barley that had been left uncut by the reapers for the poor and needy. (As widows, she and Naomi certainly qualified!) But merely gathering the grain didn't make it useful. So, after carrying the grain in the skirts of her robe all day long, a tired Ruth then had to beat the barley with a stick to separate the grain from the chaff until it was usable (2:17). Morning after morning, until the harvest was over, Ruth rose early before daybreak to get barley from the fields; and evening after evening she returned after dark to Naomi with a basket of grain and, figuratively speaking, a bucket of love. Ruth sacrificed herself and allowed God to provide for Naomi through her.

Beloved, is it possible that you know a Mara—someone God has put in your life (and perhaps even in your own family) who feels "empty" but who is actually filled with bitterness, heartache, and pain? Loving that person will mean turning to God each day, looking to Him to be your source of love, and going to Him—perhaps quite often!—for a fresh filling of His love. Loving that person will require the sacrifice of self.

Love Lived Out in You

One way we walk in love—God's love—is to look to Him to fill us with His love…the kind of love that we've been learning is an act of the will, that takes action rather than being content with mere words, that extends itself to the unlovely, that gives for the sake of loving, and that involves the sacrifice of self. Most important of all, you and I need God to help us love, and I have an assignment for you which will demonstrate God's ability to help you love the way He wants you to love: Pick the person God has placed in your life who is most difficult to love and put these principles of love into action. Then watch what happens in your heart *and* in the life of that person!

As you consider this assignment and all that you've read about in this chapter, be sure and spend some time praying to the God of love. Confess to Him all your unlovely thoughts about this unlovely person, any attitudes toward him or her that are contrary to God's loving ways, and any past failures to love him or her through your actions or your words. Ask God to enable you to follow His Son's commands to "love your enemies, do good to those who hate you, bless those who curse you, pray for those who mistreat you" (Luke 6:27-28). As we've learned, God wants to do that for you. You just need to open yourself up to receive from Him His endless supply of life-giving, life-changing love.

Things to Do Today to Walk in Love

1. Begin loving the people God puts in your path by first loving those people at home. As the saying goes, "What you are at home is what you are!" So *be* a woman who walks in God's love…at home.

2. Go to God throughout the day for a fresh supply of His love to share. At the first hint of waning love, look to the Lord of love.

3. Remember that your assignment is to serve (Galatians 5:13).

4. Remember Jesus, who "did not come to be served, but to *serve,* and to *give* His life a ransom for many" (Matthew 20:28, emphasis added).

~ 3~

Offering the Sacrifice of Joy

The fruit of the Spirit is…joy.
GALATIANS 5:22

One year on a beautiful autumn Sunday, Jim and I drove to a church in central California so that he could conduct an ordination service for one of his former students from The Masters Seminary. At lunch after the morning ceremony, we learned that we were only 45 minutes away from Sequoia National Park. So, when lunch was over and we were back in the car, Jim suggested that we drive through the park to see the fall leaves.

Well, off we went! Driving to and through the park, we enjoyed the spectacular colors and God's striking handiwork. However, as the shadows lengthened in the afternoon and the temperature dropped, we began to look for a place to warm ourselves with some hot coffee. Eventually we found the one lodge that hadn't yet closed for the winter. After parking the car, Jim and I walked along the trail toward the rustic stone building. As we crossed over a little bridge, we stopped and looked at the brook that flowed beneath it and sounded so pleasant and refreshing. Peering over the rail, we were surprised to discover the cause of the water's sweet sound. We saw piles of large, jagged rocks that were impeding the water's surface, even redirecting its path. Nevertheless, the little brook gave forth utterly joyful sounds! Both Jim and I marveled that something so traumatic could cause something so lovely!

Yet isn't this stream a picture of what real life is like—or at least of what the Christian life should be like? Our lives are filled with disappointments, crises, tragedies, heartaches, affliction, and struggles—just as Jesus said (John 16:33)! But the good news is, that as you and I encounter disquieting rocks that impede *our* progress, disturb *our* tranquility, break the surface, and redirect *our* path, God can give us the joy we need to produce sounds of praise to Him.

Beloved, Jesus desired that our joy might be full (John 16:24), but affliction, loss, stress, and pain can too easily rob us of any sense of joy. But, when we turn our gaze upon God in the midst of our suffering, we suddenly find the power we need to praise Him despite the pain and to give thanks for His goodness...even when things are not so good. Thanks to the working of His Spirit in us, you and I can experience joy that transcends circumstances and transforms something traumatic into something truly lovely.

What the Bible Says About Joy

Every year at The Logos Bible Institute, it's my privilege to take a class of women through the Book of Philippians, Paul's sparkling little epistle of joy. When I first prepared my lectures for the course, I was struck by the Bible's many references to joy, the next grace on Paul's list of the fruit of the Spirit. What do we learn about joy from the Bible, especially from the more than 70 New Testament references to joy?

First, we see that *joy is important to Jesus*. At the Passover meal He shared with His disciples shortly before His crucifixion, Jesus described the special relationship He would have with His disciples if they would abide in Him and His love. He closed this section of His teaching by saying, "These things I have spoken to you, that My *joy* may be in you, and that your *joy* may be made full" (John 15:11, emphasis added). Jesus wanted his disciples to know the joy of fellowship with Him, joy to the fullest!

Next, we see that genuine joy—which is rooted in Christ—*is an expression of godliness*. You see, joy is a sure sign of the presence of God in our lives. Put differently, our joy is "the joy of God passing through a Christian,"[1] "a joy whose foundation is God."[2] Although joy is basic to godliness, it often seems to be missing from our lives despite the fact that, as children of God, we have some great reasons to be joyful.

Reason #1—Our joy is permanent. Because our joy is rooted in our all-loving and unchanging God, our joy is permanent. In John 16:22 Jesus says that "no one takes your joy away from you." However, one thing that can rob us of the joy God provides is our failure to walk by the Spirit (Galatians 5:16). The Holy Spirit causes this fruit to grow in our lives *as* we abide in Christ and walk in obedience to His ways.

Reason #2—Our joy is always available. Since it is rooted in our faithful and ever-present God, our joy is always available. That's why you and I can "rejoice in the Lord always" (Philippians 4:4)! Whatever the circumstances of our life, we have ready access to the Source of true joy anytime we turn to Him.

Reason #3—Our joy is also inexpressible (1 Peter 1:8). Joy in the Spirit is "joy beyond speech."[3] Described as "a foretaste of the joy of heaven,"[4] Christian joy cannot be fully expressed or articulated.[5] We can't explain why we experience joy when nothing in our life suggests we should be joyful.

I hope you understand now why we must acknowledge that true spiritual joy is *not* happiness. "Happiness" is a state of good fortune and prosperity related to and dependent on our circumstances. If all is going well, we are happy; but as soon as some dark cloud or irritation enters our life, our happiness vanishes. Happiness can be a false joy and, since easy circumstances are not life's norm (John 16:33), happiness is elusive. In fact, the apostle Paul preached the truth that "all who desire to live godly in Christ Jesus will be persecuted" (2 Timothy 3:12). God's joy is a gift of grace to us as we encounter the hardship and tribulation and persecution of life in this world, and this supernatural joy, given through God's Spirit, transcends all conditions of life.

As God's children through the new birth, you and I are able to drink deeply from God's unending stream of joy—regardless of what life offers us! Pause now and praise God that our joy as Christians...

- Is not dependent on circumstances, but on the spiritual realities of God's goodness, His unconditional love for us, and His ultimate victory over sin and darkness.
- Is not based on our efforts, accomplishments, or willpower, but rather on the truth about our relationship with the Father through the Son.
- Is not merely an emotion, but the result of choosing to look beyond what appears to be true in our life to what is true about our life in Christ.

In summary, our spiritual joy is not "an experience that comes from favorable circumstances [but] is a sense of well-being that abides in the heart of the person who knows *all is well between himself and the Lord* (emphasis added).[6]

The Sources of Joy

Well, dear child of God, just as we take our empty self to God to be filled with His love, we also go to Him—the Source of true joy—when we feel empty of Christian joy. And, for five reasons, we can receive that joy inexpressible from Him.

First of all, as the psalmist knew, *God Himself* is a primary source of our joy. The psalmist reveals his aching desire to "go to the altar of God, to God my exceeding joy" (Psalm 43:4). A literal translation of this reference to God reads "to the God of the joy of my rejoicing."[7] Do you think of God as your "exceeding joy" or "the joy of your rejoicing"? Do you turn to Him, who lives in your heart, for joy? God—the only Source of true joy—wants to give you His joy. You need only to turn to Him to receive it.

Second, *God's salvation* is a great reason for joy. I'm sure you've noticed that when people explain how they became Christians, they can't help but tell their story joyfully! Isaiah, for instance, could not contain his joy when he thought about all that God had done for him. He wrote, "I will rejoice greatly in the Lord, my soul will exult in my God; for He has clothed me with garments of salvation, He has wrapped me with a robe of righteousness" (Isaiah 61:10). Because of the great price God paid to obtain our salvation through His Son's death, we are wise to regularly reflect on our salvation and what that means. Doing so in touch with the Source of joy.

Third, *God's promises* are another cause for great joy—and His promises are many. At one time, our family had a little plastic container shaped like a loaf of bread on our breakfast table. Each of the cards in that box had one promise from the Bible printed on it. Every morning one of us would close our eyes, reach over, pick a promise, and then read it as a part of our family devotions. Later that night at supper we would talk about our promise-for-the-day again and how we had seen God be true to His Word since breakfast time. Beloved, your Bible is like that plastic loaf of bread: It is filled with promises—as many (according to one calculation) as 8,000![8]

My friend Mary uses God's promises to find joy in her life of chronic illness. She writes:

> My health problem frequently robs me of joy. I often find myself in despair, depression, self-pity, and other fleshly attitudes. This week, when troubled with my affliction, I focused on the Lord. When I prayed to see the good in my pain, I recalled various promises in Scriptures. I was reminded that God is a God of comfort who comforts us in all our afflictions (2 Corinthians 1:3-4). It also helped to remember that God is in control and has a unique purpose for me (2 Timothy 1:9; Ephesians 1:11). He is using this affliction to work out His will for me—to help me be more Christlike—for my good and His glory (Romans 8:28). So I will keep on thanking Him for this [illness] daily, even though I may not fully understand the purpose behind it.

As Mary is learning, God's promises to us are a bottomless reservoir of joy which you and I can draw from at any moment by simply opening His Word and believing His promises. It's even better if you've memorized some of those promises and hidden them in your heart!

Fourth, *Christ's kingdom* is a reason for us to have joy in our lives. The fact that we who name Jesus as Savior and Lord have been welcomed into His kingdom brings great joy to the angels (Luke 15:10), and the news of souls coming to Christ should evoke joy in us as well. Such joy characterized the young church in Acts. Paul and Barnabas went from town to town describing in detail the conversion of the Gentiles, bringing great *joy* to all the brethren (Acts 15:3, emphasis added). I get a taste of this cause for joy during baptisms at my home church. Hearing each man and woman explain how God has changed their lives is truly a source of joy for me!

Finally, as we meet the challenges of life and deal with the pain that comes our way, *our future in Christ* should also bring us joy. Just like the reward we plan for ourselves to celebrate the end of a stressful season of life, we can look forward to our future in Christ—a future that holds not death, but everlasting life with God in heaven! Psalm 16:11 describes what that future will be like in the presence of God: "In Thy presence is *fullness of joy;* in Thy right hand there are *pleasures forever*" (emphasis added). Precious friend, when the trials of life seem unbearable and never-ending, you can look forward with great anticipation and assurance to your future home with God in heaven—where there shall no longer be any mourning, or crying, or pain (Revelation 21:4)—and experience deep joy despite earthly suffering.

Clearly the joy of the Lord is marvelously available to us twenty-four hours a day, every day, whatever we're dealing with! One seminary wife I know has gone back to work so that her husband can finish school. "Once when I was facing a whole day of work with many projects going," she remembers, "I was starting to feel overwhelmed and down, sorry for myself that I had to work. But God knew my ultimate desire to be fruitful, and the Holy Spirit prompted me to remember that, despite how I felt, I had access to great joy! So I ran to the Source and let God fill me with His joy until I was full."

Praise God that this fullness of joy is available to you and me, too! All we have to do is fix our focus on God—not our gloom; on the eternal—not the temporal. We experience the joy *of* the Lord when we go to Him and find our joy *in* the

Lord. True joy—spiritual joy—is found only in the things of God. You and I cultivate the fruit of joy when we ask God to keep us walking with and abiding in Him. Ask God for His grace. Ask Him to help you remember in your times of need to go to Him to be filled with His joy.

An Image for Joy

One day my daughter Katherine received an unusual phone call from a business student at her college who was making print and video catalogs of diamonds. Steve had almost everything he needed to create his catalog—the diamonds, a studio, a camera, the lights. But he needed one more thing—a pair of hands. A friend of his at The Master's College had told him, "Katherine George has the most beautiful hands I've ever seen." Well, with that recommendation, Steve phoned Katherine.

So Katherine drove to downtown Los Angeles to model diamonds for Steve's catalogs. When she arrived at the studio, Steve set up his camera and lights. Then he opened his suitcase and pulled out a piece of black velvet that was to serve as a backdrop for the diamonds. After turning on his studio lights, he removed the diamonds from his case, one by one for Katherine to model.

Instructing Katherine to slowly lift her hand up off the dark background toward the light as she modeled each ring, Steve explained, "When a diamond is placed against a dark background, the darkness makes it seem more brilliant. And, when the diamond is lifted toward a light, all of its facets are revealed and allowed to sparkle. A diamond is pretty all by itself, but putting it against a black background and lifting it up to the light enhances its radiance and glory."

Oh, my friend! What a perfect picture of joy! True spiritual joy shines brightest against the darkness of trials, tragedy, and testing! And the blacker the background, the greater the brilliance. Similarly, life's dark struggles make Christian joy more intense and our heartfelt praise more glorious. As one writer has noted, God "setteth in pain the jewel of His joy."[9]

The Sacrifice of Praise

With that image in mind, I consider *the sacrifice of praise* a slogan that is helpful in cultivating the fruit of joy. Let me explain.

When life is good, praise and thanksgiving flow automatically from my heart and lips. But when life turns black, praise and thanksgiving don't flow quite so easily! Instead, I have to deliberately choose to follow God's advice and "in everything give thanks; for this is God's will for you in Christ Jesus" (1 Thessalonians 5:18). Although I don't *feel* like praising the Lord or thanking Him, I *do* what God says, and that effort makes my praise a sacrifice. When I'd rather bask in self-pity or stay stuck in my depression, choosing to look beyond my pain makes my praise to God sacrificial. But, when I do lift such a sacrifice of praise to God out of the darkness of my trials, I find the Spirit's joy magnified in my life—just as lifting a diamond to the light against a black background enhances its brilliance!

I'm learning to offer this sacrifice of praise when I'm in pain because God calls us to be joyful...*at all times* (Philippians 4:4)! And I'm glad He gives us flesh-and-blood models in His Word. For instance, in the Old Testament, King David worships in the house of the Lord despite the aggression of his enemies. Lifting his eyes away from his predicament and looking to God his Protector, David declares that—in spite of his difficulties—"I [will] offer in His tabernacle sacrifices of joy" (Psalm 27:6 KJV).

I need God's joy—I admit it! And I (and probably you as well) most need His joy when things are black. We both need joy when we're suffering and misunderstood, when we're rejected and hated, and when we're in emotional or physical pain. But our sacrifice of praise to God gives the Spirit room to touch us with His joy that overshadows these circumstances.

It's amazing to realize that, with the sacrifice of praise, the very hindrances to our joy become the soil out of which joy blossoms. Suffering, infirmities, affliction, pain, and loss create in us the need to go to God to receive His joy. Deprivation, stress, and the demands of life—a heavy schedule, a multitude of responsibilities—compel us to go to the Father. The Spirit uses our pain, sorrow, and grief to prompt us to lift before God a sacrifice of praise. Thus, we come in touch with the unshakable joy of the Lord!

And you, beloved? I know I've shared from my own life and struggles, but whatever your current circumstances, there's no better time than now for a prayer of praise to your loving and understanding Father. Why not allow the sweet aroma of your sacrifice to drift heavenward and God's gentle presence to comfort your soul? Allow your prayer to impress on you a greater awareness of His presence. You, too, can know fullness of joy in Him.

The Sounds of Joy

It's a well-known fact that the wife of preacher C.H. Spurgeon, Susannah Spurgeon, suffered from physical disabilities that grew progressively worse year by year. Finally she reached the point where she could no longer make the transatlantic journey with her husband by ship. Then, not only did she have to endure her painful affliction, but she also had to deal with Dr. Spurgeon's absence for six to nine months at a time. Read here what she wrote one dark, cold, lonely evening when she was sitting alone (it seemed she was always alone now) beside her fire:

> The fire was letting loose the imprisoned music from the old oak's inmost heart. [As] the fierce tongues of the flames came to consume [the log's hardened] callousness...the fire wrung from him a song and a sacrifice.
>
> Oh! Thought I, when the fire of affliction draws songs of praise from us, then indeed...our God is glorified!... We [would] give forth no melodious sounds were it not for the fire which kindles round us and releases tender notes of trust in Him....Singing in the fire!...Let the furnace be heated seven times hotter than before![10]

Yes, precious friend, joy sings in the fire. Joy glorifies God through tears and pain. Joy spurs us to give thanks for God's goodness...even when circumstances are not good! Joy prompts the offering of the sacrifice of praise...even when life gives us no apparent reason to celebrate. Are these sounds of joy pouring out of *your* heart and lips? Ask God to bless you with joy in the Lord as you walk with Him through every day, o'er all the way.

Hannah's Song of Joy

Her daily life was hard and her circumstances dark, but Hannah, another woman who walked with God, nevertheless knew the brilliant joy of the Lord. As the Book of 1 Samuel opens, we learn right away that Elkanah had two wives, Hannah and Peninnah, "and Peninnah had children, but Hannah had no children" (1:2). Year after year, Peninnah flaunted her ability to bear children before Hannah, moving her to tears and prompting her to lose her appetite.

How would you cope with Peninnah's provocation if you were Hannah? And, more realistically, how are you handling what God is doing (or not doing!) in your life right now? Hannah has much to teach us.

Hannah quietly endured her pain. First, Hannah had no children and was therefore considered a failure and social embarrassment.[11] Furthermore, each day she suffered ill treatment from the woman with whom she shared her beloved husband. Then, when Hannah went to the temple to pour out her heart to God, the high priest misread her agony as drunkenness (verse 13). Despite all this pain, we never read about words of anger or self-pity coming from Hannah's lips. She looked to the Lord rather than lashing out at her provoker or her husband.

Hannah never acted out of vengeance. We also don't hear of Hannah seeking retribution upon Peninnah or Elkanah. She didn't even ask her husband to stop Peninnah's ridicule! In fact, she didn't even tell him what was going on, a report which might have turned him against her rival.

Hannah sought God through prayer (1 Samuel 1:10-16). Instead of turning to others, Hannah turned to the Almighty, knowing that He was the *only* One who understood her difficulties and the *only* One who could do something about it. In these black days of her life, Hannah looked to God to be her source of hope and joy, lifting her problems to Him and hoping in His promises. Although she could have shared her pain with her husband, she didn't. Hannah was alone...except for God. For her, joy would come from God, and God alone!

Hannah rejoiced as she offered her son to God. As she cried out to God in prayer, Hannah vowed that, if He gave her a son, she would give him back to the Lord all the days of his life (1 Samuel 1:11). God Almighty answered her prayer and gave her Samuel. And, true to her word, Hannah then gave Him back her dear boy—probably at the tender age of three years old!

But Hannah's story doesn't end here. As this godly mother took her child to the tabernacle and prepared to say goodbye to him, she offered the sacrifice of praise along with the sacrifice of her son. Hannah prayed, "My heart rejoiceth in the Lord....I rejoice in Thy salvation" (1 Samuel 2:1 KJV). You see, the source of Hannah's joy was God—*not* a human, *not* a child, *not* a son, *not* the long-prayed-for gift God had given her.

Doesn't this sobering look at Hannah's life call for us to take a personal inventory? For instance, what is God asking you to endure as you walk oh-so-closely to Him? Is pain coming from many directions? And how are you treating the people causing or aggravating your pain? Is your spirit vengeful, your tongue angry and spiteful? Are you enduring the hardship quietly? Are you allowing these hard times to press you to prayer, to fasting, to turning daily to God's Word, to worshiping weekly with His people? Are you seeking God with all your heart, soul, strength, and mind (Luke 10:27)? Do you know that you can find joy in God? Joy in the Lord can be yours—right this moment!—as you offer up to Him the sacrifice of praise.

The Supreme Model of Joy

Jesus Himself gives us the supreme model of joy in the midst of life's dark pain. There was probably no greater source of pain in the ancient world than crucifixion on a Roman cross, but we read in Hebrews 12:2 that Jesus, "for the joy set before Him endured the cross, despising the shame." Knowing that His suffering would result in great joy, Jesus looked toward His future with the Father as He endured the excruciating pain of death on the cross. As one commentator notes, "Despite the misunderstanding, the rejection, the hatred, the pain He endured from men while incarnate among them, the Lord never lost His joy in the relationship He had with His Father. And that joy He gives to each of His followers."[12] The same wondrous joy that Jesus experienced in His darkest hours is yours and mine today. Won't you look to God for that joy? Let it help you endure your dark and pain-filled days.

Cultivating Joy

Now, my friend, what can you and I do to cultivate this fruit of joy in the Lord in our daily walk with God?

- Offer the sacrifice of praise to God continually—even when you don't feel like it (Hebrews 13:15). Through the power of the Holy Spirit, this act of thanksgiving transforms our pain into praise.
- "Consider it all joy...when you encounter various trials," writes James (1:2). As I said earlier, let the very hindrances to joy become the soil out of which joy blossoms! That happens when we let life's hard times drive us nearer to the Lord, the only Source of genuine joy and real hope.
- Give thanks in everything (1 Thessalonians 5:18). Whatever is happening—good or bad—give thanks to God for His sovereignty, His perfect timing, His perfect plan, and His unconditional love.

- Bless the Lord at all times (Psalm 34:1). Offer unceasingly the sacrifice of praise (Hebrews 13:15). The Spirit can—and will—use your praise to touch you with God's joy.
- Focus on the reality of God's promises. Every time you open your Bible, read with a marker in hand and look for powerful promises that can change your outlook to one of joy. Go a step further and memorize those verses you like best and meditate on them.
- Look up. Shift your eyes and your hopes away from your suffering and focus instead on the splendor of God (Psalm 121:1-2).
- Obey God's command to be joyful always (1 Thessalonians 5:16). As author Jerry Bridges notes, "We are not to sit around waiting for our circumstances to make us joyful. We are commanded to be joyful always...we should continually be growing in joy."[13]
- Go to God to be filled with His joy whenever you need it.

Assignment for Joy

My heart hurts as I ask this question, dear friend, knowing that until we are with the Lord there will always be suffering...but what trial is causing you the greatest grief, the sharpest pain, the deepest sorrow today? Is it a physical affliction or terminal disease, an unbelieving husband, the loss of a home or a job, the deterioration of finances or health, the breakdown of a family, the turning away of a child? Is it a disappointment, a dashed dream, a disaster or disability? Is it ridicule or persecution? A difficult season as a wife or mother, daughter or daughter-in-law? Is it a strained relationship somewhere or an unknown future as you look down the road of life? Whatever your greatest trial today, let it move you to God, compel you to offer Him a sacrifice of praise, and so enable you to be touched by Him, the only Source of true joy.

Things to Do Today to Walk in Joy

1. As we discussed previously, identify the trial that causes you the greatest grief.
2. Faithfully offer to God the sacrifice of your praise (Hebrews 13:15)...even if it is offered with tears.
3. Consider that trial a joy for what God can do in your life as a result of it (see James 1:2-4 and Romans 5:1-5).

~ 4~

Experiencing God's Peace

The fruit of the Spirit is...peace.
GALATIANS 5:22

Newspaper columnist and counselor Ann Landers receives an average of 10,000 letters each month, nearly all of them from people with problems. When asked if any one problem stands out in the mail she receives, she said the greatest problem seems to be fear—people's fear of losing their health, their wealth, and their loved ones.

The medical profession sees the same fear in people. Despite what patients themselves say, the vast majority of all chronic patients today have one common symptom. In 90 percent of these cases, the first symptom was *not* a cough or chest pain, but fear...which sooner or later manifested itself in some sort of clinical symptom.

Causes for fear surround us on every side, but as Christians, dear sister, you and I have still another built-in resource for handling these fears. That resource is the peace of God, the next fruit on Paul's list of Christian graces. And what a refreshing fruit that peace is in a mad, mad, mad, mad world! In our roller-coaster society that offers no guarantees, we who are God's children can experience His peace—no matter what is happening in our life—when we walk by His Spirit. As we are blessed with the peace of God in the midst of life's trials, we experience a new closeness to Him.

Understanding the Peace of the Lord

What exactly is this peace that God's Spirit gives? Many people think of peace as the absence of problems, as the feeling that is experienced when all is well. But the peace of the Lord is not related to circumstances at all. In fact, God's peace comes to us and endures...regardless of life's circumstances.

Our Courtney and Paul live on Kauai, Hawaii, the island which experienced the ravages of Hurricane Iniki in 1992. As Jim and I drove around the island on a recent visit, we noticed not only the remaining evidence of destruction, but also the huge warning sirens on every beach and in every town. Having just been through a 6.7 earthquake in Southern California, we could well imagine something of the fear the islanders must have felt as those sirens wailed on that fateful September day. But we could also imagine the peace they must have felt when those same devices finally sounded the all-clear signal. But, can you imagine having perfect peace when the sirens are signaling a storm or when the hurricane is actually roaring around you? That, my friend, is the kind of peace God makes available to you and me for the storms of life. Notice these truths about this peace that comes from God.

- Our peace has nothing to do with our circumstances, and everything to do with knowing we have a right relationship with God.[1]

- Our peace has nothing to do with daily challenges or crises, and everything to do with knowing that our times are in God's hands.[2]
- Our peace has nothing to do with the conditions of our life, and everything to do with knowing that God is all-sufficient.[3]
- Our peace is an inward repose[4] and serenity of soul[5] that indicates a heart at rest—regardless of our circumstances—as we place complete confidence in God minute by minute.

True spiritual peace comes with *knowing that our heavenly Father is continually with us*—and indeed He is! God is omnipresent and therefore fully aware of every detail of our life—at every moment and in every place. He knows our needs—at all times and in every situation. As Psalm 139:7-12 teaches, we can never be anyplace—from the heights of heaven to the depths of the sea—where God is not present with us and available to us. Key to our peace, then, is not the *absence* of conflict, but the *presence* of God, no matter what the conflict.[6] I have to tell you that just *writing* about God's personal and continuous presence is bringing a fresh sense of peace to my soul right this minute!

Peace also comes with *acknowledging that God will supply our every need* as well as acknowledging His constant presence. For instance, when Paul asked Jesus to remove the thorn in his flesh and Jesus said no, the apostle Paul learned the truth of Jesus' statement: "My grace is sufficient for you" (2 Corinthians 12:9). Paul learned for himself the truth he wrote in Philippians 4:19—"God [will] supply all your needs according to His riches in glory in Christ Jesus"—and, in 2 Corinthians 9:8, that "God is able to make all grace abound to you, that always having all sufficiency in everything, you may have an abundance for every good deed." Do you realize what these promises mean to you and me? They mean that we will never have a real need that God is not able to meet. What a reason for peace that truth is!

Trusting God

But to enjoy God's peace, we have to actively trust Him. Jesus stated as a fact, "In the world you have tribulation" (John 16:33). But as Christians who abide in Christ there is peace (even in tribulation!) as we rest in God's presence and trust in His promises. When you and I walk by the Spirit, our life is characterized *not* by fretting, panic, and anxiety, but by the quiet peace that comes with trusting God. In the midst of life's most difficult circumstances, the Spirit's peace will guard our hearts and our minds" (Philippians 4:7), serving as a sentinel over our thoughts and emotions...despite life's turbulence.

I think of peace as *the sacrifice of trust*. And you and I make the sacrifice of trust when we face the painful and distressing realities of our life and then choose to trust God instead of panicking or falling apart. When circumstances in my life might tempt me to panic, feel terrified, become a nervous wreck, or be filled with dread, I can choose either to give in to those feelings or to trust in God and present myself to Him to be filled with His peace. And I must make this conscious choice each and every day whenever I see storm clouds looming ahead, whenever life's confusions, bewilderments, and perplexities threaten to overwhelm. You see, I can either trust Almighty God or succumb to the emotions of the flesh. Choosing to trust God—making the sacrifice of trust—causes me to experience His peace...even in the midst of tremendous uproar. We make the sacrifice of trust and experience God's peace...

when we choose not to panic...but to rest in God's presence,
when we release our terror...and trust in God's wisdom and ways,
when we reject our nervousness...and remember that God is in control,
and when we ignore our dread...and instead accept God's dealings.

Receiving God's Peace

When we are filled with His Spirit and walking in His ways, we have instant access to "the peace of God, which surpasses all comprehension" (Philippians 4:7). And that peace which comes from God—and from Him alone—comes to us through four gifts He has given to us.

God, the Son—First of all, you and I have peace through the gift of Jesus Christ, God's Son. Seven hundred years before Jesus was born in a manger in Bethlehem, the Old Testament prophet Isaiah predicted, "For a child will be born to us, a son will be given to us...and His name will be called...Prince of Peace" (Isaiah 9:6). That name, dear sister, reflects His mission. Jesus' advent to earth accomplished our salvation. His death on Calvary gave us the gift of peace with God that comes only with forgiveness for our sins: "Having been justified by faith, we have peace with God through our Lord Jesus Christ" (Romans 5:1). Our personal peace with God comes through the work of God's Son on the cross.

God, the Father—A second gift our loving God has given us is the gift of knowing Him. In the Bible, we learn all about His promises and His faithfulness so that we may trust Him in our times of need. One of those promises is found in Isaiah 26:3: "Thou wilt keep him in perfect peace, whose mind is stayed on Thee, because he trusteth in Thee" (KJV). We certainly cannot avoid strife as we walk in the world, but we can know perfect peace in the midst of turmoil as we turn to God Himself instead of focusing on our difficulties.

God's Word—The Bible is another one of God's gifts that helps us know God by revealing His law, His ways, and His purposes. When we know and love and follow God's Word, we experience God's peace to the point that *nothing* causes us to stumble (Psalm 119:165)! When you and I embrace God's Word as our standard for living and obey His commands, we experience the peace which comes with maintaining a right relationship with God.

God, the Spirit—The Holy Spirit is our personal Helper, Teacher, and Comforter (John 14:26), and the instruction, guidance, and comfort we receive from Him are indeed gifts of peace. When we abide in Christ and walk by His Spirit, we receive this peace from God.

Clearly then, as Christians, we can look to God—the Father, the Son, and the Holy Spirit—and to God's Word for peace.

Choosing the Peace of God over Panic

It's amazing to me how many situations in ordinary life can cause panic, terror, dread, fear, or doubt. For example, considering the responsibility of providing for a family or wondering about our children's safety can cause panic. For many, the memory of abuse or the anticipation of further harm can trigger dread. Terror can come with submitting to a biopsy, facing surgery, or hearing a cancer diagnosis. Pain and death can bring about fear and doubt. Danger stirs up all these emotions—as I learned during the Northridge earthquake of 1995 and its continuing aftershocks.

Such everyday causes for fear are a part of the lives of

many women I know. My heart—and prayers—went out to the student who wrote me the following note:

> I've been contemplating having a medical test done for some pains I've had in my stomach. These past two weeks the pains have increased, so I've scheduled the test for this Friday. Because I am prone to diagnose my case and I wonder about all the things it could be, my mind becomes restless and distracted, and panic sets in.

At our weekly Bible study, another woman shared that she was struggling with fear because her husband had been laid off from his job for three months and had no work or income. She asked us to pray that she would continue to choose to rest in God's peace and in the fact that He is in complete control of their situation.

Yes, the events of everyday life can indeed cause panic, terror, dread, fear, and doubt. At such times, we definitely need God's peace; and our Savior readily gives us His peace when, in those moments, we choose to trust Him. As writer and speaker Elisabeth Elliot shares, you and I must trust God "up to the fingernail-scraping edge." Praise God that we can weather the panic-causing situations of life by trusting in Him, resting in the fact that our times are in His hands, and placing our complete confidence in His all-sufficiency!

Jesus' disciples were fortunate to witness His all-sufficiency in a situation which understandably caused them to panic. Here's what happened: After a long day of teaching, Jesus and the Twelve got into a boat to travel to the other side of the lake. Luke reports that, "as they were sailing along...a fierce gale of wind descended upon the lake, and they began to be swamped and to be in danger" (Luke 8:23). As the waves broke over the boat and began to fill it with water (Mark 4:37), Jesus was asleep! The peace of God did indeed surpass all comprehension at this point! How could Jesus sleep in such a storm? Didn't He feel the turbulence? Didn't He know He could lose His life right there in the Sea of Galilee?

While the disciples panicked, Jesus remained calm. Jesus' peace came from His knowledge that His times were in the Father's hands. You see, Jesus trusted, and therefore Jesus rested. He knew that He wasn't going to die one second before God's scheduled time and that if now was His time to die, nothing could prevent it. Abiding in the Father, Jesus had complete confidence in the power and sufficiency of God.

What a sharp contrast Jesus' response is when compared with that of His faithful (or faithless?) followers! Their panic was revealed in their wake-up call to Jesus—"Master, Master, we are perishing!" (Luke 8:24). As the wind howled and the waves crashed, Jesus said to them, "Where is your faith?" (Luke 8:25). And Jesus would probably ask this same question of you and me when we find ourselves panicking. How little the disciples then—and you and I today!—seem to trust in Jesus.

It's plain to see that you and I need to remember something that the disciples didn't: Our days are in God's hands. Our God is all-sufficient to meet our needs, and the Savior is with us every step of the way. And just as the disciples could have rested if they had trusted, we can experience the peace of God when we offer the sacrifice of trust. Panic is needless, wasted energy, and stewing, fretting, and worrying signal a failure to trust our faithful Father. But when we choose to trust God, we can have the same peace in God that Christ had in the storm at sea and in many other scenes from His life. Our Jesus, even when He was threatened with death, confronted by enemies, and walking to the cross, rested in God and always acknowledged that His times were in God's hands and that His all-sufficient Father would meet His every need.

Well, dear reader, can *you* trust God this way? Can you let Him, His Son, His Word, and His Holy Spirit be channels of peace? Will you trust in God as soon as a reason to panic arises? By turning to God at just such a moment, you allow the Holy Spirit to fill you with His peace as you walk through trying times.

Choosing the Peace of God When Pressure Mounts

Perhaps even more prevalent in our lives than reasons to panic are sources of pressure. We never seem to have enough time—pressure! We want to do well as a spouse and a parent—pressure! We are called to be good stewards of finances and effective managers of a home—pressure! Jobs, friendships, responsibilities to aging parents, health problems, and even service at church—all of these bring on pressure and too easily squeeze out the peace of God.

We can thank the Lord that as we live in the whirlwind of life and the flurry of daily demands, His peace is available to us. We don't have to live in a frazzled fashion—breathless, anxious, worried, fretful, and rushed. But how?

Do you remember when Jesus went to the home of Mary and Martha? Martha welcomed Him (and probably His twelve hungry disciples) in for dinner, but she "was distracted with all her preparations" (Luke 10:40) and soon let the mounting pressure she felt to fix the meal rob her of any peace—a fact that became quite obvious.

First, *Martha's manner* was a dead give-away. Her behavior has been described as cumbered, distracted, worried, and busy.[7] She tensely scurried about, bustling and bothered, fretting and fuming, a picture of anxiety in motion. She was literally—and breathlessly—caught up in the whirlwind of life. The cook herself was in a stew, whipping herself up into a froth. Finally, no longer able to handle the pressure, she "burst in" (verse 40, *Phillips*)[8] with a few words for Jesus!

That's when *Martha's mouth* revealed her lack of peace. "Lord, do You not care…?" she asked the Master accusingly (verse 40). Pointing the finger of blame at Mary, Martha next said, "She has left me to do all the serving alone." The bossy big sister then dared to tell the Lord what to do: "Tell her to help me." Yes, besides stirring up a meal in the kitchen, Martha certainly stirred up quite a commotion in the living room with her verbal outburst!

Martha's confusion about *her mission* also robbed her of peace. She was right to be serving Jesus, but she mistakenly thought that *serving* was her primary mission. Jesus saw the confused priorities of this well-intentioned woman and commented, "Martha, Martha, you are worried and bothered about so many things" (verse 41). In her efforts to serve God, Martha failed to remember that "man's chief end is to glorify God and enjoy Him forever."[9]

So at last we come to *Martha's mindset* and the priorities which kept her from knowing God's peace: Martha was preoccupied with details and secondary issues.[10] Her service to Jesus had degenerated into mere busywork that was removed from any devotion to Him. And this focus on service rather than on the One she was serving prompted Jesus to instruct her by pointing out that her sister Mary had chosen "the good part" (verse 42) by sitting at Jesus' feet, listening to His Word, and abiding in His presence. (Oh, how many times I myself have acted like Martha!)

Now, what can we learn from Martha's sister? First of all, Mary rested at the Lord's feet while Martha was restless. She also worshiped the Lord while Martha worried about the meal. She knew the peace of the presence of God while Martha panicked at a distance. *Mary's manner* clearly revealed a soul at rest and "the imperishable quality of a gentle and quiet spirit, which is precious in the sight of God" (1 Peter 3:4).

And *Mary's mouth* rested, too. Sitting in the presence of God Himself, she had much to learn. You see, Jesus spoke the words of life...and so Mary was quiet.

Like her sister, *Mary's mission* was also to serve, but she also understood the more important priority of worship. Wanting her relationship with Jesus to be the highest priority of her life, Mary made choices which reflected that desire. She knew when to quit serving...and start sitting.

Clearly, *Mary's mindset* was pleasing to the Lord. As Jesus said, Mary had "chosen the good part, which shall not be taken away from her" (verse 42). She had her mind set on things above, not on earthly things (Colossians 3:2). She was focused on the eternal, not the temporal (2 Corinthians 4:18).

I know Mary is definitely a model *I* need for my hurricane lifestyle and, I'm guessing, a model you need, too! And so I try to remember this picture of Mary sitting...resting... worshiping...at peace...as I plan another wedding, start the messy process of remodeling after the earthquake, face a book deadline, and juggle the continuing everyday demands of schedules, commitments, and life.

And now it's time for a closer look at your own manner, mouth, mission, and mindset. What would an outside observer see in you right now—a Martha or a Mary? Are you in turmoil, or are you trusting and at peace? Are you running around in circles, or are you resting in the Lord? Are your words revealing a sense of panic and pressure, or are they words that edify and encourage, that minister grace to those who hear (Ephesians 4:29)? Are your actions reflecting the priorities God would have you set? Is your relationship with Him first, or are you too busy to sit at His feet and enjoy His presence? The woman who wrote the following words knew busyness...until the Lord interrupted. Let's learn from her.

I'm Busy, Lord!

I'm busy, Lord. Surely You can see
The thousand things that wait for me!
The dishes still lie in the sink—
I cannot stop to pray and think.

Lord, I know You understand,
For You gave these children to my hand;
And now they cry and need me so,
Lord, You understand. I'd better go.

Now I've got them all to sleep,
I'd better dust and mop and sweep.
I must thaw out the meat for stew,
And the ironing is long overdue!

And kindly my Lord answered me,
"Why do you from My presence flee?
I have so much for you today.
My child, I want to hear you pray.

"I love you, child; I want you here
To rest and listen—to shed a tear.
What if Paul had stopped to say,
'Lord, I'm too busy to write letters today!'?

"No, my child, I'm what you need,
Through household duties you can speed,
Yet when you're through, there's emptiness
If this quiet time you miss."

Oh, thank You, Lord, for showing me
How much I need to wait on Thee.

For what's an undone dish or two
Compared with sharing time with You?!

—Nancy Stitzel

May God enable us like Mary and like Nancy, the author of this poem to choose to make our number one priority "the good part which shall not be taken away"—our relationship with Him!

Walking on the Path of Peace

Well, dear one, now that we know more about God's peace, what can you and I do to live in such a way that we can cultivate this gift of His Spirit?

- We can *pray!* And we should pray first, pray often, pray continually. When we come to God in prayer and place our worries, fears, doubts, and concerns into His hands, we can be more like Mary. We'll be spending time in the presence of the Lord, enjoying fellowship with Him, learning from Him, and worshiping Him—and, yes, experiencing His peace.
- We can *pause* and turn to the Lord when a crisis or catastrophe presents itself. When we pause to acknowledge God—His presence, His all-sufficiency, His power, His love—He will make our paths straight. Furthermore, once we've turned to Him, we will again be in touch with His peace that passes understanding.
- We can *peruse* the Gospels and study Jesus' life to see the peace He experienced in stressful situations. We can learn how abiding in the Father directed Jesus' thoughts, words, deeds, responses, and reactions in difficult circumstances. We can carry these instances in our mind

and write them on the tablet of our heart so that we can follow the example of our Savior.

Things to Do Today to Walk in Peace

Do you know what challenge causes you to most act like Martha? What worry keeps you awake at night? What concern sets your mind and heart fretting as the alarm clock awakens you each morning? Please identify that item, dear one, and then make the conscious decision to trust it to God. Making this sacrifice of trust will allow *your* heart to rest in Him and enable *you* to experience His peace—even in your most difficult challenge!

~ 5 ~

Looking at Jesus' Attitudes

The preceding three chapters of this book, dear friend, have been about the circumstances of life that call for you and me to display the fruits of love, joy, and peace. First, the need for *love* is created by ill treatment, hostility, abuse, and hatred. Second, the need for *joy* springs from sorrow, tribulation, tragedy, affliction, and trials. Third, the need for *peace* comes as we face the events in life that evoke panic, fear, terror, dread, and anxiety. Oh, but how blessed you and I are to be able to follow the example of Jesus Christ, who faced these same fruit-bearing opportunities! We've already seen Jesus model each of the attitudes of love, joy, and peace. But now I want us to take a close look at Jesus in the Garden of Gethsemane, where we see Him living out all three attitudes...despite the events He faced.

As I was preparing to write this chapter, I found these words written by my pastor John MacArthur:

> Ever and always the teacher, Jesus used even this struggle with the enemy in the garden the night before the cross to teach the disciples and every future believer another lesson in godliness, a lesson about facing temptation and severe trial. The Lord not only was preparing Himself for the cross but also, by His example, preparing His followers for the crosses He calls them to bear in His name....[1]

Because you and I desire to walk in godliness, let's allow Jesus to teach us as we peer into this dark night—a physically dark night that was also the most spiritually dark night in human history as the sinless Son faced death for your sins and mine in order to accomplish our salvation.

As we look at this sacred scene from the Savior's life, you and I truly stand on holy ground! Jesus' life on earth is nearing its end and He faces every ugly word and evil deed ever directed at a person. Through God's provision of the four Gospels, you and I are allowed to witness exactly how Jesus handled this hatred, sorrow, and trauma.

The Plan

Throughout His three years of teaching, Jesus often referred to God's plan for His death, which always caused bewilderment in His disciples. For instance, in John 7:6 Jesus said, "My time [to die] is not yet at hand." But in Matthew 26, as Jesus prepared for His final Passover meal, He clearly stated the opposite: "My time *is* at hand" (verse 18, emphasis added). It was time for Him to die and to fulfill the Father's plan.

Jesus and His small band of followers were in Jerusalem to observe the Passover, and together they supped one final time. Judas the traitor had already been dismissed to do the evil deed of betraying his Master and it was nearing midnight on Thursday of the Passover week.[2] At this time, Jesus offered

His high priestly prayer for and with His disciples (John 17). Then the group sang a hymn (Matthew 26:30) and Jesus "went forth with His disciples over the ravine of the Kidron, where there was a garden, into which He Himself entered, and His disciples" (John 18:1).

The Purpose

What was it that drove Jesus to the Garden of Gethsemane? It was His situation. It was this crossroads in His life. It was the challenge He faced during His final days. His time had finally come—and what was ahead? Betrayal by His disciples. Misunderstanding from His family and followers. Rejection from mankind. Hostility and persecution. An angry mob, angry leaders, and angry people. Verbal and physical assault. An unjust sentence. The excruciating pain of crucifixion. Death. And, worst of all, momentary separation from His heavenly Father. From the human perspective, Jesus was losing all He had: His life, His family, His ministry, His friends, and His personal dignity.

Yet, His heavenly Father had commanded that He die for these sinners, and Jesus obeyed. Doing so would benefit others—including you and me!—because His death would be for sinners like us. So, acting in love, Jesus gave Himself as a sacrifice, a ransom for others (Matthew 20:28).

The Place

Facing the overwhelming challenge of the cross, Jesus went to Gethsemane (Matthew 26:36). This place was probably a secluded spot, walled in and containing some olive trees and perhaps a grotto used in the fall of the year for an olive oil-press.[3] Jesus had gone there often with His disciples (John 18:2) because it was quiet, a good spot for teaching, prayer, rest, and sleep. So, on the eve of His death, Jesus retreated to this familiar place of prayer with His little band of followers.

The People

After He entered the place called Gethsemane, Jesus did two things. First, He asked eight of the disciples to "sit here while I go over there and pray" (Matthew 26:36). Jesus left these men outside the wall or gate of the garden as sentries. Next Jesus invited three of the disciples—Peter, James, and John—to go along with Him to pray.

The Problems

Disappearing into the black darkness, Jesus began the battle. The Father's plan caused Him deep distress, and the Bible gives us glimpses into His extensive *emotional* anguish. Jesus cried out, "My soul is deeply grieved, to the point of death" (Matthew 26:38). He "began to be very distressed and troubled" (Mark 14:33), so much so that He fell upon the ground in prayer. Luke tells us that He was "in agony" (22:44). Our Lord "offered up both prayers and supplications with loud crying and tears" (Hebrews 5:7). As one commentator writes, "All the waves and the billows of distress came pouring over His soul."[4]

God's command to die also caused Jesus to suffer not only emotional turmoil, but also terrible *physical* stress: "Being in agony He was praying very fervently; and His sweat became like drops of blood, falling down upon the ground" (Luke 22:44).

Jesus was fighting another great battle in addition to these emotional and physical struggles, and that was the *spiritual* war. Knowing this, Jesus had instructed His companions, "Keep watching and praying, that you may not enter into temptation" (Matthew 26:41). Our Lord threw Himself upon the mercy of His Father and uttered, "My Father, if it is possible, let this cup [of death] pass from Me" (verse 39). On the physical level, Jesus wanted the cup to pass. No one has ever desired to taste death, and neither did Jesus. But, from the spiritual perspective, He wanted to do His Father's will and therefore added to His plea, "yet not as I will, but as Thou wilt" (verse 39).

The Process

With this submission to God's will, we see Jesus emerge triumphant from His agonizing struggle in the Garden. How did He gain the victory? How did Jesus remain steadfast in the love, joy, and peace that compelled Him to die willingly for sinners and not give in to physical and emotional desires? What was the process? And what can you and I learn so that we, too, can grow in love, joy, and peace?

As we've seen before, *love is the sacrifice of self*. For love, Jesus looked to God, the Father, who had commanded Jesus the Son to die for sinners. And in love, Jesus looked to the Father, reached out to Him for His sustaining and strengthening love, and then, offering *the sacrifice of self,* determined to do the Father's will. Jesus' love looked to the Father—and looked at us—and the Spirit enabled Him to submit to death on a cross (Hebrews 9:14). The *flesh* wanted the cup to pass, but *love* looked to the Father and said, "Not my will, but Thine be done" (Matthew 26:39 KJV). That decision led to severe and intense suffering.

Joy offers the sacrifice of praise. In joy, Jesus lifted praise to God. Scripture tells us that Jesus experienced great joy: "for the joy that was set before Him [in the Father and by the Father, He] endured the cross, despising the shame" (Hebrews 12:2).

Peace comes with the sacrifice of trust. For peace, Jesus left His problems with God. "The peace that passeth all understanding" rushed to guard Jesus' heart and mind, and He got up off that holy, tear-stained, sweat-drenched ground to go on in peace, knowing His times were in the Father's hands, saying in all peace and with total trust, "Let us be going" (Matthew 26:46).

The Product

And now please note: Nothing about Jesus' circumstances changed! After agonizing in prayer, he was *still* going to go to the cross, *still* going to be crucified, *still* going to die, but He went to the cross sustained by God's love, joy, and peace.

And note something else: This transformation, this acceptance, this turning point was not accomplished with a snap of Jesus' finger, the wink of His eye, or the wave of any wand. It came because Jesus went to the Father—in agony and with blood and sweat and tears. Lying prostrate on the earth in literal darkness as He fought the deeper darkness that settled upon His soul, Jesus looked to His Father for the Father's love, the Father's joy, and the Father's peace. As a few lines of poetry read,

> And when there seems no chance, no change,
> From grief can set me free,
> Hope finds its strength in helplessness,
> And calmly waits for Thee.[5]

No, Jesus' ultimate submission to God's will did not come easily. One time in prayer was not enough (Matthew 26:39). Twice was not enough (verse 42). Jesus turned to the Father three separate times (verse 44). And these three times in prayer were not the flinging of trite thoughts toward heaven! They were more than likely three hour-long sessions

(Matthew 26:40) of agonizing, wrestling, struggling, and fighting so that He could do all that God required of Him.

When our Savior finally rose to go forward and face the cross, He did so with love, with joy, and with peace. Filled with these graces, the Son was able to say, "Let us be going" (Mark 14:42).

The Performance

Oh, dear sister in Christ! You and I have just seen Jesus submit to His Father's will—to death on the cross! We cannot help but to ponder, to marvel! This is too amazing for us not to pause…and to praise…and to pray! Oh, dear Jesus, thank You!

But we must also look to ourselves and to our walk with the Father. How is our performance when it comes to following God's direction for our life? Speaking for myself, I know I pray so little. When something tough comes along in my day, I too often blurt out, "No way!" and go on my merry way. If something requires more than I want to give, I say, "Oh, thank you very much, but I won't be able to do that." Or I grind on, doing what I have to do—on my own, in my own flesh, and by my own power—never approaching the Father for His filling. I murmur, gripe, complain, and fret. I do my duty...but I do it grudgingly.

In times like these, I need to follow my Lord's example and go to my Garden of Gethsemane, my place of prayer. I need to turn to the Father and contend with my flesh until I realize His fruit of love, joy, and peace. I need to spend the time—however long it takes!—to allow Him to fill me with Himself until I have all of Him and He has all of me.

If you and I would, for one week or even one day, fellow follower, commit ourselves to God in this way—if we would commit ourselves to rush to Him in prayer and remember His promises when we need love, when we need joy, and when we need peace, and stay there until we have it, however long it takes—we could indeed change our world for Christ. If we would commit ourselves to spend time in the garden with the Father and to pay the price Christ paid to walk by the Spirit, overcome the flesh, and thereby experience God's love and joy and peace—well, the effects are unknown, untold, limitless! Prayer in our own garden would mean Christ in us changing our hearts, our marriages, our families, our homes, our neighborhoods, our world. And *He* can do it. But without *Him,* we can do nothing (John 15:5). Without Him, we only go through the motions, giving so little to a husband, a child, or a world that needs so much.

May my personal prayer for growth in these three attitudes of love, joy, and peace become your prayer as we visit the garden often as we walk along life's way…

> It is in prayer, Father,
> That we press ourselves to You,
> O All-Sufficient One,
> That we get…in order to give,
> that we petition...in order to praise,
> that we wrestle…in order to rest.
> We must have our time in the garden.
> We must go to Gethsemane…
> daily…first…often, if need be.
> May we hold high in our hearts and minds
> this picture of Jesus in the Garden.
> Impress it upon our souls.
> May we follow in His steps
> and refuse to rise until we have
> Your love…Your joy…Your peace.
> We pray in Jesus' name, who has taught us how
> to pray. Amen.

Section II

Actions OF THE *Fruit* OF THE SPIRIT

~ 6 ~

Resisting in Patience

The fruit of the Spirit is...patience.
GALATIANS 5:22

Each day in my own walk with God, I probably attempt the same thing you do: I try to design an ideal schedule that will guarantee me a devotional time with God, in His Word and in prayer, each morning. On a good day, when the alarm clock goes off in the morning, I hop out of bed full of good intentions and solid plans, and I experience Victory #1: I got up!

It feels so good to be up and in control of my day (so far, anyway!). What a blessing it is to enter into God's presence, revel in His Word, and linger in prayer; to settle the circumstances of my life with God before my day's responsibilities begin. And then I experience Victory #2: I had my quiet time!

Next I start going about my housekeeping chores—joyfully unloading the dishwasher, eagerly watering those impatiens, and lovingly straightening the house. Usually this happy spiritual condition extends to taking coffee and juice to Jim in bed, fixing his breakfast and lunch with a hum, and helping him load the car. After giving him a big hug and a kiss, I stand in the driveway and wave an enthusiastic "good-bye" as he drives away. Yes, I experience Victory #3: I got my husband off to work without any problems! He's happy, and I'm happy. I think to myself, "This is great! All is well! I'm on a roll. What a wonderful day this is going to be!"

But then real life—the rest of the day—begins. I remember when I was a young mother, and real life was dealing with two preschool daughters all day long. Later, real life meant managing teenagers…who soon became two more adults living in our home. And every mother knows that child-raising itself brings not only joys, but many sorrows as well.

Also, in real life the phone rings (a lot!), and I have to attend to the person and details of each call. Most calls go well. But then there are those problem calls. Someone's upset with me. Or the person on the phone says something that hurts me. Sometimes the caller reports something someone *else* has said or gives me some new information that demands a response or a decision. I may learn that I've been removed from some position or been rejected in some way.

Pain comes in a variety of packages—through a letter in the mail or a visitor to your house or by telephone. And when the "package" is opened, you and I are left confused, wounded, bewildered, baffled, and hurting. We may feel used or abused, dumped on or manipulated, heartsick or sorrowful. There was an insult, an accusation, a disagreement, an argument, a criticism, maybe even a physical blow or a lawsuit. Now what are we supposed to do?

Facing Up to the Challenge of People

When I came out of my prayer closet, the circumstances of my life were in order: I had laid before God the difficult situations of my life. I had nurtured and cultivated the attitudes of godliness there in my quiet time by drinking in God's Word and communing with Him in prayer until His Spirit had given me God's love, God's joy, and God's peace. I was ready to face life for one more day.

But—as the saying goes—where there are people, there are problems! So what can you and I do about people? How can we handle the people who cause us pain? How can we obtain Victory #4 and live in a manner that glorifies God? How can we continue to walk by the Spirit and not succumb to the flesh when we are assaulted by people?

Handling people in a gracious, Christlike manner presents a real test for us. But thank God that He gives us three more graces, three more fruit—patience, kindness, and goodness (Galatians 5:22)—for managing the strain of personal relationships. Love, joy, and peace are godly attitudes that enable us to handle the difficult circumstances of life. Patience, kindness, and goodness help us in our relationships with difficult people. One commentator noted this logical progression and wrote, "If an individual is strong in the love, joy, and peace of God, he will be able to reach out to his neighbor in a more Christlike manner."[1] Beloved, reaching out to others requires that we take action—the actions of patience, kindness, and goodness as we walk by the Spirit.

Our Calling to Patience

It's good to realize up front that as Christians you and I are called by God to be patient. God's Word instructs us to "*put on* a heart of...patience" (Colossians 3:12, emphasis added). We are to *adorn* ourselves with a heart of patience. Just as we dress our body every day by putting on clothes, we are to *dress* our spirit each morning with the godly quality of patience. How lovely to be robed with God's patience!

In addition to putting on a heart of patience, we are to "*walk*...with patience" (Ephesians 4:1-2, emphasis added). In describing the Christian life, Paul writes that we can enhance our relationships with other believers and promote the unity of the church if we conduct our lives with patience. In other words, when we see faults in other people or are annoyed by them in any way, when we want to be irritated or critical and lash out, we are to be patient instead.

Although not easy, this is a practical first step to getting along with people—as Kelly certainly realized while on jury duty. She shared that

> ...showing patience has been an everyday struggle for me while serving with a group of jurors. Some of these people are inconsiderate and unkind, and it's very easy to get mad and upset with one another. But I am learning to deal with this situation in prayer. Every time something happens which starts to test my patience, I go to God and pray that He would give me the strength to overcome my impatience and anxious attitude. It doesn't really matter where I am. I just pray at that very moment that I am tested. Unfortunately, it happens quite often, but God has really been faithful to me in helping me keep my anger and frustrations from getting out of control.

Patience, dear reader, is definitely a key to harmony in relationships, but before we can turn that key it will help us to understand the meaning of godly patience.

The Meaning of Patience

If you're like me, you probably think of patience as being able to wait a very long time for something. But much more is involved in the kind of patience that is a fruit of the Spirit, as this illustration suggests. Suppose patience were available in a can at the grocery store. What divine ingredients would be written on the label?

Ingredient #1—The first and primary ingredient in patience is *endurance.* This steadfastness of the soul under provocation includes the idea of forbearing wrong and ill-treatment.[2] Patient endurance is long-spiritedness,[3] tolerance, and slowness to wrath.[4] The old King James word "long-suffering" paints the picture of patience pretty clearly for us.

This ingredient of patient endurance is practiced primarily toward people and relates to our attitude toward others.[5] William Barclay points out that "generally speaking the word is not used of patience in regard to things or events but in regard to people."[6] As one scholar succinctly stated, "It is the quality of putting up with other people, even when...sorely tried!"[7]

Ingredient #2—The label describing patience next details the very special conditions for patience: *when injured.* You see, we need patience to endure injuries inflicted by others,[8] a patience that is characterized by long-suffering, evenness of temper, or patient endurance when injured by another.[9] Godly patience also includes the idea of forbearance of wrong under ill-treatment.[10] As one source explains, "Patience is that calm and unruffled temper with which the good [person] bears the evils of life...[that] proceed from [others]."[11] It is when you or I suffer ill treatment inflicted by other people and when we are provoked or wronged that we most need patience. Dr. George Sweeting wrote, "A large part of being kind is the patient willingness to put up with the abuse or ridicule that comes our way. Usually that patience is needed most just when it is exhausted. So often our tolerance level wears thin at the wrong time and our spirit of kindness melts away. Real love...is patient, and it never gives up."[12] Godly patience shines the brightest when pain is inflicted upon us.

Ingredient #3—Another ingredient on the label describing patience is *mercy*. God's patience is always connected with mercy[13] and bears with others for their good.[14] Patience wishes well to others and is willing to endure with them...hoping for their good.

William Barclay shares a sobering insight about mercy when he writes, "If God had been a man, He would have wiped out this world long ago, but He has that patience which bears with all of our sinning and will not cast us off. [Therefore] in our dealings with our fellow men we must reproduce this loving, forbearing, forgiving, patient attitude of God."[15] We are actually acting like God when we are patient with people!

And why does God delay the punishment of man? One day, when I was reviewing a packet of Bible verses I've memorized, I came to a verse about the second coming of the Lord: "The Lord is not slow about His promise [to come again], as some count slowness, but is patient toward you, not wishing for any to perish but *for all to come to repentance*" (2 Peter 3:9, emphasis added). Peter is suggesting here that the Lord is waiting to come again, desiring for more souls to believe and come to salvation. In other words, He is giving mankind an extended opportunity to receive Christ! Behold the patience—and mercy—of God!

This example of God's patience certainly gives you and me a good reason to wait patiently ourselves! Besides obedience to God's instructions to be patient, our motivation to practice patience should be the good of others. We should be consumed with the same thought God has for others: "If I just wait long enough, maybe something good and wonderful will happen to this person!"

Ingredient #4—Finally, written in red letters across the

label on our can of patience are these words: *"Contains no anger or vengeance!"* The Spirit's patience holds no wrath or thought of sinful revenge[16] or retaliation.[17] Patience is the grace of the man who *could* revenge himself but *chooses* not to.[18] And, as children of God, we never have any reason to avenge ourselves anyway because God has promised us, "Never take your own revenge…but leave room for the wrath of God, for it is written, 'Vengeance is Mine, I will repay,' says the Lord" (Romans 12:19). As Tertullian, the early church father, observed, "If thou endurest wrong for Christ's sake, he is a revenger"![19]

Therefore, patience withholds: It withholds vengeance, revenge, and retaliation, and endures instead. It endures ill treatment, it refuses to be angry, and it desires the offender's good.

Even very spiritual Christians struggle with this element of patience. Reading in a biography about John Wesley, I was shocked to learn that Mrs. John Wesley is rated as one of the worst wives in all history.[20] Her ugly temperament made life difficult not only for John Wesley, but also for his brother Charles, who had such trouble with his sister-in-law that he said, "I must pray or sink into a spirit of revenge!"[21]

In light of these ingredients, the definition of patience I use for myself is: *Patience does nothing*. Patience is the front end of these three fruit which relate to people—patience, goodness, and kindness—and it is the passive part of love:[22] It is love doing nothing.

As I said, this is the passive end of these three fruit, and we'll move up the "action scale" in the next two chapters. But for now, if you want to walk in patience when you've been hurt, wronged, or ill treated, do nothing! Instead of reacting and doing something outwardly negative and harmful and sinful, inwardly resist in patience. Doing *nothing* gives you and me time (even a second!) to do *something*—to pray, to reflect, and to plan to respond in a righteous manner. So, my dear friend, we must go to God for His patience...and then do nothing that will cause us to lose any of those precious contents. And, just a hint: This process is usually accomplished while kneeling in prayer!

Struggling for Patience

Think about our struggle with patience for a minute: Which is easier—to give in to emotions and anger when someone has hurt you, or to practice patience and hold back your wrath? To lash out with cruel words, or to hold back your hateful words? I know that I have very little problem letting go, losing my temper, and telling my offender exactly how I feel and what I think! But much harder for me is the godly response—God's response!—of choosing to do nothing outwardly as I resist in patience inwardly. Believe me, it takes all of God's strength to help me to do nothing! I desperately need God's Spirit to fill me with His patience. But once you and I are filled, then doing nothing as we resist in patience is how we practice patient endurance...when we're injured by others...without vengeance...and for their good!

Obviously, learning about the ingredients of true spiritual patience can make a drastic difference in our conduct toward others. This knowledge can also help us exhibit the same patience Jesus did in His treatment of others, even His enemies. But to follow in Jesus' footsteps, we'll have to lean heavily on God, because "only by strength imparted by God and by means of complete reliance on the sustaining power of His sovereign, transforming grace will [we] be able to heed [these] directions."[23] How lovely to be a Christian robed in God's patience!

Looking at God's Instructions about Patience

The Bible is an ocean of instruction regarding patience, and I want us to dip into that vast pool and discover several truths about patience, with the help of several examples.

God is patient. In 1 Peter 3:20, we are given an opportunity to marvel at the patience of God. Here we read, "The patience of God kept waiting in the days of Noah, during the construction of the ark." Do you know how long God waited? One hundred twenty years! Desiring that many would be saved, God waited 120 years before the rain and the flood (Genesis 6:3), making His salvation available to others. How sad to read that only eight people were in the ark after God waited for so long!

So now we must consider ourselves! How long can you and I wait? Think of the people in your life, your own loved ones—maybe a husband who still hasn't believed, or a child who is taking longer than you wish to yield to God, or a brother or sister whose unbelief causes your heart to break. God calls us to patience—His patience. Patience that holds on and won't give up or let go or cast off the loved one. Patience that continues to extend fresh love every day—even for 120 years! Certainly this example of God's patient waiting makes me think I could wait just a little longer! How about you?

Jesus was patient. Jesus, the Master Teacher, also instructs us about patience in relationships with problem people, even people He labels as "enemies." Jesus tells us to love our enemies (Luke 6:27) and then explains how to do just that: "Pray...for those who mistreat you" (verse 28). What a perfect picture of patience in *action!*

But what is your natural tendency when *you* are insulted or treated badly? I know that mine is to react and treat the offender in exactly the same way he or she treated me! But that kind of response makes my conduct as wrong as my offender's. That is sin upon sin, creating two wrongs. As Christians you and I are not to be returning evil for evil, or insult for insult, but to be giving a blessing instead (1 Peter 3:9). Reaction and retaliation are definitely the fleshly and wrong response. What Jesus wants from us is the godly response of patience: He wants us to do nothing in fleshly response and instead give a blessing and pray. Isn't that exactly what Jesus did when He prayed for His killers while dying on the very cross they had nailed Him to—"Father, forgive them; for they do not know what they are doing" (Luke 23:34)? Our godly response, dear sister, is prayer—kneeling to pray, being filled with God's patience…and then doing nothing.

This scene from the life of our suffering Savior is too sacred to leave without responding from the depths of our soul! If we really want to be like Jesus, we have to ask ourselves if we're willing to do what we have to do to love our enemies. Do we love Jesus enough to willfully forsake our anger and pride and instead humbly, patiently wait for God to act? Do we love those for whom Jesus died enough to endure patiently with them as He did with us? Do we really love our enemies, those who hate us and curse us and use us? It was Christ's love for such people that put Him on the cross. Therefore, if we desire to love as Jesus loves, then we have to be willing to follow in His steps (1 Peter 2:21) to resist our fleshly urges and instead be patient. Pray now for the Spirit of God to fill you with this sweet fruit.

Paul was patient. Speaking from his own experience, the apostle Paul addressed our behavior towards those who are not Christians. He tells us that we "must not be quarrelsome, but kind to all, able to teach, patient when wronged…" (2 Timothy 2:24). And why would we need to be patient in this case? Verses 25 and 26 answer this question: "with gentleness correcting those who are in opposition, if perhaps God may grant them repentance leading to the knowledge of the truth, and they may come to their senses and escape from the snare of the devil." So, in our encounters with unbelievers, we should practice patience because we are hoping for their salvation.

I thank God that's what my friend Jan did with me! Throughout junior high and high school, Jan was a constant companion and one of my best friends. In fact, we were such good friends that at college we roomed together in the dormitory until Jan moved to one sorority house and I moved to another. Then something wonderful happened to Jan. She became a Christian, and she wanted to tell me, a best friend, all about it!

So one evening after dinner Jan came to share her good news and invite me to attend her Bible study. I wish I could tell you I was sweet and behaved like a lady. Even more than that, I wish I could tell you I went with her to her meeting and embraced Christ as well. But no, I was so shocked that all I could do was ridicule her and laugh at her. Basically, I told Jan, "Prove it!" I wanted to see some big changes in her life before I was going to believe what she was telling me.

Well, through the years, Jan was faithful to grow in Christ. And she was a faithful friend to me. She kept reaching out to me, never giving up on me. I, however, gave up on her. Ten years passed, years of lost friendship as I allowed my lack of understanding to drive a wedge between us. Jan and I hadn't talked for a decade when, in another state halfway across the nation, I suddenly and dramatically became a Christian! And guess what? I wanted to call Jan immediately. I wanted to tell her about my experience...and I wanted to ask her forgiveness for mistreating her. Today I'm glad to say that we correspond and share in the things of the Lord. Jan lived out for me patience with an unbeliever, and because she desired the best for me, she remained faithful as a friend—even while being mistreated!

Sarah was not patient. Sometimes we learn just as much from negative examples as positive ones! And for us the Old Testament princess Sarah shows us a picture of a lack of patience. As Sarah and her husband Abraham followed God, they had the special privilege of hearing many of God's promises from God Himself. One of those promises was an heir for them...yet there was no child until Sarah was ninety years old and Abraham was ninety-nine. And Sarah did not handle the wait well at all!

Because her continued barrenness brought her such constant grief, Sarah became "the woman who made a great mistake."[24] Her impatience led her to propose the following plan to Abraham: Go in to my maid Hagar and conceive a child (Genesis 16:2). Although the custom of that time allowed for a man with a barren wife to take a concubine in order to have an heir,[25] this mistake produced not only historical tragedy but fierce jealousy and contention between Sarah and Hagar.

And pregnancy brought out the worst in Hagar. When she saw that she had conceived, she despised Sarah (16:4). Hagar became insolent and rebellious, acting in pride and contempt toward Sarah. This is how Hagar became the ever-present problem-person in childless Sarah's life!

How did Sarah handle this people-problem, this daily dilemma? Certainly not the way we would hope! In an ugly scene marked by Hagar's pride and disdain toward her mistress and Sarah's envy of her pregnant slave, Sarah treated Hagar so harshly that she fled from Sarah's presence (16:6).

Sarah lost her patience and persecuted her servant. Although Sarah did grow to exhibit great faith (Hebrews 11:11), here she lashed out at Hagar—probably physically as well as verbally. At this point, she is an example of a woman who lacked patience. She acted out hatred, strife, jealousy, wrath, faction, sedition, and envy—many of the works of the flesh which Paul lists in Galatians 5:19-21. No, this is *not* a pretty picture!

As I think about Sarah, a woman exalted for her faith, I ask myself, "Isn't faith what lies beneath our patience?" And the answer is yes—which takes us right back to love and joy and peace. These three fruit of the Spirit grow out of our relationship with God and the realization that He is the Author and Designer of our life and of all that enters it—even childlessness, even a Hagar. So, my friend, whenever we feel impatient, we must look again into the face of God, acknowledge Him, His wisdom, His ways, and His choices for our life, exhale...and do nothing, as we resist in patience. This is the kind of faith that makes patience grow...and makes us women who walk with God.

Hannah was patient. Very much like Sarah, Hannah, too, was on the receiving end of daily persecution and provocation. As we learned back in chapter 4, Hannah's adversary was Peninnah, her husband's other wife and a rival who provoked her bitterly year after year (1 Samuel 1:6-7). Yet Hannah was patient. And we can be sure she had all of the same thoughts, feelings, and urges that Sarah had! But Hannah handled these emotions in a godly way: She went to the temple of the Lord and prayed to Him, speaking to Him about her persecution and her pain (verses 10-16).

Yes, Hannah gives us a godly model for enduring ill treatment. We are not to fight back or lose our control. Instead, we are to run to God, hide ourselves in Him, and adorn ourselves with His cloak of patience! Only God can help us do nothing and resist in patience. It's a struggle, but you and I must constrain our natural, fleshly urges to do combat and instead draw from God's fathomless fountain all the patience we need. Then the Holy Spirit will display the glory of His patience, enabling us to successfully do nothing.

Waiting for the Judge

One evening while I was teaching on this fruit of the Spirit, I talked to my class about how to grow in God's patience. In short, I told my students to remember to *wait for the judge*. Let me explain.

In an encouraging passage written to a group of poor and oppressed Christians, the apostle James appeals to these saints to "be patient...until the coming of the Lord" (James 5:7). He tells them to "be patient...for the coming of the Lord is at hand" (verse 8). Then he says, "Behold, the judge is standing right at the door" (verse 9). Three times James speaks of the coming of the Lord and the fact that He is at hand, indeed standing right at the door. But exactly how was this information supposed to encourage these bewildered saints—and us as well?

First of all, the promise of our Lord's return brings great hope to our sore hearts, for when He does arrive, things will change (Revelation 21:3-4)! Oppression will come to an end: Our suffering at the hands of others will be over. We will also enjoy the continuing presence of Jesus. Not only that, but the Lord will reward us for the obedience we've exhibited throughout our life (Revelation 22:12). He will also take vengeance upon our enemies, judging appropriately and correcting abuses. Indeed, *everything* will be made right as Christ, the Judge, brings justice and vindicates the righteous!

I know that this image of a judge makes James's call for patience easier for me to accept and apply. It's the picture of an Old Testament circuit-rider judge like Samuel, who annually traveled his circuit, judging the affairs of the people (1 Samuel 7:16).[26] The one problem with that set-up was that people had to *wait* until Samuel showed up in their town to settle matters among themselves. And, in the meantime, possibly up to a year, they had to exist together with disputes and injustices. They had to wait patiently and do nothing...until the judge came and made everything right.

It's a tall order, but like those waiting people, you and I are to exist together with unsettled disputes and injustices until our Lord, the Judge, arrives to settle things. We are to continue to live with our adversaries and endure ill treatment from difficult people, all the while remaining patient and practicing self-restraint. We are not to turn to self-pity or complaining (see James 5:7-9). And we are not to judge, quarrel, criticize, gossip, or find fault. No, we are responsible for only one thing while we wait, and that is Christlike conduct. The Judge is responsible for everything else!

And so, dear one, with this image in mind, ask yourself, "Can I wait?" James says you can. Therefore pick the person in your life who has caused you the most personal pain—longstanding pain or pain that's related to what's happening in your life right now. Before the Lord—the Judge—select the person who is hostile, mean, or ungrateful, who ignores you, insults you, slanders you, or blocks your progress. Then—through prayer and by God's grace and His help—resist every urge to retaliate or punish that person and instead do nothing. In patience, do nothing while you wait for the Judge.

Things to Do Today to Walk in Patience

God's Word is faithful to come to our rescue as we seek to

walk with Him in the trying area of patience. What does the Bible suggest you and I can do?

- Train yourself in long-suffering. Proverbs 19:11 offers this wisdom: "A man's [or woman's] discretion makes him slow to anger, and it is his glory to overlook a transgression." In other words, learn to restrain your anger.

- Lengthen your fuse. How long can you wait? Well, make that period a little longer. How many times can you wait? Make it a few more times next time. That's where prayer comes into play. Our patient God is willing to give you His patience whenever you ask.

- Remove opportunities to sin. As Paul says, "Make no provision for the flesh" (Romans 13:14). And Proverbs instructs us that "keeping away from strife is an honor for a man, but any fool will quarrel" (20:3).

- Follow Jesus' example. No one has ever endured more abuse than Jesus did! Yet He remained absolutely sinless even under the most severe mistreatment: "He committed no sin, nor was any deceit found in His mouth; and while being reviled, He did not revile in return; while suffering, He uttered no threats" (1 Peter 2:22-23). Carry Jesus' response to suffering in your heart and mind...and try to lift your own responses to a higher level of godliness.

- Pray. This was Jesus' sure-fire method for enduring His suffering: He just "kept entrusting Himself to Him who judges righteously" (1 Peter 2:23). So, precious one, when you are injured by others, turn your aching soul heavenward. Allow God to soothe your pain as you do nothing. Let Him fill you with His patience as you endure the hurt, without vengeance and for the good of those who hurt you. After all, it was by Jesus' wounds that you and I were healed (verse 24). It was for our good that He suffered. And we are called to do the same—to be patient with others for their own good. There is no higher privilege for us as Christians.

~ 7 ~

Planning for Kindness

The fruit of the Spirit is...kindness.
GALATIANS 5:22

As we rang the doorbell, neither of us imagined what was waiting on the other side of that door! My friend Judy and I had driven for 45 minutes through the outlying hills of the San Fernando Valley to the home of another friend who was hostessing a bridal shower. Yet the door was opened by someone else...who explained that our hostess's father had passed away just thirty minutes earlier and that she had left for the hospital.

Stunned, the three of us huddled to pray for our friend and all that she was facing at that moment. But after the action of prayer, it was time for us to go into action ourselves in the kitchen! As the many guests began to arrive, Judy and I offered emergency help. When brunch was served, I worked kitchen duty while Judy moved among the women asking if they needed anything, patting them on the shoulder, and making sure everyone was comfortable. Graciously Judy chatted with each woman as she carried the heavy silver coffeepot around the room, refilling cups and removing dirty dishes and soiled napkins. Then even I, in the kitchen, could hear one guest sneer as Judy moved out of earshot, "She's too nice."

Beloved, since that morning, I've given much thought to those words, "She's too nice." What Judy did for all of us—including an ungrateful woman—was actively live out kindness, the next fruit of the Spirit. Judy modeled the grace and ministry of kindness not only for those other women, but for me as well. As you'll soon see, the highest compliment a Christian woman can receive is to be described as "too nice." When people say that of you or me, we can know we are truly exhibiting the Spirit's fruit!

Our Calling to Kindness

But...back to our walk with God! In this section of our book we're learning about the *actions* of patience, kindness, and goodness in dealing with the people in our life. As we face people each day and experience any pain they may inflict upon us, we are to be patient and be careful not to do anything sinful or harmful when provoked. This godly response is achieved when we ask God to fill us with His patience. Only He can help us to do nothing! But, having asked for patience, it is now time to make a move, to go into action, to get up and do something. And that "something" is kindness, the next fruit on the Lord's list; "the fruit of the Spirit is...kindness" (Galatians 5:22).

Just as our Lord is kind, we as His women are called to be kind, too. And, even though the fruit of kindness is borne in our lives as we walk by the Spirit, that walk involves living out several commands given to us in God's Word. One of these commands follows on the heels of a passage of Scripture (Ephesians 4:25-32) which scholar William Barclay entitles "Things Which Must Be Banished from Life."[1] In these verses, the apostle Paul warns Christians against conduct that grieves the Holy Spirit and hurts the heart of God.[2] This conduct includes various forms of meanness (bitterness, wrath, anger, clamor, and evil speaking), all of which God calls us to banish from our lives. Instead, we are to "be kind to one another" (verse 32). The Living Bible says straightforwardly: "Stop being mean…[and] instead, be kind to each other." It's obvious that our kindness is indeed an action that pleases God!

Another call to kindness is sounded forth in Colossians 3:12. Here God tells us to "put on a heart of…kindness." Kindness is one of the basic Christian virtues that helps govern human relationships. Therefore you and I are to put on kindness in all our relationships. How exquisite to have kindness characterize our life and actions!

God issues one more call to kindness in 2 Timothy 2:24. Here the apostle Paul tells us how to act toward those who are not Christians: "The Lord's bond-servant must not be quarrelsome, but be kind to all." It's a fact that kindness has been an important element in Christian witnessing since the early centuries. As one missionary reports, Christians have been known through the ages by their love and concern for others, and some of the most telling evidence of this comes not from the mouths of Christians themselves but from the critics of Christianity who were concerned that Christianity was specially advanced through their loving service rendered to strangers.[3]

And now, dear Christian, we must pause a moment and reflect upon God's charges to us to be kind. Do you consider yourself to be kind? Are you trying to "stop being mean" and to instead put on a heart of compassion and kindness toward others? Are you seeking to please God by your kindness rather than cause the Holy Spirit sorrow by any unkindness? As you spiritually prepare yourself each morning, do you choose to put on the robe of kindness? For us to walk with God means we must walk in the way of kindness.

Defining Kindness

Having acknowledged our calling to be kind, our next concern is to better understand it. It helps to know that kindness has been defined as tenderness[4] and concern for other people.[5] It is the virtue of the person whose neighbor's good is as dear to him as his own.[6] Kindness is also a sweetness of disposition[7] and a matter of the heart. Certainly God's grace of kindness should pervade the whole person, mellowing all that might be harsh.[8]

My own definition of kindness—which helps me immensely in cultivating and practicing this spirit of concern for others—is *kindness plans to do something.* While patience means doing nothing sinful while resisting in patience (see chapter 6), kindness now plans to act. Kindness, like all the other fruit of the Spirit, desires godly action and therefore plans for those actions. First we were filled with God's patience: We knelt humbly in prayer to keep from losing a drop of it by doing something rash or reactive. Now, acting out of love and filled with God's kindness as well as His patience, we get up and go looking for opportunities to do something. Do you remember that patience is the passive end of love (doing nothing when provoked)? Well, now we see kindness actively move out, preparing for the action of goodness (which we will look at in the next chapter). Kindness goes out looking, wondering, and asking, "Who needs love? How can I ease someone's burden? How can I touch another person?"

Learning from Opposites

We can learn even more about kindness when we look at

its opposites. For instance, arguing. Certain behaviors signal to us that we are not walking by the Spirit or practicing God's kindness, and one of those flashing red lights is arguing. In 2 Timothy 2:24, Paul says that the Lord's bond-servant must not be quarrelsome, but be *kind* to all. Therefore, when you or I find ourselves striving or quarrelling, arguing or quibbling, we can be sure that this behavior "is not that which comes down from above" (James 3:15), but is instead coming from our own flesh. Galatians 5:20 even lists strife, disputing, and dissension among the evil deeds of the flesh.

Imagine the home...the office...or the church without any arguing! And imagine the same energy that contention, strife, and arguing consume channeled toward kindness instead. Exactly what would you and I have to do to help make that happen? Here's a short list.

- Love others more than ourselves.
- Care for the comfort and welfare of others more than our own.
- Consider others more important than ourselves (Philippians 2:3).
- Forego quarrelling.

Matthew 11:28-30 helps us gain even greater insight into kindness from another pair of opposites. Speaking words of comfort to His followers, Jesus issues a gentle invitation: "Come unto Me, all who are weary and heavy-laden, and I will give you rest. Take My yoke upon you, and learn from Me, for I am gentle and humble in heart; and you shall find rest for your souls. For My yoke is easy [that is, kind], and My load is light." It's helpful for us to understand that a yoke was a wooden frame placed upon a person's shoulders that was meant to make his load easier to carry. However, if the load was unequally distributed or simply too heavy, that yoke would begin to chafe and rub and wear the person down. Here Jesus is contrasting His yoke and the burden He asks His followers to bear with the yoke of trying to keep all of the rules laid upon the Jews by Israel's teachers, and He says that His yoke is "easy"—which is the same word as "kind." In fact, one scholar translates the verse "My yoke is kindly."[9]

I have to admit that the vividness of this mental image caused me to ask some hard questions about my relationships with others—and maybe you would like to do the same. For instance, what is it like to be yoked with me at home, on a committee, in a project, or in a ministry? Am I an asset to those around me, a person who doesn't chafe? Am I easy to be with and kind, a person who makes it easier for other people to bear their burdens? Or am I an additional burden which others must bear, causing their yoke to chafe and rub, making it more difficult for them to pull their weight because they are yoked to a harsh, quarrelsome, wearisome woman? Do my manner and lack of kindness chafe, rub, and wear others down? Kindness means making life easier for others—not harder—just as Jesus makes your life and mine easier.

Cultivating Kindness

The book I turn to each morning during prayer time contains a sobering prompt that has helped me grow in kindness (and I hope it helps you, too). Every week, I read a prompt that instructs me to pray for "greater love and compassion for others." Well, I have to tell you that whenever I see these words, I am humbled to the core as I examine my heart and soul. This call to prayer always makes me realize how much more I need this godly quality in my life! But prayer and the following aspects of kindness have helped me to cultivate the fruit of kindness. These thoughts have given me a handle on what kindness does—and they can do the same for you.

1. *Caring is a part of kindness.* It's true that when we genuinely care about someone, we find ourselves paying attention to the circumstances of their lives and being concerned about their welfare. We get involved in their lives. As our love grows for another person, the details of that person's life become more and more important to us. It begins to matter greatly to us if they are sad or discouraged, struggling or in pain, needy or lonely. But I know for myself that such concern doesn't come nearly as easily for the problem people in my life!

I've found prayer to be one sure way to nurture care for those who bring me pain. It's true that if you and I will follow Jesus' instruction to "pray for those who mistreat you" (Luke 6:28), startling changes will occur in our heart. For starters, the bond of prayer causes us to become vitally and spiritually involved in the lives of the individuals we pray for. Also, through prayer, God changes *our* heart and mind by softening our harshness and melting our selfishness into concern for others—including our enemies!

Another act that makes a marked difference in our relationships is a decision to care for others—as one college teacher knew when she gave an unusual assignment to her seniors. She said, "Select the person on campus you dislike the most. Daily during the coming month go out of your way to do some act of kindness for that person." Later one student reported, "By the end of the month my dislike of [the woman selected] had been replaced by a growing compassion and understanding....[This assignment] helped me see things about myself—my unfriendliness, my lack of compassion, my judging without first trying to understand the causes of behavior I disliked."[10] It's no surprise that caring about others truly dispels unfriendliness, a lack of compassion, and a judgmental spirit. So...ask God to help you (as my prayer guide suggests) have greater love and compassion for others.

2. *Thinking is a part of kindness.* Another sure sign that we are growing in our concern for people is when we begin to think about others and the conditions of their lives. We'll find ourselves looking at people and thinking, "What would help her? What would help him? What does he need? What does she need?" We'll find ourselves asking God, "How can I serve this person? How can I make his or her life easier? How can I touch their life, lift their burden?" As we are learning, kindness plans to do something, and that takes a certain amount of thought and prayer before the Lord—as David models for us. When he became the king of Israel, David asked, "Is there yet anyone left of the house of Saul [the previous king], that I may show him kindness...?" (2 Samuel 9:1). You see, David was *thinking* about showing kindness to the heirs of the former king. Can you think of someone you can be kind to?

There's no doubt that the greatest training ground for thinking about the welfare of others is right in our own home. My friend Ann has thought of dozens of ways to show kindness to her family. One way involves a beautiful red plate which has in gold lettering the words, "You are very special!" A part of her joy as a wife and mother is showing simple kindnesses to a discouraged family member—such as setting that person's place at the table with her special red plate!

So, precious sister, ask God to give you a caring heart and a creative mind as you, too, begin looking around to see the needs of people in your home, your neighborhood, your work place, and your church. Hurting people are literally everywhere! One staggering statistic reports, "Ninety percent of all mental illness...could have been prevented, or could yet be cured, by simple kindness."[11] What can you think of doing today that would touch another life with kindness?

3. *Noticing is a part of kindness.* Still another way to practice kindness is to notice other people's needs. All we have to do is use our God-given capacity for observation: As the Bible says, "The hearing ear and the seeing eye, the Lord has made both of them" (Proverbs 20:12). We can *always* be watching and listening to those around us. In fact, this is one of the ways God cares for us: "The eyes of the Lord are upon the righteous, and His ears attend to their prayer" (1 Peter 3:12). And you and I can care for people in the same way God cares for us...just by paying attention and being on the lookout for people's needs.

I read of an evangelist's mother who practiced such kindness and observation: "One day he found her sitting at the table with an old tramp. Apparently she had gone shopping, met the tramp along the way, and invited him home for a warm meal. During the conversation the tramp said, 'I wish there were more people like you in the world.' Whereupon his mother replied, 'Oh, there are! But you must just look for them.' The old man simply shook his head saying, 'But lady, I didn't need to look for you. You looked for me!' "[12] When you or I begin to notice others, we'll soon know their wants and needs just as this kind and godly woman did. The Bible gives us examples of kindness as well—examples that can help you in your walk with God.

In the Old Testament, *the Shunammite woman* was a person who noticed. She noticed the prophet Elisha frequently passing by her home with no apparent place to lodge or eat (2 Kings 4:8-10). Well, kindness went into action as she persuaded him to eat food. "And so it was, as often as he passed by, he turned in there to eat food" (verse 8).

As she cared and thought and noticed, she soon realized that he had no other place to stay. Acting again on her concern, she asked her husband, "Please, let us make a little walled upper chamber and let us set a bed for him there, and a table and a chair and a lampstand; and it shall be, when he comes to us, that he can turn in there" (verse 10). This woman's eyes were open, and so was her heart and her home. In her kindness, she noticed Elisha's needs.

Another woman of the Bible who noticed people's needs was *Dorcas*. God describes her as a woman "abounding with deeds of kindness and charity, which she continually did" (Acts 9:36). Among her kind deeds was sewing tunics and garments for the widows (verse 39). What had Dorcas seen with her eyes and heard with her ears? She had noticed that the widows needed clothes—and she acted.

Of course *Jesus*, "the kindness of God" in flesh (Titus 3:4), always noticed the needs of the people around Him. In the Gospels we're told how He was moved with compassion when He looked upon the hungry multitude. He knew their needs and wanted to give them something to eat (Luke 9:13). His heart of kindness was also a rebuke to His disciples, who wanted to send the multitude away (verse 12). While Jesus cared and was concerned, the Twelve scorned the people and their needs. While Jesus was moved with compassion, they saw the people as bothersome. O for the grace to be like Jesus!

There's a story Anne Ortlund shares in her book *Disciplines of the Beautiful Woman* that shows us a woman who walks in kindness. Mrs. Ortlund writes of "a Hawaiian woman who strings a number of leis early each Sunday morning, not for anyone in particular! Then she goes to church praying, 'Lord, who needs my leis today? A newcomer? Someone discouraged. Lead me to the right people.'"[13] Yes, this is clearly a picture of kindness—a person filled with God's love going out looking; kindness planning to do something; kindness keeping a keen eye out and noticing others; kindness actively seeking those who are in need. May you and I follow in her kind footsteps!

4. *Touching is a part of kindness.* It helps us to cultivate kindness when we think of kindness as the tender touch of concern and compassion. At the bridal shower I told you about earlier, Judy's gestures of kindness included touching the women as she served them and cared for them. The same should be true of us. When we minister to others in gentle kindness, touch is something we almost instinctively give to those we care about. We can be like the apostle Paul who wrote that he was gentle among the Thessalonians "as a nursing mother tenderly cares for her own children" (1 Thessalonians 2:7). Indeed, a mother's care for a nursing infant is an image of pure and gentle tenderness!

Our Savior also demonstrated perfect kindness when He held little children. When eager parents brought their children to Him so that He might touch them, the disciples rebuked them (Mark 10:13). I can imagine them hissing, "Shoo! Get these kids out of here! Don't bother the Master. This is kingdom work!" But, after rebuking His disciples for their lack of kindness, Jesus took those little children into His arms and blessed them, laying His hands upon them (verse 16).

Yes, our Jesus was kind and tender, and He always touched the people He was caring for. He stopped and touched the coffin of a widow's only son (Luke 7:12-15). He touched the deformed, bent-over back of a suffering woman (Luke 13:10-13). He stretched out His hand and touched a man "full of leprosy" (Luke 5:12-13). He touched the two blind men's eyes (Matthew 20:29-34). The Law forbade each of these acts of touching, acts which made a man unclean and unfit to worship. Yet in each case Jesus gave His touch—and a miracle followed. The moment He touched the sufferers, they were healed, they were clean, and Jesus therefore maintained His purity in the eyes of the Law.

Aren't you glad that you and I can grow in God's grace of kindness? We can constantly ask God to work in our heart to help us care, think, notice, and touch the people He places in our life. And as we stifle and renounce our unkind emotions and thoughts about others and obey God's command for kindness from us, we can then—by the power of the Holy Spirit—practice kindness.

Becoming "Too Nice"

And now, dear one, it's time for you and me to set out on the path of becoming "too nice." In our culture today, this may not sound very appealing, but being "too nice" is exactly what kindness is. When the book of Galatians was written, the common slave-name *chrestos* came from the same Greek root word for kindness. The first-century pagans, who confused this familiar name with the unfamiliar *Christos* for Christ, began calling Christians by a nickname that meant "goody-goody"[14]—the same as being "too nice." The spelling of the two words varies by just one letter, but what an appropriate similarity! We who walk with God are indeed to be kind—to be "too nice."

My friend Judy was said to be "too nice." Why? Because she was kind, because she was serving as a "chrestos," because she was caring, thinking, noticing, and touching, and because she is a "Christos," a kind of Christ, a "goody-goody." Judy's kindness should be a goal for each of us as we continue to grow in this fruit of the Spirit. As one Bible teacher exhorted, "We need to cultivate resourcefulness in kindliness, to gain proficiency in the artistry of applying Christian love to the hearts and lives of those with whom we come in contact in the many activities and relationships of life."[15] But what are some things we could do to cultivate this artistry? I have a few thoughts.

Things to Do Today to Walk in Kindness

I've pointed out earlier that this second trio of the fruit of the Spirit—patience, kindness, and goodness—has to do with our treatment of others. The order of this listing implies that kindness is the next step we are to take after we have practiced patience when wronged. I know my natural response when someone has hurt me is to react and decide, "Well, you're off my list! I don't have to put up with that kind of treatment! I'll just withhold my love from you." But as we've been learning, moments like these are precisely when you and I need to have spiritual victory and be kind instead. This supernatural act requires God, the Holy Spirit, filling us with *His* kindness.

So, as you've done before, I'm asking you to choose your number one problem person and take him or her before the Lord in prayer. I also want you to take before God your pain, your harsh thoughts, your temptations to respond in an unchristian manner, and your confessions of times when you've given in to those thoughts or temptations. Acknowledge your unkindness as well as any times when you withheld kindness. Then go a step further and ask God to help you show His kindness to the very person who hurt you, who caused your pain, who is causing you to suffer, and who is making your life miserable. While you are suffering long and waiting patiently under ill-treatment, be kind. For love suffers patiently *and* is kind (1 Corinthians 13:4).

My friend Karen gave me a little calendar so that each day I can flip a page over and read another encouraging statement. Well, one day I learned a little more about kindness as the calendar page read, "Kindness is the ability to love people more than they deserve." Can we do that, dear friend? God says we can—and His Spirit helps us. So...

- Pray for your enemies, those people who mistreat and use you (Luke 6:28). You will find you cannot hate a person you are praying for. You also can't neglect that person. Try it! You'll find these statements to be true because prayer and hatred don't go together. Neither do prayer and neglect.
- Spend time with God owning up to any ill will you have toward an individual or group of people. Ask for God's help in demonstrating the Spirit's kindness to those people.
- Ask God to help you become known more as a comforter and less as a confronter.
- Study Jesus' life for more examples of kindness and then follow in His steps. Keep a journal of those instances of His kindness as you discover them, noting the circumstances surrounding His graciousness.
- Begin making the effort at home to live out God's command to be kind to others (Ephesians 4:32). What does your husband need? Your children? Or your roommates? What would make their life easier?
- Pray for God to fill your heart with His compassion as you walk each day and every step along the way with Him.

~ 8 ~

Giving in Goodness

The fruit of the Spirit is...goodness.
GALATIANS 5:22

Late one evening I crawled into bed clutching a book, hoping I could fulfill my nightly goal of reading at least five minutes before turning out the lamp. It had been another wild and full day and I had just about had it...but I was going to give the five minutes a try anyway. The book in my hand was a treasure I had found that morning at the bookstore, and all day long I had been relishing the thought of opening this small delight. There had been only one copy on the shelf at the store, and its title had caught my eye and piqued my curiosity: *People Whose Faith Got Them into Trouble*.[1] Finally it was time—if I could just stay awake! As I began reading this book, subtitled "Stories of Costly Discipleship," the opening words of the first chapter caught my attention so completely that I read much longer than usual. Here's what I read:

> The sound of hooves at midnight—horsemen galloping into the courtyard—and the clatter of armor as soldiers

> surround the house wake the old man. Two officers dismount and pound on the wooden door with the butt ends of their spears.
>
> Maids in disheveled nightclothes rush upstairs and urge the white-haired fugitive to hide under the bed, in a closet...anywhere. Instead, he hushes them, drapes a cloak over his frail shoulders, descends the stairs, opens the door and invites the men who have come to arrest him inside.
>
> He instructs the maids, "Quickly, prepare hot food and something to drink. Can't you see these men have ridden hard tonight? They need refreshment; give them the best in the house."
>
> Confused by this unexpected reception, the arresting officers crowd into the room and cluster around a bronze charcoal brazier on the floor.
>
> As they warm their numb hands against the cold night of February 22, 166, Polycarp, elderly bishop of Smyrna...makes every effort to see that his guests are comfortable. He personally serves the officers and soldiers alike from the warm dishes his maids have prepared.[2]

What a powerful example of Christian goodness! A man being hunted down, a man who would soon taste death by execution at a fiery stake, was showing love to his persecutors! This man was exhibiting the Spirit's fruit: *Patience* allowed him to graciously receive his captors, *kindness* thought of their needs, and then *goodness* followed through. Serving them himself, the man being led to death met the needs of those leading him. This story of Polycarp offers us a vivid example of the fruit of the Spirit in action.

Reviewing Our Progress

So far in this section of this book, you and I have examined two of the graces that help us in our relationships with people. The first is *patience.* Patience is like a seed hidden beneath the surface, germinating there, quietly and slowly incubating life. Patience silently waits in the dark earth, hidden from view, doing nothing (it seems!). This sweet fruit of patience makes it possible for kindness and goodness to develop.

Next is *kindness.* Kindness grows from the seed of patience in the dark depths of private times with God. Sprouting tiny root hairs that soon develop into a complete root system and the recognizable part of a stem, kindness pushes its head higher and higher toward heaven, stretching itself toward God, wanting to break forth and do something. At last the desires of kindness are fully formed, and the energy of a heart filled with God's kindness enables the plant to crack through the soil.

And now we behold *goodness* pushing its head through the hard, crusted soil...of our heart, of men's hearts, of the evil in the world...and blossoming into works. As we marvel at this fruit—so often sown by the pain and injuries we've suffered at the hands of other people—we can only pause and praise our Father in heaven for His wisdom in knowing how to produce loveliness in our lives, how to bring beauty from ashes (Isaiah 61:3 KJV), how to overcome evil with good (Romans 12:21), and how to transform great sorrow into greater blessing.

Beloved, only our gracious God knows how to grow us to be like Him! Just as a garden is laid out by a plan, God designs your life and mine according to a plan. He uses the people, events, and circumstances of our life to guide us along the path toward godliness, and He leads us step by step. Walking with Him—listening to His voice, humbling ourselves in prayer, following His ways, and imitating His dear Son—we show forth His glory as we bear His fruit. By studying these fruits, we've learned about God's desire for us and for our walk with Him: He wants us to be like Him. And one way to be like Him is to bear His fruit of goodness.

Getting a Handle on Goodness

Bearing the fruit of goodness will be easier if we understand three aspects of the biblical definition of spiritual goodness, aspects which relate to our conduct toward others.

1. *True goodness is spiritual in its origin*. The Bible reveals to us that God is good (Psalm 33:5; Nehemiah 9:25,35). Indeed, from cover to cover, the Bible tells the story of God's gracious goodness! One scholar defines this goodness as "the sum of all God's attributes...express[ing] the...excellence of the divine character."[3] And yet, as God's children, we can exhibit His goodness, a goodness that is so completely upright that it abhors evil.[4] What a blessed privilege to represent Him!

The Bible also shows us that God's goodness is the opposite of *man's badness*.[5] And our badness (as I mentioned in the first chapter) is why we need spiritual help from God. First, *our sin* makes human goodness impossible. As Paul writes in the Book of Romans, "There is none righteous, not even one...there is none who does good, there is not even one" (Romans 3:10,12). And second, we need God's help because of *our flesh*. The apostle Paul accurately expresses for us the struggle that exists in every human—the war with the flesh—when he cries out in despair, "For I know that nothing good dwells in me, that is, in my flesh" (Romans 7:18).

So, due to our sin and our flesh, we need God's grace and the Spirit's power to exhibit His fruit of goodness, because any and all goodness—genuine goodness—must have God in the formula.

2. *Goodness is active.* As we learned in the preceding chapter, kindness means planning to do something good for others. And now goodness moves into total action. God *in* us and His presence *with* us produces *His* goodness in us. And His goodness in us then results in active benevolence,[6] kindly activity on the behalf of others.[7] I can't think of anything that would glorify God more! Can you?

3. *Goodness is a readiness to do good.* In addition to being active, goodness is completely dedicated to helping others live well.[8] It is a quality that is ruled by and aims at what is good[9]—a readiness to do good.[10] Indeed, goodness is up on tip-toe, ready and waiting to do good.

Don't you agree that our world, our churches, and our homes need people who are actively kind; people who walk out their door every day ready to do good—not just think about it or pray about it; people who are devoted to making the lives of others better? Trying to define goodness, it helps me to understand it as *goodness does everything!* Goodness will do everything it can to shower God's goodness upon others. Goodness follows through on those wonderful thoughts of kindness, thoughts which came when we were praying, caring, noticing, and planning to act. Goodness takes the step from good intentions to actively serving others. John Wesley understood this principle and made it his rule for life...and we should, too:

> Do all the good you can,
> by all the means you can,
> in all the ways you can,
> in all the places you can,
> at all the times you can,

to all the people you can,
as long as ever you can.

Getting a Handle on Walking in Goodness

Now let me show you how God's goodness in us works itself out. The presence of the Holy Spirit within us should make a difference in the way we live and how we treat others. That's why God calls us to "walk in newness of life" (Romans 6:4); "walk in a manner worthy of the calling with which you have been called" (Ephesians 4:1); "walk in love" (Ephesians 5:2); "walk as children of light" (Ephesians 5:8); "walk in Him" (Colossians 2:6); "walk in a manner worthy of the God who calls you" (1 Thessalonians 2:12); "walk in the same manner as [Jesus] walked" (1 John 2:6); and "walk by the Spirit" (Galatians 5:16).

Walking with God (which is what this book is all about) requires that you and I make serious choices. As one fellow traveler notes, "The Spirit life includes goodness, and goodness doesn't come naturally; it always requires a decision."[11] And our relationships with others, especially with those who hurt us—the arena where we live out patience, kindness, and goodness—call for choices, too. One definite choice we can make when we're hurt by someone is to walk in *patience* and *do nothing*. Then, having made this choice (*not* to blow up, *not* tell someone off, *not* to succumb to anger, *not* to fight back, *not* to retaliate), we can move to the next choice—the choice of *kindness*—and *plan to do something*, plan to do deeds of kindness.

Do you see how God's grace released in us as we walk by the Spirit produces miracle after miracle in our lives? For instance, Miracle #1: Instead of an outburst of anger or hatred, love in the form of patience is lived out. Then Miracle #2: Our heart changes from the *natural* desire for revenge to the *supernatural* desire for the good of others. Goodness prays, "What can I do to love this person for Christ's sake?" And now Miracle #3: Goodness does everything! Goodness puts God's love into actions, follows through on our plans for kindness, and gives—indeed, pours out!—God's love to others.

Oh, dear reader, *this* kind of living—characterized by God's patience, kindness, and goodness—*is* walking by the Spirit! *This* kind of living overcomes evil with good (Romans 12:21), does not return evil for evil or insult for insult, but gives a blessing instead (1 Peter 3:9). *This* kind of living is spiritual victory—victory of the Spirit over the flesh—and evidence of God at work in our life. And *this* kind of living is godly living because only God in us can do this!

We must always remember that the fruit is His. As we practice obidience to God's commands, He produces His fruit in us. And it is also produced by His grace and glorifies him: We are told to let our light shine before men in such a way that they may see our good works, and glorify our Father who is in heaven (Matthew 5:16). However, the choice to do as Romans 6:13 tells us, to yield ourselves unto God and our members as instruments of righteousness unto God and not unto sin is ours.

This choice, my friend, is the focus of our constant battle between the flesh and the Spirit (Galatians 5:17). You and I must put forth the effort of making the right choices—God's choices. And we must turn to God for His help in gaining victory over sin. Then, miracle of miracles, our life will indeed bring glory to Him as His fruit grows and displays itself in our walk with Him!

Choosing Goodness

Some of the women in my evening Bible class were sobered by the choices they had to make on their walk with

God. Susan, for instance, was hurt by neighbors who are not Christians and who openly despise her for being one. She told me her plan of action: "I set a goal. No matter what they do or say in passing, I decided I'm going to respond in goodness—and I insist that my children do the same. We are to be Christ's examples. And it's already working! The mother has started smiling and saying hello, and I'm hoping that the father will follow soon."

Ann, too, was hurt—but by the Christian women in her Bible study. What did she do? How did she handle this? How did she respond? "I chose not to feel hurt about not being invited to join them on their outing. I chose to not feel bitterness or resentment. I just need to show my love for them."

And then there is Maria, who daily faces a hostile, persecuting boss, a person she describes as rude and abrasive. Her situation at work boiled down to a spiritual decision for her: She could react in an ungodly way or respond in godliness. She wrote, "I had to make a choice—give back what he is dishing out or show him the kindness and goodness of the Lord."

Examples like these go on and on and the choices like these go on and on, but I'm sure you get a picture of how to walk in goodness from these few glimpses. Like these wonderful women, our walk with God requires many decisions on our part as we constantly look to God, asking Him, "What is the right thing to do?"

Recognizing Goodness as an Assignment from God

Any time I've held down a job, I've always had a written job assignment. And, because the responsibilities were in writing, I always knew what was expected of me. Any time I was unsure, all I had to do was get out that description, read it again, and find direction for my efforts. Well, my friend, as believers you and I have a written job assignment, too. God has put in His Word exactly what He desires from us. And goodness, besides being a fruit of the Spirit, is something He expects of us. Indeed, we are instructed many times in Scripture to practice good works. It's an assignment from God.

For instance, consider Ephesians 2:8-10. This for me was a life-changing excerpt from our job description because it shows me both my responsibility to grow in good works and God's grace in making that possible. This Scripture tells us that "we are [God's] workmanship, created in Christ Jesus for good works, which God prepared beforehand, that we should walk in them" (verse 10). God has ordained that we live a life dedicated to good works.

Now, this passage teaches us that only our salvation makes fulfilling this purpose possible. And...exactly how was that salvation accomplished? "Not as a result of works," says verse 9! No, our works have nothing to do with our salvation. Indeed, C.H. Spurgeon once remarked that we might better try to sail the Atlantic in a paper boat than try to get to heaven on good works! Good works do *not* result in salvation, but "by *grace* you have been saved through faith; and that not of yourselves, it is the gift of God" (Ephesians 2:8, emphasis added)—and that grace is what empowers us for good works. In other words, good works cannot save, but good works sooner or later accompany salvation.[12]

Another part of the assignment God gives you and me as members of "the household of faith" is found in Galatians 6:10. Here God expresses His desire for us to extend good works to all people—not only to other Christians, but also to those who are not. We read, "Let us do good to all men, and especially to those who are of the household of the faith." And, as Dr. Chuck Swindoll acknowledges, we won't always feel like doing good. Why? Because "our tendency [when hurt] will be anything but that [of doing good]. Instead of good, we will feel like doing evil. Fume. Swear. Scream. Fight. Pout. Get irritated. Burn up all kinds of emotional BTUs. Rather than parading through that shop-worn routine, stay quiet and consciously turn it *all* over to the Lord. Let us do good."[13] Doing good to everyone is a tall order, but the Lord delights in helping us fulfill it.

Another clause in our job description—and one of my favorite formulas for interpersonal relationships—is Luke 6:27-28. These verses reveal Jesus' rule for love in our difficult relationships. He says, "Love your enemies, do good to those who hate you, bless those who curse you, pray for those who mistreat you." In other words, we are to love those who cause us pain through the *personal* response of doing good, the *public* response of blessing, and the *private* response of praying.

Abraham Lincoln was able to do just that toward a mean and insulting man named Stanton. Lincoln definitely knew how to love his enemies as Jesus instructed, as we can see in the following account:

> No one treated Lincoln with more contempt than did Stanton. He called him "a low cunning clown," he nicknamed him "the original gorilla" and said that [one was a fool] to wander about Africa trying to capture a gorilla when he could have found one so easily at Springfield, Illinois. Lincoln said nothing. He made Stanton his war minister because he was the best man for the job and he treated him with every courtesy. The years wore on. The night came when the assassin's bullet murdered Lincoln in the theatre. In the little room to which the President's body was taken stood that same Stanton, and, looking down on Lincoln's silent face, he said through his tears, "There lies the greatest ruler of men the world has ever seen."[14]

Like Jesus said, there should never be a person whom we refuse to love. In any and every case, we are to love friend and enemy alike by our acts of goodness. Thank God that He helps us fulfill this assignment by filling us with His goodness so that we have His goodness to give to others!

Putting Goodness to Work

As you and I walk through the day-in, day-out routines and responsibilities of life, we have a variety of opportunities to choose goodness. And many of these challenges come with our various roles as women—single or married. In fact, I find it sobering to notice how many times God specifies goodness and good works as the high calling for us as His women.

As women we are to learn goodness. In Titus 2:5 Paul writes to the new pastor Titus to make sure that the young women are taught by other women and encouraged by them to, among other things, "be...good" (Titus 2:5 KJV).

This, dear sister, is instruction for our daily relationships of home life. Older women are to encourage younger women to love their husbands and children (verse 4). Women of God are to exhibit spiritual goodness "while performing their tasks in the family...[and to] take care that the constant strain of domestic duties [did] not make them irritable or cruel. They must pray for the grace to remain kind [and good]."[15] This is sound advice!

As women we are to teach goodness. Once a younger woman learns goodness from older women, she is to take on the role of teacher herself and pass on to others what she's learned over the years. Titus was not to teach the women about their roles. Instead, he was to have the older women teach what is good and encourage the young women to be kind and good

(Titus 2:3-5). This means that you and I can—and should... and *must!*—use all that we have learned to help other women understand what walking by the Spirit is all about.

As women we are to be devoted to goodness. In 1 Timothy 5, Paul describes which widows the church should care for monetarily: They were to be the widows who had a "reputation for good works" (verses 9,10). And what were some of those good works? Paul writes, "If she...[has] been the wife of one man...if she has brought up children, if she has shown hospitality to strangers, if she has washed the saints' feet, if she has assisted those in distress, and if she has devoted herself to every good work" (verses 9,10). It's plain to see that the measuring stick for the widows' goodness—and ours as well—began at home: They were to be faithful wives, wise mothers, good hosts, and kind benefactresses.[16] Oh, how I pray that you and I never overlook the importance of what goes on right in our own home! Our goodness is truly to be lived out among the people who live under our roof as well as those who enter our doors.

As women we are to adorn ourselves with goodness. In 1 Timothy 2:9-10 the apostle Paul addresses the place of women in the church. Here he writes that God's desire for women was that they adorn themselves "by means of good works, as befits women making a claim to godliness" (verse 10). Speaking of Christian women, one scholar writes that good works "create that spiritual adornment which is the real glory of the Christian woman."[17]

Good works as an adornment for a woman suggests a life of selfless devotion to others, an adornment that lies not in what she puts on, but in the loving service she gives out.[18] Clearly, God wants our good works to be our chief ornaments. They are what He wants others to notice—not our clothes and not our jewelry. These good works, these selfless deeds and sacrificial actions, will reflect our walk with God.

Enjoying a Sampling of Goodness

As you and I turn through the pages of our Bible, we find many instances of goodness.

- As we've already seen, *Dorcas* was a woman "full of good works" for the widows (Acts 9:36 KJV). In her kindness, she noticed their need, and then her goodness followed through with action and made clothes for them (verse 39).
- *The Shunammite woman,* in her kindness, noticed Elisha passing through her town. Then her goodness went into action and followed through: In addition to providing his meals, she had a small room built on top of her home so Elisha could stay there every time he came her way (2 Kings 4:8-10).
- When *Rebekah,* Isaac's future wife, arrived at the town well to draw water, she saw there a tired, old man who had just completed a 500-mile journey. In her kindness she realized how weary he was from his long trek and noticed his needs. But her goodness took him water—and also watered his ten camels. Rebekah followed through on her observations with action. She did everything she could think of to ease the old servant's life and meet his needs (Genesis 24:15-20).
- *Lydia,* on the same day she became a Christian after hearing the apostle Paul speak, realized in her kindness that Paul and his companions had no place to stay. So she acted in her newborn goodness and insisted, "Come into my house and stay" (Acts 16:15). Lydia provided for

them and met their needs. She did everything she could for them.

- *Martha,* unfortunately, offers us a negative example. Oh, she did all the *deeds* of goodness, but she did them without patience or kindness or goodness. Martha crossed over the line into the works of the flesh. In our chapter on peace, we saw her complaining and out of control; "Martha the Mouth" was accusing, blaming, and slandering (Luke 10:38-42). She lived out the desires of the flesh instead of walking by the Spirit (Galatians 5:16). Martha serves as a caution signal for us, showing us how easy it is to slip from doing a good thing.

Learning from Jesus' Goodness

Of course our Jesus supplies us with the ultimate example of every grace fruit, and God's Word shows patience, kindness, and goodness all wrapped up together in Jesus. For instance, in Luke 9:51-56, our Lord is moving determinedly toward the cross. He had resolutely set His face to go to Jerusalem, where He knew He would die for mankind's sins. Jesus had sent several of His disciples ahead to make arrangements for their stay in a Samaritan village—and they did not receive Him. The Samaritans—for whom Jesus was going to die—said, in essence, "Go away. We don't want You!"[19]

Here, my friend, is a people problem! Jesus—God's love in human flesh—moved toward Jerusalem to demonstrate, in blood, His love for sinful people. And these Samaritans refused to even welcome Him into their town for one night! But look at His disciples' reaction: "Lord, do You want us to command fire to come down from heaven and consume them?" (Luke 9:54). And now look at the Lord's response. What did He think about the disciples' suggestion? He turned and He rebuked them, saying, "You do not know what kind of spirit you are of; for the Son of Man did not come to destroy men's lives, but to save them" (verses 55-56). Then Jesus led them on to another village.

Our Jesus was patience in action. *He* was the one who had been rebuffed, not the disciples! And He was definitely a man who could avenge Himself. But He chose not to. He was also kindness personified. He wanted the best for those Samaritans. And He was Goodness-in-flesh as He kept moving to Jerusalem to die for the very people—the Samaritans and those of us like them—who had rejected Him. The disciples, however, possessed no patience. They wanted revenge, retaliation, the chance to strike back! And they possessed no kindness. They wanted the Samaritans to be punished. And they possessed no goodness. They wanted to destroy the Samaritans by calling down fire and wiping them out.

Oh, how many times we take the same approach these confused, proud, foolish disciples took and respond with antagonism! It's just so easy, isn't it? So natural...and it feels so good, so smug, so righteous! But, dear friend, when you or I are hurt, rejected, abused, or snubbed, we need to make the patience that Jesus exhibited our first action—and do nothing. This choice then gives us time (even a split second!) to pray and reflect on God's way of responding to those who cause us pain. This choice to do nothing also gives us time to plan deeds of kindness so that we can then follow through with the actions of goodness. Truly, every assault upon us gives us an opportunity to live out godliness.

Walking in Goodness

Oswald Chambers writes so beautifully, "Christian character is not expressed by good doing, but by God-likeness. It is not sufficient to do good, to do the right thing. We must have our goodness stamped by the image and superscription of God. It is supernatural all through."[20] These words offer us a healthy reminder that our goal is to grow in godliness, not just to crank out works. So I urge you to pray for God's stamp on your life as you attempt to cultivate goodness in the following ways:

- Confess any thoughts or deeds that are not kind or good. Augustine wrote, "The confession of evil works is the first beginning of good works."[21]
- Take the initiative in meeting the specific needs of others. After all, "love means action."[22]
- Forget your own comfort: "When God is at work in the believer, he desires to be good and to do good....It becomes clear that the good life is not comfort, but godliness."[23]
- Advance the happiness of others: "Kindness is a sincere desire for the happiness of others; goodness is the activity calculated to advance their happiness."[24]

Things to Do Today to Walk in Goodness

As we near the end of our section on cultivating the actions of grace, again I want you to consider that person who challenges you the most, who causes you the most pain. And now I urge you to pour forth His goodness on the one who hurts you so deeply. Give every goodness you can think of and help him or her. Put kind thoughts into action and *do everything* God brings to your mind to do for that person. Act on His grace and then you will show forth His glory as you walk with Him.

~ 9 ~

Looking at Jesus' Actions

Jesus, our wonderful Master and Teacher, perfectly lived out the gracious actions of godliness we've been looking at. We saw one example at the end of chapter 5 when we witnessed Jesus praying in the Garden of Gethsemane. Do you remember? It was time for Him to die for mankind's sin. In His humanness, Jesus needed to go before His all-wise Father and come to terms with this awful assignment. And so, resisting all human and fleshly urges to rebel, panic, turn, or fall apart, Jesus instead fell upon His Father's breast in prayer. Then, after a time of earnest and intense prayer, Jesus came to terms with the upcoming events, "hushed His Spirit,"[1] and rose up from the ground filled with God's love, joy, and peace. Fortified after His time of prayer and having "thoroughly equipped Himself,"[2] Jesus gathered His sleeping disciples and boldly walked through the garden gate...

...to face people. Jesus knew that people were waiting on the other side of the gate. My friend, interpersonal problems will always be a part of the challenge of living out the Christian life, but we can learn so very much from our Lord who, even at this point, magnificently displayed God's gracious response to people. Exactly who was waiting for Jesus outside the garden?

The Traitor

As He resolutely strode toward the garden entrance, Jesus said, "Behold, the one who betrays Me is at hand!" (Matthew 26:46). The Savior most definitely knew *what* was about to happen—and He also knew *who* was instrumental in the process: It was Judas. How Christ's heart must have ached as He looked into the face and eyes of Judas—one of the Twelve chosen to be the focus of His ministry of teaching, leadership, provision, and miracles; one who had been prayed for by the Savior and fed by His miraculous multiplication of loaves and fishes; one whose dirty feet had been washed by the Savior's holy hands; one who had heard the words of life and truths of God from the mouth of God Himself. Few people have tasted the privileges Judas had enjoyed on a daily basis in the presence of our loving Jesus!

Yet there Judas stood, filled with the darkness of hell itself and the evil of Satan, a traitor and a betrayer. What grief and disappointment must have filled our Lord! What heartache and sorrow must have sickened Him! A friend, a disciple, an intimate companion—now a traitor!

The Mob

And Judas was not alone. He was "accompanied by a great multitude with swords and clubs, from the chief priests and elders of the people" (Matthew 26:47). Included in this group of as many as a thousand[3] were the officers of the temple

(Luke 22:52), a company of Roman soldiers, the chief priests and elders.[4]

Yes, Jesus had to deal with people. For the next 18 hours, He would face a host of hostile people—people who would abuse Him physically and verbally, people who would hurl not only insults at Him but also fists, whips, staves, hammers, and spears. Still to come were the high priest Caiaphas, the scribes, the elders, and the Council of the Sanhedrin (Matthew 26:57-60).

And there would be still more! The list of Jesus' enemies continues:

- Pilate—who would call for Jesus' death (Matthew 27:2).
- The soldiers—who would strip Him, mock Him, spit on Him, and beat Him (verses 28-30).
- The two thieves crucified with Him—one of whom would insult Him (Luke 23:39-41).
- The crowd—which would hurl abuses and wag their heads in mockery (Matthew 28:39-40).
- The disciples—who would flee, leaving Jesus even more alone (Matthew 26:56).

Truly, the forces of evil had gathered for the purpose of arresting Jesus and putting Him to death.

The Fleshly Response

As soon as Judas kissed Jesus, His enemies came and laid hands on Jesus and seized Him (Matthew 26:50). In the seconds that followed, we see (again!) the fleshly response of Jesus' disciples in sharp contrast to His gracious response of patience, kindness, and goodness.

Think for a minute about this troubling scene of Jesus' arrest. It happened under the dark cover of night. Possibly a thousand people were involved. There was confusion and panic. Emotions ran high as the Savior of the world met its evil head on.

And, in the heat of those emotions, "one of those who were with Jesus reached and drew out his sword, and struck the slave of the high priest, and cut off his ear" (verse 51). We learn from the apostle John that this "one" is Peter (John 18:10). Peter showed no patience. Instead, he went into action. He grabbed a sword and swung—but, as someone notes, "What a ridiculous blow! How like a man half-awake! Instead of the head, he only smote the ear."[5] No gracious patience was exhibited in Peter's desire to slash 'em, dash 'em, thrash 'em, and kill 'em! He also showed no kindness—the kindness of God that desires the best for others. Instead, Peter's action caused someone to suffer. And he certainly showed no goodness—that fruit of the Spirit that also does everything for the good of others. Instead, Peter hurt someone in his efforts to protect his Master. Peter most definitely responded in the fleshly way. He chose the easy response. He reacted. He evidenced "the deeds of the flesh" (Galatians 5:19).

The Godly Response

Jesus also went into action. Notice how His response exhibited the fruit of the Spirit.

The Godly Response of Patience—First, Jesus lived out God's perfect patience. Do you remember the definition of patience from chapter 6? Patience is endurance when injured by others, it is interested in their good, it is without vengeance, and it *does nothing*. Jesus lived every aspect of this gracious fruit. Wanting nothing done in retaliation or reaction, He told Peter, "Put your sword back into its place" (Matthew 26:52). Although Jesus definitely could have avenged Himself, He rebuked Peter's puny action by asking, "Do you think that I cannot appeal to My Father, and He will at once put at My disposal more than twelve legions of angels?" (verse 53). Instead of calling on 72,000 angels, Jesus acted in perfect patience. He did nothing and consequently was led away (verse 57) as a lamb to the slaughter (Isaiah 53:7).

The Godly Response of Kindness—And why did Jesus let Himself be led away? Because of His kindness. God's kindness is concerned for the welfare of others (even one's enemies), it desires to better their lives, and it consciously *plans to do something* for them. In kindness, Jesus had "resolutely set His face to go to Jerusalem" (Luke 9:51) in the first place. In kindness, He had agonized in prayer those three long hours. And now, acting in kindness, he met the mob head on instead of fleeing. In His divine kindness, Jesus planned to do something for His enemies: He planned to die for them!

The Godly Response of Goodness—Finally, in goodness, our Savior moved into action. Goodness is active kindness and flows out of a heart that stands ready to do good. And goodness *does everything* possible to help others live well. So what did Jesus do? He turned to the man whose ear Peter had cut off, "touched his ear and healed him" (Luke 22:51). This man was one of the enemy mob. He had come to apprehend Jesus, yet now he found himself on the receiving end of Jesus' goodness. He experienced a miracle of goodness. In fact, his healing was the last service Jesus rendered before being bound. Appropriately for our Savior and Lord, "the last action of that hand, while it was still free, was one of love, one of rendering service to men."[6]

Our Response

Truly Jesus is the God of all grace who is "able to make all grace abound to you, that always having all sufficiency in everything, you [too] may have an abundance for every good deed" (2 Corinthians 9:8)! Having seen our Savior's great graciousness in horrific circumstances, how can you or I ever again lash out at others? How could we ever again be impatient with others after witnessing the beauty and grace of our Lord's patience with His killers? How could we ever again wish evil or ill upon others after watching our Savior's kindness as He walked the lonely road to Jerusalem to die for us all? And how could we ever again strike out physically or verbally at another after seeing our Savior's healing touch for an enemy? To be like Jesus requires us to be filled with God's grace—His Spirit's gifts of patience, kindness, and goodness. To respond in His way requires looking to Him to "find grace to help in time of need" (Hebrews 4:16). Let's look to Him now in prayer...

> It is in prayer, dear Father,
> That we thank You for the people in our life
> who cause us to need Your grace so.
> We acknowledge that
> Your patience,
> Your kindness, and
> Your goodness enable us to do nothing
> harmful, to truly care, and to act out Your
> love toward others.
> In our pain...our tears...our suffering...
> we look to You, O heart of love.
> May we refuse to act or react until we have
> again looked at our Savior's actions and seen
> His patience...His kindness...His goodness.
> May we grow in these graces.
> In Jesus' name, who came not to be ministered
> to but to minister to others...
> even to the point of giving His life as
> a ransom. Amen.

Section III

Applications OF THE *Fruit* OF THE SPIRIT

~ 10 ~

Following Through in Faithfulness

The fruit of the Spirit is...faithfulness.
GALATIANS 5:22

At work my husband Jim has a terrific secretary who keeps his desk in order, but at home I'm the one who ends up with that task. One evening, while I was filing some of Jim's materials, a newspaper cartoon fell out of the manila folder. Wearing a colonial general's hat made out of paper, holding a tiny wooden sword, and standing in a George Washington pose on top of a rock, Pogo was uttering the infamous words, "We have met the enemy—and they is us!"

"We have met the enemy—and they is us" is exactly how I feel many nights at the end of another day that began with such good intentions. The discouragement comes when I realize that I, too, have watched the national average of 6.4 hours of TV; that I've eaten the foods that move one to the "20 pounds overweight" category; that I have hardly touched the to-do list (I can't even find it!); or that I have failed to open my Bible. I am truly my own worst enemy when it comes to being a disciplined woman. How greatly I need the Spirit's fruit of self-control!

In this book, you and I have been on a journey to discover the meaning of each fruit of the Spirit listed in Galatians 5:22-23. First, as we learned about love and joy and peace, we grew to understand that these lovely qualities bloom with great sacrifice.

Next we dealt with the challenge of handling people the way God desires—and the way Jesus did—by looking to the Holy Spirit for His patience, kindness, and goodness.

And now we must move on to conquer the discipline of self. If you're cringing at the thought of self-discipline, know that there is hope for meeting this challenge. That hope lies in the final three aspects of the fruit of the Spirit that God has made available to us as we walk with Him—faithfulness, gentleness, and self-control (Galatians 5:22-23). These graces enable us to triumph over weakness, impulsiveness, and laziness and win over procrastination, stubbornness, and unhealthy desires. So hang on! It may be a rough road to walk, but a pattern for victory through God's Spirit awaits us at the other end. Let's begin with faithfulness.

Insights into Faithfulness

As Christians it is vitally important that God's faithfulness be a part of our character. Why? Because faithfulness marks God's presence in our life. When you and I are faithful, we show that we are born of God and belong to Him. As we walk in faithfulness, we show forth our faithful Savior to others. Faithfulness is also critical because, as someone has said, "The final criterion God will use to judge us will not be success but faithfulness."[1] Jesus also showed the seriousness of being faithful in His parable of the talents (Matthew 25:14-30). Using this story to teach the value of faithful obedience,

Jesus praised those who are reliable and called them "good and faithful" (verses 21,23). Every woman who walks with God longs to hear these words said of her, especially by our Lord!

The following insights can help us in our understanding of faithfulness and our desire to walk in greater faithfulness.

Insight #1—The God of Faithfulness. From the opening page of the Bible to the last, we can see that God is faithful. As I was reading the Psalms just this morning, I was again moved by these words: "To all generations I will make known Thy faithfulness with my mouth" (89:1). Moses did just that when he praised God, exulting, "The Rock!...a God of faithfulness...is He" (Deuteronomy 32:4). As one scholar exhorts, "God is a Rock...and there should be something of the rock in us."[2]

This truth about God's faithfulness, dear friend, should bring comfort to both of us. When we pause to ponder God's faithfulness, strength is infused to our sore souls and we find courage to stand on Him, the Rock. Just as Jeremiah and his people did, you and I can endure our trials by counting on God's faithfulness (Lamentations 3:22-23).

The New Testament shows us that Jesus is faithful, too. Indeed His name is "Faithful and True" (Revelation 19:11). And how did Jesus exhibit His faithfulness? His ultimate demonstration is this: "Because Jesus was faithful, He 'emptied Himself, taking the form of a bond-servant, and being made in the likeness of men. And being found in appearance as a man, He humbled Himself by becoming obedient to the point of death, even death on a cross' (Philippians 2:7-8)."[3]

I certainly know that these sacred words cause me to wonder: Am I faithfully fulfilling God's purpose for my life, just as my Lord did? Am I faithfully serving those in my path—

my husband, my children, my church, my co-workers? Am I walking in humility before God so that He may exalt me (1 Peter 5:6)? Am I willing to follow in Jesus' steps of faithfulness and obedience and make every sacrifice that faithfulness requires—even that of death? When I consider these questions, I can only trust that God knows the desires of my poor, weak heart!

So, we've seen that God is faithful and Jesus is faithful. And we also know that God's Word is faithful. The aged apostle John was instructed to write down his visions because "these words are faithful and true" (Revelation 21:5). We are indeed a blessed people to be eternally experiencing the faithfulness of the Godhead and the faithfulness of the Bible!

Insight #2—The Core of Faithfulness. Faithfulness is defined as loyalty, trustworthiness, or steadfastness.[4] It is characteristic of the person who is reliable,[5] and it applies to the Christian's behavior in respect to people as well as toward God.[6] Our faithfulness to God and His will, to God and His Word, does not exclude—but includes—loyalty to others.[7] The *Ryrie Study Bible* adds that faithfulness means faithful not only in deed, but also in word.[8]

Whew! That's a lot to take in, isn't it? But this fruit of faithfulness becomes vital to us when we see that God calls us as women to be "faithful in all things" (1 Timothy 3:11). You see, faithfulness is a major distinction of Christian women and a quality God uses to benefit the church, the body of Christ. I know we've both had experiences with people who have failed to come through. We know firsthand how it feels to be disappointed or left with the full burden when we counted on someone who let us down. And...we ourselves have probably been unfaithful at times. Oh, to be more like Jesus—faithful and true!

Insight #3—The Marks of Faithfulness. What does faithfulness do? What does faithfulness in action look like? Well, if you were watching a woman who is walking with God by His Spirit, you would note these marks:

- She follows through—on whatever she has to do.
- She comes through—no matter what.
- She delivers the goods—whether a message or a meal.
- She shows up—even early so others won't worry.
- She keeps her word—her *yes* means *yes* and her *no* means *no* (James 5:12).
- She keeps her commitments and appointments—you won't find her canceling.
- She successfully transacts business—carrying out any instructions given to her.
- She discharges her official duties in the church—and doesn't neglect worship.
- She is devoted to duty—just as Jesus was when He came to do His Father's will (John 4:34).

So, my friend...take a quick inventory of your own Christian walk. Let these points stretch your understanding of the fruit of faithfulness, a fruit that is so needed in our world today! And then ask God for His strength to go to work cultivating His faithfulness in your life.

Insight #4—The Opposites of Faithfulness. A greater understanding of faithfulness comes as we consider its opposites. (You may have already thought of a few yourself!) One of those opposites is *fickle.* We've all met people who change—change their minds, change their loyalties, change their standards. Something in their nature is unstable, capricious, impulsive. Nothing seems to matter. Nothing seems too important. Nothing seems to merit commitment.

Another opposite of "faithful" is *unreliable.* An unreliable person doesn't come through, can't be depended upon, and can't be trusted with responsibility. As the saying goes, you may depend on the Lord—but may He depend on you?

Insight #5—The Essence of Faithfulness. As I considered the faithfulness of God—the strengths at the core of faithfulness, the marks of a faithful saint, and the opposites of faithfulness—I chose as my own definition the slogan "*Do it!*" or, to quote the Nike shoe ads, "*Just do it!*" Faithfulness means doing it…no matter what, doing it…regardless of feelings, moods, or desires—if the Lord wills (James 4:15).

"Do it!" has become my battle cry as I struggle daily with my own areas of weakness. Tiredness heads the list…followed closely by laziness. But when I make a decision to *do it* and look to God for His strength and purpose in *doing it,* He gives me the grace to have victory over both. Later we'll look more at the enemies of faithfulness, but for now let the motto *"Do it!"* move you toward greater faithfulness. Try it…for an hour, a day, a week. I think you'll amaze yourself (and others!) as they see this sturdy fruit grow in your life through the work of God's faithful Spirit.

The Need for Faithfulness

Understanding faithfulness is a good first step, but we must also realize that we have a need for it. I confess that, at the sound of the alarm clock each morning, I feel overwhelmed by the many hats I have to wear, the multitude of people I need to serve, and the variety of roles God asks me to fulfill. As women, you and I have many—*many!*—assignments from God which we cannot accomplish without faithfulness. For instance, the primary assignment for married women is the role of wife. We are to love our husband (Titus 2:4) and help him (Genesis 2:18), giving all that these two instructions entail—for life! And, if we have children, we are to love them (Titus 2:4) and bring them up in the things of the Lord (Ephesians 6:4), faithfully teaching and training them according to God's Word.

And then, whether we're married or single, the duties and responsibilities of the home demand a high level of faithfulness. The daily basics of housework most certainly require faithful diligence! In fact, one reason I feel a need to study "the most excellent woman" of Proverbs 31 (verses 10-31) is to examine up-close a woman who faithfully carries out her assignment to be a wise manager of the home. She inspires me in my *own* homemaking as she shows me the range of her skills and her attitude as she approaches her work.

As part of our home management, we also have the obligation of money management. Again, Proverbs 31 displays this wonderful woman's shrewdness and her understanding of finances. She was definitely an asset to her household as she oversaw the budget for the home and the servants. She made money, managed money, saved money, invested money, stretched money, and gave money to the poor and needy. This woman was truly a *faithful* and trustworthy steward.

As part of my home management, I also have the obligation of desk management. My desk really forces me to follow my maxim *"Do it."* I call it "the discipline of the desk" and mentally chain myself there many hours each day. Although your desk or personal work area may not require the hours that mine does as a writer, the desk is still the place where bills are paid and letters are written; the scene of much list-making, planning, and scheduling; and the setting for projects that bring us and others so much pleasure. I laughed out loud when I read this anecdote from the life of Winston Churchill: "A professional author said to [him] that he couldn't write unless the 'mood' came on him. The great statesman replied: 'No! shut yourself in your study from nine to one and make yourself write. Prod yourself!—kick yourself!—it's the only way.'"[9] That's another way of saying, "Do it!" when it comes to the desk.

And then there is our devotional life. I know that both you and I desire the mark of God's freshness on our life, and that is achieved only by faithfully going to His Word on a day-by-day basis. Just as a flower needs water to flourish, so we need to drink daily from God's living Word.

Plus God expects His children to be faithful in the church. After all, the church is where we are to minister our spiritual gifts for the good of the body of Christ (1 Corinthians 12:7). Serving God calls for faithfulness—to Him and to His call to use His gifts and serve His people.

The father of modern missions, William Carey was faithful in his service to God in India for 41 years. Do you want to know his secret? When asked the reason for his success as a missionary, he replied, "I can plod; I can persevere in any definite pursuit. To this I owe everything."[10] Imagine the effect you and I could have upon our world today if we would just faithfully plod on!

The Struggle to Be Faithful

After thinking about the need for faithfulness, I made a list of my own personal struggles to be faithful. As I look at that list, I see clearly that these struggles are against my flesh ("For the flesh sets its desire against the Spirit, and the Spirit against the flesh; for these are in opposition to one another, so that you may not do the things that you please"—

Galatians 5:17). The good news is that, as we yield our flesh to God and are led by His Spirit (Galatians 5:18), we can walk in faithfulness.

But walking in God's faithfulness is a three-step operation. First, you and I must *desire* to live a godly life that manifests the graces of the Holy Spirit. Next, we need to *look* to God: His power from on high is available to us, and He gives it to us freely. Finally, we must *follow* God's Word by moving out intentionally and confidently, empowered and guided by God. This three-step process can always help us in our struggles to be faithful. Read on...

Tiredness heads my personal list of struggles, and I know from talking with the many women who cross my path that they, too, face this struggle. Tiredness says, "I can't do it." Tiredness moans, "I can't get up....I can't get up and check on the baby....I can't make it to church....I can't run the errands....I can't study....I'm just too tired!" In the flesh, we think and feel that we can't do it.

But, while tiredness says, "I can't do it," God's Word says, "I can do all things through Him who strengthens me" (Philippians 4:13). You see, my flesh and God's Word are in direct opposition! Therefore I need to follow the three-step plan. If I *desire* to be faithful, *look* to God for His promised strength (Philippians 4:13), rise up and *follow* His leading, and do it anyway, then tiredness takes flight and faithfulness takes over. It's *my* heart, but *God's* strength transforms it. It's *God's* strength, but *my* will submitting to Him. It's *God's* will filling and influencing *my* will, resulting in *God's* fruit appearing in *my* life.

Laziness is another fleshly barrier to faithfulness. While tiredness is a physical struggle, laziness is a mental one. Laziness says, "I don't want to do it." Laziness whines, "I don't want to clean the house....I don't want to cook....I don't want to get involved in a ministry....I don't want to discipline my children....I don't want to go to my Bible study....I just don't want to do it."

But, while laziness says, "I don't want to do it," God's Word beckons, "Set your mind on the things above, not on the things that are on earth" (Colossians 3:2). God shows us a better way and prompts us to change our focus: "Look not at the things which are seen, but at the things which are not seen; for the things which are seen are temporal, but the things which are not seen are eternal" (2 Corinthians 4:18). In other words, we need to get our eyes off ourselves and off the people or the event prompting the "I don't want to..." and instead look straight into the face of Jesus. I am definitely more motivated to *do it*—whatever *it* is—when I remember Jesus' words, "to the extent that you did it to one of these... *you did it to Me*" (Matthew 25:40, emphasis added).

We can learn a very valuable lesson from Edith Schaeffer, the faithful wife of theologian Francis Schaeffer. Hear her thoughts about a life of serving others from a chapter entitled "The Lost Art of Serving..." reflecting the essence of Matthew 25:40 on serving unto Jesus.

> How do I regard my having run upstairs with tea, or having served breakfast in bed, or having continued for years to do this kind of thing for a diversity of people, as well as for husband and children? How do I look at it? Do I feel like a martyr? Let me tell you exactly how I see it.
>
> First, I say silently to the Lord...: "Thank You that there is a *practical* way to serve *You* tea [or breakfast in bed, or whatever it is I am doing for someone]. There would be *no* other way of bringing You food, or doing some special thing for You. Thank You for making

> it so clear that as we do things that are truly in the realm of giving of ourselves in service to others, we are really doing it for You."[11]

It's sobering to realize that all you and I do is not done only for people, but for our Savior. Serving people is a primary way for us to serve our Lord. Our ultimate motivation, as Colossians 3:23 reminds us, is "Whatever you do, do your work heartily, *as for the Lord* rather than for men" (emphasis added).

Hopelessness looms large on my list of fleshly barriers to faithfulness. Hopelessness says, "It doesn't matter if I do it." As a young mother of two preschoolers, I struggled with this feeling. The need to discipline and train my children was so constant, so draining, so demanding, and progress appeared agonizingly slow. I was tempted to come to the erroneous conclusion that "It doesn't *matter* if I do it." I can also feel that way about my efforts to follow God's plan for me as a wife. Sometimes when I try so hard, an argument, tension, or misunderstanding happens anyway, and "it just doesn't seem to matter if I do it." In both instances, I'm tempted to give up and ask, "Why try?" Fear sets in—fear that I'm failing with my children and they're not going to turn out as I desire; fear that I'm failing in my marriage and it's not glorifying God as it should. But (note the three steps) my *desire* to *follow* God's plan moves me to *look* to my Lord, and He is always faithful to encourage me. "Have not I commanded you?" He reminds me. "Be strong and of good courage; be not afraid; neither be thou dismayed" (Joshua 1:9 KJV). Yes, God is faithful—and His faithfulness is expressed to me through these words which are available to me not only every morning (Lamentations 3:23) but all day long as well!

Procrastination utterly kills faithfulness with its attitude, "I'll do it later." Procrastination announces, "I'll prepare for that class later....I'll finish (or start) that chapter later....I'll reconcile the bank statement later....I'll call the plumber later.... I'll do it later." And exactly what do I think will happen later? Do I really think the frenzy of life will slow down, that some magical minutes will miraculously open up, that new energy will mysteriously arrive and I'll feel like doing the task I'm putting off?

Both my husband Jim and I procrastinate more than we'd like! One day a Christian book catalog came in the mail, and I sat down to look through it (a good excuse for putting off some more worthy task). Listed in the books for sale was one entitled something like *Thirty Days to Overcoming Procrastination,* and the ad copy boasted helpful exercises that could be done for one month. I was thrilled! Here was help! But, rather than *do it now,* I procrastinated and grabbed a 3" x 5" card and jotted down the title and publisher so Jim could order the book from our church bookstore. Well, Jim then successfully procrastinated so long that, half a year later when he got around to ordering the book, it had been discontinued—thanks to the thousands of fellow procrastinators who had also put off ordering it! Oh, how we need our Lord's faithfulness. But, if we follow the three steps of faithfulness, we can win over the attitude of "I'll do it later" and walk in His faithfulness. So pray for a greater *desire* for this firm, solid fruit. Raise your eyes and *look* to God for His help. Then *follow* His Word which wisely prompts us, "Whatever your hand finds to do, verily, do it with all your might" (Ecclesiastes 9:10 KJV). *Do it*...just do it...and do it now!

Rationalization is an evil but subtle perspective on life, ministry, and responsibility that says, "Someone else will do it." Rationalization calculates, "Someone else will set up for the meeting....Someone else will make the announcement.... Someone else will lead the discussion....Someone else will do it." The godly woman who is faithful is "faithful in *all* things" (1 Timothy 3:11, emphasis added), all of the time no matter what. She is faithful as a servant in the church, as a member of a group, as a person with a leadership assignment. She is faithful as a wife and a mother, responding positively, enthusiastically, and energetically to those job assignments from God. She is faithful as a roommate, willingly doing her part of the work. She is faithful on the job, making sure she fulfills her assignments there.

A faithful woman will successfully defeat the unfruitful thought processes that lead to rationalizing, "Someone else will do it." How? By *desiring* to grow in faithfulness, by *looking* to God's Spirit to supply His faithfulness in weakness, and by *following* God's call that we be faithful in Christ Jesus (Ephesians 1:1) and faithful until death (Revelation 2:10). The way I chip away at rationalization is very simple: I try to be faithful for one day only. My goal each day is to be able to put my head on my pillow at night and thank God for helping me to be faithful to the tasks He gave me—today! Try this exercise yourself. Just for today, whatever responsibility you have, *do it.* This is a basic but very practical method for growing in godliness.

Apathy also gets in the way of our faithfulness. Apathy says, "I don't care if I do it." Apathy shrugs, "I don't care if the dishes get done....I don't care if I'm a good mom or wife....I don't care if I read my Bible....I don't care if I grow....I don't care if I'm faithful....I don't care if I do it." Apathy is a spiritual numbness that creeps in and corrupts the good that God intends for our life and the good that He wants us to accomplish for Him and His kingdom. But once again there is hope for this deadly perspective as you and I force our gaze off ourselves and *look* instead to our Father and His purpose for our life, as we turn our *desire* heavenward instead of inward, and as we *follow* in Jesus' steps, our Savior who lived "not…to be served, but to serve, and to give His life a ransom for many" (Mark 10:45)—including you and me.

If you, dear friend, are suffering from the crippling effects of apathy, won't you please stir up your heart? Do whatever it takes! Begin by remembering that Jesus' faithfulness accomplished your salvation. His faithfulness to die on the cross achieved eternal life for you. Ask Him to help you be more like Him and to help you cultivate His faithfulness.

Rebellion is the attitude that frightens me most. Rebellion says, "I won't do it." Rebellion stubbornly states, "I won't do what the Bible says….I won't do the laundry….I won't do what my husband asks….I won't do what the counselor advised….I won't do it." Rebellion is a hardness that we should fear because, as the Bible teaches, "The man [or woman] who hardens his [or her] neck…will suddenly be broken beyond remedy" (Proverbs 29:1). There is no deadlier attitude of the heart than rebellion—whether blatant, open, outspoken rebellion or quiet rebellion which simply and silently goes about life in its own way.

Pause now and take your pulse. Is there any part of God's Word that you know you need to heed? Is there any secret compartment in your soul that is not obeying God's ways? Is there any godly counsel you've been given that you're failing to follow? I plead with you to *look* to the Lord, ask Him to give you the *desire* to be faithful to His Word, and then *follow* in His path of obedience. Pray along with David, "Search me, O God, and know my heart; try me, and know my thoughts;

and see if there be any wicked way in me" (Psalm 139:23-24 KJV).

Are you wondering where you can get the strength necessary for all this faithfulness? Where you can get the desire? Where you can get much-needed help? Our great God has made all we need to be faithful available to us through His grace. He wants us to do what David, the shepherd-king of Israel, did when he "strengthened himself in the Lord his God" (1 Samuel 30:6). David repeatedly declared, "The Lord is the strength of my life" (Psalm 27:1 KJV).

Praise God that you and I can go to Him when we are too tired, too lazy, too uncommitted, too sick, or feeling too sorry for ourselves. In fact, moments like these are precisely when we need to call upon God and be filled with His faithfulness. We can go to Him and ask Him to fill us with His strength. We can find in Him the strength (*His* strength), the vision (*His* vision), and thereby the faithfulness (*His* faithfulness). Indeed, He is waiting to give us His faithfulness.

Women Who Were Faithful to Jesus

A great source of encouragement to be faithful is found in the extraordinary faithfulness of the women at the tomb. These dear women had faithfully ministered to the needs of the Savior by serving Him and financially supporting His ministry (Luke 8:3). But their most heroic act of faithfulness began as they followed Jesus on His last journey from Galilee to Jerusalem—on His journey to the cross, a journey that finally found this loyal band of ladies with Jesus the entire day of His crucifixion and death.

I've always admired these women. I mean, just think about what that last day in Jesus' life was like, that horrendous day the women spent at the foot of the cross! The darkness (Luke

23:44), the agony of Jesus' suffering, the mocking and jeering of the crowd, the brutality of their Lord being beaten, crowned with thorns, nailed to a cross, and pierced in His side with a spear (John 19:34), an earthquake (Matthew 27:51)—it just seems to be more than a person could bear!

Well, we know the disciples couldn't handle it! They had already denied their Savior and fled (Mark 14:50). But, in faithfulness, this sorrowing group of holy women stood as near as they could to comfort Jesus by their presence in the closing agonies of the crucifixion (Luke 23:49). If I had been one of those women, I probably would have gone home after all these gruesome events, taken three aspirin, and gone to bed.

But not these faithful women. They stayed—to the end—the bitter, awful, gruesome end! Luke reports, "The women who accompanied Him from Galilee were standing at a distance, seeing these things" (23:49). And their faithfulness did not end with Jesus' death. They waited at the cross to see what was done with His body, and then they followed and saw the tomb and how His body was laid (verse 55). Then, surely weary after a long and agonizing day, these women returned home to perform two more acts of faithfulness. First, they prepared spices and perfumes to properly anoint Jesus' body (verse 56). (And, according to Jewish Sabbath law, these preparations had to be completed before sundown!) And then these women practiced their faithfulness in another way: "On the Sabbath they rested according to the commandment" (verse 56). They were faithful to Jesus, and they were faithful to God and His holy Law.

But still we've not seen the end of their faithfulness. Hear the story from Mark:

> And when the Sabbath was over, Mary Magdalene, and Mary the mother of James, and Salome, brought

> spices, that they might come and anoint Him. And very early on the first day of the week, they came to the tomb when the sun had risen. And they were saying to one another, "Who will roll away the stone for us from the entrance of the tomb?" (16:1-3).

Do you see the marks of faithfulness in these women, dear reader? The list is long. Their beloved Jesus is dead, but hardly forgotten because they were faithful friends—faithful to His last breath...and beyond. They prepared the anointing elements in advance (not putting it off until later). They rose early (not sleeping in due to laziness, depression, or exhaustion). They went ahead to the tomb even though they knew a massive, immovable stone had been rolled in front of the entrance (no rationalizing or excuses). Even as they went, they wondered how they were going to gain access to Jesus' body, but they didn't let the thought of an obstacle deter them. They went to the tomb anyway. They followed through. They showed up. And they went early. On that morning after the Sabbath, these women went into action. These women "went with the Lord into the shadows,"[12] so to speak. Their friend still needed their ministry even though He was dead.

Whenever I'm exhausted, stretched to the limit, and tempted to give up or wait until tomorrow, I think of these magnificent women. Their love for God overruled their emotional and physical tendencies and enabled them to faithfully do the right thing. *Nothing* kept these ladies from fulfilling what they considered to be their faithful duty to a friend.

Walking in Faithfulness

I hope that after such powerful examples of faithfulness—and from a group of women who are just like you and me!—that you, too, feel the need to pause...and ponder. We *must* respond! We *must* wonder, how can we become more faithful? How can we walk in this grace, too? What can help us to cultivate God's faithfulness in our life?

Well, God's Word comes to our rescue with a few practical suggestions.

- Call upon God in prayer. "On the day I called Thou didst answer me: Thou didst make me bold with strength in my soul" (Psalm 138:3).
- Be faithful in small things. "He who is faithful in a very little thing is faithful also in much; and he who is unrighteous in a very little thing is unrighteous also in much" (Luke 16:10).
- Rely on God's strength. "I can do all things through Him who strengthens me" (Philippians 4:13).
- Fight self-indulgence. "I buffet my body and make it my slave" (1 Corinthians 9:27).
- Eliminate laziness and idleness. "[She] does not eat the bread of idleness" (Proverbs 31:27).
- Begin at home. "She looks well to the ways of her household" (Proverbs 31:27).
- Be faithful in all things. "Women must…be…faithful in all things" (1 Timothy 3:11).
- Become a "hero." I close this chapter with a prayer that the following definition of a "hero" will move you—as it has me—to desire greater faithfulness.

The Hero

> The hero does not set out to be one. He is probably more surprised than others by such recognition.

He was there when the crisis occurred...and he responded as he always had in any situation. He was simply doing what had to be done! Faithful where he was in his duty there...he was ready when the crisis arose. Being where he was supposed to be...doing what he was supposed to do...responding as was his custom...to circumstances as they developed...devoted to duty—he did the heroic![13]

~ 11 ~

Growing Strong Through Gentleness

The fruit of the Spirit is...gentleness.
GALATIANS 5:22-23

Of all the blossoms along the path we walk with God, the flower of gentleness appears so fragile, yet as we'll soon see, it develops out of the strongest of underground root systems. Before I began teaching about the fruit of the Spirit, I meditated on gentleness for one whole year—and that was one entire year devoted to cultivating gentleness in my life. Then, as I've written this book and continued my study, God has given me a second year to think about gentleness.

Come along with me and find out what makes the flower of gentleness bloom.

The Meaning of Gentleness

As you know, in this section you and I are looking at the three graces that call us to discipline ourselves in our pursuit of godliness. As we learned in the previous chapter, God's faithfulness is cultivated in us as we "do it"—as we do whatever lies in our path that must be done. And we discovered, too, how heavily we must lean upon God's strength and how deeply we must reach down inside ourselves to make the effort to follow through, to come through, to become more reliable and trustworthy. Now, as we turn to gentleness, we quickly learn that we have to depend again on God.

Gentleness means to be gentle or meek, to be lowly or humble.[1] It is a form of self-control which Christ alone can give,[2] and it manifests itself in a submissive spirit toward both God and man.[3] Gentleness is also the opposite of self-reliant arrogance.[4] And, as you'll discover, gentleness is truly grown in a hothouse—and there's a high price to pay to cultivate its bloom!

Just why is gentleness so costly?

1. *Gentleness Means Trusting the Lord*—Just as we trust the Lord for every fruit of the Spirit, so we trust Him for this one, too. In Matthew 5:5, Jesus says, "Blessed are the gentle, for they shall inherit the earth." William Hendriksen had this to say about Jesus' words:

> "The meek" [or gentle] describes the person who is not resentful. He bears no grudge. Far from mulling over injuries received, he finds refuge in the Lord and commits his way entirely to him....He has learned to take joyfully "the plundering of his possessions, knowing that he has a better possession and an abiding one" (Hebrews 10:34). Yet *meekness is not weakness*....It is submissiveness under provocation, the willingness rather to *suffer* than to *inflict* injury. The meek [or gentle] person leaves everything in the hand of him who loves and cares.[5]

It helps to note first what gentleness isn't: It is *not* resentful, it bears *no* grudge, and it is *not* involved in mulling over injuries.

And what does gentleness do instead? It finds refuge in the Lord and His ways. It endures plundering, provocation, and suffering in humble submission to an all-wise, caring Father, trusting totally in the love of God.

But, we instantly wonder, *how* can anyone bear plundering, provocation, suffering, and ill-treatment? For me, the answer boils down to one word—faith. The invisible root system of gentleness goes deep into the rich soil of faith. Faith believes that everything that happens in our life is allowed by God and that He is able to help us handle our situation. Our faith in the God behind this truth keeps us from struggling and fighting because faith believes that God will fight *for* us (Psalm 60:12).

Now do you see why I've been at work cultivating this fruit for two years? I have the feeling I'll be doing so for many more!

But how about you, precious traveller along life's way? Does your life show the fruit of gentleness? Where are you failing to submit to God and His management of your life? Do you consider God's meekness to be weakness? Do you generally bear grudges toward others, contemplate revenge, think vengeful thoughts? Or are you one who can look beyond the injury inflicted by another to the God of wisdom who uses pain in your life so that you might bear the mark of His Spirit in a mighty way? Whisper a prayer to God with me now and ask His blessing as you seek to bear any harshness in life with His Spirit of gentleness, trusting in Him.

2. *Gentleness Means Submitting to the Master*—Commentator William Barclay offers another picture of gentleness when he explains, "What throws most light on [the meaning of gentleness] is that the adjective…is used of an animal that has been tamed and brought under control."[6] This definition,

along with the fact that gentleness is highly revered by God in His women (1 Peter 3:4), caused me to search a little further—which revealed some startling concepts.

- The word *tame*, which is the opposite of wild, describes one accustomed to control by another.
- The word *tame* suggests one whose will has been broken or who has allowed himself or herself to be dominated by the will of another.
- The tame person, therefore...
  —Has been toned down and exhibits complete dependence on another.
  —Has yielded all will to another's control.
  —Unquestioningly and humbly obeys what is ordered and accepts what is given.
  —Is docile and obedient and pliable, as opposed to fierce.
  —Is easy to work with and to be with.[7]

Perhaps (like me) you're not sure you like what you're reading or what it implies!

But it helps us to think about gentleness in terms of submitting to our Master, the Lord Jesus. Don't you desire to be controlled by Him? Don't you truly yearn for Him to take complete charge of your life, to lead and guide you, to protect and care for you as you follow Him unquestioningly in faith? Don't you want to be easy to work with and be with? As one believer observed, "What makes humility [or gentleness] so desirable is the marvelous thing it does to us: It creates in us a capacity for the closest possible intimacy with God."[8] To belong totally to the Master, to want only His will, to depend completely on Him, and to yield humbly to Him and His ways brings great intimacy with God.

So breathe a huge sigh of *release* and hand over to God any part of your life that you have not yet given to Him. Thank Him—as your Master and as the Master Gardener—that He is able to care for it. Allow yourself the joy of being mastered by the Master.

3. *Gentleness Means Following Christ's Example*—I have a true confession to make: As the definition of gentleness became clearer...and tougher, I felt more and more hopeless. But when I saw in God's Word that Jesus was gentle, the meaning of gentleness became much clearer.

Our Lord, the King of kings and Lord of lords, rode on a colt as He approached Jerusalem for the last time (Matthew 21:7). This was the fulfillment of a prophecy from Zechariah 9:9 which said, "Behold, your King is coming to you, *gentle,* and mounted on a donkey, even on a colt, the foal of a beast of burden" (Matthew 21:5, emphasis added). Jesus came not as a storming conqueror or a battling king, but as the King who is meek, gentle, peaceful, gracious.[9]

Hear how Jesus describes Himself in yet another passage from Matthew: "Take My yoke upon you," He says, "and learn from Me, for I am *gentle* and humble in heart" (11:29, emphasis added). Dear sister, we follow Jesus' example of gentleness when we, like Him, find refuge in God and commit our way to Him. Jesus' gentleness was grounded in a complete trust in His loving Father, and ours can be, too, as we cultivate gentleness by following His example.

4. *Gentleness Means Bowing the Soul*—I also found a lovely word picture that helped me with gentleness. The Old Testament term for gentleness, *anah,*[10] describes a mature, ripened shock of grain with its head bent low and bowed down. Just think for a moment on the beauty of this word picture. As wheat grows, the young sprouts rise above the rest. Their heads

shoot up the highest because no grain has yet formed. In their immaturity, little fruit, if any, has appeared. But, as time passes and maturity sets in, fruit comes forth—so much of it that the burdened stalk bends and its head sinks lower and lower—and the lower the head, the greater the amount of fruit.

Oh, how I want to be this kind of Christian—a Christian with a lowered head, seasoned and mature, well past the stages of arrogance, pride, and vain emptiness. I yearn for the beauty of prostrating my soul before my Lord and bending in need toward my God!

5. *Gentleness Means Putting on a Gentle Spirit*—Wearing this gracious garment calls for a decision from us. As I mentioned earlier, God loves the quality of gentleness in His women. Look at these "elements" from 1 Peter 3:1-6:

Verse 1 speaks of *the element of submission:* "In the same way, you wives, be submissive to your own husbands." Although this particular verse focuses on submission in marriage, the exhortation appears in a very long passage on submission of all kinds. All Christians are to submit themselves for the Lord's sake to every human institution in government (2:13), servants are to be submissive to their masters with all respect (2:18), Christ submitted without a word to His tormentors (2:21-25), and wives are encouraged to be submissive to their own husbands (3:1).

Verses 1a-2 point to *the element of behavior,* suggesting that husbands "may be won without a word by the behavior of their wives as they observe [their wives'] chaste and respectful behavior." What is the behavior of gentleness? Peter says it is God-fearing and blameless conduct. It is behavior that refuses to fight, refuses to give in to anger, refuses all thoughts of violence and vengeance, and refuses to assert itself. And, beloved, we can live this out only when we rest in God's sovereignty and are confident that He controls each and every situation in our life.

Verses 3-4 address *the element of the heart:* "And let not your adornment be merely external—braiding the hair, and wearing gold jewelry, or putting on dresses; but let it be the hidden person of the heart, with the imperishable quality of a gentle and quiet spirit, which is precious in the sight of God." Rather than being obsessed with our external appearance, Peter says you and I are to be concerned with our internal condition, the condition of our heart. The phrase "hidden person of the heart" refers to the personality of the Christian woman, which is made beautiful by the ministry of the Holy Spirit glorifying the Lord Jesus and manifesting Him in and through her life.[11]

And such a heart, Peter writes, should reflect a gentle and quiet spirit. "Gentle" (which is the same Greek word used in the list of the fruit of the Spirit) refers to docile and gentle cooperation, and "quiet" refers to the acceptance of life in general.[12] Put differently, "gentle" means not creating disturbances, and "quiet" means bearing with tranquility the disturbances caused by others.[13] I must say that since discovering these simple definitions, I've been praying for daily strength from God needed not to create disturbances and not to react to any disturbances created by others.

Verse 5 instructs us in *the element of trust:* "For in this way in former times the holy women also, who [trusted (KJV)] in God, used to adorn themselves, being submissive to their own husbands." Again, faith is the only way to walk in this way—a trust that looks to God in hope, and is directed towards Him and rests in Him.[14]

Verse 6 closes with *the element of faith:* "Thus Sarah obeyed Abraham, calling him lord, and you have become her children if you do what is right without being frightened by any fear." You and I put our faith into practice as we graciously accept the details of our life which contribute to a gentle and quiet spirit.

As women of God, we are to put on all these elements of gentleness (submission, behavior, heart, trust, and faith) just as we adorn our body with clothing every day. Just as we visit the closet each morning to select garments that are appropriate, we must visit God in the prayer closet and don the garment of a gentle and quiet spirit, which is rare and precious, truly beyond price.

6. *Gentleness Means "Take It"*—My personal definition of the woman who is practicing gentleness or meekness is that she will *take it*. And what is it she takes? She bears with tranquility the disturbances others create. She endures ill treatment. She withstands misunderstandings. Carrying the image of Jesus and His suffering in her mind and heart, she takes it, thus cultivating the fruit of God's gentleness.

I know this is hard to swallow, and there are obvious moral exceptions. And, of course, we should be asking God for His wisdom (James 1:5). But, dear reader, please open your heart and mind to the beauty of this fruit. God so desires gentleness to characterize our lives! Listen to Andrew Murray's thoughts on gentleness and what it means to take it:

> [Gentleness] is perfect quietness of heart. It is for me to have no trouble; never to be fretted or vexed or irritated or sore or disappointed. It is to expect nothing, to wonder at nothing that is done to me, to feel nothing done against me. It is to be at rest when nobody praises me and when I am blamed or despised....It is the fruit of the Lord Jesus Christ's redemptive work on Calvary's cross, manifest in those of His own who are definitely in subjection to the Holy Spirit.[15]

Another believer writes these words about the strength that comes from gentleness:

> [Gentleness] is...first and chiefly towards God. It is that temper of spirit in which we accept [God's] dealings with us as good, and therefore without disputing or resisting....[It is a humble heart] which...does not fight against God and...struggle and contend with Him. This meekness, however, being first of all a meekness before God, is also such in the face of men, even evil men, out of a sense that these [evil men] with the insults and injuries which they may inflict, are permitted and employed by Him.[16]

Yes, it's true that in the eyes of the world, gentleness may look like weakness, but producing this fruit calls for the greatest of strength! Indeed, gentleness has been called "the fruit of power."[17] That's why I entitled this chapter "Growing Strong Through Gentleness."

The Posture of Gentleness

Here's another word picture to help us: One day while I was studying Proverbs 3:5—"Trust in the Lord with all your heart"—I glimpsed a fresh insight into how gentleness and meekness can be nurtured. The Hebrew word for "trust" originally expressed the idea of helplessly lying facedown.[18] But practicing this posture of trust calls for complete reliance on Jehovah. It calls for an absolute confidence that God alone knows the right way to the right ends and what benefits us. It also comes with the certainty that God is able to free us from that which does us harm. Therefore this trust—this placing of our total confidence wholly in God—is the source of gentleness or meekness. We find ourselves able to helplessly lie facedown only because we trust God's wisdom *and* His ability to protect and defend us.

Clearly, this picture of trust reveals that gentleness is opposite to much that our world exalts. Gentleness is the opposite of self-assertiveness and self-interest. It is the opposite of violence and outbursts of anger, the evidence of God at work in our life.

And here's something else to help us with our posture: Gentleness is not only outward toward people. Nor is it a natural disposition. And it's not what some have chosen to call "a phlegmatic temperament." No...gentleness (like all of the fruit of the Spirit) has to do with our relationship with God and is basically a submissiveness to the will of God. As we learned earlier, faithfulness will do it but gentleness will *take* it. And we will take it from the hands of others because we know God's sovereign and holy hand rests upon our life and He will never remove it!

Consider, too, the hothouse conditions that grow God's gentleness. Gentleness is required when wrong is inflicted upon us and when we are suffering the heat of ill treatment. And what does gentleness do under those conditions? It lies helplessly facedown. It bends, it bows, it lowers its head before the Father. It submits, it accepts, and it humbles itself under the mighty hand of God: Gentleness *takes it*.

Gentleness accomplishes all of this by not fighting. And you and I take a giant step toward cultivating gentleness in our life when we decide that we will not fight or contend or resist what God is doing in our life. We must give up disputing, complaining, murmuring, and grumbling. After all, why should we do these things if God is in control and God is allowing these trying situations?

Are you familiar with Psalm 46:10? Many of us know this verse as "Be still, and know that I am God" (KJV). But did you know that the Hebrew for "Be still" means "Stop striving"? One scholar translates this rebuke, "Quiet!...Leave off!"[19]

In essence God is telling us, "Stop it! Stop all your warlike activity,[20] for it is I, God, who is doing this!" We are to "cease striving" (NASB), to stop fighting, and instead take it—whatever it is—as being held in the hand of our sovereign and loving God. Then, as we practice this posture of a trusting heart before God and rely on Him for His wisdom and mercy and protection, we indeed grow strong through gentleness.

Demonstrations of Gentleness

These are deep and thought-provoking truths, aren't they, my friend? But aren't you glad God gives us examples of other women who have grappled with—and grown in—gentleness? Let's take a quick look at a few:

We've already met *Hannah*. Hannah found herself the daily prey of her husband's other wife, who provoked her year after year because she had no children (1 Samuel 1:6-7). Can you imagine yourself in a situation where you are purposefully vexed by another person day after day, year after year? How would you respond, how would you act, what would you do?

Well, Hannah shows us the gentle response. In her great distress, she prayed to the Lord (verse 10). Instead of getting into a verbal battle or succumbing to tattling, plotting, or scheming to get even, Hannah chose to take it and she told the Lord instead. And what enabled her to take it? Her God in whom she put her faith. She could leave her unjust mistreatment with Him—knowing that He would judge righteously (1 Peter 2:23).

Mary, the mother of our Lord Jesus, also shows us an example of gentleness. You probably know her story well—by a creative act of the Holy Spirit, Mary conceived and bore the baby Jesus. But did you know that many thought of Mary as a fornicator? Joseph, her husband-to-be, wanted to privately break their engagement (Matthew 1:19), and certain Jewish authorities referred to Jesus as one born of fornication (John 8:41). As Mary's life illustrates, exceptional privilege often goes hand in hand with sacrifice and the first thing Mary sacrificed was her reputation.[21]

Pastor and radio teacher J. Vernon McGee wrote this about Mary's submission to God's will: "She told the angel, 'Be it unto me according to thy word.' At that very moment a cloud came over her life, and that cloud was there until the Lord Jesus Christ came back from the dead. The resurrection of Christ proves His virgin birth. It was questioned until then."[22] What options were available to the young, single, and pregnant Mary? She could have tried to explain, she could have told what happened, and she could have bragged. But instead, the gentle and meek Mary took it. In fact, for 33 years she silently endured the name-calling and the misunderstanding (John 8:41).

Mary of Bethany is another woman who models gentleness for us. In a touching scene of devotion, Mary anointed Jesus' feet with costly perfume and spikenard and then wiped His feet with her hair (John 12:1-8). But then a problem arose. As the house filled with the fragrance of the perfume, Judas criticized Mary in front of everyone assembled when he sneered, "Why was this perfume not sold for three hundred denarii, and given to poor people?" (verse 5). As one commentator notes, "While the odor of the spikenard was sweet to many, it smelled of waste to others. Judas with his calculating mind quickly figured up the cost of it and called it wasted on Jesus."[23]

How would you feel, precious one, if, after pouring out your heart in worship of your Savior, you were criticized publicly? And how would you respond? Our Mary responded with godly silence. Her good intentions were misinterpreted and she was criticized—yet she took it. She quietly bowed her head and bore the pain of public ridicule...and trusted in God instead. In gentleness and meekness, Mary took it.

And what happened when she totally trusted in God, when she made the decision to respond in gentleness and take it? *God* came to her rescue! In Mary's situation, Jesus Himself shielded her against the criticism and spoke in her defense. Although Mary's good intentions were interpreted the wrong way, Jesus knew her motives...and He not only defended her, but He praised her.

Moses is another saint who teaches us much about finding strength in gentleness. As you know, God chose Moses to lead His people out of Egypt and into the Promised Land. But as Moses led, the people constantly murmured and complained against him, blaming him for all of their difficult conditions. Just look at a partial list!

- When there was no water, the people grumbled at Moses. And how did Moses respond? "He cried out to the Lord" (Exodus 15:22-25).

- After God's people failed to trust Him the first time there wasn't any water, He tried His people again in the same way. How did they handle the test this time? The people quarreled with Moses. And how did Moses respond? "Moses cried out to the Lord" (Exodus 17:1-4)

- When giants were discovered in the new land, once again all the sons of Israel grumbled against Moses and Aaron. And, once again, true to their former practices, "Moses and Aaron fell on their faces" before the Lord (Numbers 14:2-5).

- Finally, in utter rebellion, the people assembled together against Moses and Aaron. And yet again, "when Moses heard this, he fell on his face" (Numbers 16:3-4).

Did you notice Moses' pattern for handling strife? When the people complained, Moses didn't argue with them, reason with them, defend himself, or get into any kind of struggle with them. Instead, he took it. He silently endured their attack and cried unto the Lord. Moses took it—and he took it on his face, prostrate before God. Moses took it—and took it to God, appealing to God and waiting on Him to come to his rescue in these unjustified attacks.

One final attack on Moses bears looking at, and that incident—in Numbers 12—had to do with family tension (both you and I know how warm things can get in the hothouse of family relationships!). Here, Aaron (who helped Moses lead God's people) and Miriam confronted their brother Moses about his marriage to a Cushite woman (verse 1) and accused him of pride. And Moses responded with gentleness. As one Bible teacher explains, "Moses did not defend himself. Because of his humility and his gentle meekness, he did not try to justify himself or to put his brother and sister down. He knew he was being falsely criticized, and that the truth would become evident."[24]

And Moses' innocence *did* become evident: "God stepped into the scene immediately, no doubt before Moses even cried out for help. He honored Moses' response, his humility, his meekness, his willingness to bear this false accusation without a counter attack. God dealt with Aaron and Miriam.... God made things right for Moses."[25] Hear God's evaluation of Moses' heart and character: "Now the man Moses was very humble [meek, KJV], more than any man who was on the face of the earth" (Numbers 12:3). Moses lived out the grace of gentleness: He took it and did nothing, trusting everything to God's able care.

I personally find the example of these saints overwhelming. I think, "I could never be like that." But at the same time I'm thankful for them. Each of these people cultivated their godly response to ridicule and suffering in the same way that we do, beloved, and, as a result, each of them grew strong through gentleness.

As I said at the beginning of this chapter, the flower of gentleness appears to be so fragile, yet it develops out of the strongest of underground root systems—out of a life hidden in God and lived in His presence, a life that lowers its head, falls on its face, and helplessly lies facedown. We can take it, dear one—we can live out gentleness—only when we stretch our roots down deep into the soil of trust and faith until we touch the heart of God and the Rock of Ages.

My prayer is that this chapter has encouraged you to bear with tranquility the ill treatment of others as you wait to see what God will do on your behalf. As the Author of every situation in your life, He is also the Finisher of those very situations. And if—and when—He chooses to step in, *He* is wholly glorified because it is evident to all that *He* came to your rescue. And if He chooses not to step in, He is equally glorified by your gentleness because only the grace and power of God Himself *in* you can enable you to take it.

Yes, but How?

So what can you and I do to walk in gentleness? How can we become more like Hannah, Mary, Mary of Bethany, and Moses?

1. Accept—Accept everything in your life as allowed by God.

2. Pray—Prayer develops the proper posture of gentleness in us—the habits of bowing, bending, kneeling, yielding, and submitting to God.

3. Refuse to complain and grumble—To complain, one wise believer notes, "is an accusation against God. It questions God's wisdom and God's good judgment. God has always equated complaining with unbelief...[because] to complain is to doubt God. It is the same thing as suggesting that God really doesn't know what He's doing."[26]

4. Refuse to manipulate—Let God resolve the issue for you. Put your faith in Scriptures like these:

Psalm 60:12—"Through God we shall do valiantly, and it is He who will tread down our adversaries."

Psalm 37:6-7—"And [God] will bring forth your righteousness as the light, and your judgment as the noonday. Rest in the Lord and wait patiently for Him; do not fret."

Psalm 57:2—"I will cry to God Most High, to God who accomplishes all things for me."

Psalm 138:8—"The Lord will accomplish what concerns me."

Taking the First Step

If you can, take a giant first step and identify the greatest issue in your life—something from the past, or some current situation that God is asking you to live with, to bear, to take. Then grab the garment of God's gentleness and meekness and put it on. Adorn yourself with this spirit of loveliness, His spirit of gentleness. And then bow your head in the posture of prayer. Allow yourself to lie facedown and trust in the

Lord. Wait for His action and His solution. Truly, this fruit of gentleness is the fruit of power—and it is grown in us as we walk by the Spirit.

~ 12 ~

Winning the Battle of Self-Control

The fruit of the Spirit is...self-control.
GALATIANS 5:22-23

It was Friday night. Normally our church doesn't have services on Friday evenings, but our sanctuary was packed. Jim and I were sitting in the second row with our two daughters and The Master's College students who attended our Bible study. The crowd of thousands was stirring in anticipation. For me, the moment was a bit unreal. I had heard about the speaker from my first days as a Christian. I had read his classic book *Spiritual Leadership* and had studied his leadership of Overseas Missionary Fellowship. And now J. Oswald Sanders was going to speak to us in person! It was one of those once-in-a-lifetime experiences.

As Dr. Sanders mounted the five steps leading up to the pulpit, we held our breath. This saint of 92 years needed assistance. But, amazingly, as he finished his greetings and turned in his tattered Bible to begin teaching God's Word, strength and vigor came to him from the Holy Spirit, and he seemed transformed before us. We were witnessing God's power in the life of a man who had dedicated his many decades to serving and loving the Lord, a man who had walked with God for close to a century.

Dr. Sanders had spoken at the chapel service the day before, and Jim had asked him to autograph his worn copy of *Spiritual Leadership*. Jim has used this book for several decades to disciple and train men for leadership. And just as Jim had already realized, the rest of us knew this evening that we were in the presence of a man who lived out the life principles of his book.

Do you ever wonder how we can, too, grow to the spiritual stature of a saint like J. Oswald Sanders? I think the answer to that question is revealed when we consider the character quality he placed first in importance. Hear these words from his chapter entitled "Qualities Essential to Leadership":

> It has been well said that the future is with the disciplined, and that quality has been placed first in our list, for without it the other gifts, however great, will never reach their maximum potential. Only the disciplined person will rise to his highest powers. He is able to lead because he has conquered himself.[1]

Conquering one's self is what the Spirit's fruit of self-control is all about. This important gift from God is another key which, when turned, ignites the power that fuels the fruit of the Spirit. You see, self-control touches off the spiritual energy needed to kindle all of the Christian life. Let me try to show you how.

Reviewing God's Fruit

Think about the importance of self-control for a moment. I can know all about love and what it does and I can have the desire to love, but God's self-control helps me to live out that love. The same is true for joy and peace. I know I need to offer the sacrifice of praise when my heart is breaking and I want to feel self-pity, but turning the key of self-control enables God's grace to flow in me and lift that praise. Likewise, when I feel a tremendous urge to panic and fall apart, the Spirit's self-control holds me together so that I can turn to the Lord, trust Him, and experience His peace.

Patience, kindness, and goodness are also powered by the Spirit's self-control. When, for instance, every fiber of my flesh wants to be angry or get upset, the Spirit's self-control gives me God's grace to do nothing, to be patient. When hurtful circumstances make it hard for me to care about other people, only the Spirit's self-control can help me extend the godly response of kindness. And to display God's goodness—to be active in making the lives of other people easier—I once again need the Spirit's self-control.

Having just read about faithfulness and gentleness, you know how much of the Spirit's self-control it takes to follow through in faithfulness when laziness and selfishness come so easily. And we learned that gentleness takes it—but only God's self-control can give me the strength to take it.

We've come a long way together in our walk along the path of understanding the fruit of the Spirit, haven't we? Together we've learned—and, I pray, grown—as, with each new fruit, God has challenged us in deeper ways. And now the final fruit on God's list, self-control, helps it all happen. The fruit of self-control is so powerful, so essential to the Christian life, such a rock-solid foundation for our journey to be like Christ (and one that I need so badly!). "But how," we wonder, "can we ever get a grip on something this large, this important?" It helps first to get a grip on a better understanding of what self-control means.

What Is Self-Control?

In the previous chapter, the apostle Peter described the grace of gentleness as an adornment we wear when we are walking by the Spirit. However, the spiritual clothing of self-control seems more like armor! Indeed, to practice self-control will require putting on battle gear and donning a warrior's mentality. You'll soon see why.

To begin, the Greek root of "self-discipline" implies self-restraint of one's desires and lusts.[2] Plato used this term to describe the person who has mastered his desires and love of pleasure.[3] Self-control is the controlling power of the will under the operation of the Spirit of God,[4] literally a holding in of one's self with a firm hand by means of the Spirit.[5] In simple terms, self-control is the ability to keep one's self in check.[6]

Did you notice the two common denominators in these definitions? One is the control of the self—*self*-restraint, *self*-government, and *self*-command.[7] The second common thread is the object of control—our passions, appetites, pleasures, desires, and impulses,[8] all that is physical, sensual, sexual. This includes everything we see, hear, touch, think about, and hunger for. Paul took pains to list for us the works of the flesh in Galatians 5, among them, immorality, impurity, sensuality, drunkenness, and carousing. Surely no child of God would want to live a life marked by these deeds! But only the Spirit's self-control can help us avoid them.

Why? Because (as I've pointed out before) within every believer a tremendous struggle goes on between the flesh and the Spirit (Galatians 5:17). This "tug of war" between the flesh and the Holy Spirit is a spiritual duel: The flesh and the Spirit "are lined up in conflict, face to face."[9] So, to win the battle of self-control, you and I have to recognize the conflict and rely totally upon God's help and grace (Ephesians 6:10-13).

When Is Self-Control Needed?

As a fellow believer observed, "To a greater or lesser degree, if you are alive you are tempted!"[10] Consequently, you and I need God's self-control every minute of every day in every area of life where we find ourselves facing temptation. We need the Spirit's help in the battle to resist fleshly urges in the common areas of life...like food and drink, purchasing and possessions, in all matters that are sensual and sexual in nature, and in self-indulgence of any kind.

Because self-control so often relates to the body (which is the temple of the Holy Spirit—1 Corinthians 6:19), we need to keep our bodies in subjection to the Lord. The reasoning goes like this:

> If the body is the temple, then the soul is the priest of the temple and should control the temple. Therefore, the soul should govern what the body does. When the body is tempted by the lust of the flesh, the lust of the eyes and the pride of life, the soul must say no! That is self-control. That body is disciplined by the soul to glorify God in all its actions.[11]

So, dear friend, we clearly need to be alert to our need for self-control in controlling our body. Then we'll be able to see the Spirit's grace of self-control in our lives.

What Does Self-Control Do?

When you and I are walking by the Spirit, His self-control is evident in our lives. That's when we'll reflect these strengths:

- Self-control controls and checks the self.
- Self-control restrains the self.
- Self-control disciplines and masters the self.
- Self-control holds in and commands the self.
- Self-control says, "NO!" to self.

A friend of mine wrote this list on a 3" x 5" card and taped it to the bathroom mirror to help her with a problem with overeating. I think her list is a great idea, and because it's applicable to a wide variety of problems, you may want to make such a list for yourself. You may also want to put the list in your prayer notebook. I know it always helps me to be reminded of God's pattern for self-control.

What Does Self-Control Not Do?

Looking at what God's self-control *isn't* also helps us understand this important fruit of the Spirit.

- Self-control does *not* yield to temptation.
- Self-control does *not* give in to desires.
- Self-control does *not* participate in sin.
- Self-control does *not* indulge itself.
- Self-control does *not* satisfy itself.

I warned you that self-control is a fruit of strength! By God's grace, we can be this strong—strong enough not to do these things.

What Is a Slogan for Self-Control?

In this final trio of spiritual fruit, faithfulness means—"*Do it!*" gentleness means—"*Take it!*" and now for our purpose of understanding, self-control means—"*Don't do it!*" In times of temptation we are to call on God for His strength, and then *don't do it!* In other words, don't give in to emotions, to cravings, to urges. Don't think or do what you know is against God's Word. Don't pamper yourself. Don't make the easy choices. Don't rationalize. And a thousand other "don't do its!"

As one pastor well explained, "The word *self-control*

means 'the ability to say no.' It is an evidence of willpower that sometimes expresses itself in 'won't power.' It is the ability to say yes at the right time; yes to certain things, and no to others. It is that kind of inward strength that takes all the circumstances and experiences of life and subjects them to evaluation and then decides, 'This is right, this is in the will of God,' or, 'This is wrong, I will put it aside.' "[12] That is, don't do what you could—do what you should![13]

Learning from Others About Self-Control

As with the other fruit of the Spirit, God's Word comes to our rescue with vivid examples related to self-control. In fact, the Bible offers a gallery of people who did and did not possess self-control. I've selected a few of them.

David shows us self-control. Reading in 1 Samuel this week, I was impressed by King David's self-control. As we look for a moment at 1 Samuel 24, consider the events leading up to this point in David's life. After being anointed by the prophet Samuel to be king (16:13), David became the object of the jealousy and hatred of the reigning King Saul. And twice, when David played his harp for Saul, he had thrown his spear at David, hoping to kill him (18:11 and 19:10). Then, when David fled for his life, Saul and his soldiers ruthlessly pursued him.

Tired from the chase, Saul entered a cave, not knowing that David was hiding in the same cave (24:3). While David watched Saul from the shadows, David realized that he could—easily and for two good reasons—kill the king. After all, David had been anointed to be king. And, second, Saul was on an unjustified manhunt for David. There in the cave, it would have been easy for David to slay his adversary. Yet David won the battle for self-control. What did he do instead?

He "persuaded his men...and did not allow them to rise up against Saul" (verse 7) and take his life. He told them, "Don't do it!"

David not only had the opportunity to kill Saul once—he had it twice! The second time, Saul, still in hot pursuit of David, lay sleeping at night in his camp, when David and a choice warrior entered the camp and stood over the king (1 Samuel 26:7). Concluding that God had delivered his enemy to him, David's companion begged, "Please let me strike him with the spear to the ground" (verse 8). In this case, David wouldn't even have to do the deed. Someone else would kill his enemy for him! Yet David restrained his friend, "Do not destroy him" (verse 9). Again, "Don't do it!"

David also shows us a lack of self-control. After Saul's death in battle, David finally reigned as king. But then a fateful chapter of his life begins with these words: "It happened in the spring, at the time when kings go out to battle, that David sent Joab and his servants with him and all Israel...but David stayed at Jerusalem" (2 Samuel 11:1). For whatever reason, David sent others in his place and remained at home in Jerusalem instead of going to war. Do you remember the portrait of "The Hero" from chapter 10? The hero was faithful: He was where he was supposed to be, and he was doing what he was supposed to be doing. Unfortunately, this statement was not true of David here, and this point marks the beginning of his great fall—as the next scene reveals.

One evening David took a stroll on his roof and, across the way, he saw a woman bathing by lamplight in the interior courtyard of her home[14]—*David saw*. Giving in to his desires, David next sent to find out who she was—*David considered*. As lust filled his thoughts and his heart, David gave in again and again and acted upon his fleshly desires until he sent messengers and took her and lay with her (verse 4)—*David acted*.

Do you see the progression of David's sin? At every step along the path of temptation, David gave in to his desires instead of exercising self-control and stopping the forward momentum of sin. He yielded to the sensual instead of choosing the spiritual. David could have chosen to stop and turn from evil at any stage along the way.[15] At any point, David could have said, "Don't do it!" But his failure to do this ensured his fall.

My friend, the situation is the same for you and me. With just one seemingly small wrong decision, just one failure to make the godly choice of obedience, just one moment when we let down, just one unchecked look or thought, even the strongest of the strong can topple into sin. This is why we must stay oh-so-near to God, keep a close check on our walk with Him, and cultivate the fruit of self-control with each thought, word, and deed. Praise God we can look to Him at any moment and receive His help and grace...and self-control.

Achan failed in self-control, too. When Joshua was the leader of God's people, the goods in the doomed city of Jericho were under a ban: Everything was to be burned and destroyed. But Achan acted unfaithfully in regard to the things under the ban (Joshua 7:1) and took some of the contraband. After a disastrous failure in a military raid, Joshua learned from God that someone had sinned against Him. With God's direction, Joshua confronted Achan. Hear Achan explain what happened: "When I *saw* among the spoil a beautiful mantle from Shinar and two hundred shekels and a bar of gold fifty shekels in weight, I *coveted* them and *took* them" (verse 21, emphasis added).

Does anything sound familiar here? Did you notice that this is basically the same pattern of fateful choices David made? And are you beginning to see the lessons we can learn from these men? Briefly stated, those lessons are: Don't stop, don't look, and don't listen. Don't do it!

Joseph and Potiphar's wife show us, respectively, self-control and the lack of self-control. Here's how it happened. The wife of Potiphar, an Egyptian officer of Pharoah and captain of the bodyguard (Genesis 39:1), appears to have been living an empty life without purpose...until her husband purchased Joseph, the son of Jacob, to be his household slave.

And...evidently Joseph was extremely handsome (verse 6). Potiphar's wife looked with desire at Joseph and said "Lie with me" (verse 7). Suddenly Joseph had a choice to make. Choosing self-control, he successfully resisted her advance. Despite his refusal, Potiphar's wife spoke to Joseph day after day (verse 10), always extending the same invitation. And, day after day, Joseph had to again choose self-control. The day came, however, when no one was in the house but Potiphar's wife and Joseph. Filled with lust, desire, and passion, she grabbed Joseph. Again Joseph had to make a choice—and he chose to flee, leaving his outer garment behind in the woman's hand. Later this seductress used Joseph's cloak as evidence to imprison him for an act he did not commit.

This dramatic scene provides us with clear instruction on self-control. On the one hand, Potiphar's wife had no self-control. She allowed her thoughts and actions to be dictated by physical sensuality. *Looking* upon Joseph with lust...led to *thoughts*...that led to *actions* which were deeds of the flesh. In sharp contrast, Joseph shines as a positive example as he exercised self-control. He successfully resisted every opportunity to yield to temptation.

Why was Joseph able to stand strong? He explained the secret of his strength to Potiphar's wife: "How then could I do this great evil, and sin against *God?*" (verse 9, emphasis added). Joseph shows us the highest *motive* for self-control and the right perspective: He saw the incident from *God's* point of view and knew this act would be wrong. His *reasoning* was also right: He realized this deed would be a "sin against God." And Joseph's *focus* was also in the right place—not on himself, not on his desires, not on his flesh, but on God. What God wanted mattered more to Joseph than what he himself wanted.

Joseph models for us this truth: "The secret of discipline is motivation. When a man is sufficiently motivated, discipline will take care of itself."[16] As Jerry Bridges writes in *The Practice of Godliness,* "Ultimately, self-control is the exercise of inner strength under the direction of sound judgment that enables us to do, think, and say the things that are pleasing to God."[17] May that be our motive as we face the choices and temptations of life!

Struggling for Self-Control

As I was thinking about my own struggles for self-control, I listed the areas that challenge me most and cause me to turn to God for help. The first (and worst) for me is *food.* Life would certainly be easier if I didn't have to be around food. I know that God created our body to need fuel, but somehow the natural need and desire for food can so easily get out of hand. For instance, because I'm writing about food, my mouth and mind are suddenly yearning for something to eat—but it isn't time to eat. I don't *need* to eat because I just ate lunch. I just *want* to eat! So I'm forcing myself to sit here and keep my pen moving. I'm thinking, "Liz, just say no. Don't do it. Don't get up and go to the pantry. Fight it. You can have this victory with God's help. Stay seated and keep working."

Could I have something to eat? Of course. Would it hurt me to eat? Of course not—not now, anyway. But what would the blessings of not succumbing to the flesh be? For one thing, I'll continue my progress on this chapter. For another, I can have God's victory in this small thing. By saying no, I build a track record with Him and gain experience that will help me later when I face a large thing.

I also struggle with my *thoughts*—so much so that I've written an entire book on the subject. *Loving God with All Your Mind*[18] is about how to have victory over thoughts that are not true to God's Word. The book details how to win that battle by focusing on what the Bible *says* versus what our emotions and feelings lead us to *think*.

Money is another daily challenge for many, if not all, Christian women. The world comes right into our home and tempts us to spend. I had pretty much said, "Don't do it" to spending by eliminating shopping from my schedule...but almost every day some kind of catalog shows up in my mailbox, along with advertising flyers for all kinds of intriguing items! And I don't even have to send any money to get these things—my junk mail abounds with offers for free credit cards! Salespeople call me with appealing deals. (I would do better if I taped a sign on the phone that says, "Don't do it!"). All these sales pitches create a real temptation to love the things in the world (1 John 2:15).

Closely related to the issue of money is the matter of *possessions*. I'm like every homemaker who loves having a nice home with all the little touches that make it a cozy and pleasant place—all the little touches that happen to cost money! When our family moved to Singapore for a term on the mission field, we sold or gave away almost everything we owned.

But guess what? When we came back to the United States, I got to start all over again! Early every Saturday morning I left the house with $25 cash and went to garage sales. Quickly the day came when I had replaced everything—and added a few extras! At that point I came face to face with the fact that I was addicted to the thrill, the hunt, the anticipation I experienced as I drove up to each sale, salivating and tingling over the unknown. I had to start telling myself, "Don't do it" on Saturday mornings. I had to curb myself, hold myself back, and control my desires. Imagine this great struggle over what our Lord calls the "stuff in the house" (Luke 17:31 KJV)!

Last in the list of challenges I face is *coffee,* undoubtedly the most difficult bodily craving I—with God's help—have had to handle. I love the smell of coffee, the taste of coffee, and the buzz it gives. I love the warmth of coffee and the ritual of sitting down over a cup of coffee. But I reached the point when coffee was controlling my life! Coffee—not God—was my first waking thought. Coffee—not prayer—was my first waking need. Serving myself coffee—not serving my family—was my first concern each day. I got to the place where I couldn't think or function without coffee. I couldn't teach God's Word without it. I couldn't plan or write or work or drive without that warm cup in my hand. I knew I was in real trouble when I began the "drive thru" habit…not for hamburgers or french fries, but for coffee—and always a large!

The day finally came when I recognized that I had no self-control when it came to coffee. In fact, I was way out of control! Reluctantly I decided to curb my coffee drinking and bring it back under control. I had to choose to say, "Liz, don't do it" to some of my coffee.

Before you get the wrong idea, I want to say that everyone else I know seems to be able to drink coffee without any problems. Jim is one of those people. I fix him coffee every morning, but he's able to apply God's principle of moderation to his coffee intake. In all the areas I've shared—not just my coffee habit—you and I are to exercise discernment and wisdom as well as self-control.

Now your list of fleshly temptations probably looks different than mine. But the battle over each allurement is won in the same way, dear friend: by calling upon God and relying on the gift of His self-control; by asking Him for fresh strength to say, "Don't do it" one more time. Depending upon God's strength like this is the key to cultivating His self-control in our life.

Nurturing Self-Control

With its accounts of people who exhibited self-control and those who didn't, the Bible teaches much about nurturing self-control. Maybe these instructions drawn from God's Word will help you begin cultivating that important fruit.

- Begin with Christ. Is He your Lord and Master? As one wise person has noted, "The beginning of self-mastery is to be mastered by Christ, to yield to his lordship."[19]
- Monitor your input. David's problem—and Achan's too—began with looking too long at the wrong things. Perhaps it was after his fall with Bathsheba that David wrote this advice: "I will set no wicked thing before mine eyes" (Psalm 101:3 KJV).
- Stay busy. Both David and Potiphar's wives failed because they had nothing to do. So make a schedule...and keep it! Volunteer to help others. Do whatever it takes to stay busy. By doing so, you will refuse to eat "the bread of

idleness" (Proverbs 31:27), and you'll find yourself with less time to be tempted.

- Say, "No!" Solomon wrote, "Like a city that is broken into and without walls is a man who has no control over his spirit" (Proverbs 25:28). Echoing that truth is this thought: "The word *No* forms the armament and protective walls of the spiritual city....Sometimes *No* can be a hard word to say, but it is the key to self-control, the word that the Lord blesses."[20]

- *Pray*. David "was a man committed to the reality of prayer. David prayed over nearly everything...except never once in the Bible do you find David praying about his love life. Not once....It was perhaps the one area of his life he never yielded, and it almost crushed him."[21] So pray—about every aspect of your life!

God's good news for you and me, dear reader, is that we can claim His power, walk by His Spirit, exercise self-control, and win the battle over fleshly temptation. Then we will wondrously display the beauty of Christ as we walk with Him through everyday life! What a wonderful God we have who makes the storehouse of His grace—His self-control—available to us!

~ 13 ~

Looking at Jesus' Applications

As you and I have been learning about the aspects of God's fruit of the Spirit and how to experience them in our life, Jesus has shown us much about what each of them looks like lived out by God's grace. I want us to look to Him again and seek to understand this final trio that deals with the discipline of self—faithfulness, gentleness, and self-control.

When we left chapter 9, Jesus had been forcefully apprehended and led away for His trial and crucifixion. How did He handle this series of events? And what was His mindset as He faced the cross? Peter, who watched these awful events unfold, can answer these questions for us. Although he strongly denied any association with Jesus when questioned by others (Matthew 26:69-75), Peter continued to follow his Master at a distance (verse 58). And with a few brief strokes of his pen, Peter summarizes our Lord's behavior so that we may follow in His steps:

> Christ...committed no sin,
> Nor was any deceit found in His mouth;
> And while being reviled, He did not revile in return;
> While suffering, He uttered no threats (1 Peter 2:22-23).

Jesus Committed No Sin

Peter's first comment is true about all of Jesus' life, not only His final days. Throughout His earthly existence, Jesus committed no sin. You and I have probably experienced the momentary reality of committing no sin when all is well and life is good. But such favorable circumstances—a blessing from God—are times when victory comes cheaply. But picture the worst of circumstances for a moment, the kind Jesus was experiencing, the kind characterized by treachery, lying, false accusations, unjust punishment, brutality, physical abuse, fists, clubs, rods, whips, nails, and a spear. Imagine committing no sin in this environment! Beloved, that would unquestionably be the work of the Holy Spirit as He enables us to walk through difficult situations without sinning!

But why was Jesus suffering so? Why was He being so harshly mistreated? All His life He had...

> Done well,
> Done the right thing,
> Done all that God asked and required of
>   Him, and
> Successfully carried out the Father's will for
>   His life.
> Jesus had...
>   Taught God's truth,
>   Healed God's creation,
>   Fed God's people, and
>   Taken light into darkness.

> Jesus had also...
> Preached the gospel to the poor,
> Healed the brokenhearted,
> Proclaimed release to the captives,
> Restored the sight of the blind, and
> Set free those who were downtrodden
> (Luke 4:18).

As Peter explains, Jesus suffered for doing what is right (verse 20). The holy Son of God, He never in a single instance sinned. He lived His entire life without sin (Hebrews 4:15). Through the words of Peter and the writer to the Hebrews, God testifies to the complete sinlessness of Jesus. He, of all people, did not deserve to suffer in any way!

Even those who condemned Jesus knew He had committed no sin! Pilate told the chief priests and the multitudes, "I find no guilt in this man" (Luke 23:4). After Jesus returned from Herod's court, Pilate repeated to the chief priests and the rulers of the people, "Having examined [Jesus] before you, I have found no guilt in this man" (verse 14). Pilate explained further, "Nor has Herod, for he sent Him back to us; and behold, nothing deserving death has been done by Him" (verse 15). One final time Pilate asked the Jewish leaders, "Why, what evil has this man done? I have found in Him no guilt demanding death" (verse 22). No, our Jesus committed no crime. He committed no sin.

Do you realize that like our Lord and Savior who was consistently and completely victorious over sin, you and I can call upon God to help us make the right choices in life, choices which say *no* to sin? As believers, we should be primarily concerned about avoiding sin, not avoiding suffering. Scottish devotional writer Thomas Guthrie warned, "Never fear to suffer; but oh! fear to sin. If you must choose between them, prefer the greatest suffering to the smallest sin."[1] Can you make this the perspective of your heart, too?

Jesus Spoke No Sin

Jesus was not only sinless in deed. He was also sinless in word: "Nor was any deceit found in His mouth" (1 Peter 2:22). Even after careful scrutiny, Jesus' accusers failed to uncover any craftiness or trickery.[2] He had always spoken the truth. He had always spoken and acted with pure motives. Nothing of deceit or guile could be uncovered.

Furthermore, Jesus didn't talk back, but refused to answer at His trial. When falsely accused by the chief priests and elders, "He made no answer" (Matthew 27:12). When Pilate questioned Him, Jesus "did not answer him with regard to even a single charge" (verse 14). Caiaphas and the Sanhedrin challenged Him, too: "Do You make no answer? What is it that these men are testifying against You?" (Mark 14:60). Jesus' response? "He kept silent, and made no answer" (verse 61). Instead of pressing His case verbally to people who did not have ears to hear, Jesus silently submitted to harsh treatment and a cruel death which He did not deserve.

Jesus Did Not Resist

Jesus also did not resist His accusers and enemies. He refused to fight verbally or physically. We read, for instance, that while being reviled, He did not revile again (1 Peter 2:23). To be reviled means to be sharply bitten by words, to be subjected to harsh railing, to be cursed with a string of abusive words.[3] Such was the treatment our Jesus, the sinless Lamb of God, suffered! Put differently, "thus was the tender heart of the Lord Jesus wounded by totally depraved human nature."[4]

Just as Jesus didn't fight back when He was assaulted verbally, neither did He fight back when He was assaulted physically. Instead, "while suffering, He uttered no threats" (1 Peter 2:23). Here, "suffering" means being buffeted, struck with fists (Matthew 26:67). Peter is remembering the blows of the servants, the scorn of the high priest, the silent submission of Jesus, the stripes, the cross. The Greek language emphasizes that, "under sustained and repeated provocation, never once did [Jesus] break the silence. All the time during which He was the victim of abuse, He was not reviling back. All the time during which He was suffering, he was not resorting to threats."[5] One scholar points out that the words *suffered* and *threatened* have a progressive force in the original language, remarking that "even continuous suffering at the hands of the mob did not elicit from our Lord any retaliatory words."[6]

Of course sinful, retaliatory words wouldn't fit the picture of Jesus' perfect godliness! To react and respond is something you and I might do, but Jesus, when unfairly treated, did not utter threats, condemn His oppressors, or invoke judgment upon them. He kept His mouth closed. In the words of Isaiah, "He was oppressed and He was afflicted, yet He did not open His mouth; like a lamb that is led to slaughter, and like a sheep that is silent before its shearers, so He did not open His mouth" (Isaiah 53:7).

Oh, how precious is our Jesus! And how greatly my heart hurts as I think upon this scene of horror and evil. My Savior's response is sobering. It makes me think (and purpose!) that surely if He exhibited such graciousness—such faithfulness, and self-control—in these *evil* circumstances, I can do the same in my quieter sphere of life and service. Surely if He bore with tranquility the pain and suffering caused by His killers, I can quietly endure the ill treatment I receive from others. Surely if He kept His mouth shut when He was innocent, I can do the same, no matter what the false accusations and misunderstanding. But I also know that I can only do these things by the power of God's Spirit, who fills me with His faithfulness, gentleness, and self-control.

And now...a final prayer of thanksgiving...

> It is with overflowing hearts, O Father,
> That we whisper yet another "Thank You"—
> This time for the grace of Your Son
> Who demonstrated complete faithfulness to You,
> Who accepted in gentleness such unjust mistreatment, and
> Who exhibited self-control in the harshest of circumstances
> As He walked to the cross to die for us.
> May we receive Your grace...that we may
> Faithfully do all that You ask of us,
> Gently and quietly suffer all that comes our way, and,
> In control of ourselves, do nothing that dishonors
> Your worthy Name.
> In Jesus' name, our Model and Savior and Lord. Amen.

Epilogue

Planning for Greater Growth

Whew! We made it! You and I have completed our walking tour of the fruit of the Spirit! Together we strolled along the path, moving from group to group, from fruit to fruit. With God's Word as our guide, we read about each grace, each fruit—what each one is and how each can be cultivated as we walk with God.

I'm glad we were allowed as much time as we wanted with each fruit. We had time to study, time to enjoy, time to ask questions, time to discuss, and, most of all, time to appreciate. But now our tour is over; we've seen it all. We now know what it looks like to bear God's fruit in our lives.

As we leave these pages, we want to be sure to take God's message with us. It's one thing to talk about spiritual fruit, but God wants us—you and me—to live it out in our life. His Word describes for us what He wants our life to look like, what He wants others to see in us as we bear the fruit of His Spirit in real life.

God's Fruit Fleshed Out

But exactly how does the fruit of the Spirit flesh itself out in our life? I hope you can think of someone who exhibits the qualities of love, joy, peace, patience, kindness, goodness, faithfulness, gentleness, and self-control. I know I can, and his name is Sam Britten. Sam is an elder and a servant at our church, as well as director of the Center of Activities of the Physically Disabled at California State University at Northridge. Jim and I have known Sam for more than twenty years, but one of the students on campus helped us to appreciate him even more.

Judi had heard about the remarkable things going on in the center, which was just down the hall from one of her classes. So one afternoon, out of curiosity, she entered the room and stood silently watching. What she saw was Dr. Britten, down on his knees, helping and encouraging one of his disabled students. Hear what Judi—who wasn't a Christian, but who had heard of Jesus—said: "As I stood there watching Dr. Britten and saw his love and kindness and patience and gentleness with that student, I thought, 'This must be what Jesus was like!' " Daily, she was drawn to Dr. Britten's room, and again and again she saw this same scene. "Some days," Judi confessed, "I had to leave the room and go out into the hall so that I could weep. It was so moving to watch this man!"

Approaching Margie, one of Sam's assistants, Judi asked if she knew what made Sam like Jesus. Margie answered, "Oh, he's a Christian and he reads his Bible a lot and prays. In fact, we all pray together every day before the people arrive for treatment." Well, you guessed it. Soon Judi had bought herself a Bible. She began reading it and praying. She also found a church, and within a year Judi had given her heart to Jesus.

God's Word Fleshed Out in You

Dear one, this picture of Sam Britten is what this book is all about: Jesus in you and me; Jesus visible to others as we walk by the Spirit; Jesus loving and serving others through us; Jesus on display in us just as He is displayed in Sam Britten. When we walk by the Spirit, we behave as Jesus did. And, as we've seen, Jesus perfectly modeled each fruit of the Spirit. Filled with His Holy Spirit, we, too, are to cultivate these graces so that we can model Him to a needy world.

The apostle John wrote about this kind of Christlikeness in 1 John 3:2 saying, "When He appears, we shall be like Him." Then, in the next verse, he tells us how we can become like Him now: "Everyone who has this hope fixed on Him purifies himself, just as He is pure" (verse 3). And how does this purification happen, and how can we help it happen?

> Everyone who truly believes that he will one day be like Christ...surely purifies himself and relentlessly pursues godliness as a number one priority. This is the mark of the true child of God. We are to feast our eyes upon Christ, upon as much of Christ as we can find in the sacred Scriptures. We are to do everything that we possibly can: We are to wrestle and fight and pray and be disciplined in order that more and more we become like Christ—whatever the cost—knowing that every sin that is overcome, every temptation that is resisted, every virtue that is gained is another step, another step, another step, another step towards that moment when we shall be like Him.

When Dr. John Blanchard, the wise speaker of these words, finished this message, he prayed the following prayer: "We can bless You for all of Your goodness *to* us, for the enabling of the Holy Spirit *in* our lives, for every word of Scripture that has come to burn in our hearts, for every step of progress that has been made, for every victory that has been gained, for every temptation that has been resisted. And we can and do praise You as well, knowing that it is only by Your grace and power that these things were achieved."[1]

And now, my dear friend, may you and I make this prayer our own as we continue to grow in our walk with God and cultivate the fruit of His Spirit in our life.

Study Guide Questions

The fruit of the Spirit
is love, joy, peace,
patience, kindness, goodness,
faithfulness, gentleness,
[and] self-control.
GALATIANS 5:22-23

Chapter 1—Preparing for Greater Growth

God's Truth

- What is God's call to you in Galatians 5:16? What might happen in your life if you were to follow this instruction?

- According to Galatians 5:17, what conflict do believers live with? Give one or two specific examples of your struggle in this area.

- Review the "deeds of the flesh" listed in Galatians 5:19-21. Which deeds do you struggle with?

- Read Galatians 2:20, 5:24, and 6:14. What do you think these references to being "crucified" mean? How can the truths of these verses change your view of daily life and, more specifically, your view of the struggles you identified in the two preceding questions?

- What is God saying to you in Galatians 5:24-25? What does the phrase "walk by the Spirit" mean? What does walking by the Spirit look like in your life?

My Response

- Read John 15:1-8. Make a plan of action for how you will abide in Christ this week. Be specific about when and/or how you will do each of the following:

  Spend time studying God's Word

  Spend time praying

  Live in greater obedience

  Renew your commitment to Christ

Chapter 2—Looking to God for Love

God's Truth

- Read 1 Corinthians 13:4-8a. Which aspect of love is most difficult for you to live out? Because fruit-bearing involves some effort on your part, what step will you take this week toward overcoming that difficulty?

- According to 1 John 4:7-8, who is the source of love? What do verses 20 and 21 of that chapter say about how we can know if someone loves God?

- What does Romans 5:5 teach about love?

- When do you find it hardest to love? As you answer this question, look at yourself as well as other people.

My Response

- What message did God have for you in the study of Ruth's love for her mother-in-law Naomi?

- Who in your life is hardest to love? As you think about that person, read Jesus' words in Luke 6:27-28. What specific instructions about the person you have in mind does Jesus give you here? What will you do this week to obey each of Jesus' commands? Don't forget to be specific!

- According to Luke 6:35, when you love the way Jesus tells you to love, what should you expect in return? And what can you ultimately expect?

Chapter 3—Offering the Sacrifice of Joy

God's Truth

- What are believers commanded to do in 1 Thessalonians 5:16? According to Philippians 4:4, what is to be the source of a believer's constant joy? Explain.

- Read Psalm 32:3-4. How did unconfessed sin affect King David? Now look at verses 5 and 11. What did David experience once he confessed his sin? What area of sin might be interfering with your joy in the Lord? Take a few minutes to search your heart, confess your sin, and receive God's forgiveness.

- What perspective on suffering do you find in 1 Peter 1:6-8? And what reason for joy is given here?

- When do you find it hardest to experience joy in the Lord? How do circumstances generally affect your joy? What sacrifice of praise might you offer even when circumstances weigh you down?

My Response

- What message did God have for you in the study of Hannah's life and the circumstances that could have interfered with her joy? What can you do to follow her example on each of the following counts? Again, be specific.

  Quietly endure your pain

  Release any thoughts of vengeance

  Seek God in prayer

  Offer a sacrifice of praise so that God can touch you with His joy

Chapter 4—Experiencing God's Peace

God's Truth

- Personal Peace—What instruction for peace does God offer you in Philippians 4:6a and John 14:1a? How do the truths of Romans 8:28 and 1 Corinthians 10:13 encourage you to rest in God's peace?

- What clues for how to know God's peace do you find in the story of Mary and Martha (Luke 10:38-42)? How can the four Scriptures you just looked at help you experience God's peace in that situation?

- Relational Peace—Read Colossians 3:12-15. What aspect of your life should the peace of God permeate? According to Romans 14:19, Hebrews 12:14, and 1 Peter 3:11b, how does this peace happen? What is your personal responsibility when it comes to ensuring peace in your relationships?

My Response

- Personal Peace—What concerns in your life tend to cause you anxiety and rob you of peace? More specifically, what current situation tempts you to worry?

- What sacrifice of trust will you make? And what aspects of God's character will you focus on?

- Relational Peace—What message does God have for you in Matthew 5:23-24? What steps will you take to make all of your relationships right? Again, be specific about the what and the when.

Chapter 5—Looking at Jesus' Attitudes

God's Truth

- What do we know about the purpose of Jesus' life and death? See, for instance, Matthew 20:28.

- Read Matthew 26:36-46. Who witnessed Jesus' agony in the garden? According to Luke 22:45, how were the disciples handling their own distress at the time? What should they have been doing instead?

- What do Luke 22:44 and Hebrews 5:7 indicate about the intensity of Jesus' struggle in Gethsemane? According to Matthew 26:39, what was the determining factor in all that Jesus did and suffered?

- What spiritual attitude did Jesus exhibit as He faced the cross? See Hebrews 12:2.

- How do Jesus' words in Matthew 26:46 indicate that He knew God's peace?

My Response

- How do you normally handle difficult situations?

- What can you do at such times to be filled with God's love?

- What can you do in difficult situations to offer a sacrifice of praise? Think specifically about a challenge you currently face.

- In the situation you just referred to, what will you do to receive and know God's peace?

- What did Jesus do when He faced the overwhelming challenge of the Cross? What will you do to make this the habit of your life?

Chapter 6—Resisting in Patience

God's Truth

- The Greek word for "patient" has been translated in at least three ways. Use a dictionary to define each term.

  Long-suffering

  Patient

  Tolerant

- Who in the Bible best models these characteristics of patience for you? How does that person encourage you?

- Read 1 Peter 2:18-23. When does patience find favor with God? What four natural behaviors did Jesus *not* exhibit when He suffered unjustly? What approach to suffering did Jesus choose instead?

- What current situation calls for you to have patience?

My Response

- Can you think of which person or situation in your life causes you the most pain?

- Which definition of the three synonyms listed previously—long-suffering, patient, tolerant—is most meaningful to you in regards to this person or set of circumstances?

- Now consider Jesus' example (1 Peter 18:23). What attitudes and behaviors do you think God desires from you in your suffering? How can you achieve these attitudes and behaviors?

  By doing:

  By not doing:

Chapter 7—Planning for Kindness

God's Truth

- Read the following references to God's kindness. Luke 6:35—To whom does God extend His kindness? Romans 2:4—What is the intention of God's goodness? Romans 11:22—What is the opposite of God's goodness?

Ephesians 2:7 and Titus 3:4-5—What is the result of God's gentleness and kindness toward you?

- According to 2 Corinthians 6:6 and 2 Timothy 2:24, what qualities should characterize God's people?

- What commands does God give believers in Ephesians 4:32 and Colossians 3:12?

- Read 1 Corinthians 13:4. What does a failure to be gentle indicate?

My Response

- Who in your life tempts you to be unkind? What interactions with people especially challenge your efforts to be kind?

- Now choose one particular person who tends to bring out the opposite of kindness in you. Based on the discussion which closes the chapter, design a specific plan of action that will help you exhibit the fruit of kindness in your dealings with that person.

Chapter 8—Giving in Goodness

God's Truth

- According to Matthew 5:45, what are some ways God practices goodness—and who benefits?

- What commands to Christians do you find in Galatians 6:9-10—and who is to benefit?

- What do the following verses say about goodness? Note those words addressed specifically to women.

  Luke 6:27

  Ephesians 2:10

  1 Timothy 2:9-10

  1 Timothy 5:1

  Titus 2:5

- What is God saying through these passages?

- Why do you need the help of the Holy Spirit in producing good works? See Romans 7:18-19.

My Response

- Read the parable of the talents in Matthew 25:14-26. How does the man of means describe the servants who benefitted him? How does he describe the servant who did nothing with his money? What is the connection between wickedness and laziness? Between goodness and faithfulness?

- Why do you often not do what is good and beneficial to others?

- How does knowing that the practice of goodness is a fruit of the Spirit both challenge and encourage you?

Chapter 9—Looking at Jesus' Actions

God's Truth

- In Matthew 26:47-68, who were the people or groups of people Jesus faced? List the different kinds of treatment He received from them.
- Now read Matthew 27:27-44. Add to your list of unkind people in Jesus' life and the unkind treatment He received from them.
- Did Jesus deserve the treatment He received? Was He guilty or innocent? Explain why you answered as you did.
- What could Jesus have done to defend Himself? What did He do instead?
- What do you learn from the way Jesus treated the man whose ear had been cut off (Luke 22:51)?

My Response

- How do you usually respond to people who cause you pain?

- Exactly what can you do to resist in patience?

- What steps will you take to plan for kindness?

- What will you do to give in goodness?

Chapter 10—Following Through in Faithfulness

God's Truth

- Define "faithfulness" in your own words.

- What do the following verses show you about faithfulness?

  Lamentations 3:22-23

  Romans 3:3

  Revelation 19:11

Revelation 21:5; 22:6

- In 1 Corinthians 4:2 and 1 Timothy 3:11, who is it that God is calling to be faithful? Why do you think God needed to call these individuals to faithfulness?

- In what circumstances do you especially need to hear God call you to greater faithfulness?

My Response

- Think back through your week. List any instances at home, in your relationships, or in ministry when you were unfaithful, when you proved unworthy of the confidence placed in you, when you didn't follow through on your commitments and responsibilities.

- What generally causes you to be unfaithful? What kept you from being faithful in the situations you listed previously?

- What does your unfaithfulness warn you about or indicate about your spiritual walk?

Chapter 11—Growing Strong Through Gentleness

God's Truth

- How does Jesus describe Himself in Matthew 11:29? What invitation does He issue His followers here? What effect has your acceptance or rejection of this invitation had on your life?

- What did Jesus say in Matthew 5:5 about those who are gentle? What do you think He means here? Make this question the focus of some study time if you're not sure.

- According to 1 Peter 3:4, how does God regard a gentle spirit?

- What does God command in the following verses?

  Galatians 6:1

  Ephesians 4:2

  Colossians 3:12

1 Timothy 6:11

2 Timothy 2:24-25

Titus 3:1-2

- Why is gentleness so important to God?

- Why is gentleness so important to your walk with God?

My Response

- Gentleness is submissiveness to the will of God. In light of this definition, take a look at your life. In what, if any, areas of your life are you resisting God's will? What would help you bow before God in submission?

- What *thoughts* could help you cultivate gentleness in your life?

- What *actions* do you equate with gentleness?

- Outline a plan for growing in the Christlike quality of gentleness.

Chapter 12—Winning the Battle of Self-Control

God's Truth

- Read 1 Corinthians 9:24-27. What does Paul describe here? What must be done to compete in the games (verse 25a)? According to Paul, what is his real opponent? What is Paul doing to control his opponent? What does this passage teach about self-control?

- Now read 1 Corinthians 7:1-9. What area of life is Paul addressing here? What does this passage teach about self-control?

- According to 1 John 2:16, what are three areas where we are especially vulnerable to temptation? What is the source of these areas of temptation? What source of strength for standing strong against these temptations does John identify here?

My Response

- What are two areas of life which call you to exercise self-control?

- What do the following guidelines from God's Word say to you regarding those areas of temptation you just identified?

  Proverbs 4:14-15

  Proverbs 4:23

  Matthew 26:41

  1 Corinthians 10:31

  Colossians 3:16a

- What ideas from "Nurturing Self-Control" will you put into practice today (see pages 188-89)?

Chapter 13—Looking at Jesus' Applications

God's Truth

- Read 1 Peter 2:22-23. What does Peter tell you about Jesus here? Was He guilty of any sin?

- What does Hebrews 4:15 tell us about Jesus? How do you think He gained His victory over temptation? Explain how His victory over sin testifies to the presence of faithfulness, gentleness, and self-control in Jesus' life.

- Now read 1 Peter 2:19-20. What two kinds of suffering are contrasted in verse 20? Which kind of suffering finds favor with God? What is the right reason for you to suffer? And what does the issue of suffering have to do with the fruit of self-control?

My Response

- Evaluate the evidence of the following fruit in your life. Give a specific example or two of when you've seen the Spirit's grace gifts in your life and list areas which especially challenge you in each of these areas.

  Faithfulness

Gentleness

Self-control

- What does Isaiah 53:7 tell you about Jesus? What does Jesus' example teach you here?

- What specific step can you take to live out God's grace and follow through in faithfulness?

- Also, what specific step can you take to live out God's grace and grow strong in gentleness?

- And what specific step can you take to live out God's grace and win the battle of self-control?

Epilogue

- I feel privileged to know Sam Britten, a godly man who exhibits love, joy, peace, patience, kindness, goodness, faithfulness, gentleness, and self-control. Who in your life fleshes out the fruit of God's Spirit? Give specific examples from that person's life—and thank God for his/her model.

- As we wrap up our study of the fruit of the Spirit, note what stands out from your reading, Bible study, and prayer.

  The most challenging biblical command

  The most encouraging truth from the Bible

  The most memorable word picture

  The most vivid Bible character

  The most significant new insight into Jesus

  The most important insight into yourself

- In closing, thank God for these lessons He has taught you...and ask Him to help you nurture these seeds He has planted by yielding to the work of the Holy Spirit so that His Spirit can continue to bring love, joy, peace, patience, kindness, goodness, faithfulness, gentleness, and self-control to full fruition in your life as you walk with Him.

Notes

Chapter 1—Preparing for Greater Growth

1. Merrill E. Unger, *Unger's Bible Dictionary* (Chicago: Moody Press, 1972), p. 382.
2. Alfred Martin, *John, Life Through Believing* (Chicago: Moody Bible Institute, 1981), p. 92.
3. Everett F. Harrison, *John, The Gospel of Faith* (Chicago: Moody Press, 1962), p. 91.
4. William Barclay, *The Gospel of John,* Vol. 2, rev. ed. (Philadelphia: The Westminster Press, 1975), p. 176.
5. Everett F. Harrison, *John, the Gospel of Faith,* p. 91.
6. Ibid.
7. H.D.M. Spence and Joseph S. Exell, eds., *The Pulpit Commentary,* Vol. 17 (Grand Rapids, MI: William B. Eerdmans Publishing Company, 1978), p. 295.
8. Albert M. Wells, Jr., ed., *Inspiring Quotations Contemporary & Classical* (Nashville: Thomas Nelson Publishers, 1988), p. 158.
9. John MacArthur, Jr., *Liberty in Christ* (Panorama City, CA: Word of Grace Communications, 1986), p. 92.
10. Phill McHugh and Greg Nelson, "Much Too High a Price." Copyright 1985 River Oaks Music Company/Careers–BMG Music Publishing/Greg Nelson Music. River Oaks Music Company Admin. by EMI Christian Music Publishing. All rights reserved. Reprinted by permission.
11. Henry Varley, *Moody Monthly,* June 1976, p. 97.

Chapter 2—Looking to God for Love

1. William Barclay, *The Letters to the Galatians and Ephesians,* rev. ed. (Philadelphia: The Westminster Press, 1976), p. 50.
2. H.D.M. Spence and Joseph S. Exell, eds., *The Pulpit Commentary,* Vol. 20 (Grand Rapids, MI: William B. Eerdmans Publishing Company, 1978), p. 293.
3. George Sweeting, *Love Is the Greatest* (Chicago: Moody Press, 1975), p. 20.
4. Edith Schaeffer, *What Is a Family?* (Old Tappan, NJ: Fleming H. Revell Company, 1975), p. 91.
5. Jerry Bridges, *The Practice of Godliness* (Colorado Springs: NavPress, 1987), p. 246.
6. William Barclay, *The Letters to the Galatians and Ephesians,* rev. ed., p. 50.
7. Mrs. Charles E. Cowman, *Streams in the Desert,* Vol. 1 (Grand Rapids, MI: Zondervan Publishing House, 1965), p. 97.
8. *The Amplified Bible* (Grand Rapids, MI: Zondervan Publishing House, 1970), p. 302.
9. John MacArthur, Jr., *Liberty in Christ* (Panorama City, CA: Word of Grace Communications, 1986), p. 88.

Chapter 3—Offering the Sacrifice of Joy

1. John MacArthur, Jr., *Liberty in Christ* (Panorama City, CA: Word of Grace Communications, 1986), p. 90.
2. William Barclay, *The Letters to the Galatians and Ephesians,* rev. ed. (Philadelphia: The Westminster Press, 1976), p. 50.
3. William Barclay, *The Letters of James and Peter,* rev. ed. (Philadelphia: The Westminster Press, 1976), p. 178.
4. H.D.M. Spence and Joseph S. Exell, eds., *The Pulpit Commentary,* Vol. 22 (Grand Rapids, MI: William B. Eerdmans Publishing Company, 1978), p. 6.
5. W.H. Griffith Thomas, *The Apostle Peter* (Grand Rapids, MI: Kregel Publications, 1984), p. 162.
6. John MacArthur, Jr., *The MacArthur New Testament Commentary, Galatians* (Chicago: Moody Press, 1987), p. 166.
7. A.A. Anderson, *New Century Bible Commentary, The Book of Psalms,* Vol. 1 (Grand Rapids, MI: William B. Eerdmans Publishing Company, 1972), p. 336.
8. Herbert Lockyer, *All the Promises of the Bible* (Grand Rapids, MI: Zondervan Publishing House, 1962), p. 10.
9. Margaret Clarkson, *Grace Grows Best in Winter* (Grand Rapids, MI: William B. Eerdmans Publishing Company, 1984), p. 21. Quoting from *St. Paul* by Frederick W.H. Myers, 1843–1901.
10. Charles Ray, *Mrs. C. H. Spurgeon* (Pasadena, TX: Pilgrim Publications, 1979), pp. 82-83.

11. *Life Application Bible* (Wheaton, IL: Tyndale House Publishers, Inc. and Youth for Christ/USA, 1988), p. 402.

12. John MacArthur, Jr., *The MacArthur New Testament Commentary, Galatians,* p. 166.

13. Jerry Bridges, *The Practice of Godliness* (Colorado Springs: NavPress, 1983), p. 134.

Chapter 4—Experiencing God's Peace

1. Kenneth S. Wuest, *Wuest's Word Studies in the Greek New Testament,* Vol. 1 (Grand Rapids, MI: William B. Eerdmans Publishing Company, 1973), p. 160.

2. William Barclay, *The Letters to the Galatians and Ephesians,* rev. ed. (Philadelphia: The Westminster Press, 1976), p. 50.

3. Howard F. Vos, *Galatians, A Call to Christian Liberty* (Chicago: Moody Press, 1971), p. 107.

4. Charles F. Pfeiffer and Everett R. Harrison, eds., *The Wycliffe Bible Commentary* (Chicago: Moody Press, 1973), p. 1297.

5. H.D.M. Spence and Joseph S. Exell, eds., *The Pulpit Commentary,* Vol. 20 (Grand Rapids, MI: William B. Eerdmans Publishing Company, 1978), p. 262.

6. Albert M. Wells, Jr., ed., *Inspiring Quotations Contemporary & Classical* (Nashville: Thomas Nelson Publishers, 1988), p. 152.

7. Curtis Vaughan, ed., *The New Testament from 26 Translations* (Grand Rapids, MI: Zondervan Publishing House, 1967), p. 265.

8. Ibid.

9. The shorter catechism of the Presbyterian *Book of Confessions.*

10. Gien Karssen, *Her Name Is Woman* (Colorado Springs: NavPress, 1975), p. 161.

Chapter 5—Looking at Jesus' Attitudes

1. John MacArthur, Jr., *The MacArthur New Testament Commentary, Matthew 24–28* (Chicago: Moody Press, 1989), p. 167.

2. Ibid., p. 166.

3. William Hendriksen, *New Testament Commentary, Matthew* (Grand Rapids, MI: Baker Book House, 1973), p. 916.

4. Ibid., p. 917.

5. Mrs. Charles E. Cowman, *Streams in the Desert* (Grand Rapids, MI: Zondervan Publishing House, 1965), p. 104.

Chapter 6—Resisting in Patience

1. Howard F. Vos, *Galatians, A Call to Christian Liberty* (Chicago: Moody Press, 1971), p. 108.

2. Kenneth S. Wuest, *Wuest's Word Studies in the Greek New Testament* (Grand Rapids, MI: William B. Eerdmans Publishing Company, 1973), p. 160.
3. Charles F. Pfeiffer and Everett F. Harrison, eds., *The Wycliffe Bible Commentary* (Chicago: Moody Press, 1962), p. 1297.
4. John MacArthur, Jr., *Liberty in Christ* (Panorama City, CA: Word of Grace Communications, 1986), p. 92.
5. Charles F. Pfeiffer and Everett F. Harrison, eds., *The Wycliffe Bible Commentary,* p. 1297.
6. William Barclay, *The Letters to the Galatians and Ephesians,* rev. ed. (Philadelphia: The Westminster Press, 1976), p. 50.
7. Alan Cole, *The Epistle of Paul to the Galatians, Tyndale New Testament Commentaries* (Grand Rapids, MI: William B. Eerdmans Publishing Company, 1965), p. 167.
8. John MacArthur, Jr., *The MacArthur New Testament Commentary, Galatians* (Chicago: Moody Press, 1987), p. 167.
9. Howard F. Vos, *Galatians, A Call to Christian Liberty,* p. 108.
10. Kenneth S. Wuest, *Wuest's Word Studies in the Greek New Testament,* p. 160.
11. Merrill F. Unger, *Unger's Bible Dictionary* (Chicago: Moody Press, 1972), p. 829.
12. George Sweeting, *Love Is the Greatest* (Chicago: Moody Press, 1974), p. 53.
13. John MacArthur, Jr., *Liberty in Christ,* p. 92.
14. H.D.M. Spence and Joseph S. Exell, eds., *The Pulpit Commentary,* Vol. 20 (Grand Rapids, MI: William B. Eerdmans Publishing Company, 1978), p. 287.
15. William Barclay, *The Letters to the Galatians and Ephesians,* rev. ed., p. 51.
16. Kenneth S. Wuest, *Wuest's Word Studies in the Greek New Testament,* p. 160.
17. Charles F. Pfeiffer and Everett F. Harrison, eds., *The Wycliffe Bible Commentary,* p. 1297.
18. William Barclay, *The Letters to the Galatians and Ephesians,* rev. ed., p. 51.
19. D.L. Moody, *Notes from My Bible and Thoughts from My Library* (Grand Rapids, MI: Baker Book House, 1979), p. 323.
20. William J. Peterson, *Martin Luther Had a Wife* (Wheaton, IL: Living Books, Tyndale House Publishers, Inc., 1983), p. 42.
21. William J. Peterson, *Martin Luther Had a Wife,* p. 62.
22. H.D.M. Spence and Joseph S. Exell, eds., *The Pulpit Commentary,* Vol. 20, p. 294.
23. William Hendriksen, *The New Testament Commentary, Colossians and Philemon* (Grand Rapids, MI: Baker Book House, 1964), p. 155.
24. Herbert Lockyer, *The Women of the Bible* (Grand Rapids, MI: Zondervan Publishing House, 1967), p. 158.

25. Herbert Lockyer, *The Women of the Bible,* p. 158.
26. Charles Caldwell Ryrie, *The Ryrie Study Bible* (Chicago: Moody Press, 1978), p. 420.

Chapter 7—Planning for Kindness

1. William Barclay, *The Letters to the Galatians and Ephesians,* rev. ed. (Philadelphia: The Westminster Press, 1976), p. 154.
2. William Barclay, *The Letters to the Galatians and Ephesians,* rev. ed., p. 158.
3. Ruth A. Tucker, *From Jerusalem to Irian Jaya* (Grand Rapids, MI: Zondervan Publishing House, Academie Books, 1983), p. 27.
4. John MacArthur, Jr., *Liberty in Christ* (Panorama City, CA: Word of Grace Communications, 1986), p. 93.
5. John MacArthur, Jr., *The MacArthur New Testament Commentary, Galatians* (Chicago: Moody Press, 1987), p. 168.
6. William Barclay, *The Letters to the Philippians, Colossians, and Philemon,* rev. ed. (Philadelphia: The Westminster Press, 1975), p. 157.
7. H.D.M. Spence and Joseph S. Exell, eds., *The Pulpit Commentary,* Vol. 20 (Grand Rapids, MI: William B. Eerdmans Publishing Company, 1978), p. 262.
8. John MacArthur, Jr., *The MacArthur New Testament Commentary, Colossians* and Philemon (Chicago: Moody Press, 1992), p. 155.
9. William Hendriksen, *New Testament Commentary, Matthew* (Grand Rapids, MI: Baker Book House, 1973), p. 505.
10. John M. Drescher, *Spirit Fruit* (Scottdale, PA: Herald Press, 1974), pp. 221-22.
11. John M. Drescher, *Spirit Fruit,* p. 210.
12. John M. Drescher, *Spirit Fruit,* p. 206.
13. Anne Ortlund, *Disciplines of the Beautiful Woman* (Waco, TX: Word, Incorporated, 1977), pp. 96, 98.
14. Alan Cole, *The Epistle of Paul to the Galatians, Tyndale New Testament Commentaries* (Grand Rapids, MI: William B. Eerdmans Publishing Company, 1965), p. 167.
15. C. Norman Bartlett, *The Gospel in Galatians* (Chicago: The Moody Bible Institute, 1964), p. 134.

Chapter 8—Giving in Goodness

1. John W. Cowart, *People Whose Faith Got Them into Trouble* (Downers Grove, IL: InterVarsity Press, 1990).
2. John W. Cowart, *People Whose Faith Got Them into Trouble,* pp. 13-14.
3. Merrill F. Unger, *Unger's Bible Dictionary* (Chicago: Moody Press, 1972), p. 420.

4. Charles F. Pfeiffer and Everett F. Harrison, *The Wycliffe Bible Commentary* (Chicago: Moody Press, 1973), p. 1296.

5. Merrill F. Unger, *Unger's Bible Dictionary,* p. 420.

6. H.D.M. Spence and Joseph S. Exell, eds., *The Pulpit Commentary,* Vol. 20 (Grand Rapids, MI: William B. Eerdmans Publishing Company, 1978), p. 262.

7. W.E. Vine, *An Expository Dictionary of New Testament Words* (Old Tappan, NJ: Fleming H. Revell Company, 1966), p. 165.

8. John MacArthur, Jr., *The MacArthur New Testament Commentary, Galatians* (Chicago: Moody Press, 1987), p. 168.

9. H.D.M. Spence and Joseph S. Exell, eds., *The Pulpit Commentary,* Vol. 20, p. 262.

10. Kenneth S. Wuest, *Word Studies in the Greek New Testament,* Vol. 1 (Grand Rapids, MI: William B. Eerdmans Publishing Company, 1974), p. 160.

11. Howard F. Vos, *Galatians, A Call to Christian Liberty* (Chicago: Moody Press, 1973), p. 108.

12. Stuart Briscoe, *The Fruit of the Spirit* (Wheaton, IL: Harold Shaw Publishers, rev. ed., 1993), p. 105.

13. Charles Caldwell Ryrie, *The Ryrie Study Bible* (Chicago: Moody Press, 1978), p. 1781.

14. Charles R. Swindoll, *Come Before Winter* (Portland, OR: Multnomah Press, 1985), p. 196.

15. William Barclay, *The Letters to the Corinthians,* rev. ed. (Philadelphia: The Westminster Press, 1975), p. 120.

16. William Hendriksen, *Exposition of the Pastoral Epistles, New Testament Commentary* (Grand Rapids, MI: Baker Book House, 1976), p. 365.

17. Ibid., p. 188.

18. Ibid., p. 107.

19. Donald Guthrie, *The Pastoral Epistles, Tyndale New Testament Commentaries* (Grand Rapids, MI: William B. Eerdmans Publishing Company, 1976), p. 75.

20. William Hendriksen, *Exposition of the Bible According to Luke, New Testament Commentary* (Grand Rapids, MI: Baker Book House, 1978), p. 558.

21. Oswald Chambers, *Studies in the Sermon on the Mount* (Fort Washington, PA: Christian Literature Crusade, 1960), p. 53.

22. Albert M. Wells, Jr., ed., *Inspiring Quotations Contemporary & Classical* (Nashville: Thomas Nelson Publishers, 1988), p. 82.

23. Neil S. Wilson, ed., *The Handbook of Bible Application* (Wheaton, IL: Tyndale House Publishers, Inc., 1992), p. 369.

24. Dan Baumann, *Extraordinary Living for Ordinary People* (Irvine, CA: Harvest House Publishers, 1978), pp. 83-84.

Chapter 9—Looking at Jesus' Actions

1. James Stalker, *The Life of Jesus Christ* (Old Tappan, NJ: Fleming H. Revell Company, 1949), p. 120.
2. Ibid., p. 121.
3. John MacArthur, Jr., *The MacArthur New Testament Commentary, Matthew* 24-28 (Chicago: Moody Press, 1989), p. 194.
4. Ibid., p. 183.
5. James Stalker, *The Trial and Death of Jesus Christ* (Grand Rapids, MI: Zondervan Publishing House, 1972), p. 13.
6. William Hendriksen, *Exposition of the Gospel According to Luke, New Testament Commentary* (Grand Rapids, MI: Baker Book House, 1978), p. 989.

Chapter 10—Following Through in Faithfulness

1. Albert M. Wells, Jr., ed., *Inspiring Quotations Contemporary & Classical* (Nashville: Thomas Nelson Publishers, 1988), p. 69.
2. H.D.M. Spence and Joseph S. Exell, eds., *The Pulpit Commentary,* Vol. 20 (Grand Rapids, MI: William B. Eerdmans Publishing Company, 1978), p. 287.
3. John MacArthur, Jr., *The MacArthur New Testament Commentary, Galatians* (Chicago: Moody Press, 1987), p. 169.
4. John MacArthur, Jr., *Liberty in Christ* (Panorama City, CA: Word of Grace Communities, 1986), p. 95.
5. William Barclay, *The Letters to the Galatians and Ephesians,* rev. ed. (Philadelphia: The Westminster Press, 1976), p. 51.
6. Alan Cole, *The Epistle of Paul to the Galatians, Tyndale New Testament Commentaries* (Grand Rapids, MI: William B. Eerdmans Publishing Company, 1976), p. 168.
7. William Hendriksen, *Exposition of Galatians, New Testament Commentary* (Grand Rapids, MI: Baker Book House, 1974), p. 225.
8. Charles Caldwell Ryrie, *The Ryrie Study Bible* (Chicago: Moody Press, 1978), p. 1777.
9. Richard Shelley Taylor, *The Disciplined Life* (Minneapolis, MN: Dimension Books, Bethany Fellowship, Inc., 1962), p. 37.
10. Vanita Hampton and Carol Plueddemann, eds., *World Shapers* (Wheaton, IL: Harold Shaw Publishers, 1991), p. 17.
11. Edith Schaeffer, *Common Sense Christian Living,* pp. 88-89.
12. Herbert Lockyer, *The Women of the Bible* (Grand Rapids, MI: Zondervan Publishing House, 1967), p. 101.
13. Richard C. Halverson, "Perspective" newsletter, 10/26/77.

Chapter 11—Growing Strong Through Gentleness

1. John F. MacArthur, Jr., *Liberty in Christ* (Panorama City, CA: Word of Grace Communities, 1986), p. 95.
2. William Barclay, *The Letters to the Galatians and Ephesians,* rev. ed. (Philadelphia: The Westminster Press, 1976), p. 52.
3. Howard F. Vos, *Galatians, A Call to Christian Liberty* (Chicago: Moody Press, 1971), p. 108.
4. H.D.M. Spence and Joseph S. Exell, eds., *The Pulpit Commentary,* Vol. 20 (Grand Rapids, MI: William B. Eerdmans Publishing Company, 1978), p. 262.
5. William Hendriksen, *Exposition of the Gospel According to Matthew, New Testament Commentary* (Grand Rapids, MI: Baker Book House, 1975), pp. 271-72.
6. William Barclay, *The Letters to the Galatians and Ephesians,* rev. ed., p. 52.
7. *Webster's New Dictionary of Synonyms* (Springfield, MA: G. & C. Merriam Company, Publishers, 1973), p. 812.
8. Albert M. Wells, Jr., ed., *Inspiring Quotations Contemporary & Classical* (Nashville: Thomas Nelson Publishers, 1988), p. 91.
9. William Hendriksen, *Exposition of the Gospel According to Matthew,* p. 765.
10. Merrill F. Unger, *Unger's Bible Dictionary* (Chicago: Moody Press, 1972), p. 709.
11. Kenneth S. Wuest, *Wuest's Word Studies from the Greek New Testament,* Vol. 2 (Grand Rapids, MI: William B. Eerdmans Publishing Company, 1974), p. 78.
12. Alan M. Stibbs, *The First Epistle General of Peter, The Tyndale New Testament Commentaries* (Grand Rapids, MI: William B. Eerdmans Publishing Company, 1976), p. 125.
13. Robert Jamieson, A.R. Fausset, and David Brown, *Commentary on the Whole Bible* (Grand Rapids, MI: Zondervan Publishing House, 1973), p. 1475.
14. Kenneth S. Wuest, *Wuest's Word Studies from the Greek New Testament,* Vol. 2, p. 81.
15. Albert M. Wells, Jr., ed., *Inspiring Quotations Contemporary & Classical,* p. 92.
16. W.E. Vine, *An Expository Dictionary of New Testament Words* (Old Tappan, NJ: Fleming H. Revell Company, 1966), pp. 55-56.
17. W.E. Vine, *An Expository Dictionary of New Testament Words,* p. 56.
18. Derek Kidner, *The Proverbs* (London: InterVarsity Press, 1973), p. 63.
19. Derek Kidner, *Psalms 1–72* (Downers Grove, IL: InterVarsity Press, 1973), p. 176.
20. Charles Caldwell Ryrie, *The Ryrie Study Bible* (Chicago: Moody Press, 1978), p. 841.
21. Gien Karssen, *Her Name Is Woman* (Colorado Springs: NavPress, 1975), p. 132.
22. J. Vernon McGee, *Luke* (Pasadena, CA: Thru the Bible Books, 1986), p. 24.

23. Herbert Lockyer, *The Women of the Bible* (Grand Rapids, MI: Zondervan Publishing House, 1975), p. 105.

24. Gene A. Getz, *Moses, Moments of Glory...Feet of Clay* (Glendale, CA: Regal Books, 1976), p. 138.

25. Ibid., pp. 139-140.

26. Don Baker, *Pain's Hidden Purpose* (Portland, OR: Multnomah Press, 1984), pp. 86-89.

Chapter 12—Winning the Battle of Self-Control

1. J. Oswald Sanders, *Spiritual Leadership,* rev. ed. (Chicago: Moody Press, 1980), pp. 71-72.

2. Robert Jamieson, A.R. Fausset, and David Brown, *Commentary of the Whole Bible* (Grand Rapids, MI: Zondervan Publishing House, 1973), p. 1275.

3. William Barclay, *The Letters to the Galatians and Ephesians,* rev. ed. (Philadelphia: The Westminster Press, 1976), p. 52.

4. W.E. Vine, *An Expository Dictionary of New Testament Words* (Old Tappan, NJ: Fleming H. Revell Company, 1966), p. 114.

5. Charles F. Pfeiffer and Everett F. Harrison, *The Wycliffe Bible Commentary* (Chicago: Moody Press, 1973), p. 1297.

6. John MacArthur, Jr., *Liberty in Christ* (Panorama City, CA: Word of Grace Communities, 1986), p. 96.

7. H.D.M. Spence and Joseph S. Exell, eds., *The Pulpit Commentary,* Vol. 20 (Grand Rapids, MI: William B. Eerdmans Publishing Company, 1978), p. 287.

8. Kenneth S. Wuest, *Wuest's Word Studies from the Greek New Testament* (Grand Rapids, MI: William B. Eerdmans Publishing Company, 1974), p. 160.

9. Archibald Thomas Robertson, *Word Pictures in the New Testament,* Vol. IV, p. 311.

10. Bruce Wideman, *Presbyterian Journal,* July 30, 1975, p. 7.

11. Robert C. Gage, *Cultivating Spiritual Fruit* (Schaumburg, IL: Regular Baptist Press, 1986), p. 126.

12. Dan Baumann, *Extraordinary Living for Ordinary People* (Irvine, CA: Harvest House Publishers, 1978), pp. 118-19.

13. John H. Timmerman, *The Way of Christian Living* (Grand Rapids, MI: William B. Eerdmans Publishing Company, 1987), p. 146.

14. Charles R. Ryrie, *The Ryrie Study Bible* (Chicago: Moody Press, 1978), p. 476.

15. *Life Application Bible* (Wheaton, IL: Tyndale House Publishers, Inc. and Youth for Christ, 1988), p. 475.

16. Albert M. Wells, Jr., *Inspiring Quotes Contemporary & Classical* (Nashville: Thomas Nelson Publishers, 1988), p. 58.

17. Jerry Bridges, *The Practice of Godliness* (Colorado Springs, CO: NavPress, 1987), p. 164.
18. Elizabeth George, *Loving God with All Your Mind* (Eugene, OR: Harvest House Publishers, 1994).
19. Jerry Bridges, *The Practice of Godliness,* quoting D.G. Kehl, p. 175.
20. John H. Timmerman, *The Way of Christian Living,* pp. 147-48.
21. Luis Palau, *Heart After God* (Portland, OR: Multnomah Press, 1978), p. 70.

Chapter 13—Looking at Jesus' Applications

1. D.L. Moody, *Notes from My Bible and Thoughts from My Library* (Grand Rapids, MI: Baker Book House, 1979), p. 362.
2. Kenneth S. Wuest, *Wuest's Word Studies from the Greek New Testament,* Vol. II (Grand Rapids, MI: William B. Eerdmans Publishing Company, 1973), p. 67.
3. Kenneth S. Wuest, *Wuest's Word Studies from the Greek New Testament,* Vol. II, pp. 67-68.
4. Ibid.
5. Alan M. Stibbs, *The First Epistle General of Peter, Tyndale New Testament Commentaries,* p. 118.
6. Kenneth S. Wuest, *Wuest's Word Studies from the Greek New Testament,* Vol. II, pp. 67-68.

Epilogue—Planning for Greater Growth

1. John Blanchard, "The Most Amazing Statement in Scripture" (Grace to You, P.O. Box 4000, Panorama City, CA 91412).

Beautiful in God's Eyes

Elizabeth George

HARVEST HOUSE PUBLISHERS
EUGENE, OREGON

Italicized text in Scripture quotations indicates author's emphasis.

Acknowledgment

As always, thank you to my dear husband, Jim George, M.Div.,Th.M., for your able assistance, guidance, suggestions, and loving encouragement on this project.

BEAUTIFUL IN GOD'S EYES

Published by Harvest House Publishers, Eugene, Oregon 97402
www.harvesthousepublishers.com

Library of Congress Cataloging-in-Publication Data

George, Elizabeth, 1944–
Beautiful in God's eyes / Elizabeth George.
p. cm.
Includes bibliographical references.
ISBN-13: 978-0-7369-1538-0
ISBN-10: 0-7369-1538-9
1. Women—Religious life. 2. Bible. O.T. Proverbs XXXI, 10-31—Criticism, interpretation, etc. I. Title.
BV4527.G458 1998/2005
248.8'43—dc21 97-41991

In loving memory of

Lois George Onesti

Godly mother to my husband, Jim,
gracious mother-in-law to me,
loving grandmother to our daughters,
Katherine and Courtney.

Because of her faithful obedience,
we have known God's ideal—
a woman beautiful in His eyes.

We rise up and bless her!
Proverbs 31:28

Contents

An Invitation to Beauty

I have a real love for the book of Proverbs in the Bible...because that's where I first met "the Proverbs 31 woman" (Proverbs 31:10-31). She's the incredible woman who models for all women—young or seasoned, married or single—all that is beautiful in God's eyes.

Since first discovering the treasure of the Proverbs 31 woman, I've tried to model my life after her. I have sought and prayed to duplicate her actions and attitudes in developing strength of character and pursuing the responsibilities, opportunities, and dreams God gives me. And I have tried to follow after her wisdom in creating a home-sweet-home, nurturing my marriage, and raising my children.

And you'll fall in love with her too! In this remarkable woman you will find instruction, encouragement, a model to follow, and the motivation to keep you looking to God for a lifetime. And most important of all, you'll find out about true beauty—God's kind of beauty!

I'm glad you're joining me in scaling the heights of this godly beauty. God's excellent woman is someone we can follow without hesitation. And, my friend, you will never be the same after moving verse by verse through Proverbs 31:10-31! You'll grow personally and spiritually as you discover what God considers beautiful—and then apply it to your life. To help you, I've included practical *How-To's of Beauty* in each chapter. And, for even greater progress (for you or your study group), I recommend the book *Beautiful in God's Eyes Growth and Study Guide*.

You and I cannot be who God wants us to be on our own power, so each chapter ends with *An Invitation to Beauty* reflective section. This "look in the mirror" gives you an opportunity to gaze into God's eyes, search your heart, and seek God's beautiful will for your life.

My heartfelt prayer as we begin, dear friend, is that you will…

- let God use this teaching about His kind of beauty to transform your heart and your life.
- share this picture of beauty from the Bible with your daughters and anyone else who is interested in God's brand of beauty.
- truly desire to become like the woman of Proverbs 31—a woman who is beautiful in God's eyes!

May it be said of you, "Many daughters have done well, but you excel them all" (Proverbs 31:29)!

In God's beautiful love,

Elizabeth George

~ 1 ~

A Rare Treasure

Her Character

"Who can find a virtuous woman?"
Proverbs 31:10 (KJV)

Have you ever felt overwhelmed by a larger-than-life challenge you suddenly found yourself facing? Well, I experienced such a moment as our tour bus drove into the hotel parking lot at the base of the massive natural fortress called Masada. Jutting straight up from the shore of the Dead Sea, these fortifications built by Herod the Great towered some 1300 feet above us. It was already casting its dark and foreboding shadow over our group as the guide told us to get a good night's rest to fortify ourselves for the 7:00 AM climb up this ancient wonder the next day.

I felt as if I were standing at the base of Mount Everest! "What am I doing here?" I wondered. "How did this happen? I'm just a submissive wife who came to the Holy Land with her husband to study the *Bible!* I never bargained for *this!*" But now I was expected to climb up this steep mountain with the rest of the (much younger) group!

And, my new friend, I want to quickly admit that I have all these same feelings again as you and I stand at the beginning of this book about being beautiful in God's eyes, looking up at *her*—the beautiful (and successful and wonderful and perfect) woman of Proverbs 31. She certainly appears to be larger than life. She's "up there," so far away, so far removed, so beautiful, so superior, so impossible. Or so it seems....

But wait! Let me finish my story about Masada. I dutifully ate a healthy dinner and went to bed early, just as the guide had instructed. But I also worried all night long—Should I eat or not eat before such a strenuous climb? Should I wear jeans or shorts? How much water should I carry?...On and on my thoughts and fears churned. I definitely didn't get the prescribed good night's sleep!

Finally it was 6:30 in the morning—time to act. I threw on my clothes (shorts because of the brutal heat), grabbed the largest water bottle (I skipped breakfast), opened the door of our room, walked to the footpath—and I climbed Masada! I didn't want to, but I did it. It wasn't easy, and I stopped for many rests—many, *many* rests! My lungs hurt, and my legs hurt. People passed me by as I struggled. But I made it! By tapping into the deepest resources of both my mental and physical strength and by continuing to put one foot in front of the other—by taking one step after one step after one step—I finally arrived at the top of the world! (I only discovered later that the "top of the world" was sea level!) I had done what had seemed impossible—and that accomplishment was glorious!

Now, dear fellow climber, you and I face the rather daunting Proverbs 31 woman! Perhaps just as I struggled with a lack of desire to climb a mountain, you've struggled to even *want* to be like her. Maybe you've tossed and turned as you've counted the cost of such an endeavor, sensing that it will require much from you. And possibly you've suffered as other women have passed you by in their efforts to become more like her.

Whatever you're feeling, whatever your past experiences with the challenge of Proverbs 31, I invite you to come along with me now. Let's hold hands if we need to as, accepting God's invitation to become beautiful in His eyes, we climb together. Along the way we're going to tap into the grace of God's power and the Spirit-driven resolve to become all God wants us to be—and we're going to take one step at a time. After all, the Proverbs 31 woman *is* the "virtuous woman" (Proverbs 31:10), and by mastering one virtue at a time, one verse at a time, you and I are going to fully grasp her rare beauty and, by God's grace, realize it for ourselves. Pray with me now and ask God to guard you from scorning the height of His standard, from discounting this woman's superior beauty, from downplaying her virtues, or from writing her off as old-fashioned or impossible. May God's desire for you be your desire for yourself!

An Alphabet of Character

But where, you might wonder, did this woman come from? How did the woman of Proverbs 31 become a standard for godly beauty? Believe it or not, she began with a real flesh-and-blood woman!

Once upon a time there was a young prince who would someday be king, but he had many lessons to learn before then. So his mother sat down with him beside the hearth at home and taught him not only how to be a godly king but also how to find an outstanding wife.

Most scholars agree that Proverbs 31 reflects that wise mother's instruction to her young son. Verse 1 says, "The words of King Lemuel, the utterance which his mother taught him." In verses 1-9 she covers the basics of leadership, and then she describes in verses 10-31 the kind of wife he should seek, one who is indeed a rare treasure. Perhaps due to her son's young age, this wise mother organizes the list of qualities he is to look for in a wife according to the letters of the Hebrew alphabet. Taught this way, this alphabet of character could be quickly learned, easily memorized, regularly recited, and permanently etched into the tablet of his young heart (Proverbs 3:3). When the mother reached the last letter of the alphabet and finished extolling the qualities of a virtuous woman, this ode of praise became for that young prince—and for us—God's alphabet of feminine character.

As you and I begin learning the alphabet, I want us to remember two words of hope. First of all, Proverbs 31 was spoken by a woman. These are not the words or instructions of a man expressing some personal and unrealistic fantasy. True, a man (King Lemuel) is writing to us, but he is repeating a *woman's* opinion of what a woman should be! This fact inspires and encourages me. I appreciate this kind of woman-to-woman instruction as I learn more about what God finds beautiful. I want to understand the makeup of true godly beauty, and who better to show me that beauty than a beautiful-in-God's-eyes woman?

Second, even though this mother begins her alphabet with a question—"Who can find a virtuous woman?" (Proverbs 31:10)—she fully expects her son to find such a woman of character. In fact, in ancient Jerusalem, when a man married, others inquired, "Has he found a virtuous woman?"[1] Knowing such a woman is out there (verse 29), she encourages her son to look for her. The mother's faith that such a woman exists encourages me. You see, the Proverbs

31 woman is real! And you and I can be this woman—not just admire her, but *be* her! She may seem untouchable, an ideal we can't possibly attain, but she isn't. In fact, God takes great care to show her to us at other places in the Bible: He points us to Ruth, who was "a virtuous woman" (Ruth 3:11); He tells us that "a virtuous woman is [note present tense] a crown to her husband" (Proverbs 12:4 KJV); and He states that "*many* daughters have done virtuously" (Proverbs 31:29 KJV). Many!

Yes, the virtuous woman is a rare treasure—a distinctive, exceptional, extraordinary, superlative treasure—but according to God, the Author of all beauty, you and I can become all that she is. You and I can become beautiful in His eyes.

A Picture of Beauty

Since *Beautiful in God's Eyes* is the title of this book, let me clarify before we go any farther that God's idea of beauty is probably quite different from what you and I consider beautiful. (His idea of beauty is certainly far different from the world's!) So, as you read, keep in mind that Proverbs 31:10-31 presents a picture of *God's* idea of beauty, and—as God says about Himself—"My thoughts are not your thoughts, nor are your ways My ways....My ways [are] higher than your ways, and My thoughts than your thoughts" (Isaiah 55:8-9). Just as God is in a category of His own, so is His idea of beauty!

Understanding God's kind of beauty was Step One for the young prince, and it's Step One for you and me as well. (Remember Masada? It's climbed one step at a time!) So first we have to grasp the meaning of the word *virtuous*: "Who can find a virtuous woman?" (Proverbs 31:10). The meaning of the word *virtuous* can be likened to the two sides of a coin. *Power of mind* (moral principles and attitudes) makes up the image on one side, and *power of body* (potency and effectiveness) makes up the other. Neither of these powerful traits seems to be very beautiful, but consider how God addresses them in His Proverbs 31 picture of beauty.

A *powerful mind*—In God's picture of His beautiful woman, He shows her mental strength in a composite of the internal qualities that keep her (and that will keep us) from giving up, giving in, dropping out, or quitting short of the goal to be and do what God desires. Right now look at the Proverbs 31:10-31 picture from afar. We'll take a closer look at each characteristic as we move through this book and up our mountain! God's beautiful woman is

- Pure—She is a woman of virtue (Proverbs 31:10).
- Honest—Her husband trusts her (verses 11-12).
- Industrious—She is busy from sunup to sundown managing her interests and expanding her enterprises (verses 13-19, 21-22, 24, 27, 31).
- Thrifty—Her skill with finances enables her to care for her loved ones and increase her property (verses 14, 16).
- Strong in character—She faces the daily challenges of life (and death!) with undaunted courage (verse 25, 29).
- Kind—Compassion for the unfortunate governs her life and sweet speech flows from her lips (verses 20, 26).
- Wise—Walking in wisdom is her way of life (verse 26).
- Holy—She wholeheartedly loves the Lord (verse 30).

These internal qualities enable God's beautiful woman to manage well her life, her time, her money, her mouth, her home, her relationships, and her self.

A *powerful body*—And how, we wonder, does the Proverbs 31 woman *do* all that God desires of her? When we turn over the "coin of definition" we clearly see that her life requires physical energy and vigor. Observe the beautiful—and strong—Proverbs 31 woman at work.

- She works willingly with her hands (Proverbs 31:13).
- Those willing hands plant a vineyard (verse 16).
- They also operate a spindle and distaff (verse 19).
- She works from early in the morning (verse 15) until late at night (verse 18).
- She nurses the needy (verse 20).
- She weaves the cloth for her family's clothes (verse 21), for her household needs (verse 22), for her own clothing (verse 22), and for sale as a professional (verse 24).
- Never idle, she watches over and builds her home (verse 27).

This virtuous and very industrious woman needs physical strength and ability to do the work of her life, the work of love.

An Army of Virtues

And now, dear reader, having considered this special woman's moral and physical strength, we must look at one final element that is crucial to understanding what a virtuous woman is. I know it doesn't sound very attractive or feminine or beautiful, but she is an army—an army of virtues! That's the essence of God's description of her character. Let me explain.

The Hebrew word for *virtuous* is used 200-plus times in

the Bible to describe an army. This Old Testament word refers to *a force* and is used to mean *able*, *capable*, *mighty*, *strong*, *valiant*, *powerful*, *efficient*, *wealthy*, and *worthy*.[2] The word is also used in reference to a man of war, men of war, and men prepared for war. Change this definition to the feminine case and you begin to grasp the power at the core of this woman! Just as mental toughness and physical energy are the primary traits of an army, they also mark God's beautiful woman.

I know this is a lot to absorb, so you may want to go back and read this important section again. As you and I stand together staring at the awesome Proverbs 31 woman, we need to understand as much as possible what God means when He describes her as a virtuous woman. After all, understanding her character—the goal of this chapter—is our first step toward becoming virtuous Proverbs 31 women ourselves!

"Who can find a virtuous woman?" is the question of Proverbs 31:10. With this query God points out that His kind of woman is extraordinary—indeed, a rare treasure—when it comes to her inner strength and outward accomplishments. She's also an utterly awesome army of virtues. And with God's help you and I can become awesome, too! Here are some initial steps.

The How-To's of Beauty

1. *Cultivate the desire*—Based on Moses' prayer in Psalm 90:10 ("The days of our lives are seventy years; and if by reason of strength they are eighty years"), imagine yourself sitting back and enjoying your eightieth birthday! A host of people has gathered to celebrate with you at this special party in your honor. Suddenly a fanfare announces the arrival of your birthday cake. As it's wheeled in, you marvel

at how big it is! It has to be because it has 80 candles on it, and every one of them is lighted. In fact, the heat from their blaze makes you wish you hadn't worn a sweater!

Now for the challenge: If the Lord allows you to live to enjoy such a birthday party, what do you want to have accomplished by the time you blow out the candles that represent 80 years of life?

My friend, I'm praying right now that your answer to this crucial question will indicate your heartfelt desire to be a woman of character, a woman who is beautiful in God's eyes!

2. *Give it time*—How did God's beautiful woman become such a rare, exceptional, extraordinary treasure, such a woman of strong godly character? In a word, it took *time*! Nothing this grand happens overnight; nothing this grand just happens! What kind of time does the development of virtuous character require?

Time reading God's Word—Make daily time for reading God's Word your highest priority. Maybe this story will help you understand why reading the Bible cultivates beauty.

When I was in Israel, a foremost exporter of diamonds, I learned that one step in the process of diamond production is polishing the gem. A diamond is never released to the marketplace until the person assigned to polish it can see the image of his own face reflected in the jewel.

Well, dear one, you are a diamond in the rough, and you gain the power of character—you begin to more clearly reflect your heavenly Father's face—as His Holy Word smoothes and polishes your character. As you spend time gazing into God's Word, the light of His truth brightens your motivation to live your life for His glory. When you read the Word of the Lord, He uses it to scrub and scour away your fears, your laziness, your doubts, and your sinful ways. God uses His Word to transform you into a woman of divine power who more brilliantly reflects His beauty.

Time memorizing God's Word—Besides reading God's Word daily, set up a plan for regularly memorizing Scripture. My plan involves working on Scripture while I take my daily walk. Sure, the exercise contributes to my physical power (and even my physical beauty as it keeps the pounds off!), but the Scripture verses I memorize *while* I am walking give me the mental and spiritual force I need to "climb" toward God's kind of beauty—for one more day.

Time with other women—Surround yourself with women who encourage your spiritual growth (Titus 2:3). I know from experience there's nothing like relationships with sisters in Christ. God has blessed me with my "faithful five," five women who are endeavoring to spend the 80 years of their lives (Lord willing!) becoming God's beautiful women. We are committed to loving, encouraging, and praying for one another along the way. Fellowship with these women who delight in living for God spurs me on in my heart's desire to be a beautiful woman of character.

Time reading biographies of God's saints—Begin a reading program—even for five minutes a day. I've found that time spent getting to know the great saints of the faith is time well spent. Being touched by the lives of God's "army" of women gives me a fresh infusion of strength as I consider their physical strength and their mental endurance.

- Amy Carmichael was a missionary to India who never took a furlough from ministry in her 55 years of serving.

- Susanna Wesley was a mother of 19 children (ten of whom died before the age of two) who taught and raised her children (including John and Charles Wesley, the founders of the Methodist movement) at the same time that she managed the family farm during her husband's imprisonment and endured religious persecution from her neighbors.
- Elisabeth Elliot served as a jungle missionary, suffered the loss of one husband by martyrdom and another to a lingering cancer, and raised her daughter as a single mom.
- Edith Schaeffer forsook a life of comfort to forge a new ministry with her husband Francis in Europe. At L'Abri, she suffered from local persecution, terrifying avalanches, a lack of medical care for a child with polio and another with a rheumatic heart condition, and later the death of her husband after a five-year struggle with cancer.
- Ruth Graham faithfully looked after five children while their father and her husband Billy served the Lord away from home for many months each year.

On and on the list of God's beautiful women goes—and you and I can draw enormous strength from their example.

Time today—Dedicate the remainder of your day (and your tomorrows) to God and live it His way. "As now, so then," one wise saying instructs. It's true that if we want to be God's beautiful woman at that eightieth birthday party—or at any other time—we have to be her today! After all, today is what our tomorrows are made of. That truth is behind Moses' plea for God to "teach us to number our days that we may gain a heart of wisdom" (Psalm 90:12). You see, as we try to live our life today as *God* wants us to live it, and as we cultivate the character qualities *He* says are beautiful, then we will be beautiful and wise today—and, in God's hands, the tomorrows will take care of themselves.

Time over a lifetime—You and I don't ever need to be discouraged or feel overwhelmed by God's standard for beauty because He gives us, day by day, a lifetime to reach it. Hear what beautiful and wise Edith Schaeffer says about the Proverbs 31 woman: "Certainly all the admirable things written about this woman did not take place in one year. It seems to me it is a summary of the great diversity of accomplishments and results of her work and imagination and talents over a long period of time."[3]

An Invitation to Beauty

Whew! I feel as if I've already climbed a mountain by just trying to describe God's beautiful woman. Maybe you do, too, after trying to absorb the richness of her portrait.

I'm also feeling somewhat tentative (do I really want this?), fearful (what if I fail?), and sober (it will be a hard climb!). And at moments I even wonder, "What difference will it make if I try to live such a virtuous life?" But that kind of thinking ends when you and I remember that the description of this special woman is in God's Word: she is *God's* portrait, and she reflects *God's* idea of beauty and *God's* design for excellence. *He* knows the value of the work He has given us to do for Him and what it takes mentally and physically to accomplish it. Perhaps we are beginning to realize why this woman of strength is "a rare treasure"!

Why not join me in whispering a plea to God for strength—*His* strength? Why not declare with me your desire to become a woman who, like an army, moves through the challenges and duties of life with valor, courage, bravery, stamina, endurance, and power—*His* power? I know you want the same thing I want—to truly be a woman who is beautiful in God's eyes, to enjoy His approval, His "well done, good and faithful servant" (Matthew 25:21), His acknowledgment that "*you* are a virtuous woman" (Ruth 3:11)!

~ 2 ~

A Sparkling Jewel

Her Value

"Her price is much higher than jewels."[1]
PROVERBS 31:10

It was a dream come true! I was finally going to meet her! I'm talking about the Proverbs 31 woman, the woman who is beautiful in God's eyes, the woman we'll be getting to know throughout this book. My husband Jim was taking students from The Master's Seminary to Israel for some intensive study, and he invited me to come along!

You see, he knew. He knew that for 25 years I had done everything I could to learn about this beautiful woman. He knew I had memorized many versions of Proverbs 31:10-31. He also knew (from our checkbook!) that I had made her exemplary life a special study project for that same quarter-century, investing in a library of books about the Proverbs and about her. And he knew the pursuit of her exemplary lifestyle was a personal lifetime goal of mine. Yes, Jim definitely knew what meeting her would mean to me. As I said, a trip to her homeland to meet the Proverbs 31 woman was a dream come true!

So I did what many women do before a trip—I made lists! Of course the list of things that had to be done before I could leave home and office for a month was long. The packing list was long, too, and so was the shopping list of items to pick up before we departed. But I carefully—and prayerfully—created another list before we left, a list so personal and so important that I carried it in my Bible during the entire trip. I titled it "Things to See" and noted every cultural aspect from Proverbs 31:10-31 that I wanted to see for myself in Israel. I was on a mission. "Who can find a virtuous woman?" Proverbs 31:10 asks. Well, I was going to find her!

The first item on my "must see" list was *jewels*. I wrote this down because Proverbs 31:10 (the verse this chapter is about) begins with a statement about the value of her character: "Her price is much higher than jewels." I wanted to see firsthand the jewels in the land of Israel that reflect the value of God's beautiful woman so I could take another step toward understanding her better and appreciating her more.

Searching for Treasure

You and I began our search for God's beautiful woman in chapter 1 as we listened in on a mother teaching a class of one—her young son—about true feminine beauty. Her lesson stressed what an extraordinary and exceptional treasure a truly godly woman is. And now as we read on, we see that the mother reiterates the woman's value by referring to jewels: "Her price is much higher than jewels" (Proverbs 31:10).

- "Her worth is far above rubies," one translator tells us.[2] The rich red ruby is truly a unique gem, and because of their rarity, large rubies even surpass diamonds of equal weight in value![3]

- "Her value is far beyond pearls," another translation states.[4] Consider that only twenty pearls are found in 35,000 pearl oysters—and only three of those are gem quality![5]
- "Far beyond corals is her worth," still another reading of the Bible declares.[6] Corals are delicate "flower-animals," and only a few are quality enough to be polished and regarded as precious stones.[7]

Rubies. Pearls. Corals. Take your pick. Each of these sparkling jewels is quite rare *and* valuable. Each is hard to harvest and few are found. And that's the imagery our young prince's mother uses to impress upon him how extraordinary a woman who is beautiful—in God's eyes—would be. Once found, she would be of inestimable value!

Now let me tell you, my beautiful friend, what I found on my personal treasure-hunt in Israel. As I told you, my list of "Things to See" had jewels right at the top. So, when our study group spent a day in the Israel Museum, I dashed in and began searching for jewels. On and on the museum's displays went, and on and on my search continued. Covering every hall, I found not a single jewel! The jewels—along with every other item of value—had been carried away by conquering armies in days gone by.

But what I did find in the museum was as telling as what I didn't find. You see, the Israel Museum is filled with artifacts that have been unearthed in that country, and these artifacts represent the nation's rich and long history. What were some of the relics that give us clues into the life lived by God's beautiful woman? I feasted my eyes on...bones and coffins! Walls were covered with shields and swords, body armor and instruments of war! Cases displayed dishes and cookware made out of mud! Stone olive presses and millstones for grinding grains were also on display. These were not at all what I had expected!

What lesson did such primitive items offer? They were a voice which spoke of hard times—of struggling to survive, of eking out a living, of barely managing to exist. These items spoke of work and war, labor and loss. There was little—if any—beauty, color, or evidence of pleasure. Everything I saw was stark, bleak, and basic, testifying to a life that was stark, bleak, and basic.

Then it hit me! I suddenly realized that God's beautiful Proverbs 31 woman was the sparkling jewel in her husband's life! She brought the love, the color, the joy, the life, and the energy to the home. Yes, life was bleak in Israel, and everyday life focused on just surviving in that dry, rugged land. Food, clothing, and shelter were all-consuming daily concerns. But, with a wife who was a sparkling jewel, a man would find life bearable. In fact, with God's beautiful woman beside him, he possessed treasure untold!

The How-To's of Beauty

I said God's truth hit me—and it hit me hard! Emotionally I staggered as I realized the magnitude of God's plan for me (and for you, too!): I am to supply beauty in the lives of my husband and children as we struggle through life together. I am to light up the home with sparkle no matter how hard times are.

I hope you are catching a vision of your life as a sparkling jewel to those who face hardship, pain, weariness, drudgery, or sorrow. Being a jewel in the lives of those He blesses us with is a tall order from God, but He knows you and I can—by His beautiful grace—fill it!

Just as gems increase in value as time passes, we who

are God's beautiful women—His jewels—should, too. So here are some exercises to help us enhance our sparkle and brighten up our life as well as the lives of those around us.

1. *Grow in practical skills*—Married or single, we who are God's women need to sharpen the skills necessary for managing a home (or apartment or dorm room).

Homemaking—I well remember the sad tears of a college graduate about to marry whose mother had financed swimming lessons, encouraged her athletic efforts, and driven her to swimming pools, swim practice, and swim meets for 20 years. My friend could swim—but she couldn't cook or clean!

Another woman had the same problem. Actually I should say her *husband* had the problem. One day he showed up in Jim's office at The Master's Seminary. You see, he went home every evening after his classes and his job to—nothing! Nothing was cooked, nothing was cooking, nothing was in the cupboard or refrigerator *to* cook, and his wife also had nothing of a plan for what to cook in mind. She was clueless! And he was helpless—and hungry!

Money management—God's beautiful women also need a working knowledge of personal finances. We need to know about paying bills, managing a checkbook, reconciling a bank statement, nurturing savings and investments, and holding the reins on those charge cards. Jim says that one of my greatest gifts to him has been taking care of our family finances. By managing his paycheck I've given him back hours of time every week for 30-plus years, hours he can spend on other responsibilities at home, at work, and at church. As you and I work our way through Proverbs 31:10-31, you'll notice again and again the keen business head on God's beautiful woman!

Time management—Diligent time management is key to running a home (and a life!) smoothly. Time is the most precious commodity God gives us, and He expects it to be redeemed (Colossians 4:5) and used for His purposes (Ephesians 2:10). Life itself is made up of minutes, and those minutes must be managed wisely and well. I encourage you to begin the daily habit of planning and scheduling. If you don't know how to begin, invest in some time management books or talk with the women you know who excel in this practical skill.

2. *Grow in emotional stability*—Certainly to be a sparkling jewel in anyone's life, you and I need to be growing in emotional stability. After all, the mistress of the home determines the general emotional atmosphere under her roof; her emotional state sets the standard and the tone. Proverbs speaks numerous times of the shrewish woman who is rottenness to her husband's bones (Proverbs 12:4) and the brawling woman whose husband can no longer endure living in the same house with her (21:9 and 19; 25:24). I know neither you nor I want to be this kind of unattractive woman. Our desire is to live out an epitaph found on a gravestone. The husband of 60 years said of his wife that "she always made home happy." What a wonderful tribute to his sparkling jewel!

Since this book is about becoming a virtuous woman—a woman of mental, emotional, physical, and spiritual strength—here are three guidelines for gaining some emotional stability so that you, too, can make your home happy.

Master your tolerance—By this I mean your endurance. Emotional stability gives every soldier in every army the invaluable ability to continue on when the going is tough, and that's what I'm calling you to do. I'm calling you to learn endurance, something I've been working towards for decades. Ever since I discovered that God's beautiful and virtuous woman is an army of virtues, I've been trying to learn a soldier's ability to persevere, and I turn to God to be my Helper.

When I face difficult circumstances or painful times, I pray something like this: "God, Your Word says You have already given me all things that pertain to life and godliness (2 Peter 1:3). And Your Word says I can do all things—including handle this—through Christ who strengthens me (Philippians 4:13). By Your grace and through Your Spirit, I can do this. Thank You for enabling me to meet the challenge!"

With this prayer I acknowledge the marvelous resources I have in the Lord and then bear down physically and mentally like a soldier and march right through what lies before me. I endeavor to quietly...and calmly...and determinedly...endure life's challenges as they roll in and out with the regularity of the ocean's surf. You see, my goal—my prayer—is always that I will not give in, give up, or quit. Instead of becoming incapacitated by emotions, I want to be that soldier who is beautiful in God's eyes, and I know you join me in that desire.

Master your temper—I'm using *temper* to refer to "heat of mind" (as *Webster's* says) and passion. When it comes to temper, God's Word tells us a few things about a woman of strength:

- She nurtures a peaceful heart (Proverbs 14:30).
- She knows how to wait (Proverbs 19:2).
- She does not strive (Proverbs 19:11).
- She restrains her spirit (Proverbs 25:28).

This description may seem like another impossible dream, but let me reassure you that God uses our faithful devotion to Him and our careful attention to His standards day by day, incident by incident, challenge by challenge over a lifetime to flesh out in us His divine beauty, a reflection of His image.

I started down this path of mastering my temper by first creating a "resolutions" page in my personal prayer notebook. This list (you can tell I'm a list maker!) contained the deadly sins I was holding up to God daily with a heart-plea for Him to help me eliminate them out of my life (Matthew 5:29-30). One such unbeautiful habit on that list read, "Stop screaming at the children." I hope you get the picture!

Master your tongue—Speaking of deadly sins, don't most of them involve the tongue? Blessing and cursing do indeed proceed out of the same mouth (James 3:10). Our words can either "speak like the piercings of a sword" or "promote health" (Proverbs 12:18). To bring the sparkle of God's beauty into a home, you and I need to live out a few more wise proverbs. Specifically, we need to:

- Speak less often (Proverbs 10:19).
- Speak only after we think about what we're going to say (Proverbs 15:28).
- Speak only what is sweet and pleasant (Proverbs 16:21 and 24).
- Speak only what is wise and kind (Proverbs 31:26).

In light of this topic, I can't resist passing on to you one of our family's all-time favorite devotionals from the *Our Daily Bread* series. The morning Jim read it at the breakfast table, my daughter Katherine drew five stars and wrote the word "Mom" on it. That day was May 17, 1982—a red-letter day for our family. Maybe this will help you, too.

> A woman developed a very serious throat condition. The doctor prescribed medication but told her that her vocal cords needed total rest—no talking for six months! With a husband and six children to care for, it seemed an impossible order, but she cooperated. When she needed the youngsters, she blew a whistle. Instructions became written memos, and questions were answered on pads of paper she had placed around the house. The six months passed, and after she recovered, her first comments were quite revealing. She said that the children had become quieter, and then remarked, "I don't think I'll ever holler again like I used to." When asked about the notes, she replied, "You'd be surprised how many, written hastily, I crumpled up and threw into the wastebasket before I gave them to anyone to read. Seeing my words before anyone heard them had an effect that I don't think I can ever forget."[8]

I got the message: Speak less often...and only after thinking about what I'm going to say. And speak only what is sweet and pleasant...only what is wise and kind! These are God's guidelines for beautiful speech.

An Invitation to Beauty

Don't you want God's kind of practical beauty and inner strength in your life, too, dear sister? Don't you deeply desire to be beautiful in His eyes, to be a blazing jewel who adds sparkle to the lives of others?

We must pay a price if we are to become priceless, if we

are to become women whose "price is much higher than jewels." Such rare beauty of character is hard-won as is the beauty of the jewels we so prize. Gems are hard to begin with, and these rough, hard gems need to be cut. All the flaws, all that is unlovely about them, need to be removed. Once cut, these gems are polished to add to their luster and increase their brilliance, to allow color to shine through, and to create its "fire," a rainbow-like sparkle. Our sparkle comes by such a process, too, as—married or single—we gain greater emotional stability and sharpen our practical skills. With these two core elements inside, we who long to be God's beautiful gems will indeed sparkle.

Oh, dear one, God, our Master Craftsman, is holding your heart (and mine) in His hands. Will you look into His eyes, see His love for you, and choose to let Him do His purifying work? Will you yield to Him the flaws in your life that inhibit your "fire," your sparkle? Will you ask Him to help you not succumb to any harmful emotions? And will you do your part to grow in emotional stability and to polish your skills? These two traits—your character and the skills that reflect that character—are so desirable to Him and so valuable to others. Let God work His beauty process in you!

And now, on to a closer look at another sparkling feature of the woman who is beautiful in God's eyes.

~ 3 ~

A Solid Rock

Her Loyalty

"The heart of her husband safely trusts her."
PROVERBS 31:11

I once read about a couple who exchanged their wedding vows on top of the Rock of Gibraltar, the famed rock island at the entrance to the Mediterranean Sea. The groom explained that they wanted to found their marriage on a rock. Well, far better for a husband than saying one's vows on the Rock of Gibraltar is establishing a marriage on the rock of Jesus Christ and the bedrock loyalty of his wife! When a man marries a woman who is mentally, emotionally, physically, and spiritually strong, he can confidently build his life, his work, and his home, trusting in her rock-solid character to be a cornerstone for his efforts.

Believe me, after studying in Israel and living in Jerusalem for three weeks, I know a lot about rocks! Climbing through the hill country day after day meant taking on the characteristics of a gazelle as we walked up, over, around, between, and back down the rocks. And the tells we visited—those layers of remains from Old Testament cities—consisted of layers upon layers of rock and stone, all resting on a foundation of bedrock.

But the most exciting rock I saw was a cornerstone. I took a picture of it (in fact, I'm looking at it as I write) because God speaks of His women as "cornerstones" (Psalm 144:12 KJV). I chose the cornerstone at the excavated base of the south end of the Temple Mount, the site of Herod's Temple (where Jesus worshiped). Supporting the massive foundation of the Temple, this ancient cornerstone has sustained the weight of 75-foot-high stone walls for more than 2,000 years. Twenty feet long, the standard height-of-a-man high (six feet), and at least eight feet across, it still holds the weight of the entire Temple wall.

This remarkable cornerstone had been carefully selected because Herod wanted a firm foundation for the wonder he was building. This most important building had to be stable, so Herod chose a rock that was more than adequate enough to be the cornerstone. Definitely a solid rock, it has not budged despite 2,000 years of battles, earthquakes, elements, and the erosion of time—and neither has the wall on top of it!

Like that wall, your marriage can be strengthened as you, my sister in the Lord, become—by His grace—a virtuous woman of strength who stands steady as a rock. The cornerstone I have a picture of may not be beautiful and most of it is buried and out of sight, but Herod's Temple was splendid! I want you to carry this image of a cornerstone with you through this chapter because the picture of a wife standing as steady and strong as a rock is at the heart of Proverbs 31:11.

The Language of Loyalty

I thought I knew all about trust, but I have to admit I

found three surprises as I studied the statement "the heart of her husband safely trusts her" (Proverbs 31:11). These surprises taught me even more about the importance of being a rock to my husband Jim.

Rest—First consider "the *heart* of her husband." The Hebrew word for *heart* actually refers to the mind where doubt, anxiety, and restlessness fester. But the heart (the mind) of a husband who can trust a loyal wife is a heart at ease, a heart at rest. Our calling as God's women is to live life in such a solid way that our husband never worries or wonders about our character or our management of our home, our finances, or our time! Then he can truly build his life on the cornerstone of our loyalty, his heart resting in—and on—the steady support of his wife.

Encouragement—Next comes the trust factor: "The heart of her husband safely *trusts* her." The Hebrew word for *trust* translates "to be of good courage, to take heart and to feel confidence."[1] Therefore, a man married to one of God's beautiful women feels confident—he is encouraged—by his ability to trust in his wife![2] Her loyalty is a daily ministry of encouragement to him. Because of his confidence in her (he "safely trusts *her*"), he is encouraged and strengthened for his tasks.

Trust in God—Throughout the book of Proverbs trusting in any person or pursuit other than God is equated to foolishness (see Proverbs 3:5). But God makes one exception to His principle: Whereas a man usually enjoys wealth as a result of his trust in *God*, here in Proverbs 31:11 his profit is a result of the value of *his wife*—in whom he can solidly trust. He trusts his wife in the same way he trusts God![3] "The heart of her husband safely trusts in *her*"—and in the Lord!

As one translator sees it, "The heart of her husband has faith in her"![4] Imagine, a calling to work together with God to comfort and support our mate. What an incredible privilege and ministry!

Checklist for Loyalty

These three surprises give me a lot to think about. It's staggering to realize that because of me (when I follow God's guidelines, that is), my Jim can enjoy rest, confidence, and a deeper trust in the Lord.

As I considered the impact our loyalty has on our hardworking husbands, I again skimmed Proverbs 31:10-31 and jotted down a personal checklist for loyalty. If you're not married, this is still relevant. Remember, after all, that this mother is advising her son to search for a *single* woman who *already* possesses this beautiful quality of loyalty! Any and all of God's beautiful women should be worthy of this description: faithful, true, and constant; a solid rock in terms of her character, her marriage, her family, her relationships, and her ministry. So, whether we are married or single, our goal is for this priceless virtue to become a jewel in our crown (Proverbs 12:4)!

Here's my personal checklist for loyalty in ten different spheres of daily life. Why not consider how you measure up against God's standards? Are you building your life, your home, and your marriage on these rocks?

Money—Can your husband's heart and mind rest because of your diligent management of his (and your) assets (Proverbs 31:27)? Can he depend on you to be thrifty, wise, and debt-free?

Children—Are you a devoted mother, dedicated to

training up obedient children who love the Lord, who love their father, and who bring honor to their names (Proverbs 31:1-2)?

Home—Is your husband encouraged by the knowledge that all is well—and will be well—at home because of your focused efforts to run an orderly home (Proverbs 31:13,27)?

Reputation—Is your husband's heart at rest because he knows that you will do him good and not evil all the days of your life, never causing any questions about his character to arise (Proverbs 31:12,23)?

Fidelity—Can your husband trust and even rejoice in your lifelong faithfulness to your wedding vows (Proverbs 5:18)?

Emotions—Does your husband rest in the knowledge that he can depend on you to be emotionally steady and stable, avoiding blow-ups and flare-ups (Proverbs 14:30)?

Happiness—Are you a fountain of joy, delighting yourself in the Lord (Psalm 37:4) and refreshing the hearts of those at home?

Wisdom—Can your husband trust you to handle the challenges, difficulties, and crises of life with godly wisdom (Proverbs 19:14)?

Conduct—Can your husband count on you to conduct yourself with graciousness (Proverbs 11:16), discretion (Proverbs 11:22), virtue (Proverbs 31:10), and dignity (Proverbs 31:25)?

Love—Positive progress in the preceding nine areas is progress in love! You see, love is known by its actions. Your active care for your husband's assets and the details of his life is powerful evidence of your love for him (Proverbs 31:29).

I hope you are beginning to appreciate how highly God values loyalty in you and me! Do you understand why loyalty is so beautiful in His eyes—and in your husband's? Here in Proverbs 31, loyalty is number one on God's list of character traits, and you (and I) can take specific, concrete steps—daily and for the rest of your life—to lay a firm foundation of loyal character and earn a greater degree of trust from everyone you meet.

The How-To's of Beauty

1. *Take trust seriously*—We need to take seriously whatever God says whenever He speaks! And God says "a virtuous woman"—a woman who's faithful, a wife who's loyal—can be trusted. The best way to begin laying this cornerstone of godly beauty is to place it at the top of your daily prayer list. Ask God to transform your character.

2. *Keep your word*—I remember listening to some college women share prayer requests at their weekly Bible study in our home. They earnestly and eagerly wanted others to pray that they would become "women of their word," women who were true to their word. That's a good goal for us, too. So challenge yourself to do what you say you'll do, be where you say you'll be, and keep the appointments you make.

3. *Follow through on instructions*—The degree to which we follow through on instructions is a measure of our faithfulness and our loyalty. In Genesis 3:1-6, for instance, we see how Eve failed her husband—and God—when she failed to follow the Lord's guidelines regarding the tree of knowledge and ate the forbidden fruit (Genesis 2:17). Her failure to

follow God's directions sent the world reeling. Her sin—her desire to do things her way and not God's way—toppled a perfect creation and required the sacrifice of His only Son to bring us back into fellowship with Him (2 Corinthians 11:3; 1 Timothy 2:14).

So one way you can build trust is to do what you've been asked to do. Try not to second-guess the whys behind instructions. And don't get too creative with directions. Ask questions if you need to, but in the end your goal is to follow through. If your husband wants the paper canceled today, do it. If he needs his clothes picked up from the cleaners, do it. If he asks you to have the oil changed in the car, do it. If he's on a special diet, fix it. *His* heart can be at ease because he knows that *you* are carrying out his desires for the home, the family, and the finances. Furthermore, your compliance is evidence of God's deep character buried in your heart!

4. *When in doubt, check it out!*—One day a wife who was working on building her husband's trust in her took his car to be worked on. While the car was up on the rack, the mechanic noticed a "what-you-ma-call-it" that needed to be replaced. When he asked her if she wanted it replaced ("So glad we caught it! You sure wouldn't want that to break while you're out driving! Won't take but a minute—and a few more dollars, of course—if we do it right now"), she was ready to blurt out an enthusiastic "Yes!" when she remembered her goal. When she called her husband to check it out, he said it was something he could easily—and cheaply—replace. And then he thanked her for calling! She could sense his grateful heart, a heart that rested because she checked with him first. Her wise actions built her husband's trust in her, served him well, and saved them money—all at the same time!

So, when in doubt, check it out. Call your husband and get his input. (P.S. Seeking counsel like this is also a mark of wisdom. Proverbs 28:26 says, "He that trusts in his own heart is a fool.")

5. *Be accountable*—When Jim and I were teaching our teenage daughters Katherine and Courtney about accountability and trustworthiness, we let them leave the house only after they let us know where they would be and agreed to check in if their plans changed.

And I do the same thing as a wife! You see, I want Jim to know where I am every minute. This goal becomes quite a challenge when I travel to speaking engagements. Jim is usually with me, but when he isn't, I phone, I fax, I e-mail, and I leave a travel itinerary complete with all names, locations, phone numbers, fax numbers, flight numbers, and flight times. I call him from every airport—with every plane change—and from every conference site. We even have a toll-free 800 number and 50-state cell phone coverage so I can call him from Anywhere, U.S.A., without any hassle. It's very important to me that Jim knows exactly where I am. Even when I run my daily errands at home, I let him know where I am going and when I'll be back.

Your husband should know where you are at all times. Keeping him informed speaks loudly of your willingness to be accountable to him and nurtures his trust in you and your relationship. Besides—returning to Eve's story—didn't Satan deceive her (Genesis 3:1) when she was away from her husband's protection and failed to check in?

An Invitation to Beauty

And now, my loyal friend and beautiful sister, it's time to

turn our hearts to the Father and look full into His wonderful face. As we discussed, whenever God speaks, we need to take His word seriously. And here in Proverbs 31:11 God states His desire that we exhibit one of His personal attributes—His faithfulness. You and I trust the Lord because we can count on His faithfulness. David, who trusted God, proclaimed, "You are my rock" (Psalm 31:3). God asks you to show forth His kind of faithfulness to your husband; He asks you to be a solid rock for your husband to trust in and lean on.

Do you want to be beautiful in God's eyes? Do you want to reflect His loyalty and faithfulness in your life? Then you need *His* marvelous grace, power, faithfulness, and strength—so that you can be dependable in all areas of life. You need to choose to be a woman of your word (and His!) and a woman who follows instructions in the details of daily life.

This chapter is entitled "A Solid Rock," and, dear one, that's exactly what you'll be for your mate (and others) as you consistently live out your loyalty to him. Life is difficult and filled with hardships, and your husband carries a heavy load of responsibility. He needs a solid rock to rest his soul upon, and you have the privilege of being that kind of rock! Will you extend to your husband the gift of a heart at rest? Will you provide him an oh-so-needed rock to rest on? Will you begin today to make the virtue of loyalty a lifetime aim as God transforms you into one of His treasured cornerstones (Psalm 144:12)?

~ 4 ~

An Unfailing Prize
Her Contribution

"He will have no lack of gain."
PROVERBS 31:11

"Here's something I think you'll want to read," Jim said as he handed me the business section of our daily newspaper. (And I think you'll want to read this chapter, too!) The feature article offered the following advice for, as the title said, "Building Your Nest Egg":

- Keep track of your expenditures.
- Cut back on spending.
- Shop wisely.
- Stay out of debt (especially credit card debt).
- Save six months' worth of living expenses for emergencies.
- Set aside money each month for savings and investments.
- Invest aggressively.[1]

I had to blink! My newspaper was describing the wisdom God's beautiful woman already possesses...and practices! As a master in micromanagement, she's already following this advice and making an invaluable contribution to her family's financial well-being.

The Spoils of War

Along with the sterling virtues God's beautiful woman possesses, her financial contribution to her household makes her invaluable to her husband and her family. Because she herself is an unfailing prize, her husband "will have no lack of gain" (Proverbs 31:11). Let me explain.

A *military prize*—The word "gain" derives its significance from the cultural setting of Proverbs. In those days when one army defeated another, the victorious ruler and his soldiers carried off the spoils of war. These spoils were the prizes of war and comprised wealth in a time when there was no coinage.

With this verse from Proverbs 31 in mind, I stood a long time in the Israel Museum studying a 15' by 50' clay relief found on a wall in Babylon. It pictured the historic siege of the great Palestinian city of Lakish in 701 BC (2 Chronicles 32:9). The left side of the picture detailed the raging battle taking place at the gate and around the walls of the city. The right side showed the victors carrying off the prizes of war—people for servants, livestock for food, and treasures of silver, gold, jewels, and clothing.

A *peaceful prize*—But wealth could be acquired without facing the threat of death in battle. There were other, more peaceful ways to obtain wealth. A man could, for instance, lie, cheat, or steal; he could borrow money; he could become an indentured servant, hiring himself out for long periods of time in faraway places.

A *personal prize*—The woman who is beautiful in God's eyes, however, determines that by her personal contribution to her husband's finances "he will have no lack of gain" (verse 11). She doesn't want him to lack anything, but she also doesn't want him to be forced to leave her, his children, or his home to go off to war—to endanger his life—in order to bring home the spoils to pay off debts or increase his personal wealth. And she certainly doesn't want him to be tempted to obtain money by unrighteous means! So she chooses to give of herself—her mind, her strength—to do the work and make the necessary contribution so that her husband will "have no lack of gain." We easily see that she herself is the gain, the wealth, the unfailing prize!

The "Warrior"

She is also a warrior. We defined the word *virtuous* in chapter 1 as meaning an army, and that idea is repeated here. The Hebrew and Greek languages give us a vivid metaphoric picture of this woman, this unfailing prize, as a mighty warrior who utilizes her abilities for the benefit of her husband's domain.[2]

This startling image dramatically conveys the commitment of God's beautiful woman to her husband and his wealth and welfare. She is a warrior of undying allegiance who dedicates her life and energies to the well-being of her husband and his household. *She* battles daily on the home front so that *he* doesn't have to engage in war or experience a "lack of gain"!

The Beauty of God's Plan

I know this may sound crass, unspiritual, and quite unbeautiful, but much of Proverbs 31:10-31 deals with money. God's 22-verse portrait of His beautiful woman clearly shows her daily involvement in managing, making, and multiplying money. When I read this, I wondered why money management is so important in God's eyes, and learning why was a good exercise for me. Here are some of the reasons money matters to God.

God is honored—This teaching from Proverbs 31 about family finance—about making, managing, and multiplying money—is God's design for His beautiful women. He is honored when we follow His plan.

Your husband is blessed—Money management is a ministry to your husband which gives him relief of mind *and* release of time. Even if your husband oversees finances in a general way, you are the one who runs the home and therefore manages the money on a day-to-day basis. You can, for instance, manage the food budget, save money by using coupons, shop wisely, and cook instead of buying prepared foods or eating out.

Your children benefit—As your children see firsthand how you, a mother who is beautiful in God's eyes, handle money, they will be greatly blessed. They will learn many lessons as they watch you manage money, make money, save money, and give money away (children notice our faithful giving at church!). Your children will develop a healthy respect for money, an appreciation of stewardship, an ability to be disciplined with finances, and personal savings goals and money management skills of their own. You will be training them for life by your example.

Your home is built—The Proverbs teach that "every wise woman builds her house" (Proverbs 14:1) and "through wisdom a house is built" (Proverbs 24:3). What characterizes the house wisdom builds? "The rooms are filled with all precious and pleasant riches" (Proverbs 24:4). How can you build such a home? By keen oversight of the finances. Yours will be a house of plenty—truly a home-sweet-home!

Your character grows—Proverbs 31 clearly shows that, in God's eyes, wise money management is a virtue. And God calls us to nurture the sister virtue of self-control in the area of money. Usually the one person you have to especially watch if you're going to save money is *yourself!* After all, every decision *not* to spend money is money saved! When you learn to do without, when you learn to say no, you reap great rewards: The savings grow, the expenses fall, and the bank account builds—all of which motivates you to continue your wise money management!

A Personal Story

In the early days of our marriage, Jim handled our finances. He paid the bills, balanced the checkbook, and kept our files and records. But as his life became more complicated, money management became more burdensome. I didn't like seeing him stay up late at night, hunched over the checkbook, and I hated those mornings when he had to dash off last-minute checks before he headed out the door. I dreaded the days of paperwork he faced before and after his long missions trips. And I dared not look at what was lying in those piles of paperwork I dutifully dusted around on his desk! Our lives were marked by mad scrambling to get to the post office, waiting in line the "day-of" to make on-time payments, and the frustration of finance charges, late fees, and overdraft penalties.

Memorizing Proverbs 31:10-31 and studying the life of God's beautiful woman helped me realize that I could ease Jim's life by taking over some of this responsibility for him. Under his tutelage I learned the basics of bookkeeping, bill paying, and banking, and I began contributing to our financial well-being. No, I didn't have a job or bring in a paycheck at the time, but let me tell you some of the ways I did contribute financially—and still do today.

- I paid all bills on time, saving on finance charges and late fees. That meant money in the bank.

- We opened a savings account and signed up to have some money automatically withdrawn from each of Jim's paychecks and deposited into that account. That meant fewer trips to the bank, less paperwork, and more savings.

- We reconcile all bank statements the day we receive them. That means that we know our current financial condition. It also means no bounced checks and therefore more money in the bank.

- The checkbook shows an up-to-the-minute balance, signaling to us exactly where we stand every day of the month. That means savings realized by not overspending.

Needless to say, Jim was greatly relieved when I started to contribute to our financial health and strength in these ways. The time my labor redeemed for him was spent in other productive ways around the house and in ministry. Our evenings took on a lighter tone, and our mornings were more relaxed. We experienced a wonderful sense of freedom as we gained control of our finances.

But my contribution didn't end with the four steps outlined above. They were only the beginning! I took flight and began reading to learn better money management skills, principles, and methods. This led to a study of advanced finance and instituting more ways to save, increase, and manage Jim's salary. I took my role of money management seriously and have come to excel in it—and you can, too!

The How-To's of Beauty

My prayer for you is that you won't be like I was—a carefree, uninformed wife who threw up her hands saying, "Oh, I don't know anything about the money! My husband takes care of all of that!" These words might have sounded like respect and submission to some, but they were actually words of ignorance, foolishness, immaturity, and weakness.

My prayer is that you will learn how to increase revenue and make a contribution to your budget whether you're married or single. Here are some steps you can take toward becoming a beautiful money manager, an unfailing prize!

1. *Own the assignment*—Obviously you will want to follow your husband's desires when it comes to this vital area of money. But you can understand financial matters, know how to handle them, and make your contributions (don't forget those grocery store coupons!) even if your husband does all the paperwork. You can find unlimited ways to contribute if you first own God's assignment to become business minded, to make a contribution in the area of finances.

2. *Bone up on money management*—Read and collect information on personal finance. Learn what others are saying and doing to manage, earn, and save money. For starters, put into action the "Building Your Own Nest Egg" ideas you read about at the beginning of this chapter.

3. *Talk it over with your husband*—If you're married, you need to follow your husband's leadership (Genesis 3:16; Ephesians 5:22-24). He's the head of the household and you are his householder, his manager (1 Timothy 5:14; Titus 2:5). So before you attempt a "takeover" or institute any major financial reforms, be sure he approves of the plan.

I put these first three how-to's together and began reading books and articles about household budgeting during Jim's years in seminary—years when we had next to no money! One article I found suggested "Fifteen Ways to Put More Money in the Bank."[3] I implemented the ones I could (like saving sales receipts for tax deductions on April 15), but I took other ideas to Jim for his consideration and input. These more complex proposals involved our joint property. I wasn't about to decide on my own whether we should raise the deductible on our car insurance and drop collision and comprehensive insurance on older cars. I'm sure you get the picture about how and when to get your husband involved!

4. *Get set up for better money management*—Start some kind of record-keeping system. See what a local stationery store or office supply center has available. Look for books on tracking your expenses. Consider investing in a bookkeeping program for your computer or look into on-line banking. Ask your bank about computerized bill paying. Arrange for bill payments to be automatically deducted from your checking account. (I was thrilled yesterday to sign up for this kind of

service through our local gas company! That's one less bill in the mailbox, one less check to write, one less stamp to purchase, one less due date to worry about, and at least 15 minutes redeemed!)

Besides gathering knowledge and supplies, you may need to set up a desk area, a specific place for you to sit and manage your finances. Let this be the place where you put everything related to money management, where you perform the actions involved in managing your finances, and where you can file and find important information.

Once you own God's assignment, learn more about money management, agree with your husband on your role (whatever *he* determines it to be!), and get set up, you will be making an important contribution to your household. I guarantee it!

An Invitation to Beauty

Well, I know it isn't at all glamorous and it doesn't seem very lovely, but God considers your contribution in the financial arena of your home quite beautiful!

Dear one, this book is all about virtue, character, godliness, and spiritual beauty. But keep in mind each step of the way that God's kind of beauty is lived out in practical life, in practical places (at home), and in practical ways (money management)!

So glance again through those sacred verses, Proverbs 31:10-31. Ask God's Spirit to open your eyes to the many references to this beautiful woman's thrifty and wise money management. She was truly an unfailing prize to her husband and a tribute to her God. And that's what I want for you!

~ 5 ~

A Spring of Goodness

Her Mission

"She does [her husband] good and not evil
all the days of her life."
PROVERBS 31:12

As I sit at my desk and begin a chapter about God's beautiful Proverbs 31 woman who does her husband "good and not evil all the days of her life" (verse 12), I've decided to christen it "A Spring of Goodness." This title is prompted by the two framed photos of my smiling husband Jim that sit on my desk. I snapped the two shots at En-gedi where the Old Testament hero David hid from King Saul and his 3,000 mightiest hand-picked warriors (1 Samuel 23:29–24:2). Jim stood in the exact place for both pictures—but each has its own tale to tell!

In the first picture, Jim is standing in front of a rushing torrent of water falling 100 feet into a teal blue pool. We visited this basin of refreshment on the same day we climbed Masada, the day's second dusty, dirty, dry, and, of course, steep trek! The trail was also very rocky. In fact, this place was a perfect hideout for David exactly because of all its rocks and caves. After trudging up, up, up, and up, over, and around rocks and boulders, we finally reached our destination—these life-giving waterfalls of En-gedi. En-gedi means "fountain of the wild goat" (you have to be one to get there!) or "spring of the kid."[1] And it was definitely a refreshing sight for sore eyes—and a refreshing treat for tired feet!

The small year-round spring that feeds these falls creates a cool, calming, and invigorating oasis in the desert wilderness. Laughing children splashed and played and entertained themselves. Adults waded, relaxed, and soaked their weary feet. A shadow cast by the shear rock wall and the lush green undergrowth and trees served as a cool, welcoming embrace after a day of physical exertion, heat, thirst, and sandstone. How easy to imagine what this refuge meant to David! That one little spring provided everything he needed for safety, for life. David may even have been looking at the rocks around the spring when he described God as his "rock and fortress" (Psalm 31:3), "the rock that is higher than I" (Psalm 61:2).

Now let me tell you about the second photograph. Jim stood in the same spot, but turned his body 180 degrees. The background for this picture is the Dead Sea, a body of water so vast that it claimed the full expanse of my camera range! Forty-nine miles long, ten miles wide, and 1,300 feet deep, the Dead Sea is fed by the Jordan River at the rate of six million gallons of fresh water a day. But the Dead Sea is a salt sea and therefore virtually useless. As the saying goes, "Water, water, everywhere, but not a drop to drink!" Situated in an arid desert land, parched for lack of water, the Dead Sea is good for nothing. There is so much of it, it's so blue and so inviting—yet it poisons those who drink! Truly it is a Dead Sea...and a sea of death!

A Heart of Goodness

Now let's return to the picture of the woman who is beautiful in God's eyes, the woman of Proverbs 31:10-31. A faithful mother—who herself is living out God's picture of true beauty—is impressing upon her royal young son what really matters in a wife. She's showing him snapshot after snapshot of God's beautiful woman so he'll recognize her when he sees her.

With this next picture in the album, with the snapshot of verse 12, we peer right into the heart of God's beautiful woman, and we're startled because it is so clean, so pure, so lovely. Hers is a heart of goodness! How refreshing in this day of selfishness—of self-centeredness, self-confidence, self-esteem, self-image, and self-assertion—to come across a selfless spring of goodness. No wonder this woman is beautiful in God's eyes! But how is her heart of goodness demonstrated?

The presence of good—"She does [her husband] good," Proverbs 31:12 tells us. God's beautiful wife is intent on lavishing every possible good upon her husband. She lives to love him, and so she does him good at every opportunity. She operates her life and his home in a way that routinely benefits him with good.[2] Her waking prayer each day is to do her dear husband good—to love him, serve him, honor him, advance him, spoil him, and ease his life. Far from looking for any payoff, notice, or praise, she finds following through on God's assignment to do her husband good reward enough!

And where does all her goodness come from? How can she keep up this kind of giving for a lifetime? First of all, as God's beautiful woman, goodness is part of what God weaves into her character. Doing good is who she is; doing good—no matter what—is what she's all about! Besides, she's a woman who fears the Lord (Proverbs 31:30), and He is the One who calls her to do her husband good. She takes seriously her God-given mission to be a spring of goodness in her marriage. After all, *her heavenly Lord* has ordained goodness as her behavior toward *her earthly lord*, her husband (Proverbs 31:12). And she finds her highest happiness in doing just that—and doing it "heartily, as to the Lord [her heavenly One] and not unto man [her earthly one]" (Colossians 3:23).

The absence of evil—"She does her husband good and *not evil*" (Proverbs 31:12). As a fallen creature (Psalm 14:1; Romans 3:12,23), God's beautiful woman of Proverbs 31 experiences the same temptations toward evil that you and I do, but—by God's grace—she stands strong against them. At every opportunity to give in to selfishness, resentment, anger, disapproval, or disagreement, she perseveres against evil and instead chooses to follow after God's plan to do her husband good—not evil. As one gentleman notes, "Life is difficult enough for a man who makes his way in this world without adding to that burden a wife who does not understand or support him."[3]

The influence of a lifetime—The good which the Proverbs 31 woman does her husband and the evil which she doesn't do are to characterize "all the days of her life" (verse 12). That's the timeframe God has for her mission: She is to overflow with goodness into her husband's life "all the days of her life"! She is to take seriously and literally her marriage vows to do her husband good "till death us do part." Being a spring of goodness for her beloved husband is her lifelong calling. She is to be sweet tempered and constant today…tomorrow…twenty years from now…fifty years from now…until death parts the partners. Sickness, poverty, old age, and mistakes are not to dampen her commitment to be a positive influence in her husband's life.

An Example of Goodness

For years I've enjoyed the daily blessing of the devotional series *Streams in the Desert* by Mrs. Charles E. Cowman.[4] For a long time, though, I had no idea what soil her powerful words of comfort grew out of! Only later did I learn her story and, with it, the how and why these volumes of hope and comfort were assembled.

Charles Cowman was founder of the Oriental Missionary Society. As he neared the end of a five-year Gospel crusade in Japan, he commented to his wife, "I have been having such heart pain at night." Despite agonizing physical pain, Charles completed the crusade. Then he returned to the United States for rest and recovery...only to suffer a severe heart attack and a paralyzing stroke. His time of chronic illnesses and suffering was truly like nights without stars—six years of them!

To counter their despair, Lettie Cowman determined to use God's promises as an antidote. Collecting countless books and magazines, she searched for words that would encourage both of them, and she read those words day in and day out to her suffering husband. In the darkness of her sorrow, she dug brilliant nuggets of hope out of the rich mine of God's promises to share with her dear Charles. Studying the Scriptures, she found the soul-sustaining power and comfort they both so desperately needed.[5]

Dear one, Lettie Cowman was not only a solid rock for her husband's soul, but she was also a spring of goodness until his dying day. When he was healthy, she was his helpmate in Japan. But in his twilight years she remained loyal to him and to her Lord, spending six years of her life bringing spiritual refreshment to her dear and dying husband. While managing his home, his finances, and his ministry organization during those dark years, she also fed her husband's soul divine truth.

I pray your heart is moved by this beautiful woman's strength. And I trust you are beginning to grasp what a real-life beautiful-in-God's-eyes woman looks like. She's tender, but she's also tough (ever the army)! She's a rock, but she's also a spring. Prompted by God and empowered by a heart full of His goodness, she bears down, follows through, and finishes the task. She's on a mission from God to "do her husband good" (Proverbs 31:12), and she takes that mission seriously, faithfully working to fulfill it.

I don't know what Lettie Cowman looked like from the outside, but you and I do know her heart. I don't know anything about her physical stature, but you and I do know about her strength to endure, to serve, and to remain loyal to her husband to the end. Like all of God's beautiful women, Mrs. Cowman spent "all the days of her life" (Proverbs 31:12) living out God's plan that she be a perpetual spring of goodness to her husband. In Mrs. Cowman's case, her life was indeed a stream in the desert!

The How-To's of Beauty

How can you live out a lifelong ministry of refreshment to your husband?

1. *Beware the enemies of goodness!*—"She does her husband good and not evil all the days of her life" (Proverbs 31:12). Imagine "good" and "evil" in the same verse! These are such sharply contrasting behaviors—the one so desirable and the other so dreadful. Obviously the possibility of a wife doing her husband evil is a reality or God wouldn't mention

it. In fact, the Bible itself offers plenty of examples. Scan this list of women who failed to be a spring of goodness for their husbands.

- Eve, created to be a helper for Adam, invited him to join her in her sin (Genesis 2:18 and 3:6).
- Solomon's wives drew his heart away from God (1 Kings 11:4).
- Jezebel stirred up her husband Ahab to commit acts of abominable wickedness (1 Kings 21:25).
- Job's wife counseled him to "curse God and die" (Job 2:9).
- Rebekah willfully deceived her husband Isaac (Genesis 27).
- Michal despised her husband David (2 Samuel 6:16).

What are some heart-issues that could cause such chaos in a marriage? First of all, *a tendency to compare* leads us down a dark path (2 Corinthians 10:12). I know how easy it is to compare my husband, my life, my marriage, my financial condition (the list can go on!) to other people. Comparisons—as well as expectations, dreams, and fantasies (all of which come with disappointment guaranteed!)—can quickly change my heart that should be focused on God's personal plan for *my* life...with *my* husband...in *my* God-ordained circumstances...as I travel on *my* God-appointed mission of goodness.

Why not pause right here and thank God for your husband and for the path He has put you on? While you pray, make the commitment to tend to your tendency to compare! At the same time, decide to do a better job praising your husband and thanking him for contributing to your welfare.

Nurturing *a growing root of bitterness* is another sure way to foster evil rather than good. Allowing bitterness to even begin to take root—bitterness toward our husband or our circumstances—causes trouble and ultimately defiles other people, especially those closest to us, especially our husband and our children (see Hebrews 12:15).

So once again turn to God in prayer and thank Him for every detail of your life. Gratitude that has us looking to God—not our husband or our circumstances—is the weapon with which you and I can do battle against any budding bitterness. Try it. You'll find that you simply cannot be thankful and bitter at the same time!

Finally, watch out for *a sagging spiritual condition*. Problems in a marriage may point to problems in the spiritual life. Staying close to God—by reading His Word, by praying, and by walking in His grace—fills our hearts and makes them the spring of goodness we desire them to be. The following prayer focuses on the vital link between living close to God and lavishing goodness on our precious husbands. (Only the gender has been changed!)

> That I may come near to my husband, draw me nearer to Thee than to him.
> That I may know my husband, make me to know Thee more than him.
> That I may love my husband with the perfect love of a perfectly whole heart, cause me to love Thee more than him and most of all.
> That nothing may be between me and my husband, be Thou between us, every moment.
> That we may be constantly together, draw us into separate loneliness with Thyself.
> And when we meet breast to breast, O God, let it be upon Thine own.[6]

Please make this prayer your own. Allow God to fill your heart with His great love until it is filled to overflowing as a spring of goodness right into your husband's life. I invite you to pray this prayer and pray it often!

2. *Follow God's plan*—Our mission of fulfilling God's pattern for goodness in marriage is empowered by Him when we plan and practice goodness.

Plan to do good—A wise proverb says, "Do they not go astray who *devise evil*? But mercy and truth belong to those who *devise good*" (Proverbs 14:22). Sharing his insights into this verse, a visiting preacher at my church pointed to Adolf Hitler, the Nazi leader who masterminded the murder of six million Jews. He noted that Hitler "devised evil," that he planned evil, as meticulously as a bride plans her wedding. What are you planning? You and I can choose to plan for good or plan for evil, but as God's beautiful women we are called to do *good!* So make it your goal to set sail today—and every day—on a course of doing your husband good all day long.

Practice your plan—Don't be content with merely planning to do good. Follow through on your good intentions! Put your plan to work. Hopefully, the following ABCs will help your spring of goodness to gush!

Some ABCs of Goodness

A Always contribute spiritually. Don't discourage your husband about God's plans as Job's wife did (Job 2:9).

B Bless his name. Allow "the law of kindness" (Proverbs 31:26) to rule your words whenever you talk about your husband.

C Control your spending. Be sensitive to the family's financial situation.

D Discipline, raise, and train his children. Proverbs 31 is the faithful teaching of a godly mother to her husband's child.

E Encourage his dreams. Fan the flames of his personal aspirations.

F Follow his leadership. Eve brought sorrow of heart to her man—and to the world—by not following him.

G Give your husband the joy of a happy home. Don't be the contentious, brawling wife of Proverbs 19:13.

H Habitually exhibit a steady, predictable, even-keeled nature. Be sure there's no Dr. Jekyll and Mrs. Hyde in your home!

I Indulge in praising him. A *good* word makes a heavy heart glad (Proverbs 12:25). Let your mouth be a spring of goodness!

J Join him in sexual pleasure. Rejoice his heart and satisfy him "at all times" (Proverbs 5:18-19).

K Keep up your spiritual growth. Seeking the Lord regularly is the best way to contribute goodness to your husband.

L Look not at what others have. Be content—and delighted—with your husband's provision for you.

M Make prayer a part of your ministry to your husband. Nothing creates a deeper spring of goodness in a heart!

N Now try your hand and heart at finishing this alphabet of goodness! Refer to it daily—and, of course, do it!

Just a note here. I know that Proverbs 31:12 refers to the husband mentioned in verse 11, making its application obvious for married women. But Proverbs 31:10-31 is every bit as much a description of a single woman as it is a married woman. Remember that the young man hearing these instructions from his mother was single, and he will be seeking these virtues in an unmarried woman! Clearly, God's goal for all of His women—married or single—is that we be a perpetual spring of goodness!

An Invitation to Beauty

Now, my beautiful friend, can you look full into God's wonderful eyes of love and wisdom and choose to do good (and not evil) to your own dear husband? Even if he doesn't seem so dear to you right now, you are still to be a refreshing spring of goodness to him. After all, your husband is a part of God's sovereign plan to grow you into a more beautiful woman. That growth may mean some stretching, some reaching, and it will definitely mean some heavy-duty dependence on God's beautiful grace. But know that blessings untold await you as you follow God's plan for greater beauty, and that plan includes doing your husband good.

So, regardless of the details of your marriage, realize that your husband is the husband God wants you to devote "all the days of your life" to "doing good" to. As you draw upon your resources in Him, the strength of the Lord (Psalm 62:7) and the mind of the Lord (1 Corinthians 2:16) will sustain you, and He who is always faithful will fill your spring of goodness to overflowing.

~ 6 ~

A Fountain of Joy

HER HEART

"She seeks wool and flax,
and willingly works with her hands."
PROVERBS 31:13

Join me for a moment or two on a walk Jim and I took through the streets of Old Jerusalem. It was not a pleasant walk (adventurous, yes; educational, yes; pleasant, no!) as our senses were assaulted with various sights, sounds...and smells!

Crowds of people were everywhere—shoppers jostling us in their hurry, merchants and hawkers shouting and grabbing at us as we passed by their wares. Animals used for transportation and delivery purposes made their different noises—and left various sights and smells behind! Raw meat with the accompanying layers of flies grew old and rank with the heat of the day. Vegetables and fruit, too, began to droop and reek.

In the midst of this sea of humanity a thousand buses were belching fumes and depositing tourists, dump trucks were contributing their diesel fumes, and the sounds of construction work came from the renovation sites. Add to this scene the midday heat, the relentless sun, and your incredible thirst—and you may have a sense of our experience. And there was no relief in sight!

And then our guide Bill led us through one of the many closed doors that line the streets of the Old City…right into paradise! Suddenly—in a single second—we found ourselves standing in the walled courtyard of a home with a flower garden and a small patch of lush, green grass. Blooming vines grew up the walls in the shade of several olive trees and palm trees. Seven pillars supported the second story of a U-shaped, three-sided structure (I was reminded of the home in Proverbs 9:1!), and their graceful arches shaded a walkway. In the very center of this lovely scene was a fountain! Imagine—coolness and shade and water and grass and greenery after the dust and heat of the street! Imagine—silence after the clamor of the crowds, hawkers, and animals! Yes, it was paradise!

But I want to tell you more about that fountain. In the architectural tradition of its day, the entire house, the verandah, the garden, and the walkways were built around that fountain.[1] Singing with joy, that fountain provided the only sound we heard. With its gurgles and gushes, its bubbles and busyness, that lovely fountain said, "Welcome to a place where everything is cared for and every care met!"

When I think of this fountain, dear one, I think of you and me. You see, as God's beautiful women, you and I are to be the fountain of joy at the heart of our home, the center of all that is beautiful and the hub of all that happens there. Proverbs 31 is all about being a fountain of joy—of life, of love, of nourishment—for others. That's why I'm praying that we will each be a fountain of joyful energy, a joyous heart at the center of our home, a faithful and diligent worker who willingly, enthusiastically, and continually makes home happen.

A Willing Worker

The primary ingredient for success in any venture is hard work, and that is especially true when it comes to running a home. In this verse, the wise mother painting the Proverbs 31 portrait addresses the ideal heart attitude God's ideal woman would have toward this hard work: "She *willingly* works with her hands" (Proverbs 31:13)! The woman for her son would be a willing worker, one who tackles her work diligently and cheerfully. She literally "puts her hands *joyfully* to work"[2] and makes her hands "active after the pleasure of her heart."[3]

Exactly what kind of activity is this diligent woman involved in? Weaving is a major part of the work the Proverbs 31 woman has to do (verses 13, 18, 19, 21, 24). The Jewish women of her day were responsible for making the clothing for the family,[4] and wool and flax were the two basic elements needed for weaving. So, with energy and enthusiasm, "she seeks wool and flax" (Proverbs 31:13). After first gathering these unrefined substances, God's beautiful woman then carries out an entire manufacturing process. She starts with raw materials and ends with finished garments—choosing, buying, processing, dying, spinning, weaving the cloth, and finally making the clothing. And Proverbs 31:13 says she does all this with willing hands and a joyful heart!

Throughout Israel's history, much of the people's clothing has been made out of *wool*. The large outer garment common to the region called for this heavy, warm fiber. Those willing to do the work—and God's beautiful woman is!—would dye the wool as they prepared it. Under the keen eye and in the skillful hands of the Proverbs 31 woman, her threads turn brilliant crimson (verse 21), canary yellow, Phoenician purple (verse 22), and dragon's blood red. Then they are ready to be passed through her creative heart and hands, first woven and then made into clothing. Decked out in these colors, her family is quite spectacular against the backdrop of her sun-drenched land.[5]

The Proverbs 31 woman also works with *flax*. She uses the fiber of this slender herb for spinning, but it has to be gathered, separated, twisted, and bleached before it can be woven into fine linen and used to make inner garments, tunics, and sleepwear (verse 24). Processing the flax involves the painstaking steps of drying, peeling, beating, combing, and finally spinning it. In fact, the more flax is beaten, the more it glistens.[6] But no labor was too taxing for our model of a joyful and willing worker!

A Worker of Beauty

Many women do the chores at home because they have to, they're expected to, or they're told to. But the woman who is beautiful in God's eyes throws herself wholeheartedly into her work. Like that fountain in the center of the garden, at the heart of its home, she joyfully sings, hums, and whistles as she works, delighting in her work. She lives out God's exhortation, "Whatever your hand finds to do, do it with your might" (Ecclesiastes 9:10). Far from murmuring at life's demands, she sets a worthy example and finds pleasure in the work of her hands. With zeal, enthusiasm, and gusto, she puts her heart into her work. She goes all out. She doesn't merely do her work; she does it willingly and joyfully!

Our beautiful woman's heart is a fountain of joy. She is filled with love for her God (verse 30), love for her family (verses 28, 29), and love for her home (verse 27). Graced by this love in her heart, she lives a life that overflows with energy, industry, delight, and creativity. Her willing heart transforms her approach to even the mundane chores in her home. This powerful joy of her heart energizes her hands for willing labor.

Some scholars have translated verse 13 to read that the Proverbs 31 woman works with the *pleasure* of her hands, with *willing* hands, with *merry* hands, with *inspired* hands![7] I like all of these thoughts and the attitudes they reflect, and I hope you're getting the picture. Her joyous heart and the busy hands it energizes transform everything she touches into something of beauty.[8]

The How-To's of Beauty

When I think about God's beautiful woman and the abundant energy and obvious joy that distinguishes how she does her work, I want it! I want for myself that same kind of energy and joy when I approach the tasks at hand—and I'm sure you share my desire. Well, I've been experimenting over the years with what I call my "attitude helpers." Besides helping me get more work done, they've helped me do my work with a willing, joyous heart. I hope these ideas help your fountain of joy bubble and flow!

1. *Pray daily*—Pray for those you serve and for yourself. Pray specifically about your attitude toward your work. Because God listens and responds, prayer changes things. Our Lord can turn your heart into a fountain of joy. In fact, prayer can give you the God-given perspective that lifts your duties in the home out of the physical realm and transports them to the spiritual realm (see Colossians 3:23 and number three on the next page).

2. *Recite Scripture*—Make a list of verses right out of God's Word that encourage you to be joyous in your work. My favorite is Psalm 118:24—"This is the day which the Lord has made; [I] will rejoice and be glad in it." When we have verses like that in our heart and recite them as we work, we will find ourselves "rejoic[ing] in the Lord always" (Philippians 4:4)!

3. *Do your work as unto the Lord*—When things really seem unbearable and my perspective becomes skewed, another verse comes to my rescue. Colossians 3:23 says, "Whatever you do, do it heartily, *as to the Lord and not to men*." I must remember that the *What*, the *Who*, and the *Why* of my work is God Himself! This reminder adds fresh joy to my empty heart.

4. *Tackle your tasks*—As you face each task, make the conscious choice to tackle it energetically, creatively, and joyfully.

Energetically—Whatever chore you face, take on the challenge and "do it with all your might" (Ecclesiastes 9:10)! That's how Nehemiah and the people approached the task of rebuilding the walls of Jerusalem (Nehemiah 2)—with "a mind to work" (4:6)! They were on a mission! And so are you!

Creatively—Thomas Kinkade, the acclaimed "painter of light," approaches each new painting with a creative heart. He developed this approach during the art-student phase of his life when he worked in a gas station. Hear what he says:

> The work was routine, the hours were inconvenient, the pay was minuscule. My surroundings were grimy, the

> clientele grumpy. And yet I still managed to have fun at that job. I observed an endless parade of humanity who came through the doors. I made up stories about them in my head and sketched them from memory. I played games with myself to see how quickly I could make change or reset the pumps. And I took pleasure in serving, in knowing I helped people get through their day.[9]

You knew Thomas Kinkade as a creative artist. But he is also a creative worker who clearly has a loving heart!

Joyfully—Just as the heart of God's beautiful woman is a fountain of joy, yours can and should be, too. Sometimes when I read this verse about her happy heart, I feel jealous. I want her joy, her willingness to work, the pleasure she derives from what she views as her labors of love. I think key to her joy is the fact that she looks at her work with anticipation rather than dread. She sees tasks as challenges rather than drudgery. Her positive outlook springs not merely from love for her family, but also from her joyful habit of looking at each demanding task of life and deciding to do it, to do it well, to do it unto the Lord, and to enjoy doing it!

5. *Look for the benefits*—I love these thoughts of Edith Schaeffer, a woman who learned how to see the good in the work of granting her husband's daily request for an afternoon tea tray. Here's how she approached the task and the benefits she found in doing so:

> First, I say silently to the Lord: "Thank You that [this] is a *practical* way to serve *You* tea.... Thank You for making it so clear that as we do things...in service to others, we are really doing it for You."

> Second, I go on to remember something of this sort: "Now Fran [her husband] really needs this...refreshment...a bit of blood sugar...good nourishment, too, for whatever is coming next."
>
> Third, I then walk up the stairs...think[ing]: "Who is keeping their waistline? Here I am doing my aerobic up-and-down-the-stairs exercise."[10]

Edith looked for the benefits she received as she served others. Doing so can lighten the burden of your tasks (and mine) just as it did for her.

6. *Pause and rest*—There's nothing wrong with a well-earned rest. God warns against idleness (Proverbs 31:27) and a sluggardly lifestyle (Proverbs 21:25), but He never condemns our physical need for rest. So pause when you need to and refresh yourself in the Lord (Isaiah 40:31). Schedule a nap each day if it energizes your work.

7. *Watch what you eat!*—One year when I was reading through my Bible, I marked every reference to food, and I discovered that food is an important subject in the Bible. What we eat should be important to us as well. A worthy goal is to eat for energy and health. To see if you're reaching that goal, make a practice of noticing your energy levels. Does the food you eat give you energy or put you to sleep? Do you experience low periods during the day? When—and why? Doing God's job assignments with a willing, cheerful, joyous, energetic heart requires physical energy. Be sure you're giving your body what it needs.

8. *Value each day*—I climbed Masada one step at a time, and that's how you and I will achieve the excellence of God's beautiful woman. The Proverbs 31 woman enjoys the rich

blessings of her children's and her husband's praise (verses 28-31), but she earned it by willingly doing her work one day at a time and one task at a time. How we live each day is our "one step at a time" toward her excellence and the kind of praise she received.

So what can you do today? How will you live? How closely will you walk with God? Know that He will use this twenty-four-hour period to make you more the person He wants you to be. In God's economy, nothing is wasted, so He's certainly not going to let this day—whatever tasks it holds—be in vain!

An Invitation to Beauty

What a blessing to know that you and I can bring a gift to our home that no one else can offer—the gift of a heart filled with joy! Your joyful heart can minister to the people at home, the place of home, and the work at home.

Such a heart can even help you find joy in the work you do at home. After all, every task you do out of a joy-filled heart greatly blesses those you love and serve. When you serve with a heart of joy, you refresh and revive tired souls and hurting spirits. Like a fountain of refreshing water in the dusty, dry desert streets, a heart God fills with His love ministers life and health. Besides, whether you realize it or not, dear one, your heart attitude determines how much *you* enjoy your work as well as what the atmosphere of your home will be. When you choose to work with a willing, happy heart, *you* become a beautiful source of joy to all, a fountain of God-given joy!

~ 7 ~

An Enterprising Spirit

Her Provision

"She is like the merchant's ship;
she brings her merchandise from afar."[1]
Proverbs 31:14

One Christmas season Jim and I were invited to a special holiday open house at the home of a precious saint, a member of the Sunday school class of seniors Jim was pastoring. As the guests took turns sharing their childhood memories of Christmas, our hostess told her story as well. She described to us a custom in the country where she grew up: On Christmas Eve the wealthy people of the town would open their front drapes and allow others to press their faces against the windows and look inside their elaborate homes. Many times as a child our friend had stood peering through exquisite panes of beveled glass at the furnishings, decorations, Christmas trees, and food in these residences. On that one rare evening of the year, she could look through those windows and admire the bountiful richness of those who lived inside.

As you and I consider how God's beautiful woman

provided for her loved ones, I feel as if He is allowing us to press our faces against the windows of her house. Through the window of His Word, He gives us a glimpse of what her enterprising spirit looks like and how it impacts the way she loves her family. We find every beauty and provision imaginable in her home. God's beautiful woman spares no effort to provide the best she can for her beloved family.

A Spirit of Adventure

Proverbs 31:14 reads, "She is like the merchant's ship." This image may not seem too appealing at first, but consider for a moment how the woman who is beautiful in God's eyes is indeed like a merchant's ship. We can easily imagine, for instance, that she scours the marketplace for goods that will enhance the quality of life under her roof. She spares no cost in terms of money, time, or effort when it comes to contributing to the well-being of those she loves.

"She brings her merchandise from afar," verse 14 continues. The Proverbs 31 woman gladly expends her energy to gather up special goods from around the world for her household—and they truly came from afar. Just look at the process!

The ships—Merchant ships have sailed between Phoenicia and Egypt since 2400 BC. Stopping in every port throughout the Mediterranean Sea, they traded their cargo for other goods. Second Chronicles 9:21 tells us that these merchant ships completed their route once every three years.

The supplies—The long waits, however, paid off in unusual and exotic goods for those at home. The ships that went to Tarshish (modern-day Spain) brought home gold, silver, ivory, apes, and monkeys (2 Chronicles 9:21). Cedar was shipped out from Lebanon. Dye came from Tyre. Spices, nuts, balm, and grain were exported from Egypt. Greece contributed oil, wine, honey, and exquisite pottery to the international marketplace. All kinds of woolen goods, pieces of art, hand-crafted objects, and exquisite jewelry were transported—sometimes by desert caravan, other times by boats via canals and rivers—to the ports of each continent to be loaded onto the merchant ships.

The superhighways—Merchandise brought into seaports was then carried by caravan back to the inland cities. In fact, ceaseless camel-caravans flowed through the homeland of our beautiful woman. Throughout history Israel has been at the crossroads of every major trade route in the Middle East. When I was there, I traveled the King's Highway and the Great Trunk Road, the two key routes which made the Promised Land a world trade center.

The shops—Finally, after all the caravans and ships, goods from around the world arrived in small shops of all sizes, shapes, and styles. Permanent shops opened onto a square or street, creating a bazaar or arcade in a central location. Portable shops were set up under makeshift awnings near city gates and in the open streets. And whenever a camel caravan arrived from points as far south as Sheba (modern-day Iran) or as far east as Babylon and India, a market appeared instantly wherever the camels knelt. Imagine the buzz of excitement as dry goods, grocery items, tin utensils, leather goods, sweetmeats, and other valued rarities arrived by camel in the village streets!

A Spirit of Mission

Now, my patient friend, let's look more closely at how our beautiful woman from Proverbs 31—*like* these merchant ships—is on a mission to bring her merchandise from afar. *Her family* is the primary reason she searches far and wide. She has mouths to feed and a house to furnish and decorate—and, as she sees it, her loved ones deserve nothing but the best. So, motivated by her heart of love, she goes the extra miles (literally!) to provide the best for those at home.

But the Proverbs 31 woman is also motivated by her *creativity*. She's an artist! Let me give you an example. Since her home has no refrigeration, she shops daily for the ingredients she needs for each day's meals. This responsibility could easily become a drudgery, but shopping at the exotic foreign market booths feeds her imagination—and her family—and allows her to express her creativity in day-in-day-out life. In those stalls she discovers color, beauty, and variety, the unique, and the exquisite. This adventure stimulates creativity in her recipes and meals, her weaving and homemaking. Mundane, routine, daily provision became a creative adventure for her!

A Spirit of Satisfaction

This book is about beauty as seen through the eyes of God, and here we are, talking about…shopping! But realize the enterprising spirit of this woman who is beautiful in God's eyes sets her apart from others. Like the merchant ships of her day, she sets sail and glides on and on… searching…looking for…seeking out…and obtaining what she wants to provide for her family. Motivated by love for those she cares for, she sets forth on her mission with vigor and anticipation, willing to explore beyond the familiarity and convenience of her neighborhood market. She "sails away" to the faraway corners of the city and returns laden with exactly what her family needs. As she puts forth the effort, this special homemaker enjoys a sense of satisfaction as she provides what's best for her family:

- Health resides under her roof because she sets nutritious foods before her family.
- Savings result as she searches, bargains, and barters to provide the necessary and the beautiful for her clan.
- Culture enters her doors as she brings home not only goods from far-off, exotic places but also the tales heard and the information gathered while making her purchases.
- Variety spices up life in her home as foods and furnishings from afar greet and treat those within.
- Quality goods are enjoyed by all because of her keen eye and uncompromising standards.
- Beauty satisfies, invigorates, and ministers to the souls who abide there.

The How-To's of Beauty

By now you and I can sense that the enterprising spirit which God holds up to us in this chapter doesn't come without effort. A sailing vessel doesn't just naturally or automatically cut rapidly through the waters with its sails billowing! Such beauty comes at a price for the Proverbs 31 woman (and for us, too). Having caught a breeze stirred up by her busyness and bobbing in the wake of her energy and accomplishments, look at how—in God's grace—you can nurture such an enterprising spirit and then set sail on your own.

1. *A heart of love*—Without love we are nothing

(1 Corinthians 13:2), and, I might add, without love we will want to do nothing! So...

Pray—Ask God to reveal and heal any area in your heart that keeps you from loving your roles as a wife, mother, and home manager.

Make home your first priority—Even if you aren't within its four walls as much as you'd like to be, cherish your home and those who reside there. Your family—not your job or profession, your hobby or your volunteer work—is to be first in your heart!

Spend time with other women—Listen to other women who speak with heartfelt love about their husband, their children, and their home (Titus 2:3-5). You'll find their enthusiasm contagious.

2. *A vision of loveliness*—God's beautiful woman appreciates beauty and its ministry to those it touches. As a creative individual, nurture your own vision of loveliness and offer your family your personal expressions of beauty.

Surround yourself with beauty—When confined to his bed in his later years, the great Impressionist artist Henri Matisse, ordered exotic plants and brilliantly colored parrots brought into his bedroom. These additions stimulated the art he produced from his sickbed during those final years. Inspired by Matisse, I painted my office walls red, hung them with my favorite pictures and paintings, and decorated with objects (a calendar featuring great art of the world, a crystal bud vase with a single fresh cut rose, a rock found on the West Texas prairie by my aunt and painted to portray a kitty curled up in its basket for a catnap) that push me to be more creative. Cocooned in loveliness, I seek to produce what is lovely. My office itself invites me to write.

Make your vision of loveliness a reality—Spend time with people who are creating beauty. Study magazines. Visit gift shops and attend home shows. Pay attention to any loveliness you encounter along the way and learn from what you see. Finally, let the furnishings and decor of your home be an expression of beauty.

I remember so well coming back to my own home after staying in the house of a woman who had a vision for loveliness, and I had been changed by my visit. When I stood at the entrance to her living room and took in the exquisite beauty that welcomed me into the haven she had created for her family, I thought, "Why, she's an artist!" My initial impression wasn't of money spent; I didn't think, "Look at all the stuff she's bought!" Instead, I was struck by the arrangement of things—by little touches like placing Grandmother's lovely hand-crocheted doily on the arm of a chair, displaying a shell found on the beach, and having a low-hung lamp spotlight a tiny table and its miniature fern. She had also removed some curtains so that the containers of exotic, blooming kaffir lilies lining her porch seemed like part of the room. And she had sparkling clean windows. This woman with a vision for loveliness had simply taken what she had, tweaked it a bit, and made it remarkable!

3. *God's assignment to love*—Love your family in the practicalities of daily life.

Start with the basics—Every individual needs the basics of food, clothing, and shelter. As one author asks, "Are you too tired to cook meals and keep the house in order? Do you want to eat out all the time?'"[2] Or are you energetically providing the basics your family needs?

Become a wise shopper—Focus on saving money. Look for bargains. Avoid impulse buying by carefully considering every purchase (Proverbs 31:16). Know what you need and what you don't need. Learn what is quality and what isn't—and also how to say no! Remember one of the keys to money management: all money not spent is money saved! Sometimes I say no by deciding not to shop at all. Other times I say no by shopping by catalog, foregoing the time and temptations of wandering through stores and malls. Still other times I say no by seeing how many things I can take out of my shopping basket before I go through the check-out stand, and then I mentally add up my savings.

Search for the unusual—Wait a little longer and search a little farther until you find something basic that's also a bit unique. The Proverbs 31 woman shops in the city's *bazaar*, but she is looking for the *bizarre*! Ever the artist, she has an eye for the unusual. She delights in picking up the odd item, something imported, something sure to bring oohs and aahs from family and friends—and that something rewards her enterprising spirit!

Consider bartering—List your skills and then seek to sharpen them. They will be your currency as you barter for what you need. So figure out what you need and what you can give in exchange for it. Bartering like that has worked for me. My book *Loving God with All Your Mind*[3] was first transcribed from my teaching tapes by a seminary wife from New Zealand in exchange for a used car my husband made available to her husband for three years. They needed a car—and had no money. I needed help—and had no money (or time). So we bartered!

Become "the resident artist"—Consider yourself on assignment to bring beauty into your home. Once a week my friend Karen—the resident artist in her home—sails away at 4:00 AM to the flower mart in downtown Los Angeles to bring fresh flowers into her home and onto the patio and porch. (She also uses the flowers to make bouquets for those who need a little beauty to cheer them up.) By the time I call her at 7:30 AM, Karen is already busy adding touches of beauty here and there throughout her home—and she's doing this for just pennies! Karen challenges herself to do something new and creative in her flower arranging week by week. Like Karen, figure out exactly how you—the resident artist in your home—can create beauty there. Also ask yourself, "What area of creativity could I work on improving and developing?"

An Invitation to Beauty

Now, my beautiful enterprising friend, it's time to look deep into God's eyes of love and acknowledge the desires of His heart for your life. Through His Word, our wise Father calls you to be an enterprising homemaker and wife who adds touches of beauty to her home. This call requires some effort, but it's a call to great blessing!

Is your heart in tune with God's great heart of love? Do you cherish those at home whom He has given you to provide for? Are you giving your utmost as you work to provide for your family? Proverbs 31:14—albeit an image of a merchant ship—actually addresses a matter of the heart, a matter of love. You see, only love—God's gracious love—can motivate you to lay aside selfishness and exert the physical energy needed to set sail on behalf of others. And only the love of God, filling you to overflowing, can supply you with the necessary emotional endurance to forego personal ease and sustain the relentless activity of a lifetime of enterprise for the good of others.

Won't you ask God to give you greater resolve and renewed energy so that you can sail off toward the endearing—and enduring—quality of an enterprising spirit? Truly, such a spirit is beautiful in God's eyes!

~ 8 ~

A Pattern for the Household

HER DISCIPLINE

"She rises also while it is yet night,
and gives food to her household
and work to her maids."[1]
Proverbs 31:15

I couldn't sleep—and a full-blown case of jet lag was the reason! Jim and I had arrived in Jerusalem the day before after 15 hours of flight time and a stopover in London. We had already been awake for several hours in our hotel room inside the Old City of Jerusalem, waiting for daylight and an excuse to throw on some clothes and begin our 21-day study course in the Holy Land. We'd been too tired the day before to appreciate much of what we had taken in through blurred eyes, but now we were ready—if the sun would just come up!

Finally there was enough light to merit a walk up to the roof of our hotel. Standing shoulder to shoulder in the dawning light, we heard church bells from distant corners of the Old City heralding a new day. As the sky brightened in the east, we could see the centuries-old walls fortifying the Old City of Jerusalem, the flags flying atop David's Citadel, and a panorama of the Temple Mount where Christ had walked—and will walk again in the future. It was a breathtaking sight: we were looking at places that haven't changed in hundreds of years! We were in Jerusalem!

Then I saw her. On a rooftop nearby a woman was hard at work. Her laundry was already hung on a line. Her front door was open, allowing the morning air to cool the stone house before the day's heat set in. Her porch was already swept and scrubbed, and now she was at work on her rooftop. Cutting some fresh flowers that grew there in pots, she then carried them into her home along with several ripe lemons picked from her rooftop citrus trees.

This opportunity to watch a real-life Jewish woman brought Proverbs 31:15 alive—"She rises also while it is yet night, and gives food to her household and work to her maids." The spectacular view I had been enjoying made me glad I had gotten up early (although jet lag gets most of the credit!), but now I was freshly challenged by this hard-working woman to keep on trying to live out the kind of disciplined life that is beautiful in God's eyes. "Thank You, God," I whispered, "for the Bible made alive! Thank You for this glimpse—here in Your land—of a woman who gets up early and lovingly tends to the ways of her house."

This chapter is about how you and I can lovingly tend to the ways of our house. The beautiful mother who is teaching her son the ABCs of godly womanhood (Proverbs 31:10-31) knows full-well the benefits a well-disciplined woman can bring to her household, and she points her son (and us!) to three disciplines for a woman's success in the home.

Discipline #1: An Early Start

According to Proverbs 31:15, the woman who will bless her home "rises also while it is yet night." Back when Proverbs 31 was written, a woman got up early for a number of reasons.

Tending the fire at home—First, she tended the lamp. This small lamp (more accurately, a saucer filled with oil with a wick of flax floating in it) was kept burning all night so that the household fire could be lighted from it in the morning. God's beautiful homemaker got up several times during the night to replenish the oil so that her lamp didn't go out (Proverbs 31:18). These night risings were also ideal opportunities to get a headstart on some of the food preparation for the next day. She could grind a little corn, set a few things out, and lay the fire.

Tending the fire of her heart—Proverbs 31:30 says that God's beautiful woman fears the Lord, and an early start gave her time to tend to her daily prayers and the keeping of God's Law. She knew the Law said to love the Lord with all your heart, soul, and might (Deuteronomy 6:5). Our Proverbs 31 woman must tend not only the fire at home, but also the fire of her own heart's love for the Lord.

Tending the fires of their hearts—This godly woman also knows that the Law of Moses instructed her to teach and train her children in the knowledge of God and His laws (Deuteronomy 6:7). God's beautiful mother first fills her own heart with God's truths. Then, just like the careful mother teaching Proverbs 31 to her son, she teaches those truths to her children and talks of them all day long in the classroom called "home."

An early start is essential when these crucial tasks are on your list!

Discipline #2: Food for the Family

The woman who is a blessing in her home "gives food to her household" (Proverbs 31:15). Her family's daily bread was a major reason for her early rising. They depended on her to provide them the food they needed. Even today three out of four people in the Middle East live entirely on bread and other foods made from grains.[2] Bread was—and is—truly the staff of life and a mainstay with every meal. And there can be no bread until the grain is ground (the first duty of each day). Then the dough is mixed, and finally the small pita-like flat breads are baked on hot rocks and ashes.[3]

But there is an exciting image behind this verse! The Hebrew word used here for "food" actually means "prey" and refers to the prey of a lion. God's beautiful woman is likened to a lion hunting for the prey it needs to survive. She is pictured as a lioness prowling at night ("she also rises while it is yet *night*") to obtain food for her household.[4] Besides being an army (Proverbs 31:10), a warrior (verse 10), a worker (verse 13), and a powerful ship (verse 14), she is now a lioness (verse 15)! The images of these verses continue to point to her tremendous strength and courage. The prowess of this woman is so great that she provides for the needs (food) of the others (household) under her charge.[5]

And that "household" includes anyone fortunate enough to be under her roof on a given day! "Household" is a collective term used for a unit of people, a group, everyone in the entire house.[6] Her list of lucky VIPs includes her husband (her most important VIP), her children (these junior VIPs are next in line), any extended family (in those days many family members lived in the same house), her servants, and her guests.

Discipline #3: A Plan for the Day

"She gives...work to her maids" (Proverbs 31:15). "Work" or "portion" refers to something due to another, a prescribed portion or allowance.[7] It's assumed that God's beautiful woman gives a portion of food to her maids as members of her household, but she also gives them work. She issues them a "decree" or work "ordinance" which outlines their daily work assignments.[8] She has her own work to plan and organize, but her maidservants also need their assignments—their "portion"—for the day (verse 15). Eager not to lose a minute of the day's work time, she has to be ready for them—early!

A Pattern for Success

God's beautiful woman lived out a pattern for success that worked in her day and time, but you and I can have success today, centuries later, by following her pattern for her household: She got up early (a simple but not necessarily easy thing to do!). Just count her many blessings!

Time alone—A chief complaint I hear among women is that they have no time alone. It seems the kids are always there (with their needs—and noise) and the phone is always ringing (with still more needs—and more noise). The TV is usually blaring (more noise!), and Mom just never seems to find any peace and quiet. Early rising gives you that cherished quiet time. In the still of the pre-dawn morning, you can have some precious time alone.

Time with God—When you get up a little early, you can use the time to seek the Lord and spend a few moments in prayer, asking His blessing upon your day and your household. A Mother's Day article I read featured an interview with Anne Graham Lotz, daughter of Ruth Graham, who wrote of her mother: "No matter what time I arose in the morning, I would see the light from [Mother's] room. When I arrived downstairs she'd be at her desk reading one of 14 different Bible translations. This was one way Mother taught me that it is through the Word and prayer that I can know God. She knows God well."[9] (And she rises early to do it!)

Time to plan—In your time alone, you also have time to think, and that's how effective planning gets done. A few quiet minutes alone before the rush of the day begins means time for the planning that is essential for a well-ordered home. Hear one top time-management expert's praises of early rising: "I do almost all my planning early in the morning. I...average...three and a half hours a week at it. I wake up around 5 AM, before anyone else in the house, and I put this quiet time into my most important activity—planning."[10]

Time to get the jump on the day—There's no doubt that getting up early starts a chain reaction of benefits. Rising early is your first step toward redeeming time! Look at what that time can mean for you: Time with God—for guidance and strength. Time alone—for planning. Time to exercise—sometimes it's the only time! Time to get a jump-start on the day—for wise use of the hours to come. Time for breakfast—for fuel. Time for family devotions—for focus as a family. When you make early rising a discipline for each day, you take an important step toward setting an orderly tone and establishing a predictable pattern for your household.

A Personal Story

Thanks to my husband, Jim, I regularly experience the benefits of early rising (most days, anyway)—and let me tell you why.

As a new seminary student, Jim returned home from class each day praising a man named Mr. McDougal. Jim would say over and over, "You have to meet Mr. McDougal! He's a professor, he has a wife and a family, he's a student himself in a doctoral program at UCLA, he runs every day, *and* he pastors a church."

One day Jim finally asked Mr. Don McDougal how he accomplished all that he did. "He gets up every day at 4 AM!" Jim exclaimed when he told me the story later. While I was busy thinking, "That's great for *him*," Jim announced, "We're going to start getting up at 4 AM!"

Facing such an early hour was difficult (and still is!), but the benefits were immediate. For one thing, that much-sought-after time with God became a reality. Suddenly I had time to linger in God's Word and I had time for unhurried prayer. Furthermore, for the first time ever, I was able to plan my approach to the hectic day ahead, a day filled with young children and household chores.

But there was even more to be gained by my early rising. I was able to start an exercise program—which I still follow each morning. I could also unload the dishwasher, make all my phone calls to eastern time zones before 8 o'clock, do our bookkeeping, write letters, type, file, study the Bible, and create Bible study materials—all before 7:30 in the morning. Even today I have a file labeled "Early AM" and keep in it an ongoing list of the tasks I can do early each day.

So, if you want some time without any interruptions, some time of quiet peace and solitude, try rising early in the morning. You may have to get to bed a little earlier. But after all, what are you missing? Perhaps a little TV? You do need time for family, but you'll be surprised how much time you can buy back from non-essentials when you are motivated to get up early.

Well, Jim graduated from seminary many years ago, but I still try to get up early. Like the woman on her rooftop in Jerusalem, I open up all the doors and windows in the summer to cool the house. I, too, get my laundry started and water our flowers. Although I don't grind grain, I do grind our coffee beans and get the coffee pot going for Jim. When Katherine and Courtney were at home, I checked on them and then shut their doors so my early-morning noises wouldn't disturb them for the few extra minutes they had before their alarm clocks went off...and they, too, rose early!

What are some of the "noises" I make around our house in the morning? Well, the coffee bean grinder! (After all, first things first!) The opening of windows and doors. The running of sprinklers. The emptying of the dishwasher. The setting of the breakfast table. The making of lunches. The taking out of trash. The hum of the treadmill if it's a bad-weather/no-walk day.

And the noises cease and all gets quiet—very quiet! Then, before the onslaught of another day's busyness, I sit down and worship the Lord and behold His beauty (Psalm 27:4). You see, I know what's coming! My day will be fast-paced and full. If I'm not "full" myself, I'll fail to handle the day's demands in the beautiful way God has in mind. Going to Him for strength is not an option—it's a must! I know I can't be the warrior I need to be, I know I can't even make it through the day, if I don't have the strength and courage only He can give me. I can do all things beautifully—including handle one more frenzied day—only through His strength (Philippians 4:13). His peace is not an option either. I know there's only one way to conquer anxiety—and that's by receiving from God His peace which passes all understanding (Philippians 4:6-7). Do you see why my early morning hours are priceless?

The How-To's of Beauty

I'm sure you've heard a lot about getting your beauty rest, but it's much more important to be getting God's kind of beauty by rising early. Of course you need to rest, but early rising brings the beauty of order and discipline to life. So instead of living a life marked by the helter-skelter of things lost, forgotten, or misplaced, characterized by running behind and never getting around to it, and punctuated by "oops!," "eek!," and "oh, no!"—cultivate the discipline of getting up early. How?

1. *Determine a time*—You probably won't start your day at 4:00 AM (we did because Jim had to leave the house at 5:30). But figure out what time you want to have completed your planning, your preparations for the day, and your ideal morning routine, and then work backwards. That's the time you need to get up. When you do, I bet you'll love having a schedule that works—and so will your family!

2. *Get to bed*—You can only burn your candle at both ends for a while before you burn out! So try moving your bedtime up an hour. At least be *in* your bed an hour earlier!

3. *Say a prayer!*—Pray as you turn out your light. Center your day's-end thoughts on the Lord and all you desire to accomplish for Him and His kingdom with your upcoming fresh new day. Your lights-out communication with God sets your mind on the next day's work and transfers something physical—getting up a little earlier—into the spiritual realm.

4. Get *up!*—And thinking about the amount of life you're buying back when you get up early is certainly motivation to do just that! A time-management authority says this:

> [If you] can do nicely with six hours of sleep instead of the eight you now may be getting, saving those two hours a day, Monday through Friday, would give you an extra forty hours—one additional work week—every month!...Just one hour less sleep per night would mean: six extra work weeks per year, which adds up, over a working lifetime, to more than five years. Think what you could accomplish in an extra five years!—"Up and at 'em!"[11]

An Invitation to Beauty

My dear and beloved reading friend, I hope you're catching a vision of the important role you play in your home. Oh, you may have a job, a career, even a prestigious title outside the home, but even so *you* are the key to a well-run home, the key to the order and efficiency of your entire household! In the words of this chapter's title, *you* set the pattern for your household. So when you take (and make) the time to plan, to organize, to micro-manage for the smooth functioning of your home, you give your family—and yourself—a gift no one else can give them. You give your husband the gifts of peace of mind and a sense of order and well-being as his heart trusts and rests in your management. And you give your children a pattern for how to run their own lives. As they watch you plan and manage and then taste the sweet results, they learn how to live their lives for the Lord.

God's beautiful Proverbs 31 woman models for you (and me) the discipline of early rising. Time spent praying and planning in the early hushed part of the day gives you a master plan that works for your home and sets a pattern of order for your life.

So, as the time-management expert advised, "Up and at 'em!"

-9-

A Field of Dreams

Her Vision

"She considers a field and buys it;
From her profits she plants a vineyard."
Proverbs 31:16

Artists like my friend Margaret tell me that the most difficult part of the human anatomy to draw is the face. Mastering the skills to accurately represent facial features is the final frontier for any artist. As you and I enter this chapter about the Proverbs 31 woman, we begin to see her face take shape as a few revealing characteristics are sketched for us. So far we've watched her hands work with delight (verse 13), marveled at the heart her husband trusts (verse 11), and been impressed by her swift feet as they take her afar for her family's provisions (verse 14).

But now the mind of God's beautiful woman is opening up to us as He, the Original Artist, reveals its impressive abilities. In the preceding chapter we watched her use her keen mind to plan and organize. Now, in verse 16, we see that she uses her mind as a visionary *and* a businesswoman.

You may have heard about the findings of "right brain-left brain" research. Supposedly one side of the brain controls our *creative* functions and the other all that is *practical*. Well, God's beautiful woman has fully and gloriously developed both sides of her brain! In the creative realm, she's a visionary—a person given to dreaming and imagining.[1] She wants what's best for her family and dreams of making that "best" happen. But she doesn't stop there. She puts the practical part of her mind to work to make her dreams happen. You see, she's a businesswoman as well as a visionary.

Triple Action

Although this chapter is about dreams and visions (and active imaginations!), we can learn much from the three concrete actions which God's beautiful woman takes in Proverbs 31:16 as she works to make those dreams come true. The same three steps can help you and me make our own dreams become reality.

Step #1: Consideration—Imagine the following scene. Our beautiful woman of Proverbs 31 rises early one morning, feeds her family, sees her husband off to work, sets her servants into action, and, like that merchant ship, sails out the door on her rounds of daily shopping. While she's conducting business in the town market, she hears about a local field that's just come up for sale. Heart racing, she discreetly asks a few questions and gathers some preliminary information about the property.

Why the racing heart? Because she has a dream—a vision born out of love—that will better her dear family. She's always been on the lookout for a chance to make that dream happen, and this field definitely looks like a golden opportunity to increase her husband's wealth and status and thereby improve her family situation. But how does she respond to news that the property is for sale? Does she impulsively rush to the landowner and buy the field? Does she reach into her tunic, whip out her clay credit card, and blurt "Charge it"? No.

"She *considers* a field," the Bible tells us (Proverbs 31:16). Donning her businesswoman hat, she carefully looks at the field to determine whether or not it would be a wise investment. In her heart, she wants a field, but choosing instead to let her mind take control (like a good soldier), she sets out to learn all she can about the piece of land.

- The value of the property—Collecting information about said property, she *considers* its worth. Not relying only on hearsay or even on expert opinions, she examines the land for herself.
- The state of the finances—Evaluating the family finances, she *considers* whether there is adequate money to purchase and improve the property without endangering the family's welfare.
- The inventory of time—She *considers* her time commitments to her family to determine whether she has the time which the ownership of the field would require.
- The review of priorities—Her family is her primary area of ministry and responsibility, so she wisely *considers* whether working on the field will threaten those priorities.

The Proverbs 31 woman realizes that she has much to learn, ponder, and pray about before she makes any kind of real estate investment.

Finally, after due consideration and consultation with

the Lord, I believe she brings the matter to her husband. Armed with a businesswoman's facts and statistics, she shares her vision. Laying out her report, she points to the many reasons why this property is desirable and exactly how it will benefit her husband and the family.

Now why would this very capable woman go to her husband? I can think of several reasons—all of which are entwined in her great strength of character. *As a woman of virtue* she doesn't act independently from her husband, her God-ordained head (Genesis 3:16). *As a woman of strength* she doesn't act impulsively (Proverbs 19:2). *As a woman of wisdom* she doesn't act without advice (Proverbs 12:15). And, *as a wife*, she doesn't want what her husband doesn't want (Proverbs 19:14). God's beautiful woman lives her life to please God, and a part of pleasing God includes pleasing her husband (Genesis 2:18). She is a team player, wanting what her husband wants and helping him move in the direction he's chosen for his family. Together they are a solid unit, so they move forward...together! They build their life...together! They make their dreams come true, hers of increased financial strength for her family (verse 16) and his of service in his community (verse 23)...together!

Blessed with his approval (how could he not approve, what with her track record, her business head, her work ethic), she takes the next step toward owning her field of dreams.

Step #2: Acquisition—"She considers a field and *buys* it," Proverbs 31:16 reports. As one scholar remarks, "There is no way we can interpret this to say less than what is obvious. This woman apparently does buy and sell land...."[2] In verse 16, the term "buys" is from the business world, denoting buying and selling, the give-and-take of business dealings.[3]

So we see that the Proverbs 31 woman takes possession of her field of dreams.[4]

Before I traveled to Israel, I had always imagined her field as being something of a ranch or a farm. But after seeing the fields of the Holy Land, I now know that her field was basically a lot, a piece of land measuring about 50 feet by 80 feet. Each owner first cleared the area of its many large rocks and used them to build a stacked-stone wall around the lot. Then the owner tilled and planted the land. The work was difficult, tedious, and time-consuming.

But where, we wonder, does God's beautiful woman get the money to buy a field? How does she finance her field of dreams? The cash comes from her shrewd money management. Her thrift pays off in daily life as well as in this business deal. All her efforts—her management, her work, her industry, her bartering, her weaving, her sales, her doing without, her saying "no"—furnish the capital that make her dreams come true. As someone has said, "Hard work is the yeast that raises the dough!"

Step #3: Renovation—"She considers a field and buys it," Proverbs 31:16 says; "From her profits she *plants* a vineyard." Despite what this verse seems to suggest, two different pieces of property and two separate business transactions are referred to here. "Field" and "vineyard" are different words for distinctly different kinds of property. Our beautiful woman does not purchase a field and then plant a vineyard there, but rather she purchases both a field and a vineyard.[5] With her hard-earned, well-managed, faithfully saved money, she not only buys a field but also selects and plants a vineyard with the best plantings her funds could buy.

Why a vineyard? Her choice of crops was wise. In her dry homeland where water is so scarce, grapes and wine were staples. Everyone needs fluids to drink, so by owning her personal vineyard God's beautiful woman takes care of her precious family. What is leftover she sells to others, earning more money for her next dream. Everyone benefits! "With the fruit of her hands" (KJV) she plants "fruit" so that her family will be well supplied with the essentials as well as the conveniences of life.

The How-To's of Beauty

When you and I, in quest of our dreams, seek and follow God's wisdom and add our own hard work to the pursuit, everyone benefits. Here's a beauty plan for making your dreams come true.

1. *Desire God's beauty*—Ask the Lord to build in your heart a treasure-house of beautiful virtues. Ask Him to supply you with:

- Patience—so that you will wait before you act when opportunities arise
- Prudence—so that you will carefully think things over while you're waiting
- Prayerfulness—so that you will seek the Lord's wisdom while you are waiting and thinking
- Petition—so that you will willingly consult your husband—or parents or pastor or boss—after you've waited and thought and prayed
- Purpose—so that God will guide your heart in the right direction, in His direction
- Perseverance—so that you will do whatever it takes to make your dreams come true

2. *Devote yourself to God's goals*—And that means family

comes first! Your goal is to build your house (Proverbs 14:1), build an honorable name for your family (Proverbs 22:1), and build up the next generation (Proverbs 31:28). Never mind what you're going to get in return. Don't worry about what your building efforts will cost you personally (and I'm not talking about financial cost!). Forget about whether or not others will be grateful for your selfless service or whether they will even notice it. As God's beautiful woman, you don't do what you do to *get* anything: You do what you do because of who you are, because of the person God is making you into—a virtuous woman, a woman who is beautiful in His eyes! Selfless service is the greatest beauty of all. It's the beauty of our Lord!

3. *Your husband is paramount*—Remember how "the heart of her husband safely trusts" the Proverbs 31 woman (verse 11)? In verse 16, we've seen another way that trust is built. That way involves your willing submission and subordination of your personal desires to those of your husband. Note again that this is done willingly. (God's beautiful woman does everything willingly—verse 13!) As you strengthen godly virtues and put them to work in your everyday life, and as you consult with your husband on the issues at home, you, too, will build his trust in you. Your husband will be smiling inwardly as you present your cases. He'll be trying to keep a straight face, thinking, "Here she goes again! She's truly amazing! Where does she get her ideas? And where does she get her energy? I sure am fortunate to have her as my wife!" He'll be like the husband of Proverbs 31:28-29 who praises his wife as "the best of all."[6]

4. *Creativity abounds!*—As you continue to set self aside and serve others, you'll be surprised by the multitude of opportunities God gives you to creatively show your

love. Your mind and heart will burst forth with "hidden art" (as Mrs. Edith Schaeffer calls our creative efforts in the commonplace activities of life).[7] Consider the source of the ideas I heard about recently at a time management seminar for busy women. Do you know where the speaker learned the magical methods she was passing on to us? At home—organizing a home, a husband, and five children! I've also been in classes like "Cooking Meals in Under 20 Minutes." It's the same success story: Some super-busy, pressed-for-time woman discovered creative shortcuts as she served her family.

My special friend Kris, with three little ones and her husband still in school, purchases her children's clothes at "The 99¢ Store" and pulls out her hot-glue gun, a few doo-dads (spare buttons, a dried flower, a leftover piece of rick-rack) and creates stunning clothes for her children—for next to no money! When she caught a vision for what she could be doing, her field of dreams became an ongoing booth in a craft fair. Now she sells her creative efforts to other moms for their children—and helps pay for her husband's education at the same time. A business was born in the kitchen as Kris stood at the ironing board. Her dream came—and then became a reality—because all the necessary ingredients were present: focus on the family, loving provision, dutiful service, and a spark of creativity!

5. *Dare to dream!*—If you could improve your family's financial status, what would you love to do? Combining your love for family, the personal desires of your heart, and your own creative bents, what direction would you go? Like the Proverbs 31 woman, who is both creative (verses 13,18,21-22,24) and driven to provide for her husband, children, and home, you can use your creativity for practical purposes.

So don't forget to dream! God's beautiful woman's supervision of her home, her oversight of the budget, her labor for her family, her doing without, her thrift, her saying "no," and her time spent getting the best bargains—all of these efforts pay off in money saved and lead to her dream becoming reality. Clearly, one of her financial goals is earning and saving money she could use not for herself, not for trifles, but for making her dreams for her *family* come true! Because of her dreams, her *family* is served. *They* benefit. *Their* life is improved. It's crucial that you, too, be ever-conscious of money. You just may want to follow your dreams someday, so be sure you'll have the finances to help your dream take shape.

6. *Do the work!*—How do dreams become reality? The progression for God's beautiful woman went like this:

Her virtue (verse 10) led to
her willing heart (verse 13), which led to
her industry (verse 13), which led to
her savings (verse 11), which led to
her investments (verse 16), which led to
her prosperity (verse 25).

Behind every success story is plain ol' hard work—powered by love for family, a vision of their well-being, a dream about how to make that happen, and God's gracious blessing!

An Invitation to Beauty

Now for you, my friend with hidden talents galore! I could be writing these same beautiful truths about *you*! I want you to dream right now, to consider your field of dreams. Turn off the TV. Turn off the radio, the music, whatever it is that keeps you from thinking creatively, from dreaming and wondering and planning.

Now describe your dream—or ten of your dreams! Then start through this process for making your dreams come true: *First, consider your dreams*. Pray. Count the cost. Pray. Gather information. Pray. And talk to your husband. *Next, do the work*. Money comes from hard work, so do what you need to do in the way of saving, earning, and managing. Once you have the finances, you can begin the work of acquiring your "field," your materials, your start-up supplies. *And move forward*. Be careful not to neglect your home or family. After all, you're taking on the dream to benefit them. You're not on this earth to primarily build a business: You're building your house (Proverbs 14:1), an honorable name for your family (Proverbs 22:1), and the next generation (Proverbs 31:25, 28)! So, I repeat, behind every success story is plain ol' hard work—powered by love for family, a vision of their well-being, a dream about how to make that happen, and God's gracious blessing!

~ 10 ~

An Eager Attitude
Her Work

"She girds herself with strength,
and strengthens her arms."
Proverbs 31:17

I smile every time I think about the results of a survey I took several years ago. During a teaching series entitled "The Wise Homemaker," I asked a hundred women just like you and me, "What keeps you from getting your housework done?" Their answers fell in this order:

#1 Reason: Poor use of time

#2 Reason: Lack of motivation

#3 Reason: Failure to plan

#4 Reason: Procrastination

I'm smiling and nodding now because I can certainly relate! The items on the list make perfect sense to me!

Here's how the progression usually goes for me: My

poor use of time is always linked to a lack of motivation, indicating to me that I'm unsure about what I'm trying to accomplish! You see, when I don't know *why* I'm trying to accomplish something, when I have no goals or only unclear ones, I remain totally unmotivated and use my time poorly.

And planning? Well, doesn't a lack of goals mean that there's nothing to plan for—or at least an uncertainty about what to plan for?

And then there's procrastination. I certainly put off what I'm not sure I'm trying to do. As I said, it all makes perfect sense to me.

So, if you're like me, dear friend, you and I can both thank God that He has shown us His beautiful Proverbs 31 woman who uses her time—indeed, every second of it—and uses it well! She knows her goal: She's on assignment from God to build a home (Proverbs 14:1) and is therefore highly motivated. She wisely plans her days so that each one of them moves her toward her goals and dreams. She works—and she works *hard*—never procrastinating, always using her time well, focusing her plans and her energy on making her dreams come true. I hope you join with me in a heartfelt "Thank You, Lord, for Your beautiful woman!" Where would we be without her model and inspiration?

As we've looked at Proverbs 31 verse by verse, you and I have marveled at the two sides of God's beautiful woman: She is both mentally tough and physically strong, as her attitudes and her work reveal. We see these two sides again in verse 17, looking first at her mental strength, her attitude. You see, without mental toughness, we'll never get around to doing the actual physical work!

Preparation for Work

How does God's beautiful woman—whom we've seen

described metaphorically as an army, a warrior, a ship, a lioness, and a farmer—get her work done? What is the key to her success in all that she tackles?

First, "she *girds herself* with strength," Proverbs 31:17 tells us. These words, carefully chosen by the female teacher, suggest the *attitude toward work* her young son should look for in a wife. Let me explain the imagery.

Three thousand years ago when this poem was written, women (and men) wore flowing garments. To perform physical labor, they had to first gather up their dress and secure it with a girdle-like belt. Only then would they have the unlimited movement they needed for heavy labor. This girding of the gown was necessary preparation for serious work[1] as well as prolonged effort.[2]

The girding action was also a psychological trigger for her attitude. Much like putting on an apron, work clothes, exercise clothes, painting clothes, or gardening clothes, much like rolling up your sleeves, the action of gathering one's dress was key to preparing to act. This preparatory action and the appropriate clothes encouraged a "let's go" attitude toward the task at hand.

Second, "she girds herself *with strength*" (Proverbs 31:17). The Hebrew emphasis on the Proverbs 31 woman's physical strength and endurance suggests her unwavering commitment to work and her ability to work hard. A part of her strength comes from her *choice* to engage in hard work, and the girdle is a symbol of the mental and physical strength she wears as she enters the arena of her labor. Her girding herself with strength reveals that she is motivated to do her work and prepared for the activity. This phrase could also be translated, "She dressed herself in strength!"[3]

The Bible speaks of "strength unto strength" (Psalm 84:7), and that's what God's beautiful woman enjoys: As she disciplines herself to work, that discipline results in greater strength and endurance![4]

Finally, we see that she "strengthens her *arms*" (Proverbs 31:17). This reference to her physical strength tells us that she is ready to work. She has prepared herself for the effort physically as well as mentally. Like a lioness, she is physically able and strong.[5] As one translation exclaims, "How briskly she girds herself to the task, how tireless are her arms!"[6]

A Personal Formula for Work

If I were paraphrasing Proverbs 31:17 today, I would say, "When it comes to work, the woman who is beautiful in God's eyes is ready, willing, and able!" As I've thought about this quality in God's beautiful woman, I've decided that her mental attitude is the key to the volume of work she accomplishes, and that attitude reveals the following four qualities of the heart.

Commitment—Work is a matter of the heart, and where there is no heart commitment, little (if any) work gets done. I know in my early homemaking days I had to make a commitment to step into the homemaking arena. I loved reading, brooding, and watching TV. But one evening I heard a Christian woman I admire say, "I don't do anything sedentary!" I thought about that statement for days (and I still think about it—and her—every day!), and I finally made a pledge to be more active, to keep moving, to always be doing something. After all, as another proverb teaches, "In all labor there is profit" (14:23)!

Willingness—Our willingness to do the job plays a large role in how easily we accomplish our work and how much we get done. We can have a heart commitment to do the work, build the home, serve the family, and carry out God's plans, but we must also be willing to actually do it! As a woman of God, a virtuous woman, we've enlisted in the army, so to speak; we've signed on; we've volunteered. So now we have to be mentally ready and willing to do or give whatever is necessary to answer the call to duty!

Motivation—For me, motivation is key to the work I do because motivation is the "why" of anything I do. I'm constantly thinking and praying about what I want for my life, my marriage, my family, and my home *and* what I want to contribute to my church, to God's people, and to others. I want what the Proverbs 31 woman reaped in her life: to have God as the driving force behind all I do; to enhance Jim's life; to give the church, the world, and the next generation two godly daughters; to give the gift of order and beauty in the home to my family; to be a generous giver of whatever my church needs me to give; and to touch the lives of other women with the love of Christ. Beloved, this is what I want (and I think it's what God wants), and I want these things badly enough that I'm motivated to do the work—from sunup to sundown—to make it happen (Lord willing!). These goals provide motivation for a lifetime, and give me strength of mind as I tackle the work involved.

Discipline—Ouch! For me, this is the one that hurts. Up to this point, everything has been dreams, desires, goals, and talk! But, as the second half of Proverbs 14:23 so rightly states, "Idle chatter leads only to poverty!" Discipline is necessary for turning talk into action and reaching goals. Here's how it happens for me. I can want a clean house, but discipline is what gets me out of bed when the alarm goes off. Discipline is what gets me up off the couch or out of the easy chair. Discipline is what makes me walk over to the pantry and pull out the vacuum cleaner and cleaning products. Discipline is what keeps me moving when I want to take a break. Discipline is what pushes me to finish fully instead of leaving some things undone or done halfway. Discipline is what makes me put everything away when I'm done!

And this discipline is all a matter of the mind! We fight the battle to get any kind of work done in the mind. That's where we make our choices; that's where we decide how to spend our time and energy. That, my fellow pursuer of beauty, is why mental toughness is basic to work. When we're mentally tough, we'll win the battle over laziness, procrastination, disorganization, and other enemies of productivity.

The How-To's of Beauty

Let me pass on some methods that help me "work up" a better attitude and even an eagerness about my work.

1. *Embrace God's will for your life*—If you're uncertain about what God's will for your life is, you're seeing it expressed right here in Proverbs 31. So study these verses of the Bible carefully. Put the message in your words and then own it, love it, tackle it, be committed to it, and dedicate your life to it!

2. *Stay in God's Word*—Allow the Spirit of God to energize your heart, mind—and strength—through the power of God's Word. After all, fundamental to who she is, God's beautiful woman loved and feared the Lord (verse 30). Her goals were derived from His Word, her strength was empowered by His Word, and the grace to persist was given through His Word and His Spirit!

3. *Develop a vision*—Having a vision of the big picture, of your goals, of the ministry possibilities of what God is calling you to do, will mean an eagerness about what you're doing. Think for a moment about how your daily environment is a direct result of your vision for your home and family, your vision for the beauty and order of a well-run home and for peace under your roof. Broaden your horizons and also nurture a vision for the future of your family members and the contribution they can make to society. Allow a prayer like this one to fuel your vision: "Lord, make us masters of ourselves that we may be the servants of others."[7]

4. *Tap into the why*—I may be repeating myself, but it's vital to know *why* you are doing what you do. The *why* will motivate the work. Some unknown teacher has accurately set forth this truth: "The secret of discipline is motivation. When a man [or woman] is sufficiently motivated, discipline will take care of itself." You can know what needs to be done and possess all the necessary skills to get it done, but until there is motivation—an understanding and passion for the *why*—the job probably won't get done!

5. *Pray for an eager attitude*—When you turn off your light at night, pray about the work that awaits the next day. Ask God to help you greet the day with an eager attitude (see Psalm 118:24). Then, when the alarm wakens you, thank God for another day in which to serve Him and love your family.

6. *Create a schedule*—A schedule will help you plan your work. You'll know what's coming and where you're going, and you'll be able to anticipate the pace and envision your next task.

7. *Develop a routine*—The more work you're able to

fit into a daily routine, the better. Those things you do everyday (spending time with the Lord, getting dressed, exercising, making coffee, watering the lawn, unloading the dishwasher, making the bed, bringing in the newspaper, tidying up, fixing breakfast, lunch, and dinner, running errands, etc.) take less time when they're part of a routine. Your goal is to be able to say, "This is when I *always* walk...tidy up...pay the bills. This is the day I *always* clean the house...get the groceries...wash the clothes...pull the weeds." Then you'll be able to glide more effortlessly from one task to the next. Also, because you're used to your routine, you'll have fewer decisions to make, less thinking to do, and less indecision to battle. You'll perform many tasks by rote, leaving your mind free to pray, dream, and plan. Knowing what's coming can also generate an eager and energetic expectation about the next tasks.

8. *Read books on time management*—Proverbs 31 is a portrait of the excellent woman, the excellent wife, the excellent mother, the excellent homemaker, *and* the excellent time manager! She's the best of all, and that's God's challenge to you and me. So study organizational systems and make them work for you. Learn the best, fastest, most effective and efficient methods for doing your work. Reading about time management will stimulate your eager attitude *and* offer tips on improving your skills so that you, too, can excel in your work!

9. *Tackle the worst first*—There's no reason to live your days under a cloud of dread because of some challenging or unpleasant task you need to tackle. Simply do that task first! Having the monumental thing out of the way makes the day go more smoothly and easily. Having cleared the major

hurdle of the day early on, you'll have fresh energy as you dive into your more pleasant work.

10. *Play music*—One afternoon at about 3:00 I called my friend, another Karen. I had to wait a moment while she turned her music down—one of Bach's lively Brandenburg concerti. She explained, "I always play loud music in the afternoons when I start to sag. It keeps me going!" That's good advice. Try it.

11. *See how quickly you can work*—Try to beat the clock. Better your times. Make doing your chores a game. The reward is having more time for your own creative pastimes and your field of dreams. With your housework done, you can concentrate on a cottage industry just as God's beautiful woman did with her weaving. Besides, just thinking about topping off your day with such pleasure will fuel an eager attitude for your work.

12. *Consider yourself*—Consider the message in this poem and pray that you will not be your own roadblock.

> All that stands between your goal
> And the deeds you hope to do
> And the dreams which stir your soul—
> Is you![8]

An Invitation to Beauty

Thank you for staying with me! I so desperately want you to make it to the peak of this woman's glory! I'm excited about this woman who is so beautiful in God's eyes, and I'm trying so hard to capture some of her beauty that I sometimes think smoke is coming right off these pages!

As I was just now re-reading this chapter's section on motivation (please read it again!), my heart was freshly moved for you. I know I was listing all the things I want for *my* life, but, beloved friend, I passionately want them for *you*! Why? Because these selfless acts of generous love are what *God* wants from us—and we are supremely blessed when we walk in His paths (Psalm 16:11).

I also want you to experience the unutterable joy and fulfillment that come from acting on the desires of your heart, desires which God has placed there (Psalm 37:4); I want you to experience the exhilaration and continuing motivation that come with such noble efforts. So please pause, pray, pour out your heart to God—with tears if they flow—and, relying on His grace, persist in the divine work God has given you to do for Him!

-11-

A Taste of Success

Her Confidence

"She perceives that her merchandise is good,
and her lamp does not go out by night."
Proverbs 31:18

As we begin another chapter about true beauty, I want to tell you in advance that this verse may be my personal favorite. I'll tell you why in a minute, but first a few statements.

First of all, I know that each and every verse of this exquisite Proverbs 31 portrait of the beautiful-in-God's-eyes woman is powerful, potentially life-changing, and crucial because it comes from God Himself. I also know from the study of Proverbs 31:10-31 that my husband, children, and home are to be paramount as I live according to His ways. As a married woman, my greatest fulfillment and highest reward come in the arena of the home. Living according to God's priorities brings me real blessing and joy.

But verse 18—this little gem tucked in the middle of this outpouring of instruction—offers me motivation for a lifetime. You see, verse 18 is the spark that ignites the flame of a full-fledged business for the Proverbs 31 woman, for me, and perhaps for you, too. As we've seen, God's beautiful woman does all things well, and she enjoys the success that results from attaining her standards of excellence. We've also seen her willingness to work hard and to save pennies by bartering and bargaining. Through thrift, hard work, and saying "no," she builds a savings account that supplies her with the capital for some real estate ventures. Having taken care of her family and seeing that her home is well cared for, she now starts up her own little business.

Excellence in All Things

How did her business begin? How did it come to be? The wise, royal mother who is teaching this alphabet of wisdom shows us and also offers us a formula for success—in a word, *excellence*! When you and I pursue excellence in all things (Proverbs 31:29), we can experience the kind of success enjoyed by God's beautiful woman.

Excellent taste—Proverbs 31:18 opens with, "She perceives that her merchandise is good." The word *perceive* is the same Hebrew word that is translated *taste* in Psalm 34:8—"taste and see that the Lord is good." So we see that God's beautiful woman tastes and perceives that her merchandise is good. By trial she finds out that her work is good. By taking risks, trying new ideas and methods, and refining her efforts, she learns that what she's producing is good. She can be confident about her work, and she is.

Excellent goods—But what exactly is the merchandise she perceives as good? First, this woman has purchased a field and planted it with crops, and she has planted another field with vines (verse 16). The yield from her land—corn, grapes, wine—is greater than what her family needs, so she sells the extra produce.

This excellent woman also sells her weaving. Remember all her effort processing the raw wool and flax (verse 13), spinning her yarn (verse 19), and weaving it into exquisite works for her family, home, and self (verses 21-22)? Perceiving that her woven clothing is good (she must have gotten a lot of compliments!), she confidently creates and sells her handiwork to others (verse 24).

Excellent results—The merchandise that the Proverbs 31 woman sells is "good" (verse 18). Put differently, her merchandise is *profitable*—and it is profitable because it is *good!* All she does is done first for her family and nothing but the best will do for them. She would never offer her loved ones something shoddy or quickly thrown together. Her standards of excellence mean the work she does is top quality. So, when a little of this "best" is leftover, she sells it. Because her merchandise is good, it has a ready market and brings a good price.

Excellent pursuit—Next, verse 18 reports that "her lamp does not go out by night." God's beautiful homemaker confidently follows through on her financial enterprise even at the cost of late-night efforts. She likes what she "tastes," and that spurs her on to continue her work even into the night. Her creative efforts and the financial gain that results motivate her to even greater industry and diligence. Because trading conditions are good, she burns the midnight oil to make the most of them while they last.[1] Her intellectual perception ("she perceives") turns into physical exertion ("her lamp does not go out by night") as she pushes forward to both benefit her family and express herself creatively in her work.

Before we move on, let me add a quick note about the lamp mentioned here. When dusk arrived, a lamp needed to be lit if any activity were to continue. As I've mentioned, these lamps were actually flat saucers with pinched edges, and they held olive oil and a flax wick. The lighting of the lamp signified several things about a home.

- First of all, a lighted lamp meant that work was going on so light was needed. Much work was certainly going on in the home of God's beautiful woman!
- Hospitality was another reason the lamp was used. Its light signaled to needy travelers that comfort and refreshment were available.
- A light—shining because precious oil was being burned—also meant prosperity (Proverbs 21:20).
- Finally, a lighted lamp meant wisdom: Someone inside had the practical wisdom to keep a lamp burning so that the kitchen fire could be lighted in the morning. And remember who got up periodically during the night to make sure the lamp didn't go out or burn out (verse 18)!

All said, God's beautiful woman is a busy woman, not only giving her maidens tasks, but working herself late into the night as well as early in the morning (verse 15). She works outdoors in her field and vineyard during daylight hours (verse 16) and inside her home day and night (verse 18) as she tends to her profit-making projects.

Well, my dear friend, we shouldn't be surprised that her business is successful. After all, our beautiful woman doesn't avoid hard work—and, in her skilled hands and with God's blessing, it's good and profitable work (verse 18)! She's doing something she enjoys (she works willingly with her heart and hands) at the same time that she helps gain financial security for her family (she does her husband good, and he has no need of gain). She's also free to be creative in her clothing designs, and her management of these efforts makes a profit for her family. The joy of creating and the satisfaction of selling motivate her to continue. On and on the blessings and benefits of busyness and business continue. A cottage industry has been born!

A Stimulus to Excellence

I call the little business of God's beautiful woman her "Proverbs 31 Project." And now I want you to pray about what is it that you do—or might do—to contribute to the finances at home. I hope this roll call of some of the many women I know who work late into the night will stimulate and inspire you. Let their Proverbs 31 Projects spark your imagination and encourage you to keep your lamp burning at night!

- My daughter Courtney oversees the taxes and prepares all the returns for her household, and her Paul gladly gives her any tax refunds as pay. This was the beginning of her own small business—which she does at home—compiling tax returns for others as well.
- A registered nurse I know picks up medical charts from her local hospital every evening, checks them at home, and delivers them the next day with the appropriate paperwork done. She also picks up a paycheck! She simply modified her profession and moved it home when her first baby arrived.
- A seminary wife bakes all her own bread—and takes orders from people like me for their daily bread! She

also sends baked goods to school with her husband to sell in the student lounge at break time. Voilà! Money for educational expenses!

- My husband's former secretary took her typing skills home when her first baby came along. She types student papers—and transcribes tapes for me—right from her home!
- Then there's my "pool person" friend! To save money, this true Proverbs 31 woman asked her husband if she could clean and maintain their pool and collect the same monthly fee he was paying a pool man. So she began keeping her pool clean—and pocketing the money for her family's needs. When her neighbor saw her sparkling pool, he asked if she would clean his, too. Today Kathy does every pool on her block, and she uses the money for her family's needs.
- And then there is my Lisa, a sharp woman with a husband, two young toddlers, and a home. But she also has a master's degree in English, a heart filled with compassion, and an incredible ability to write. Lisa is my editor—and a capable editor for many others. She's a master manager of her time and energy and—just like God's beautiful woman (verses 15 and 18)—rises early and stays up late to turn her passion into a profession—and some profit!

In light of these ideas, why don't you take some time to evaluate your dreams, abilities, and interests? Pray about an area you can develop so that you can help improve your family's financial situation and add your name to my list. (If you already hold down a job outside the home, challenge yourself to be more creative once you're home. Don't just give at the office!)

Even as you consider a Proverbs 31 Project, let me remind you that you make a significant financial contribution simply by taking care of the home. We've talked about the money you save by systematic bill paying, wise shopping, careful menu planning, and healthy food preparation. Add to that tasks like yard work, housecleaning, and perhaps cleaning your own pool that you do yourself rather than paying someone else to do. The wise saying is certainly true: "Money saved is money earned."

It's OK if your lifestyle doesn't allow for a formal Proverbs 31 Project. I know that every woman is different, and every woman's situation is different (eight children? no children?). But if God has gifted you with special creative abilities, a mind for business, some marketable professional skills, the blessing of spare time, an empty nest, or some initial capital, by all means think about and pray about how He would have you put these gifts to work for your family.

The How-To's of Beauty

Now some tips on determining your personal Proverbs 31 Project.

1. *Listen to others*—Are you getting compliments for something you do? We usually take our gifts for granted. We tend to think, "Oh, everyone can do this! It's so easy!" and we fail to notice that no one else is doing it—or doing it with the same excellence, flair, or boldness. Sometimes we may even think, "Oh, that's not so great! Others do a better job!" instead of thanking God for the abilities He's given us and trying to use those abilities in a broader way.

2. *Move forward*—Did you goof? Did the recipe fail, the paints run? Were you unable to find the exact words for your writing (I can relate!) or the right notes for your

music composition? Did you over-fertilize your prize roses? Move forward from these experiences with the attitude of inventor Thomas Edison who failed thousands of times before he invented the light bulb: "Don't call it a mistake. Call it an education!"[2]

3. *Develop your skills*—To be successful in your Proverbs 31 Project, you need to continue to develop your skills and techniques. My daughter Courtney enrolled in a culinary school to further develop her wonderful cooking skills. She has an ability and the desire to do more in the kitchen, and she has "tasted" enough success to dare to dream of future enterprises involving food preparation. Whatever it takes to develop your skills, commit yourself to it. You'll not only develop skills but confidence as well.

4. *Redeem your time*—Buy back time from less important activities and use it for your Proverbs 31 Project, for personal creative efforts, for your "merchandising." As I focused my mind and energy on my writing and speaking, I noticed that a few once-regular activities completely disappeared. I no longer spend hours watching television, shopping, attending luncheons, going on outings, or talking on the telephone. One of the few activities I make extended time for now is my "work," and I willingly extend it far into the night! (It's 10:30 PM right now!)

5. *Take risks*—Be creative. Try new things. Express yourself. Adopt my friend Julie's attitude toward her flower arranging—"Be bold!" in whatever enterprise you are exploring.

6. *Do your best*—"Whatever your hand finds to do, do it with your might." That's the wisdom of Ecclesiastes 9:10.

God's beautiful woman certainly works with all her might and all her heart. All she does, she does with excellence. As a result, her merchandise is good!

7. *Do your projects unto the Lord*—In both the Old Testament and the New, in Proverbs 16:3 and Colossians 3:23 respectively, we are told to commit our work to the Lord and to do our work as unto the Lord. With Him as the reason for your work, with Him as your Boss, with His glory as your goal, you'll experience the blessing of His strength and His guidance. With Him as your stay, you'll also find staying power for staying up!

8. *Manage for profit*—As we see in this profile of God's beautiful woman, profit can be gained in several ways. We can strengthen our family's financial situation by money saved, by money earned, and by money invested.

9. *Know what you're doing is important*—In Psalm 34:8, David calls us to "taste and see that the Lord is good." The meaning of see is "convinced"—and usually the hardest person to convince about the value of your efforts is you! Remember that this chapter is about the confidence of God's beautiful woman—her confidence in her God, her God-given talents and abilities, and her use of those gifts for the good of her family and other people.

10. *Family first*—Jesus teaches that if the tree is good, the fruit will be, too (Matthew 7:15-20). For God's beautiful woman, her family comes first. All that she does, she does for them. Because her family's good is the desire of her heart and the focus of her actions, the fruit of her efforts is good. She isn't motivated by greed, but only by her concern for her dear family. That motivation prompts her to do her best,

and God uses her to bless her family and others (Proverbs 31:20,24) in a variety of ways, including financially.

So take a second to check your motives. Are your efforts fueled by the right motives? As my wise pastor exhorts, "You take care of the depth and let God take care of the breadth." In the case of becoming beautiful in God's eyes, you take care of your family and let God take care of how He chooses to bless and expand any business efforts.

An Invitation to Beauty

I hope and pray that, by reading this chapter about God's beautiful woman, you are encouraged to:

- Pour your greatest energy and most fervent efforts into your family and home.
- Pray for discernment about the area you excel in, what area you may be able to expand into a Proverbs 31 Project.
- Pursue your skills and sharpen your expertise.
- Plan for a few late nights of creative effort.
- Prepare to taste success!

~ 12 ~

A Little Night Work

Her Diligence

"She stretches out her hands to the distaff,
and her hand holds the spindle."
Proverbs 31:19

It happens every day. The sun that lights the world and energizes our life and our work starts to sink, signaling to our weary minds and bodies that another day is winding down. You and I both know the order of events from this moment on: Soon there will be supper to serve, the dishes and the kitchen to clean up, baths to give, teeth to brush, stories to read, kids to tuck in, and then it will finally be time to call it a day and go to bed.

It's been a long day and a full day—full of challenges, creativity, service, and work. And...ooooh...it's going to feel so good to be in a horizontal position, to rest our weary mind and body, to draw up the covers and close our eyes—until we rise up before the next new day dawns! These are the kinds of thoughts and feelings that enter our mind via a tired body as God closes His curtain of darkness on the activities of another busy day.

But wait a minute! As we read on in Proverbs 31, we discover an added dimension to God's beautiful woman, another trait that causes us to completely reevaluate how we approach our evenings! Just when you and I thought we were done for the day, God's beautiful teacher presents Lesson #12 (we're halfway through!) on what it means to be beautiful in God's eyes. Her young son listens as she again points to the diligence of the Proverbs 31 woman who does a little night work before going to bed.

Behind the Scenes

It's true that work, work, and more work lie behind every success. You and I are considering the wonderful success story of the Proverbs 31 woman. Clearly, she's a woman of diligence—ever persevering, continually industrious, and constantly busy. Delighting in her family and her work, she rises early to take care of her household and continues to work at the other end of her day, too. She puts her evenings to good use.

In the preceding chapter, we saw that God's beautiful woman foregoes a little beauty rest for a little night work: "She perceives that her merchandise is good, and her lamp does not go out by night" (Proverbs 31:18). But what, we wonder, does she do in the evening? Proverbs 31:19 may provide an obvious answer: "She stretches out her hands to the distaff, and her hand holds the spindle." When evening arrives, God's beautiful woman shifts her activities from outside in her fields to inside her home where she works by lamplight (verse 18). Yes, she's put in a long day, but she keeps on working in the evening. In her day it was perfectly natural and permissible to retire when night fell, but our heroine stays up to work...just a little longer.

And, according to Proverbs 31:19, she's working with a distaff and a spindle. Mentioned nowhere else in the Old

Testament, these ancient objects were used in spinning wool.[1] In skilled and experienced hands, the distaff and the spindle converted processed wool and flax into yarn and thread. These two implements were definitely the tools of the cloth-making trade for the Proverbs 31 woman.

Earlier in verse 13 we saw that she uses her energy to bring in, dress, clean, and untangle her wool and flax. Now at night, as her body slows down, she sits and spins, perfecting the wool and the flax for her weaving. She knows that the monotonous work of spinning must be completed before she can be more creative and begin her weaving.

This kind of behind-the-scenes preparation is necessary before any great work can be accomplished. For instance, before there can be a painting, the canvases must be stretched and mounted. Before a dress can be sewn, the pattern must be cut out. Before an opera can be sung, the scales must be practiced. Before a book can be written, the research must be done. Before a wall can be painted, the baseboards must be masked. Before a meal can be cooked, the ingredients must be cleaned, chopped, and measured. Such behind-the-scenes work may be mundane, routine, unglamorous, dull, unchallenging, and even a "no-brainer," but such preparation is fundamental to beauty and usefulness.

So God's beautiful woman willingly, cheerfully, heartily, and gladly (verse 13) spends her evenings doing the tedious, unexciting—but very necessary—work from which her great works of art are born.

The How-To's of Beauty

When I first began working at night rather than plopping down in front of the TV with a bowl of Cheetos and a Coke, I struggled! Making the commitment to use my evenings to help my family and ministry and developing self-discipline in a new area, I gradually learned to use my evenings in useful and creative ways. (It's 9:15 PM as I write this!) Now I value my evenings that were, for so long, a hidden treasure.

In fact, finding this gift of time for a little night work opened up a whole new life for me. Christian Development Ministries was birthed by Jim and me one evening ten years ago. A wiser use of my evenings has given me the time to sit beside Jim at the helm of our ministry organization and to develop and use my spiritual gifts to enrich the lives of Christian women. I shudder to think what I would be doing (or *not* doing!) if I had continued to throw away God's gift of evenings!

As one time-management expert advises about some often-wasted hours, make your evenings and weekends count![2] Hopefully some of these first steps that revolutionized my life—and my evenings—will encourage you to do just that.

1. *Evaluate your evenings*—I recently heard the highest-paid sports agent in the world talk about a skill he practices every day. Speaking on the importance of time, he stated that he plans his day (every single one of them—even his weekends) in 20-minute increments. Do you know how you spend every 20 minutes of your evenings? Answering this question can be quite an eye-opening exercise!

2. *Plan your evenings*—One Sunday morning at church I walked right past a friend of mine. Thankfully she grabbed my arm as I went by so I could share in a wonderful thing that had happened to her—she had lost 40 pounds! (That's why I walked past her—I didn't even recognize her!) When I asked her how she had done it, she told me that she had decided to exercise every night after she got home from work. Her goal

for the new year had been to incorporate that one activity into her life, specifically her evenings. In other words, she planned her evenings—and she's definitely enjoying the payoff!

I try to plan my evenings in advance because, by the time they roll around, I'm too tired to put forth the mental energy it takes to even think about doing something useful! So I created what I call my "PM File" (the bookend to my "Early AM. File"). In my "PM File" I keep a running list of activities I can do at night.

For instance, I assemble my Bible study workbooks a hundred at a time. I autograph my books for Bible study groups. About once a week I answer my correspondence. (Sometimes I've dictated so late into the night [I've seen 2:00 AM before!] that the words are barely intelligible.) Paying bills, bringing the checkbook up to date, and reconciling our bank statement are good nighttime activities for me. Night is when I go through junk mail and catalogs, keeping a large trash can nearby! Our clothes get folded at night, and any ironing that needs to be done gets done after the sun goes down. As a teacher and writer, I need lots of illustrations, so in the evening I sift through books of quotations, biographical notes, and art books. At night I major on the minors, keeping my reading content on the light side. I save the heavy-duty commentaries and research books for the daylight hours (and energy)! And I don't know about you, but I have lots of piles around the house, so on some nights I sort through a pile or two.

Create your own "PM File" and plan your evenings to include a little night work. Your file might include clipping coupons, looking through your recipe box, and making menus. Following in the steps of God's beautiful woman, you could mend, knit, crochet, or do embroidery and cross-stitching.

Work on making your Christmas gifts at night—and then wrap them after the sun goes down. Read your favorite magazines, the newspaper, or a professional journal at night. Use the evening to pursue your own special interests. If you like art, classical music, cooking, gardening, or history, why not rent an educational video to watch instead of evening TV? Or listen to an audiotape and take notes.

Maybe you want to watch TV with your family—or at least be in the same room with them. I meet many women whose husbands want them right there beside them on the couch during the evening programs. Well, author Anne Ortlund lists 22 things you can do then. Here's a sampling: Look over your calendar and plan ahead, give yourself a pedicure, write a letter to an old friend, do your nails, bring your recipe file up to date, put all those old photos into albums, polish the silver, and write your pastor an encouraging note.[3]

The point is, my beautiful sister, to save your daylight hours—your prime energy time—for the work that demands the most from you physically and mentally. When dusk begins to darken the day and your energy starts to fade, instead of zoning out, kicking back, and plopping down, follow the example of our beautiful and diligent woman: Simply change activities. After all, Proverbs 10:4 tells us, "She who deals with a slack hand [and is negligent] becomes poor, but the hand of the diligent makes one rich." In other words, the lazy person reaps nothing, but those who are diligent succeed. So plan for diligence!

3. *Prepare for your evenings*—If you set up a "PM File," you'll have some specific options for your evenings and know exactly how to plan for them. So before the sun goes down and you get too tired, set out the supplies you need for your

little bit of night work. If I'm going to assemble Bible study workbooks, I set up my assembly line right on the coffee table. If I'm working on bookkeeping, I set up the card table in the family room so I can be with my family while I work. I have a friend who created a letter-writing caddie to hold stationery, postcards, notecards, stamps, envelopes, pens, and her address book. You could set something like that by your husband's easy chair and write away. My friend Judy has her art easel standing in her cozy family room. My treadmill and exercycle are permanent fixtures in our family room—a constant reminder to me to keep trying!

I've even discovered some tricks for getting more done in an evening. One of those tricks is exercising or going for a walk to get my energy level up for the evening's activities. Another trick is telling myself, "Now, Liz, just do one more thing." Whenever I finish one effort, I remind myself that I can do just one more thing. Before I know it, I've been doing just one more thing all evening long! Or I tell myself, "Just five more minutes and I'll quit!" (I once read that "the difference between an amateur and professional is about five minutes more."[4] And once again, I'm surprised and thrilled when all those "five minutes more" add up to three or four hours of additional work getting done.

4. *Use your evenings!*—It's great to evaluate, plan, and prepare, but ultimately you must use your evenings. And that calls for effort! God's beautiful woman "stretched out her hands to the spindle" (Proverbs 31:19). What do your hands reach for at night? A snack? Another romance novel? A favorite video? Your pillow? The remote control? This chapter is about diligence; it's an invitation to you to make your evenings productive.

If you hold down a job outside the home, you may find

it especially challenging to use your evenings once you're home. Here's how one woman does it, described in a chapter she wrote entitled "Working Women, Read This First."

> The evening? Checking clothing needs and making breakfast preparations the night before....As soon as I greet everyone, I gather up the laundry for the day and start the washer. Then I cook. Dinner is our family time, and I try to keep it pleasant and unhurried. After dinner, I transfer laundry to the dryer and clean up the kitchen. (Each evening, as I cooked dinner, I mixed up a batch of dough for our traditional Christmas cookies and breads. I refrigerated them all, and then on one night I had a baking orgy.) The cleaning of refrigerator, range, and cupboards, I've moved to evening. Sometimes, if I've had a rough day, I take a 30-minute nap. Right now, with [my] writing schedule so tight, I spend more time at the typewriter. Whatever I'm doing, I keep an ear open for the dryer's stopping so that I can snatch out the clothes....I schedule the last 30 minutes before bedtime for self-improvement. This includes exercises, skin, teeth, and nail care.[5]

This beautiful woman has so many dreams and so much to do that she simply doesn't have time for talking endlessly on the phone, sprawling out to watch TV, or kicking back after a hard day. No, she knows that her home is to be the site of her best work and her true fulfillment. That's one reason why her family time, home-making chores, creative baking, and writing projects motivated her throughout the evening. Once you get yourself going on a little night work, you'll find yourself motivated to continue, too!

5. *Use your mind in the evenings*—Even if you're doing

dull, routine work, your mind can be active. With a little prompting, creative sparks can fly while your hands are busy. As God's beautiful woman spins her raw materials, she probably imagines what she could make with the yarn and linen, maybe even pausing to sketch her ideas. Designing in her head while her body rests and her hands sail, she creates her unique garments, deciding which ornaments would complement the fabric, what kind of design to embroider across the yoke, etc., etc. Whatever your "no-brainer" task is, assign your brain a creative task, choose a fun or serious subject to think about, or train yourself to dream!

An Invitation to Beauty

Speaking of dreaming, I want to challenge you to dream! First, name something you love to do, something personal, a passion you carry in your heart. Do you realize you just might be able to turn that "something personal" into "something professional" by doing a little night work? I know many women who have two professions—one by day and one by night.

For instance, my mother was a Shakespearean scholar and teacher by day and a seamstress by night. As I grew up, she made all of my clothes, continuing to send me a package of newly sewn clothes every week I was away at college. Mom used her nights—often until two o'clock in the morning!—to sew all the curtains, throw pillows, dust ruffles, and pillow shams in our home. Her hands worked magic as she made all our bathrobes, even whimsically whipping up doll clothes for my "babies" and a Christmas coat for our dog! My mother lived out a lovely line of poetry that states, "A woman's love is like a light, shining the brightest in the night."[6]

I know others who also have two professions. One of my friends is a grade-school teacher by day and a gifted tole painter by night. Another is a school principal by day and a writer by night. Another friend is a mother of preschoolers by day and a master oil painter by night.

Again I ask—and urge—you to consider how doing a little night work could help your dreams for your family, for your home, and for some personal creative outlet come true. How can you, like God's beautiful woman, turn a personal passion into a professional line of work? Whisper a prayer to God, the Creator of all things beautiful, and ask Him to guide your heart—and hands—toward a little diligent night work that will help you realize your dreams.

~ 13 ~

A Helping Hand

HER MERCY

"She extends her hand to the poor,
Yes, she reaches out her hands to the needy."
Proverbs 31:20

God's beautiful woman is impressive, isn't she? She excels in trustworthiness, supportiveness, diligence, industry, thrift, creativity, organization, and micromanagement. But aren't you encouraged to see that mercy is the next item on the list of her outstanding qualities? Truly beautiful in God's eyes, the Proverbs 31 woman works hard for her profits, but those profits benefit people beyond the boundaries of private family life as "she extends her hand to the poor, yes, she reaches out her hands to the needy" (Proverbs 31:20). Her efforts and her virtues benefit her precious family, but she is ever ready to bestow the soft grace of mercy to the unfortunate. Although she's busy with her household, she's not so busy that she forgets the needs of others. Without this godly mercy, her industry and activity could make her harsh and hurried; she'd be too busy to care.

Her Hand

For twelve chapters you and I have been marveling at God's beautiful woman and her strong, energetic body. Now, Proverbs 31:20 focuses our attention specifically on her hands.

The first part of the verse reads, "She extends her *hand* to the poor." The beauty of God's merciful woman opens up (just like her hand) as we open up the Hebrew language here. The image of the single extended hand reveals her generous, giving nature. For instance, if money is needed, she reaches her hand into her purse and shares her wealth. If bread is lacking, she offers a homemade loaf. If warm clothes are missing, God's merciful and generous woman provides one of her own handmade woolen coats (verse 21), the result of months and months and nights and nights of personal labor (verses 13, 18-19). (In her day, a woolen garment could cost over two months wages!)[1] As one woman writes, "I sharpen skills and needles (not my tongue) when neighbors dress in rags and suffer."[2] When it is in her power to do so, the Proverbs 31 woman extends her hand with whatever item is needed (Proverbs 3:27). God's beautiful woman lends a helping hand at every opportunity!

Her Hands

The verse continues: "She [also] reaches out her *hands* to the needy." For the woman who is beautiful in God's eyes, generosity doesn't end with the mere giving of things. The plural word "hands" signifies those activities requiring two hands. Nursing the sick, for instance, requires two hands. So does caring for babies, young children, the elderly, and the sick. The Proverbs 31 woman uses her hands for ministry. She's not afraid to roll up her sleeves and touch those who are suffering. Whatever the need, she holds out her hands—her literal, open, upturned palms—to offer any profits or profitable activities.[3]

Her Heart

It's good to see God's beautiful woman giving, but, as the wise mother and instructor points out to her boy (and to us), this woman's heart is involved. The verbs "extends" and "reaches out" suggest that her giving stretches as far as her means will allow.[4] This kind of stretching, as you know, requires a heart—a generous heart of love and compassion, a heart after God (verse 30). This dear woman gives to the poor and needy with her whole heart.[5]

As she "stretch[es] out" (KJV) her mercy and compassion, she stretches out her heart. Rather than folding her beautiful hands for moments of relaxation, or using them to clutch her profits, or keeping them frantically busy in order to gain greater wealth, she extends her outstretched hands to those around her who are in need! She is aware of these people, sympathetic to their needs, and ready to help, and her full heart and full coffers spill over to liberally and plentifully bless others. Rather than drawing a tight circle around her family and shutting others out, she follows her heart, opens the circle, and takes them in. Her circle of love includes all who need her help.

Her Heeding of God's Word

When I speak, I usually allow some time for questions and answers. For years now, I've kept a handwritten question from one such session. It read, "From your study of Proverbs 31, please comment on the fact that no reference is made to the woman's involvement in 'ministry' kinds of activities."

As I look at God's beautiful woman, I definitely see that one of her ministries is taking care of the poor and the needy (verse 20). Her giving is generated not only from her heart, but out of obedience to and in worship of God. As a woman who fears the Lord (verse 30), she walks in obedience to His Word. And hear now the Word of the Lord on this subject of mercy—and note the blessing God promises:

- "If there is among you a poor man...you shall not harden your heart nor shut your hand from your poor brother, but you shall open your hand wide to him and willingly lend him...whatever he needs" (Moses' Law, Deuteronomy 15:7-8).
- "He has shown you, O man, what is good; and what does the Lord require of you but to do justly, to love mercy, and to walk humbly with your God" (Micah 6:8).
- "The generous soul will be made rich, and he who waters will also be watered himself" (Proverbs 11:25).
- "He who has pity on the poor lends to the Lord, and He will pay back what he has given" (Proverbs 19:17).
- "He who has a bountiful eye will be blessed, for he gives of his bread to the poor" (Proverbs 22:9).

As we continue to learn what is beautiful in God's eyes, we see that caring for the poor and needy is one of His primary concerns. This beautiful, God-fearing woman knows that fact because she knows God's law and takes His commands seriously. So, I ask you, have you ever considered that perhaps the great blessing upon her home is *because* of her generosity to the poor and needy? That perhaps she is wealthy not because she is a hard worker, a capable manager, or a smart businesswoman, but *because* God blesses her generosity? God's people are God's way of caring for the poor and needy, and He blesses those who care for them in obedience to His Word!

Her Sisters of Mercy

Do you remember when you and I began our climb to the heights of God's beautiful woman? We both found tremendous comfort in the fact that this woman is real, that by God's grace we, too, can attain her level of excellence. Others have also obtained her greatness of character. In her ministry of mercy and giving, God's beautiful woman joins other women in the Bible, fellow sisters of mercy, who live out God's kind of mercy. These beautiful-in-God's-eyes women include Abigail who fed David's 600 men (1 Samuel 25); the starving widow of Zarephath who took in the prophet Elijah (1 Kings 17); the Shunamite woman who regularly fed and lodged the prophet Elisha (2 Kings 4); and Dorcas who clothed the widows in the early church at Joppa (Acts 9). The Proverbs 31 woman is added to this elite list—and you can be, too!

The How-To's of Beauty

Once you begin moving along the gracious path of giving, you'll have no trouble finding golden opportunities to extend God's mercy to the poor and needy. Would some first steps toward becoming a bountiful giver help? Try these for starters.

1. *Begin at home*—Each sunrise presents fresh opportunities for you to show mercy to others, and those opportunities won't go unnoticed. Your children will benefit greatly as they view firsthand the life of a giving mother—a woman who is beautiful in God's eyes.

Edith Schaeffer is such a mother, a woman who extends a helping hand. Regularly the "hobos and tramps" who traveled on the freight cars past her home knocked at her back door asking for a "cup of coffee, ma'am, and maybe some bread?" She never turned one away, but instead she saw each of these men as an opportunity to do something for "one of the least of these" (Matthew 25:40) and perhaps entertain "angels unawares" (Hebrews 13:2). Employing her "hidden art" of hospitality, she toasted nuts, made two generous sandwiches, and heated leftover soup. "For *me*? Is this for me?" was always the bewildered reaction when she stepped through the door from her kitchen holding a tray set with her good china, a bouquet of flowers, a lighted candle—and a copy of the gospel of John to read while he ate and take along with him when he went on his way. Only later did Mrs. Schaeffer discover that her house was marked with chalk—a sign to other tramps that a handout was available. "No matter," Edith smiles. "It was part of our first child Priscilla's education which nothing else could give her!"[6]

2. *Give regularly to your home church*—Most churches minister to the homeless and needy. So through your financial support of your church (1 Corinthians 16:2), you can indirectly lend a helping hand and extend your hand to the poor (Proverbs 31:20). My church stocks a "deacons' closet" for the homeless. Plus a portion of all giving to our church is used to support our missionaries. Your giving to your local church extends in many directions and even around the world.

3. *Keep your ear to the ground*—Take time to notice people around you who are in need. Then purchase double groceries and share them with a struggling couple. Or clean

out your wallet when an offering is taken for a special cause. You can also pass your children's clothes on to a young family who's fallen on hard times. When you go to garage sales, pick up needed items that could help others (an aluminum walker for a shut-in, a baby crib for an unwed mother). You can prepare a special meal for a woman undergoing chemotherapy. To reap the many blessings that come with such a ministry of giving, you must keep your ear to the ground. Then these golden opportunities won't pass you by!

4. *Support a worthy organization or person*—Right now I'm studying the women who followed Jesus and supported Him financially (Luke 8:2-3). They set a noble example for you and me because—just as they did—you and I can encourage many individuals and organizations with our financial gifts. You can contribute directly to a mission organization or support a missionary family you know. You can assist in the training of seminary students by giving to scholarship funds or helping with the purchase of textbooks. You can support young people who are going on a summer missions trip. Why not ask God how you can extend your hands and be involved in His work?

5. *Pray about a personal project*—As you're asking God about where He wants you to be involved in His work in the world, ask Him to direct you to your own personal ministry project which you can support financially. You might be surprised how God answers those prayers—as the following story illustrates.

Sitting in a missions conference, I was personally challenged when I learned how the Central American Mission (CAM) organization began. Two Canadian women, whose husbands owned a coffee plantation in Costa Rica, sat sharing a cup of tea one afternoon in 1879. Deeply concerned for the spiritual needs of the people in that part of the world, and realizing their personal limitations, they began asking God to provide a solution. In February 1891, the first missionary arrived from the United States. Out of the prayers of two women like you and me CAM was born! When you pray, God may touch your generous heart and give you that kind of vision for ministry. Wouldn't that be wonderful?

6. *Err on the side of generosity*—Evangelist Billy Graham smiled proudly as he said this of his wife Ruth: "She manages the fiscal affairs of the household—with...more generosity than precision!"[7] How lovely to have a generous heart! You see, like flowing water, money is less useful when it becomes stagnant. You don't want to be like the Dead Sea in Israel, vast and fed with fresh water but useless and dead because the water has no outlet!

Just a caution: If you're married, be sure you work with your husband to set a policy. Find out his views on giving and know where he wants to help out financially. Agree with him and honor his choices. Then set your mind, body, hands, and heart to work on those endeavors.

7. *Live out love*—When asked what love looks like, the early church father Augustine replied, "Love has hands to help others. It has feet to hasten to the poor and needy. It has eyes to see misery and want. It has ears to hear the sighs and sorrow of men. This is what love looks like." What a blessing you are to others as you live out this kind of love. It truly is beautiful in God's eyes!

An Invitation to Beauty

Now, dear one, it's time to evaluate ourselves. It's wonderful to excel in your home, to lead the way in management skills, to perfect your God-given abilities, to shine as a professional, to know that your husband is happy, to keep a tight rein on the family finances, and to watch your savings increase and investments soar. But God highly esteems this great mark of beauty in your life—mercy!

More than any virtue we've looked at so far, mercy reflects the presence of the Lord in your heart and your life. Mercy adds the lovely fragrance of the Lord to who you are and to all you do. Mercy pleases the Lord and is beautiful in His eyes. So I'm praying right now that you will sincerely desire and ask God to help you be a generous, helpful, loving, merciful, truly-beautiful-in-the-Lord woman who delights (and excels!) in giving a helping hand to any and all who are in need. Do it—in the name of the Lord!

~ 14 ~

A Double Blessing

Her Preparation

"She is not afraid of snow for her household,
for all her household is clothed with scarlet."
Proverbs 31:21

No one, Jesus proclaimed in His famous Sermon on the Mount, was ever arrayed in clothing as splendid and grand as King Solomon of the Old Testament (Matthew 6:29).

But the family of the Proverbs 31 woman may have come close!

What joy her loved ones stir in her heart—and what joy she brings them as they wear the masterpieces she spins and weaves and decorates. They step out into the bleak streets of Israel clothed like royalty. When her family walks down the street, people can't help but notice!

Now before you start thinking that God's beautiful woman is out of balance here, that she's overly concerned about appearances, that we've found a flaw, and before you write her off as a spendthrift or a clotheshorse, remember something that this godly woman knows to be fact: "Charm is deceitful and beauty is vain" (Proverbs 31:30). Far from being conceited or worldly, God's beautiful woman once again demonstrates her concern and care for other people, her creativity, and her great ability to work. Only this time her efforts are visible to all because now her character expresses itself in her family's clothing.

Looking to the Future

It's a fact! It snows in Israel! I had a hard time imagining this while Jim and I experienced its extreme heat during our studies, as we hiked the dry, barren hills, as we worried more about carrying enough drinking water than about what we wore or how we looked! Even though I have a picture clipped out of the *Los Angeles Times* of devout Jews worshiping at Jerusalem's wailing wall in a foot of snow, I still struggled to imagine snow in Israel.

So I asked our instructor Bill Schlegel, an American who has lived in Israel for thirteen years. "Yes," he heartily nodded, "believe it!" Then he described Jerusalem's wet, cold, windy winters that people endure in their frigid stone buildings, on stone streets, and behind stone walls and with little or no heat. Bill himself went without heat one winter for two months, and that winter it snowed 15 inches—twice! Despite the unrelenting heat I experienced, one can count on snow almost annually in Palestine.

God's beautiful woman knows that snow comes to her homeland, but "she is not afraid of snow for her household" (Proverbs 31:21). Why? Because she's prepared for the future, whatever it will hold. Ever looking ahead, she wisely provides for her family. "All her household is clothed with scarlet," verse 21 concludes.

Now this foresight and her proactive efforts shouldn't be a surprise to us. For thirteen chapters we've seen the

Proverbs 31 woman's great heart of love, her wisdom, her willingness, her ability to plan ahead, and her management tactics. We know that she's a planner who is always looking to the future and planning for it (verses 15 and 27). I can easily imagine that, long before a single snowflake even thought of forming, a scene like this occurred:

Rising early one morning (verse 15), this oh-so-beautiful-in-God's-eye's woman turns her prayer concerns to her dear family. As she lifts each of them to God in prayer and considers ways to express her love to them, she grabs her "to do" list and jots several notes to herself: "Prepare for winter. Get wool. Locate some red dye. Spin yarn. Weave fabric. Make winter coats." She will bless her family with the winter clothing they need!

"Extended Care" Living

But notice just who is fortunate enough to be blessed in this way. The verse says, "*All* her household is clothed with scarlet" (Proverbs 31:21). Everyone who lives under this beautiful woman's roof is handsomely and warmly clothed with scarlet cloaks of wool for winter.

You see, the Proverbs 31 woman takes care of everyone. That's why I'm calling her kind of care "extended care"! We've seen in verse 20 her care extended to the poor and afflicted. Whether the need is food or clothing, nursing assistance or help cleaning a house, she offers it.

But God's beautiful woman also extends her care to her extended family. Consider who would be living under her roof. We've met her husband and heard that there are children. Also in her day (and for many of us, too) elderly parents are a part of the household. Married children—and their children—are probably there. So are orphaned nieces and nephews and widowed relations. And, oh yes, the servants (verse 15)! Quite a group depends on her provision, and she provides generously. "All her household is clothed with scarlet!"

Clothes Fit for a King

And what does it mean that God's beautiful woman clothes her family members in "scarlet"? The color reveals much about her provision.

- *Warmth*—Red, or scarlet (meaning "to shine"), indicates the retention of heat.[1]
- *Stately appearance*—Scarlet is the color of kings' clothing[2] and signifies dignity,[3] luxury, and magnificence.[4]
- *Quality*—Only the best will do for this beautiful woman's family. The fact that they are clothed with wool—and with scarlet wool at that!—speaks of the quality clothing she provides. Then, as well as now, very few people owned more than one woolen overcoat.
- *Double thickness*—I'm sure you've felt the difference between cheap, thin wool and that which is rich and heavy. Well, one meaning of the Hebrew word for scarlet is "double," and of course God's beautiful woman would only make quality, double-thick clothing, extending a double blessing to her brood.
- *Double dipped*—Wool has to be dyed the color scarlet, and to become truly scarlet, wool was dipped into the dye more than once.
- *Costly*—Because of the dye and the added labor and time, scarlet robes were luxurious and costly.[5]

It's amazing that the mere mention of scarlet clothing reveals so much about the heart of the seamstress and conveys such a powerful message from that heart to the heart of those for whom she sews!

The How-To's of Beauty

Even more amazing is that you and I are able to send the same powerful message of love. Our family members will be blessed when we care enough to prepare and provide for their future needs. Just as God's beautiful woman, armed with her calendar and a "to do" list, takes the time to anticipate her family's future needs and prepare for them, so can you. Here are a few items to put at the top of your "to do" list.

1. Determine future needs—Lay out a one-year calendar and determine your future needs. Think about the maintenance work you need done inside your home—winterizing, summerizing, or cleaning the upholstery, drapes, and carpets. Wool clothes need to be moth-proofed and stored. Firewood needs to be ordered.

Next, think through your outdoor responsibilities. Do you have a swimming pool to be emptied, roses to be pruned back, or gutters to be cleared out? When do you need to prepare your garden, plant your seeds, and bury your bulbs?

And which special family occasions are coming up? Is someone graduating, getting married, or having a baby? Have you marked all the birthdays and anniversaries on your calendar? You already know you have Thanksgiving and Christmas and Easter—and vacations—to prepare for! And the list goes on with back-to-school preparations, open houses, special guests for dinner, family reunions, etc.

Mark every anticipated future event and need on your

calendar. Your goal is, just as it is for God's beautiful woman, to be far-sighted, to look forward through your eyes of love and, acting in wisdom, prepare!

2. *Prepare for emergencies*—This item was slow in making sense to me, but after the 6.8 earthquake my family went through in Southern California in 1994, it tops my list! Caught without a single flashlight, we now have one in every room...and purse...and drawer...and suitcase...and car. And I never leave home without one!

But this call to preparedness applies to everyone everywhere, not just to others living in earthquake country. My parents lived in tornado country—and they were prepared. My daughter Courtney lived in Kauai where there are hurricanes. Do you live in a picturesque snowy region—where there might be avalanches? Or along a beautiful river bank—that may flood with too much rain?

Let me repeat myself: Everyone everywhere needs to prepare for emergencies. Each of us needs to practice fire drills, determine emergency plans, and gather first-aid supplies, emergency food, and water. God's beautiful woman is "not afraid" (verse 21) because she is *prepared*, and—with a little preparation—you can enjoy that same peace of mind.

3. *Care for the clothing*—Top on the list when it comes to caring for your family's clothes is keeping the clothes clean. So pick a day to be wash day, and don't forget—this one is hard for me!—the laundry isn't done until it's washed, dried, folded, pressed, *and* put away! Your goal is to provide clothes that are ready to wear, and that means sewing on those loose or missing buttons. Also see that clothes are protected—moth-proofed, stored, and covered—when necessary. The dollar value of your clothes adds up. Just ask your insurance agent!

In the day of the Proverbs 31 woman, clothes were actually used as money for deposits and trade (Proverbs 20:16).

4. *Consider quality*—Just as the Marines only need "a few good men," your family only needs a few good clothes. It's obvious (by the scarlet color) that God's beautiful woman concerns herself with providing quality clothes for her family—not quantity!

5. *Consider comfort*—The comfort, protection, warmth, and health of your family is undoubtedly a major concern for you, and that's a concern that God's beautiful woman shares. In fact, there's no doubt that her concern for her family's comfort is the motivation behind the scarlet garments. The clothing is red, of double thickness, and of high quality for a reason: Such a coat would be warm as well as beautiful—a double blessing!

6. *Consider beauty*—The woman who is beautiful in God's eyes models His standards for us in all of her life, including how she provides clothing for her family. Since she is a professional weaver and artist, wouldn't you imagine that the clothes she provides for her household are beautiful? Obviously they were colorful and fine, intricately woven with beads, jewels, and gold thread (Proverbs 31:21,22,24). But knowing the virtues of the Proverbs 31 woman, I'm confident that her expression of beauty is never overdone. The clothes she makes are simply another expression of her great love—which you can express to your family, too, straight from your own beautiful heart.

Now, dear reader, I simply can't leave this subject without telling you about my friend LaTonya, a mother of five girls. It makes my day when I see her with her smiling husband and those five darling daughters all dressed up on Sunday morning. I can't imagine the time it takes LaTonya to braid, ribbon, and barrette all the little pigtails, ponytails, and hair-dos! From their polished little patent-leather shoes to their starched-and-ironed dresses, from their scrubbed-until-they-shine faces and glistening hair to their tiny purses and Bibles, they are little testimonies to LaTonya's loving care. Her family is truly blessed by her devotion to provide for them—and yours will be, too!

An Invitation to Beauty

At first glance a chapter on clothing and preparation doesn't look terribly important, does it? But, dear one, this chapter is about yet another virtue this woman who is beautiful in God's eyes possesses. It's about preparation.

First of all, know that the work of preparation is important to God and that He will guide your planning. After all, He provides for us. His very name is "Jehovah-jireh, God will provide"! You and I mirror this aspect of His character when we provide for our loved ones, and our provision happens more easily—if not more bountifully—when we plan and prepare. Second, when we work to provide clothing for our family and when we prepare for their future needs, our actions speak forth a loud message of love. Then, having prepared for the seasons of life and having placed your trust in our caring, loving, gracious, all-sufficient God, there is never a place in your home for fear. Blessed by your preparations *and* by God's provision, your loved ones are indeed doubly blessed!

~ 15 ~

A Tapestry of Beauty

Her Handiwork

"She makes herself coverings of tapestry;
her clothing is silk and purple."
Proverbs 31:22 (KJV)

Before you and I catch our first—and only!—glimpse of the woman who is beautiful in God's eyes actually doing something for herself, I want us to pause and look back at the path we've been traveling. Since we began our climb in the first chapter (remember Masada?), we've taken step after step toward God's kind of beauty, guided along by His lovely Proverbs 31 woman.

We've seen in the wonder of her character that God's beautiful woman is truly a person of virtue and excellence. We've seen how her strength of mind and body enables her to handle well the challenges and demands of daily life. We've marveled at her constant, deep love for her husband and children, a love which she lives out in her actions. She finds no sacrifice for them too costly. And far from stopping at her doorpost, her love extends beyond her family to the needy in her household and community. We have no doubt about her capable management, her creativity, or her awesome diligence.

As I mentioned earlier, mere survival was the paramount issue for people of the Old Testament as each new day dawned in their destitute land. But we've seen this woman, who is an army of virtues, not only provide the essentials of existence, but provide abundantly—so much so that she has enough to give to the poor and some to sell to those who can afford it! Now, with the basics of food and clothing for her family taken care of, she turns her attention to decorating her home. We are allowed to peek into the home of God's beautiful woman and even catch a glimpse of her. But I don't want to race ahead of our text. First her beautiful home!

House Beautiful

What woman doesn't delight in making her home a place of beauty? And God's beautiful woman is no different. In fact she surpasses them all (Proverbs 31:29)!

Proverbs 31:22 says, "She makes herself coverings of tapestry." At first glance this sentence seems to be describing her wardrobe, but the "coverings of tapestry" are actually her home furnishings. Some translators of the Bible call these furnishings carpets, woven coverlets, and upholstery.[1] One version even says, "She makes her own quilts"![2]

As we've seen, weaving plays an important role in the life of God's beautiful woman and in her Middle Eastern culture. A creative artist with an end product in mind, she gathers wool and flax and then works the raw materials into a usable state. Spending many late night hours with her distaff and spindle, she spins her wool and flax into yarn and thread, weaves it into fantastic fabrics only an artist could envision, and uses it to clothe her family—in the red of royalty, clothing fit for kings! But she has leftover yarn, fabric, creativity, and energy! So why not make tapestries of beauty for the home, tapestries also fit for kings?

So, with busy hands and an overflowing heart of love, God's beautiful woman sets about making tapestry for pillows, blankets, cushions, drapes, rugs, wall hangings, tablecloths, runners, mats, and upholstery to adorn her home. Our beautiful weaver also designs and makes napkins, hand towels, sheets, quilts, coverlets, and bedspreads. A variety of colors, textures, patterns, and styles adds beauty and warmth to her stone house, transforming it into a delight for the senses. She truly is an artist! Each object of her handiwork is a masterpiece!

This fact is supported by an image hidden in the wording of verse 22 and created by the word *makes* ("she *makes* herself coverings of tapestry"). Our Proverbs 31 woman makes the tapestry in the basic sense: She uses her hands to do this hard work. But *makes* also means "spreads" or "decks." The Hebrew language paints a picture of an enticing bed of comfort and luxury.[3] When God's beautiful woman is finished, her bed is "spread" with colorfully woven pillows, mattresses, coverlets, and tapestry.[4] Indeed, her entire home is "decked out," a rich tapestry of beauty!

Beauty Check

Before we leave the Proverbs 31 woman's house and home, let's take a look around our own home at the tapestry of beauty we're weaving for our House Beautiful.

Check #1: Pretend you're a visitor—Walk through the place where you live. What do you see? What would a guest notice? What mood does your home invite? What pleases you about what you see—and what would you like to improve? Any eyesores? Clutter? As the homemaker—the maker of your home—you are in the position to generate powerful impressions and create a welcoming atmosphere and beautiful environment.

Check #2: Plan several home improvements—God's beautiful woman is certainly a do-it-yourselfer! Keep that in mind as you take inventory of your home. What projects are you working on? Right now I'm hunting for some red paisley sheets to make into curtains for my office window. Do your cabinets need a fresh coat of stain or polish? Are there grease spots on your carpet you could remove with a little elbow grease? Do your windows need a good cleaning? What repairs have you been putting off?

Not all home improvements cost money. In fact, the greatest improvement of all can be cleaning up and removing clutter! (I'll be cleaning out my bedroom closet when this book is done! I'm terribly convicted just writing about clutter!) Some of the most dramatic improvements come from your heart and mind. I'm talking about putting a single flower in a bud vase, displaying an item of color or interest, rearranging furniture, adding knickknacks to the coffee tables, and using some personal treasures to add your caring touch and unique flair to your decor.

Check #3: Pass it by your husband—God's beautiful woman has her priorities in order. The first item on her list is clothing for her family. After that comes the house. Be sure—with your husband and your checkbook—that now is the right time to spend money on home decor. After all, God's beautiful woman knows how to wait (Proverbs 19:2).

Check #4: Put in some overtime—And I mean put in some overtime at home, not at the office. God's beautiful woman works long and late (Proverbs 31:18). So set aside a Saturday or an evening or two for a home-improvement project.

Wherever home is for you, it's an expression of *you*—*your* virtues, *your* abilities, *your* love. You may not be able to determine the kind of home you have, but you can determine its beauty. You control whether it's clean, organized, and orderly. You also choose your favorite colors, styles, and moods.

But maybe your home is hardly ideal. Well, consider some of the places your sisters in the Bible called home! Eve cared for a garden. Mrs. Noah managed an ark. Sarah was queen of a tent. Esther lived in a palace in a foreign land. Mary spent time in a stable. Peter's mother-in-law offered the gift of hospitality in her stone dwelling. So no matter how often the place you live changes, *you* are the beautiful woman with the beautiful heart who turns it into a home. *You* are in charge of the handiwork and decorations that make your residence a "Home, Sweet Home"!

I faced a real homemaking challenge when our family served as missionaries in Singapore. Over there, both the houses we lived in were concrete—walls, floors, and ceilings. (In fact, when we cleaned the house, we just turned on the hose and hosed it down and out!) There on the equator, far away from all my family and friends, I nevertheless "built" my home, giving it all the touches of warmth and love I could (Proverbs 14:1). Then, returning to the United States, we faced more challenges as we moved four times in two months, sleeping in sleeping bags on the floor in two of those places. But each place was home because I was determined to make it one! Even four sleeping bags lying in a row can be beautiful in a place you're making home!

A Touch of Class

At last! Everyone has been well taken care of. Those in need are warm. The family members are striking in their garments of red. The house is beautiful and able to minister love and peace to all who pass through its doorway. Now it is time for God's beautiful woman to think about what she herself will wear. It's time for her to put on the ornaments suited to her station and means.

First we see that "her clothing is silk and purple" (Proverbs 31:22). Ever the artist and a grand lady, she gives her clothing a touch of class. God's beautiful woman deserves silk and purple—and it becomes her! As a woman of virtue, wisdom, strength, and dignity, she is precisely the caliber of woman who should wear such regal clothing. Her clothing is simply a reflection of her character.

Although Proverbs reports that her clothing is made of silk, that word is better understood as fine linen, the fabric she weaves from her flax. Elegance has emerged as she has sewn, and now, when touched by the sun, the fine white linen glistens like silk. What she fashions for herself to wear reveals her inner clothing of "strength and dignity" (verse 25).

We also learn that her clothes are purple, colored by a rare and costly dye extracted in minute quantities from a shellfish found on the eastern shores of the Mediterranean Sea.[5] God's beautiful woman probably exchanged her handiwork for this rare, expensive dye when the merchant ships came in. The purple is clearly another indication of her hard work and shrewd management.

A Touch of Taste

All this talk of expense and exquisiteness may sound proud or showy or frivolous, but we need to keep in mind a few facts.

First of all, God's beautiful woman does not have a closet full of clothes. She has a few quality items, each of which took her months (maybe even a year) to make for herself.

Second, Proverbs 31 is a poem of praise. Along with her many virtues, she is praised for the beauty of her wardrobe. Her clothes are cut from fantastically woven handmade fabrics, they are adorned with detailed needlework, and they are warm, rich, and regal in color—and she does all this herself, starting with raw flax and wool (verse 13) and ending with splendid garments.

Also don't forget that God's beautiful woman never forgets her priorities. She would never slight others in order to parade in finery. Such selfishness would be neither praiseworthy nor beautiful! She rightly places herself last.

Finally, remember that these words of Proverbs 31 are the words of another noble woman. And who knows a woman better than another woman? King Lemuel's mother makes a special point of telling him how the woman of his dreams should be dressed. This knowing mother focuses on:

- The *position* in society which God's beautiful woman holds—She is a woman of dignity, wealth, and high ranking, and her clothing is suitable to her station.

- Her *practice* of hard work and skillful management which pays off in practical ways—She has the finances and is willing to invest the time and effort to dress according to her position.

- Her *professional status*—As she sails along the cobblestone passages that crisscross Jerusalem, she is a walking advertisement for her skillful handiwork. A seamstress certainly should not dress shabbily!

- Her *praiseworthy character*—The virtuous wife is robed in what speaks of her true character and dignity.

With this perspective in mind, we gladly join with the young prince's mother as she exults, "Give her of the fruit of her hands, and let her own works praise her in the gates" (Proverbs 31:31)! This woman who is altogether beautiful in God's eyes is fully deserving of her finery.

The How-To's of Beauty

Considering what God is saying to us in Proverbs 31:22 about our personal wardrobe, I believe His message comes down to three main ideas.

1. *Your care*—Taking care of your clothes is as important as the clothes themselves. Your level of care shows up in the mending of a tear, the sewing-on of a button, the removal of a spot, the washing of dirty clothes, and (don't forget that most important final step) the ironing-out of wrinkles and the ironing-in of creases! The way you care for your clothes reveals something of your character and what you value. So consider the general condition and overall appearance of your clothes. What message might the way you take care of your clothes be sending? Beauty begins with cleanliness and neatness.

2. *Your reflection*—You're not the only person affected by your appearance. How you dress and how you look also sends a message about your family. When you maintain a certain level of cleanliness and dignity in public, you can be a positive reflection on your husband and his name, his reputation, and his (and your!) children.

The husband of God's beautiful woman "is known in the gates" (verse 23), but not as the poor man who's married to a slob or the man whose wife is a mess. (As one clever author notes, "MRS. in front of your name does not mean *miserable rut of sloppiness!*"[6]) No, the husband of the Proverbs 31 woman is known in the gates as the man who is married to a *lady*, a meticulous, gracious, attractive woman of character.

And it's no different for you or me! How we look is a direct reflection on our husband and our children—and even our parents and the company we work for! Other people can form their opinions of your entire family based on their perception of you, which can be based on how you look. That being the case, I try to follow this bit of advice: "Be different, if it means being cleaner, neater, and better groomed than the group. It is always better to arrive for any function looking slightly better, rather than slightly worse than the others."[7]

3. *Your standards*—As women seeking the kind of beauty God highly esteems, you and I want to follow His standards. And exactly what are those standards? *Modesty* heads His list, which continues with *soberness* (meaning acting or dressing in a proper and sensible manner), *moderation*, *discretion*, and *chasteness* (see 1 Timothy 2:9 and Titus 2:5). These words may sound old-fashioned, but these qualities flow out of a heart intent on godliness (1 Timothy 2:10). And our loving Lord is always more concerned about the clothing of your heart than He is with how you clothe your external, outer, physical body: "Do not let your beauty be that outward adorning of arranging the hair, of wearing gold, or of putting on fine apparel; but let it be the hidden person of the heart, with the incorruptible ornament of a gentle and quiet spirit, which is very precious in the sight of God" (1 Peter 3:3-4). Amen!

An Invitation to Beauty

Now it's your turn to express yourself creatively in the beauty of your home and your clothing. Everything in its time!

The Proverbs 31 woman who is beautiful in God's eyes is a weaver, but you are a weaver, too. You can weave your own tapestry of beauty right in your own home—wherever home is! What will you need? In a word, love. With threads of love woven by hands of love and expressing a heart of love, you can creatively transform even a camper into a home. That transformation occurs anywhere and anytime your heart and handiwork come together.

Know then, dear weaver of beauty, that God has given us opportunity upon opportunity to not only express our love but to be creative as we share that love. Your decorations of both home and wardrobe can bless so many by their beauty. We read in the psalms that "the heavens declare the glory of God; and the firmament shows His handiwork" (Psalm 19:1). On a smaller scale, your handiwork can also bring glory to God *and* show forth something of His beauty. So set your heart in motion, your mind to spinning, and your fingers to work and see what handiwork you can generate to glorify your wonderful God!

~ 16 ~

A Man of Influence

HER HUSBAND

"Her husband is known in the gates,
when he sits among the elders of the land."
Proverbs 31:23

Although our culture may not value it, one of the wife's most important roles is to support her husband. A woman who is beautiful in God's eyes knows how to do just that. Let me give you the example of Susannah Spurgeon, the wife of Charles Spurgeon, famed preacher at London's Metropolitan Tabernacle. His ministry was thriving, but he became concerned that he might be neglecting his children, so Charles Spurgeon returned home earlier than usual one evening. Opening the door, he was surprised to find no children in the hall. Ascending the stairs, he heard his wife's voice and knew that she was engaged in prayer with the children. She named each of the children in prayer. When she finished her prayer and her nightly instructions to their little ones, Spurgeon thought, "I can go on with my work. My children are well cared for."[1] Imagine! Because of her faithfulness and diligence at home, Mrs. Spurgeon gave the world Charles Haddon Spurgeon, his words which continue to stir and convict hearts today, and their two sons, who also became ministers.

Marriage to a Man of Influence

At this point of Proverbs 31, we finally learn something about the husband of God's beautiful woman! You and I were introduced to him in verse 11 as a trusting husband who rests his soul safely upon the character of his beautiful-in-God's-eyes wife. He's the fortunate man she is committed to doing good to all the days of her life (verse 12). We've witnessed the meals she prepares for him (verse 15), as well as her management of his home (verse 15) and finances (verse 11). And, thanks to her handiwork, he is splendidly clothed in scarlet (verse 21). "Who can find a virtuous wife (verse 10)?" Well, this man has! God has definitely graced him with one of His truly beautiful women!

In addition to being richly blessed by God through his wife, this man is himself a blessing to many. You see, he is a man of influence. Let me explain.

"Her husband is known in the gates, when he sits among the elders of the land" (Proverbs 31:23). In the days of the Proverbs 31 woman, cities were walled around for protection, but gates allowed for entrance and exit. These gated entrances contained one or more large rooms built into the city wall. In fact, whenever Jim and I visited any sizable city, we saw evidence of the thick stone walls that once protected it and the many spacious chambered gates. Some of these compartments were set aside as guard rooms, complete with a well for water, a place for a fire, and inside steps leading up to the top of the wall. Other chambers served as official government offices.

And exactly what happened in the gates as the townspeople passed through them in their daily comings and goings? In the coolness and protection of these stone rooms, legal and governmental decisions were made. Deliberations took place. Political issues were settled. Official proclamations and edicts were read. Matters of public welfare were transacted. Judgments were administered. Legal questions were decided.

This is the place where the husband of the Proverbs 31 woman is "known" (verse 23). In fact, known to be a reputable man, he "sits among the elders of the land." Clearly, he makes a notable contribution to public life. Recognized as a leader, he is in a position to influence the life of the community. He may even have had a seat in the gate, signifying his status as a man of importance and an able counselor. He may have been one of the elders, the judicial body which ruled the land. This prestigious group met daily in the town gate to transact any public business or decide cases that were brought before them.[2] Whatever the specific situation, we see that this man is well known because he sits in the council chambers with other respected civic leaders who are conducting legal business.[3] An honored citizen, he is held in high esteem by the townspeople and the officials of his community and, therefore, is truly a man of influence.

Behind Every Good Man

Do you remember the setting for the teaching of Proverbs 31:10-31? A young prince—a leader in the making, a king to be, a ruler in process, a future man of influence—is learning the ABCs of life (Proverbs 31:1). His wise and beautiful-in-God's-eyes mother is herself married to a leader, a king, a ruler, a man of influence. So, faithful, passionate teacher that she is, she has been describing for her young son the kind of wife a man of influence needs. So far we've seen that this woman must be fit for a king, as powerful and effective in her realm as he will be in his, and, like him, earning the respect and esteem of the community as she serves. Clearly, God's wise mother knows that behind every good man stands a good woman! (As a more modern "proverb" puts it, "Generally, when a man climbs the ladder to success, his wife is holding the ladder!")

As I think about the husband and wife pictured in Proverbs 31, I think of them as a pair of bookends. Both of them are pillars in the community, both are known in the gates (verses 23 and 31), and both are committed to the good of others (verses 20 and 23). Although their spheres of influence are different, they both exhibit the same virtuous character as they live with the same purpose, that of serving others. Just as wise Solomon noted, "Two are better than one" (Ecclesiastes 4:9). As evidence, consider how this matched set works together.

- He contributes to the community; she is his helpmeet (Genesis 2:18).
- He is successful in the realm of city management; she is successful in the realm of family and home management.
- He is happy at work; she is happy working at home.
- He is respected and held in high esteem; she preserves and advances his honor by her conduct and example.
- He is deferred to as a solid, influential citizen; she brings credit to him.
- He is a counselor, a man of common sense and not-so-common insight; she speaks with loving wisdom.

- He exerts his influence on the life of the community in the city gates; she influences the community from home.
- He is known for his solid character and important contributions; so is she.
- He has achieved some worldly wealth and social status; she improves his financial situation as well as his social standing by what she is to him and what she does for him as a wife.
- He has reached his professional aims; she has helped him do so by her diligence and frugality.
- He has earned prestige; she is respected for her creative handiwork.
- He is a virtuous man; she is a virtuous woman.
- He is crowned with honor; she is his crown (Proverbs 12:4).

A Woman of Influence

Oh, my dear friend, it's vital that you and I understand the inestimable contribution we can make to our husband as he pursues his career and serves the Lord in his job. First consider how this man of influence is his wife's gift to the people. He's out there in public. He leaves home daily, following God's plan for his life and making a difference in the community, if not the world!

Behind him, however, stands this wonderful, beautiful woman. One reason he can succeed and thrive in his position of influence is the fact that he has no worries at home. In fact, his honorable and prosperous home enhances his reputation. By virtue of his *wife's* character and *her* ability to manage the home, *he* is able to serve in his position of influence. *She* enables *him* to sit in the gate among the elders of the land. The well-ordered home which *she* runs reflects positively on her husband as *he* has risen in worldly wealth and social power. Furthermore, *her* diligence and thriftiness at home have enabled *him* to dream his dreams and reach them. The influence our beautiful woman has had on her husband has clearly helped him become a man of influence in the community.

Now I want to ask you whether you see your husband's service "out there" as your gift to the people he serves. After all, *you* are the one who fills him up and sends him off to be a blessing to others. He is *your* contribution to society, to the company he works for, to the people in his office, to his customers, to his students, to his flock—whatever the case may be.

And he is your contribution whether you hold down a job or spend every waking minute at home. You support him not because you may or may not earn a paycheck yourself. Your support is a matter of your heart and your home; the issue is how you take care of him, his home, and his children. It's about your beautiful contribution to his well-being.

The How-To's of Beauty

Exactly how do you and I make that valuable contribution? How do we support our husband and beautify his life? Here are some ideas.

1. Praise him—Every human being appreciates words of sincere praise, and your husband is no different. So, as Proverbs 3:27 says, "Do not withhold good from those to whom it is due, when it is in the power of your hand to do so." It is definitely in the power of your hand—and heart and mouth!—to praise your man, so do so today and every day of your life (Proverbs 31:12). As someone has quipped, "He can't read it on his tombstone when he's dead!"

2. *Encourage him*—Every human being—including your dear husband—also needs encouragement. Correction can help, but encouragement can help far more, as an unidentified husband realized. Marveling about his wife, he wrote, "You see some hidden, struggling trait, encourage it and make it great!" Proverbs 12:25 says, "A good word makes the heart glad," and a good word from you gives your husband courage to face life's challenges. So open that beautiful mouth and speak words of wisdom and kindness. Let love and encouragement flow (Proverbs 31:26).

3. *Take care of your marriage*—The truth isn't very romantic, but in case you haven't noticed, marriage is work! Martin Luther observed, "Marriage is not a joke. It must be worked on, and prayed over."[4] As a wife, you are called to pray for your husband and to respect him (Ephesians 5:33). The Amplified Bible explains it this way: "Let the wife see that she respects and reverences her husband—that she notices him, regards him, honors him, prefers him, venerates and esteems him; and that she defers to him, praises him, and loves and admires him exceedingly."[5] This is a tall order, an order for a lifetime! But if you follow through on this calling from God, you'll be a beautiful wife—and a wife who enjoys a beautiful marriage.

4. *Take care of your family*—The husband of the Proverbs 31 woman is a man of influence on his job and in his community because his wife is a woman of influence in the home. And here's another calling from God—and another of His standards of beauty: You are to take care of your family. You are to take seriously the meals, the schedule, the

clothing, the counsel and training you give the children. By running his home smoothly and effectively, you contribute to both your husband's public reputation and his usefulness in the church (see 1 Timothy 3:4-5). Nothing credits a man as much as a beautiful-in-God's-eyes wife and a beautifully behaved family!

5. *Take care of your home*—Be sure all is well at home. Tap into God's great grace for help to handle the daily drudgeries and even the unexpected challenges of life. Ask the Lord to help you delight in watching over the ways of your household (verse 27).

6. *Take care of your finances*—Your wise money management is a gift to your husband. It buys him some financial freedom to follow his abilities and his heart into an occupation of choice rather than necessity. By keeping watch over your family day by day, by holding down the spending, upping the savings, and increasing the earnings, you follow in the footsteps of God's wise and beautiful woman.

7. *Let him go*—When Jim first began serving on our church's pastoral staff, I struggled to get used to his absences, his late hours, and his seven-day-a-week calling. The following words from a wife's prayer of relinquishment showed me a better way to support and serve Jim; they helped me to let Jim go.

> God...I declare afresh that my husband belongs to You, not to me. I have yielded all right to him—all right to his time, his understanding, his attention, his love. I will take what You give back as privileges to be used for my enjoyment and for Your glory as long as You see fit to give these privileges to us.
>
> I purpose to refuse [to let] any thoughts of self-pity,

> criticism, jealousy, or resentment creep in when these precious privileges are denied—when his time is taken up by others…when he seems to have failed in consideration and love.
>
> Lord…help Yourself to my husband's life to spend it however You choose to let him spend it, regardless of the disadvantages to me personally.[6]

These words express a significantly more beautiful attitude than clinging, whining, complaining, nagging, and begrudging your husband the time he needs to do what he needs to do.

8. *Support his dreams*—A pastor's wife I greatly admire helped me tremendously when Jim entered seminary to prepare for a life of ministry. When I asked for her Number One piece of advice for a struggling seminary wife, she responded with a four-page letter. Her wise advice included the following: "Dream with your husband about the effect of his ministry. Share in the expectation and excitement together. Later on the goals you establish will issue from 'the dream.' It will carry you during dry and trying times and help you remain faithful to the Lord, always seeking His best. 'The dream' keeps your focus on our great God and not on the day-to-day situations."

These words express a heart attitude that must indeed be beautiful in God's eyes. So, whatever your husband's job, his place of employment, his sphere of influence, pour your strength into him by supporting rather than ignoring, belittling, or even laughing at his dreams.

9. *Realize that your behavior is a reflection on him*—The husband of the Proverbs 31 woman "is known in the gates" (verse

23) for, among other things, having a worthy wife! Is that one of the reasons your husband is known and respected?

An Invitation to Beauty

Isn't Proverbs 31:23 a beautiful and empowering verse of Scripture? If you're married, I hope you are realizing that you and your husband are not two separate entities pursuing two separate causes in two separate directions. No, you are like a pair of bookends. You stand together as a unit, facing together and managing together all the facets and challenges, all the causes and concerns, all the opportunities and dreams that make up your life together. Rejoice that you are equal in influence and contribution, although you live out that influence and contribution in separate arenas. Rejoice when your husband is the center of attention, when he excels, when he is recognized and honored. Rejoice in the privilege of following Jesus' footsteps and giving your life for your husband in sacrificial love, making the supreme sacrifice of your self for him.

As you face this challenge, I invite you to pray and ask God to help you support your husband in ways that will strengthen him and glorify God. Make a Proverbs 31:12 commitment to do your husband good all the days of your life by praising him, encouraging him, nurturing your marriage, serving your family, tending to your home, watching over the finances, supporting his dreams, and praying for his success—that he may be a man of godly influence in his work and his community.

~ 17 ~

A Creative Professional

Her Industry

"She makes linen garments and sells them,
and supplies sashes for the merchants."
Proverbs 31:24

I love hearing the success stories of artists and entrepreneurs. (In fact, I have folders full of these remarkable tales!) Whenever I hear about a woman our society labels "successful," I wonder, "How did it happen? What steps did she take? Where did her knowledge and skills come from?" Amazingly, as each woman's story unfolds, two common essentials for success emerge: She developed *something personal* into *something professional.*

As I write this chapter, I can think of many women who fit this description of success. They are accomplished, energetic, ever-learning. And best of all, they are dedicated to teaching women like you and me the skills for homemaking, decorating, food preparation, crafts, gift making, gardening, and scrapbooking. These wonderful women love their homes and love being busy and creative. And they want to show others how to do the same and experience the same joy and fulfillment.

When I think of women like this, I can't help but recall God's assignment to His women to be "teachers of good things" (Titus 2:3). I know I am greatly blessed to have grown up in the Lord and in the church in the shadow of an army of these industrious women who actively pass on what they know.

Whatever skills and talents God has given to you, and whatever knowledge you possess that has turned *something personal* into *something professional*, I hope you will take every opportunity to better the lives of others. I pray that you will dedicate yourself to heeding God's assignment to you to fill others with the "good things" that you know and they yearn to know!

You and I may never take our skills to a business or professional level, but each of us can set our hearts on creating beauty in our homes for those who enter. Like God's beautiful Proverbs 31 woman, we can develop an eye and a heart for beauty. Our homes provide the perfect soil for the joyous creativity that will result. In fact, you and I can nurture our own creative enterprises right there and right now by giving our wholehearted attention to our daily work at home (something personal). With the joy of the Lord as our strength (Nehemiah 8:10), we can transform our daily work into enduring works of art.

The Birth of a Business

Just as the pattern in a piece of wood repeats itself in cut after cut, so weaving is ingrained in the soul of the Proverbs 31 woman. It's definitely her "thing"! Just look at the number of times the little prince's mother mentions our beautiful woman's weaving: she seeks wool and flax for her fabrics (verse 13); she sits up late processing her raw materials by candlelight (verses 18-19); she gives her warm handmade garments to the poor (verse 20); and she regally decks out her family, her home, and herself with her handiwork (verses 21-22).

Now young King Lemuel's mother points once again to the dignity and beauty of the Proverbs 31 woman's skills as a weaver: "She makes linen garments and sells them, and supplies sashes for the merchants" (verse 24).

Moving systematically through this poem of praise, you and I have watched this woman who is so beautiful in God's eyes expand her sphere of influence and industry. Now we realize that her efforts have overflowed the banks of hearth and home and crossed over the boundaries of community. She has created a full-fledged industry that reaches to the markets of the known world. Her handiwork—originally created at home from a heart of love for those near and dear to her—is now at the heart of a thriving business. The beautiful work of her hands is carried by merchant ships and camel caravans to the ends of the earth. In case you were bothered by her not being a "career woman," you can see that she is—and is she ever! The selling of her items to foreign markets speaks of the quality of her work, explains her prosperity, and proves that she is a creative professional.[1] Something personal became something professional!

The Expression of Creativity

Clearly, in the case of God's beautiful woman, her God-given creativity plus the desire to better her family finances added up to a profession. Something personal (her ability and her desires for her family) became something professional (her cottage industry).

And it all began with an outlet for her creativity: "She makes linen garments" (Proverbs 31:24). First she made the linen fabric itself, and then she made the clothes from it.

The fineness of her linen made it soft and usable for bedclothes, undergarments, or lightweight tunic-like smocks worn in the summer on a bare body. Her linen garments were thin and fine—and therefore costly!

This beautiful woman's handiwork also includes sashes, and we see that she "supplies sashes for the merchants" (verse 24). Like a belt or girdle, a sash was worn to gather the flowing garments (still worn in Israel today) so that movement was easier. Leather belts were common, but a linen sash or belt was more attractive and more costly, woven with gold and silver thread and studded with jewels and gold. These were the works of art she "supplies...for the merchants."

The Enrichment of Estate

For the Proverbs 31 woman a business was born when something personal to her became something professional. Her business grew out of her personal creativity *and* her personal desire to enrich her estate. So "she makes linen garments and *sells* them" (verse 24). God's beautiful woman merchandises her goods, producing them for the specific purpose of economic trade. Intent on improving her family's financial situation and knowing that her merchandise is good (verse 18), she moves her handmade goods out from the home and into the local markets.

The sashes she supplies to foreign merchants offer her a second source of income. Canaanite and Phoenician traders come by caravan and ship to choose out the best, the most exquisite, the most extraordinary goods to carry to distant places, and her sashes certainly qualified. Ever the businesswoman, she trades, exchanges, barters, and sells her sashes and linen garments (verse 24).

A Personal Story

For me, this verse has been a special challenge. The

thought of "something personal" becoming "something professional" has sparked my thoughts and fueled my energy for a long time. Just like God's beautiful woman, my "thing" just happened: It grew out of something I did every day without ever thinking much about it. You see, my "thing," my something personal, was studying the Bible. Becoming a Christian at age 28, already married for eight years and the mother of two preschoolers, I fell in love with my Bible. Through it God gave me answers to many questions and direction for my confused life. Whenever I wasn't sure about something (how to discipline my children, how to be a better wife, how to run my home, how to manage my time), God's Word always had the answer. So I made sure I spent some time each day studying my Bible.

Well, "some time each day" adds up over the decades. In the still quiet times around our house (usually *very* early in the morning or at night after Katherine and Courtney were asleep), I studied, I read, I memorized, I outlined, and I broke down God's Word into paragraphs and topics and passages. One day, when I was asked to teach a Bible study, I realized I already had the makings of about ten Bible study workbooks to choose from, all originating in my daily quiet time. As I began teaching, using my handmade-at-home-early-in-the-morning materials, women from other churches wanted to use these materials for their studies, and Christian Development Ministries was born. Soon tape albums accompanied the workbooks, and now many of those studies have become books like this one, thanks to Harvest House Publishers.[2]

Earlier, I encouraged you to find a Proverbs 31 Project—something that you do well and love to do that can bring in a little something financially for the family. Developing Bible studies and writing books has become my Proverbs

31 Project. I want to invite you to find a project, too. Look again in chapter 11 for examples of real-life women who have found their "thing." And don't forget two of God's guidelines, drawn from Proverbs 31:

- *Your family is first.* Be careful not to neglect your family to pursue your own interests. With God's help and good time management, you can take care of your family and work on your Proverbs 31 Project. Everyone is cared for *and* everyone benefits when your "something personal" (your diligent activity, willing work, attention to family finances, and wise management of the people and place of home) leads naturally—and with God's blessing—to your "something professional."

- *Give it time.* As I've said, a little time each day adds up over a lifetime. Doing something to advance your "something personal" each day ultimately adds up to something very special from which "something professional" can be born! One of my favorite quotes promises that "fifteen minutes a day devoted to one definite study will make one a master in a dozen years."[3]

The How-To's of Beauty

Once you've identified what your "thing" is—your "something personal," the area where you excel and express yourself—you'll want to actively and consciously cultivate a higher level of creativity. Here are some criteria for creativity that I try to work on every day.

1. Alertness—To nurture your creativity and stay excited about your project, make it a practice to notice how other people express themselves. Keep up with what's happening in your field. Try to stay on the cutting edge of your "thing." Stay alert and aware of other people's creative efforts. For instance, my friend Judy is an artist who stays motivated and stimulated by going to the Los Angeles County Art Museum the first Tuesday of every month (which is the "free" day). Another friend is an interior decorator who spends time walking through the fully furnished model homes in Southern California. Still another friend is a designer who wouldn't miss the latest issue of *Architectural Digest* magazine. Another artist friend has a weekly appointment for teatime with herself to linger over and study her latest issue of *Victoria* magazine. You'll continue to grow creatively if you stay alert and aware of the expressions of creativity all around you.

2. *Planning*—Of course you'll want to set aside time for planning your projects and developing your skills and abilities. But I also want to encourage you to use every spare minute you can find to plan and create in your mind. For instance, when Jim sold my car recently, we realized that, in the four years I had it, I never set the automatic station stops on my car radio because I've designated my car time for thinking. I carry a small dictating machine with me and speak right into that important tool my thoughts, plans, and dreams as well as any reminders to myself. The next time you're in the shower or alone in your car, use the time to plan rather than to zone out or fire up the radio. While you're waiting at the doctor's office, plan! While you're in the checkout line at the grocery store, plan! Keep your mind thinking about how to do what you do better.

3. *Initiative*—It takes initiative to make the phone call to enroll in a class that will help you develop your skills. It takes initiative to go to a specialty store and purchase a

magazine that targets your area of creativity. It takes initiative to subscribe to a journal, magazine, newspaper, or educational cable station that will help you in your creative pursuits. It takes initiative to bring your dreams down to earth and finally set up a work station, the sewing machine, or the easel. It takes initiative to find out where to send your sample line of greeting cards, your manuscript, your book ideas, or your magazine article. It takes initiative to plan a weekend at a conference that addresses your area of interest and desired expertise.

And taking initiative—this crucial step toward a more creative lifestyle—is difficult for many women. As one of God's beautiful women, you need to not only know what you want to do in order to benefit your family, but you also have to act on that desire. Every morning, write down one thing you can do that day to turn your "something personal" into "something professional." That step may be only making a phone call or buying a helpful resource. Or it may be spending 15 minutes doing what you love. But keep in mind that 15 minutes a day will make you a master in a dozen years!

4. *Hard work*—Hard work is essential for success in any venture, and that's exactly what God's beautiful woman does: "She willingly works" (Proverbs 31:13). Besides running the home and getting meals on the table, this dear woman weaves (verses 13,19,21,24), and she excels at it to the stature of professionalism (verses 18,24). Through this Proverbs 31 Project, she provides clothes and extra income for the family. She worked hard to get her enterprise going, and she continues to work hard.

Maybe this is a good place to tell you another reason Proverbs 31:24 is such an exciting verse for me. First let me acknowledge that you may be feeling overwhelmed by the productivity of the Proverbs 31 woman. After all, she has her husband, her children, and her servants to take care of, and her food, her marketing, her fields, the production of the family's clothing, and even the poor in the community to tend to—and we haven't even gotten to the housework yet (verse 27)! The list goes on and on!

But, for me, the crowning achievement of this godly and beautiful woman is her little enterprise. By putting in the time required at home to fulfill God's high calling for her as a wife, mother, and homemaker, she improved her weaving skills and perfected her time management skills...until she excelled in her creative efforts. Then, when she realized that her merchandise was good, she worked even harder to get the work at home done faster so she could follow her dreams and have more time to be creative. Her hard work buys her the time she wants and needs to pursue her talent, to excel in her field, and to run her cottage industry. She is truly worthy of her well-deserved, hard-earned praise (verse 31)!

An Invitation to Beauty

I certainly hope and pray you are encouraged by the industry (pun intended!) of this magnificent woman who is beautiful in God's eyes! Our society focuses so much on self-fulfillment, self-image, and self-esteem. But the good news in Proverbs 31 is that *God* provides all that you need in these areas. After all, there is no greater fulfillment than knowing that you have loved and cared for your family and home. When you (and I) take care of your "something personal" first—the people at home—and do it well, God can grow you personally and even propel you into "something professional," something creative, some avenue where you can express the creative gifts and talents He has given you. If you have no idea where to begin your pursuit of your "something professional," start right this minute asking God to reveal what He would have you do. Just one hint. Your cottage industry will probably grow out of something you are already doing…or dreaming of doing!

~ 18 ~

A Wardrobe of Virtues

Her Clothing

"Strength and dignity are her clothing;
she shall rejoice in time to come."[1]
Proverbs 31:25

I don't know you as well as I would like, but I do know a few things about you. First of all, I can be sure you are a woman who desires God's beauty in her life or you wouldn't be reading a book with the title *Beautiful in God's Eyes*. That's a given.

And I'm also sure about some other details of your everyday life. You get up (and together we're working on doing that a little earlier!), you (I hope) join with the psalmist in saying, "This is the day which the Lord has made; we will rejoice and be glad in it" (Psalm 118:24), and then, at some later time in your morning, you get dressed. (How am I doing?) Opening your closet door, you take a look. Thinking through the events scheduled for your fresh new day, you finally select the clothes suitable for your activities and put them on.

Well, dear one, that's exactly how God's beautiful

woman greets the days of her life. She, too, rises up to praise the God she loves so much, and she, too, considers the activities of her day and then selects the appropriate garments to wear. She doesn't have a lot of clothing to choose from (in fact, the heavy woolen cloak people wore in her day served as their blanket at night), but she has what's adequate and proper.

The Clothing of Character

But the woman who is beautiful in God's eyes adorns herself daily with clothing that doesn't hang in her closet. Proverbs 31:25 says, "*Strength* and *dignity* are her clothing." These two prized ornaments are the most impressive part of our virtuous woman's attire because they are the clothing of godly character.

Once again we see that *strength* is an attribute of God's beautiful woman—and that strength manifests itself in a variety of ways. The Proverbs 31 woman has, for instance, faithfully built up economic strength, so she faces daily life and the prospect of old age with ample monetary reserves. Also, having made diligent preparations, she is ready to meet temporal changes (like a snowy change in the weather [verse 21]) with confidence. Her great trust in the Lord (verse 30) strengthens her for sorrow and care. Although, being a woman, she is considered "the weaker vessel" (1 Peter 3:7), she is strong in wisdom (verse 26) and in the knowledge of God (verse 30). Besides developing physical strength through the demands of her day-to-day work, she has gained social strength by her upright heart, her virtues, and her dignified conduct (verse 25). As the finishing touch to this wardrobe of virtues, her powerful mind gives her an inward vigor and resolution. Yes, strength for life is her clothing.

Dignity is another ornament this woman, who is beautiful in God's eyes, wears consistently. The literal Hebrew translation is "splendor."[2] Apparently her noble spirit gives her the aura of majesty. We marvel at her virtuous character, her regal bearing, and her godly behavior. There is nothing common, low, or little in her wardrobe of character. Her greatness of soul—coupled with her gracious conduct—spells goodness to all who are blessed to know her. All that she is, is touched with the beauty of dignity.

Joy for a Lifetime

Clothed in her rich wardrobe of virtues, God's beautiful woman "shall rejoice in time to come" (verse 25). Not only does she live in the present with utmost joy, but, in the words of another translator, "she *smiles* at the future."[3] When she looks forward—whether to a new day or to her death—"she laughs at the time to come."[4] As author Anne Ortlund shares, this woman's ability to smile and laugh at her future "puts the lines on her face in the right places"![5] Having made all human provision possible and knowing that God will take care of the rest, God's beautiful woman faces the future with joy for a lifetime. Faithful herself with the temporal matters of life, she trusts God for the eternal.

As we've noted, the Proverbs 31 woman wears only a few jewels. She wears none of the usual cheap trinkets—the anxieties, the worries, the fears—which detract from the appearance of so many others. Instead, her beauty is unmarred by concern for life's uncertainties. Whether she's thinking about the past, the present, or the future, she experiences only pleasure. She's done her job. She's carried out her God-given assignments and lived out her virtues a day at a time, every day of her life. Looking backward, she has no regrets. Looking forward, she has nothing to dread. Living in the present, she knows only the joyous challenge of tapping into God's provision and putting her powerful mind and body to work for one more beautiful and joy-filled day!

The How-To's of Beauty

These days, books, conferences, and counselors all offer to help me learn about "God's will" for my life. My choice for instruction is Proverbs 31! I love to study this passage about God's beautiful woman because it gives me—and you—concrete guidance. Every single day of our life we can know exactly what God's will for us is by reading Proverbs 31:10-31. Married or single, young or old, stay-at-home mom or working woman, we are to be about the business of becoming beautiful in God's eyes. The same virtuous traits which the young prince's mother spells out for him to seek in a wife are the traits which we are to pursue. If we do, we too will be clothed with God's strength and dignity and able to smile at the future.

As you know by now, I'm a strong believer in the value of goals. (Sometimes I even drive myself crazy! I have lifetime, ten-year, five-year, one-year, half-year, monthly, weekly, and daily goals written down, and the daily goals often are specific to the hour. In fact my timer is ticking right this second—sounding out for me a 30-minute goal!) I find it easier to set goals for daily life if I break the complexities of life into seven categories.[6] As we look at the how-to's of clothing all of life in God's garments of virtue, consider the following seven areas of godly living. And remember that right now—today!—is the day that counts. It's the only day we have. When you and I take life one day at a time, when we wake up every day for the rest of our life and dress for success in God's wardrobe of virtues, we will find ourselves clothed by God with virtues that will supply us with a lifelong harvest of joy.

1. Your spiritual life—We've been talking about our clothes closet, but first let's consider your prayer closet, that place where you nurture your love for the Lord (Proverbs 31:30). That's the closet you want to visit first each day. God called to His holy city, "Awake, awake; put on your strength, O Zion; put on your beautiful garments" (Isaiah 52:1)! He calls you and me to do the same, and the most beautiful garment in your wardrobe of virtues is your love for Him. As young Lemuel's mother stresses, "A woman who fears the Lord, she shall be praised" (verse 30). *She* is the one who is truly beautiful in God's eyes!

When you emerge from the sacred communion of your prayer closet, you'll be wearing the clothing of righteousness. You will have exchanged your spirit of heaviness for God's festive garment of praise (Isaiah 61:3). You'll also be ready for battle, having donned the whole armor of God (Ephesians 6:12-18). And no one will fail to notice the fragrance of Christ and the aroma of life in Him (2 Corinthians 2:14-16) that flows from your soul.

Why not set yourself the goal of seeking the Lord early (Psalm 63:1)? If you haven't already done so today, stop right now, put this book down, and spend time with the only Person who can make you genuinely beautiful—God Himself! You can smile at the future when you receive God's "strength for today and bright hope for tomorrow"[7] each day of your life.

2. Your family life—Whatever your circumstances, you have a family. You have parents, sisters, brothers, grandparents, aunts, uncles, nieces, nephews, or cousins to love. If you're married, you have a husband and in-laws and maybe some children to love, and you are to be pouring your life into them just as God's beautiful woman does. We all have the family of God, the body of Christ, the church.

If you want to reap the kind of rewards God's beautiful woman reaps (verses 28-29), put your family first—and be sure they know that's where they stand! Take care of their physical needs of food (verses 14-15) and clothing (verse 21). See that you run a neat, clean, orderly home (verse 27). Pour out your love—lavishly, unselfishly, creatively, and joyously. And, if your service, your care, and your love seem to be unnoticed, or you feel unappreciated, or you never hear a "thank you," keep in mind the perspective and call of Colossians 3:23— "Whatever you do, do it heartily *as to the Lord* and not unto men."

That beautiful, godly principle doesn't always earn us rave reviews, though. Just this week a friend called, sounding a little downhearted. As we talked, she shared that her sister had pointed out that she was "too nice" to her children—fixing sack lunches and leaving food in the oven for late-arriving, working adult children. I wish you could have heard the sermon I preached from Proverbs 31! God's beautiful woman takes care of her family—whatever age and whatever stage! A part of her permanent clothing is the apron of "too nice": "The fruit of the Spirit is...kindness [and] goodness" (Galatians 5:22-23)!

3. *Your financial life*—God's beautiful woman can smile when she looks to the future because she has kept watch over the household finances. She has set goals and reached them. What financial goals do you have for your day, the week, this month, and the year?

One day during the writing of this book, I got a glimpse

of my daughters' goals when I received e-mail messages from both of them. Katherine was asking for all my recipes from those days when times were hard, and Courtney was telling me that she had started shopping for groceries only once every two weeks—which challenged her creativity toward the end of the second week! With these two real-life, practical, and simple methods, you can save money, too.

You can also save on clothing by waiting for sales, saying "no," and shopping only one day a week. (You burn out really fast when you have to get everything done on the same day! Believe me, you'll want to rush home and never go "out there" again!) As I shared earlier, you can also save finance fees by staying on top of the bill-paying (see chapter 4). You can open up an automatic savings account. You can ask your husband for an allowance—and save it!

The next time you're in the car or shower, think about what you might do to bring in some income. I have a girlfriend who assembles furniture for an office furniture store. She works on the family room floor after her kids are in bed. My Lori and her daughter Bethany helped me out by making my bulk mailings and workbook assembling their Proverbs 31 Projects. Another woman I know (a senior citizen) sticks labels onto cassette tapes while caring for her 100-year-old mother! With a dollars-and-cents mindset and a willingness to do the work, you can make a significant financial contribution to your future—and your present!

4. *Your physical life*—(Oh, no! We knew this would come up sooner or later!) Proverbs 31:25 speaks of the strength of God's beautiful woman. While strength is a garment in her wardrobe of virtues, it is also a part of her physical makeup. She did, after all, strengthen her body and arms *for* her work and *by* her work (verse 17).

In order to follow in her steps, I want you to set a few goals for your physical health and strength. Would you feel better if you trimmed down a little—or do you need to beef up? Strong muscle tone means fewer back, shoulder, and neck strains. (This one's a must for me! One box of my books weighs 32 pounds, and I have to lift them seven days a week and carry them up and down stairs and in and out of airports!) Exercise means fewer worries about arthritis, osteoporosis, and clogged arteries. Proper food fuels your work and betters your all-around health. You'll feel better today—and in the future you'll be smiling, too—if you tend to this vital aspect of your life and make time in your schedule to get moving.

5. *Your mental life*—The Bible calls us to love God with all our mind (Luke 10:27). (I feel so strongly about this subject that I wrote an entire book on it, *Loving God with All Your Mind.)*[8] I do believe that, as Christians, we will give an account to God for the use (and misuse) of our mind. God makes us in His image with the ability to think and learn, analyze and create (Genesis 1:27; James 3:9). Indeed, we have the mind of Christ (1 Corinthians 2:16)! Not surprisingly, then, Scripture tells us again and again what to do with our mind. (So far, I've counted 31 exhortations regarding the right and wrong ways a Christian can use her mind!)

Now for a personal challenge: How do you use your mind? If I asked how you use your *minutes*, I would be asking for the same information because every minute you're awake, you're using your *mind*. Here are some ideas for how to use your mind in constructive ways.

- As a woman desiring to become more and more beautiful in God's eyes, make sure that, first and foremost, you use your mind to read God's Word, memorize it, and meditate on it.

- You can also think through the issues of Scripture—the role of women in the church, etc.
- You can think, pray, and plan—just as the Proverbs 31 woman does. (That's one of the main reasons she can smile at the future: She has thought about it, prayed about it, and planned for it!)
- You can set a goal to read a good Christian book or biography every month.
- You can read a time- or money-management book.
- Worthwhile books on marriage, mothering, and homemaking are also available.

"Dear Abby" writes her thoughts: "Just for Today... I will improve my mind. I will not be a mental loafer. I will force myself to read something that requires effort, thought and concentration."[9] I urge you to clothe yourself with *strength of mind* and then use that strength for God's glory and the furtherance of His purposes.

6. *Your social life*—Obviously we need to set aside great amounts of time for the Lord and for our family (that's what God's beautiful woman—and this book—are all about!), but we also need to spend time with a few good friends. Proverbs tells us that, while it's difficult to be "best friends" with a lot of people, it's important to have a few. "A man who has [many] friends must himself be friendly, but there is a friend who sticks closer than a brother" (Proverbs 18:24).

Which of your friends stick closer than a brother? Does your schedule reflect time set aside for those special people?

When you are together, do you make it a point to encourage each other in the Lord, in your spiritual journeys? Are your best friends on your daily prayer list?

7. *Your professional life*—After the preceding chapter, you can better understand what I mean by the phrase "professional life." It's your enterprise, your industry, your contribution, your expertise, your "something personal" that becomes "something professional" and advances your family financially. Maybe you have a job, a career, a license, a credential, or a hobby that pays. Whatever your professional life consists of, keep your skills sharp and your knowledge up-to-date. Make sure you're always reaching for higher levels of excellence. Continue the exercises concerning creativity (stay alert; plan and dream; take initiative to develop your skills and abilities; work hard). Do whatever you have to do to stay motivated, excited, and moving forward in your unique area of expertise and skill. If God wills, you may be doing that special work for a long time! That's what this chapter is about, about securing your future as much as humanly possible. Our job is to do all we can. God's job is to take care of the rest!

You've met her before in this book, and once again Edith Schaeffer sets an example for us. She is a woman fully clothed in strength and dignity and able to smile at the future. At age 87 she was busily writing her eighteenth book. Today, she continues to wear her wardrobe of virtues, serve the Lord, love her family, take care of her physical health, and feed her mind—at age 90!

As you peer into your future, what do you pray God will enable you to be doing at age 87 or 90? "Whatever you do, do all to the glory of God" (1 Corinthians 10:31)!

An Invitation to Beauty

Being able to rejoice in the future requires clothing yourself today with the garment of strength and the ornament of dignity. So here are a few "just for today" thoughts.

Just for today...give your life afresh to God and proceed full-faith ahead into your beautiful day. Just for today... wholeheartedly pour out your love and care for your family and be "too nice"! Just for today...think about your positive contributions to the family finances. Just for today...take your physical "strength" seriously and exert yourself. Just for today...eliminate the misuse of your mind and instead use that brain power God has given you to grow more beautiful in character. Just for today...reach out and encourage your best friend in her spiritual journey. Just for today...take one small step toward your "something professional." Finally, just for today...make the commitment to wake up every day of your life and repeat this pattern for beauty. Then you, too, can stand fully robed in your virtues, look down the corridor of time toward your unknown future, and rejoice!

~ 19 ~

A Law of Kindness

HER WORDS

"She opens her mouth with wisdom,
and on her tongue is the law of kindness."[1]
Proverbs 31:26

Well, how are you doing so far on our climb toward excellence? I thought we had better pause a moment and see how we're faring. We're getting ready to take a giant step, and I want to be sure you can make it! In chapter 1, you and I decided to look steadfastly at God's idea of beauty and take the necessary steps, one after the other, to reach the heights of His ideal. And we're making wonderful progress!

Just think of all we've learned—and, I hope, begun to put into practice. We've found, for instance, that getting up just a little earlier *is* possible! We see that running our life and home on a schedule is paying off! Nurturing our marriage is bringing great personal satisfaction. Energy flows as we busy ourselves in constructive activity. Finances are firming up as we diligently manage, save, and earn money. Our involvement in ministry blesses us—and others.

Taking care of our family's needs brings us deep joy. And God is using our obedience to work His godly character in us. God's ways do work!

But now, dear one, as we approach another virtue of beauty—indeed a crowning glory!—we must once again count the cost of our journey. This virtue just may be the one that truly separates the women from the girls in God's army. I warn you, it's probably the hardest to achieve! I'm talking about controlling the quality of the words that come from our mouth.

Oh, we've come a long way and climbed a far piece, but this matter of the tongue trips up many women in their journey toward becoming beautiful in God's eyes. Beautiful speech is hard-won. It's a minute-by-minute challenge. As one of the apostles writes, "If anyone does not stumble in word, he is a perfect man" (James 3:2)!

I'll be frank. Being committed to our home, running the household in an organized manner, excelling in meal preparation and homemaking, supporting our husband's advancement, giving generously to charity, and bringing in income are all easy—compared to opening our mouth with wisdom and kindness. Why do I say that? Because actions are externals, but speech is a matter of the heart: "Out of the abundance of the heart [the] mouth speaks" (Luke 6:45). To be truly beautiful in God's eyes, you and I must push ahead and take this next difficult-but-beautiful step toward more godly speech. God wants His laws of wisdom and kindness to govern our speech—and our heart.

A Fountain of Life

Before we consider the words that we speak, remember that the setting of Proverbs 31 is the deadly dry land of Israel. Hardship was—and is—the rule of the day. Survival was—and is—a day-in, day-out challenge. Brutal heat and life-threatening thirst are two facts of daily life. I wish I could adequately describe for you how great and how relentlessly daily the people's concern about having adequate water is in this parched and arid land. Given your choice of food or water, you would always choose water!

Against this harsh background, the writer of Proverbs paints this image: "The mouth of the righteous is a fountain of life" (Proverbs 10:11 NASB). The writer knows how important water is in sustaining life, and he compares godly speech to life-giving water. He likens the effect of godly speech on our emotional needs to that of water on our physical needs. Just as finding a fountain in the desert was the same as finding life, being in the presence of a woman who speaks words of wisdom and kindness is like finding life!

Wise in Speech

The speech of God's beautiful woman truly is a fountain of life to those around her. Lemuel's mother continues, "She *opens* her mouth with wisdom" (Proverbs 31:26). Note an important thought right away. The wording suggests that her mouth is not always open! She's not a yapper or a compulsive talker or a jabber-mouth. Unless she has something wise and kind to say, her mouth is shut.

When she does speak, "she opens her mouth with *wisdom*." She is wise in what she says and how she says it. Wisdom has long been defined as "the use of knowledge in a practical and successful way."[2] Simply scan through Proverbs 31 and note the practical topics young Prince Lemuel's mother covered. She herself opened her mouth to impart wisdom—practical knowledge for living—to her precious son.

Kind in Heart

As Proverbs 31:26 continues, we see that "on her tongue

is the *law of kindness*." Not only does the woman we're admiring let wisdom guide her speech, but she also limits it according to the law of kindness. All that she utters is in the *spirit* and *manner* of a gentle and benevolent heart, revealing a kindly disposition and a fear of unnecessarily offending.[3] She acquires wisdom and limits her words accordingly. She is never hurtful or destructive with her words. As the Greek translation puts it, "she places order on her tongue."[4]

Now think for a moment about the daily life of God's beautiful woman. She has her husband—whom she is intent upon encouraging and blessing. She has children—whom she must instruct, train, and discipline. Servants—who need directions for the day—reside in her home. Merchants and buyers—who must be dealt with as she barters, bargains, and buys—are on her trade route. Every person in her life means words must be spoken, and the Proverbs 31 woman makes sure her words are wise and kind.

A note of interest (and challenge!) here: In ancient Jewish marriages, not only was the content of a woman's speech important, but *the volume of her voice* was important as well. A woman could be divorced without a marriage settlement if she had a loud voice! How was "loud" measured? By the ability of her neighbors to hear her speak while in her own house.[5] Take heed!

Absence of Malice

What's true in art is also true of speech: What is *not* present makes a louder statement than what is. In light of that, consider what is absent from the words of God's beautiful woman.

For starters, there is no gossip, slander, or unkindness toward others. Kindness would never do that! Nor is there any complaining. As a woman who fears the Lord, God's beautiful woman knows that because He maintains perfect control over the circumstances of life, she really has nothing to complain about! Wit, humor, and jesting—especially at other people's expense—are not how she wants to make her mark. Our beautiful lady would rather be known for her wisdom than her ability to entertain. And, opening her mouth wisely, she certainly says nothing indiscreet or unwholesome. Meaningless talk of trivia and trifles has also been erased from her speech. As a successful estate manager and businesswoman, she could be tempted to speak with an assertive voice, but again kindness rules her rhetoric.

As one student of human nature has so aptly noted, "Those who are not gracious talk of the wrong things. Those who are gracious but not wise talk too much." Wisdom and the law of kindness prevent both errors.

Listening to God's Beautiful Women

When looking through Scripture for wise women who observe the gracious law of kindness, I found two of God's beautiful women who shine forth as models for us in this delicate and difficult area of controlling our tongue.

Hannah is a woman who opened her mouth *very little* under *very difficult* circumstances! Married to a man who had another wife, Hannah endured not only childlessness as her rival bore child after child, but also cruel and ongoing provocations from that woman (1 Samuel 1:1-7). Again and again insult was added to injury, yet Hannah chose to say nothing in response.

With great agony of soul, she went to the house of the Lord (the right place and the right Person) to pray about her situation (the right solution). The intensity of her praying caused the high priest to think she must be drunk, and he said scornfully, "How long will you be drunk? Put your wine away from you" (verse 14). But dear, noble Hannah answered with wisdom and according to the law of kindness, graciously explaining her pain and appealing to his understanding. In the end, she received his priestly blessing.

Abigail, whose name means "source of joy," is a woman who lived out the proverb "The mouth of the righteous is a fountain of life" (Proverbs 10:11 NASB). Married to the foolish, alcoholic Nabal (his name even means "foolish"), Abigail used some carefully chosen words to successfully walk a tightrope of danger. When her husband rebuffed David's kindnesses and mistreated his men (1 Samuel 25:10-11), her servants reported Nabal's insulting behavior to her. She intercepted David on his mission to annihilate all that belonged to Nabal—including herself and the servants. Acting quickly—and with wisdom and kindness—Abigail met David with abundant food for his 600 men.

Then, prostrate on the ground before the enraged David, Abigail begged his forgiveness. With her sensible reasoning and words of wisdom spoken in accordance with the law of kindness, she successfully persuaded David not to take vengeance on her husband. Returning home to find her husband too drunk to listen, she wisely said nothing of the danger that had been avoided until the next day. Abigail worked wisely to keep both David and Nabal from making rash moves. She lives on in history as a wise woman, a skillful negotiator, and a persuasive speaker.[6]

It's encouraging to know that you and I can follow in the footsteps of these two wise and beautiful women!

The How-To's of Beautiful Speech

Oh, my dear friend, I wish I had space to tell you of the

years I've been struggling toward beautiful speech! I detailed at length my battle with gossip in my book *A Woman After God's Own Heart*.[7] I've been learning how and when to talk to and about my husband and children (less is always best!). I've stumbled through the preschool, school-age, teenage, and young-adults-living-at-home years of raising my girls. I can only say that I know *God knows* how desperately I was trying—and I keep trying because this principle of wise and kind speech is God's beautiful plan and His clear standard for my life and my lips.

The Book of Proverbs, tucked into the middle of your Bible, offers invaluable, eternal wisdom, including some of God's rules for godly speech. I'm delighted to share a few of them with you—the ones that have helped me the most and still do!

1. *Establish two guidelines*—God's beautiful woman set two guidelines for her speech: 1) Speak only if the words are wise, and 2) speak only if the words are kind (Proverbs 31:26). By following these same two guidelines, you will always have something to say that's worth saying (wisdom), and you'll say it in the right way (with kindness)! You can know a lot, but if you speak unkindly, your words will be less effective.

2. *Think before you speak*—"The heart of the righteous *studies* how to answer, but the mouth of the wicked pours forth evil" (Proverbs 15:28). Literally pause and think about your words before you speak them. Make it your goal to carefully select wording that measures up to God's standards of wisdom and kindness. When you aren't careful, evil "gushes like a torrent"![8] Rash speech and quick temper betray a shallow and less than beautiful character.[9]

3. *Learn to wait*—When something unpleasant happens,

make it your first "law" to do and say nothing. If you must respond at the moment, be sure your words are soft because "a *soft* answer turns away wrath, but a harsh word stirs up anger" (Proverbs 15:1). Then wait. Waiting buys you time to:

- Search the Scriptures and find out what God says about how to handle the situation.
- Seek counsel and find out what other wise people say. As Proverbs 15:14 cautions, "Where there is no counsel, the people fall." Proverbs 28:26 warns, "He who trusts in his own heart is a fool."
- Pray for a kind heart and a wise solution for the situation.
- Calm down! Cool down! Back off! As Proverbs 17:27 says, "A man of understanding is of a calm spirit." Only when we are calm can we hear good counsel and make wise decisions.
- Weigh the problem. Decide whether the situation is something to pass over (Proverbs 19:11) or whether you need to "open" your mouth and address (with wisdom and kindness, of course!) the people involved.
- Consider the person involved: Is the offense out of character, or is it becoming a pattern? Is it a one-time failure or another in a string of repeated misbehavior?

4. *Add sweetness to your speech*—Wisdom possesses great charm when sweetened with the right words. That truth is behind Proverbs 16:21—"Sweetness of the lips increases learning." Speaking pleasantly will always make others more willing to listen and be instructed. It's true that a spoonful of sugar makes the medicine go down!

5. *Add persuasiveness to your speech*—Besides being kind

and speaking sweetly, know what you're talking about. Your speech will always be an indicator of what is in your mind, and you want to display knowledge when you speak. When you speak with authority, when it's obvious you know what you're talking about, your words will be persuasive. True wisdom cannot fail to make a good impression.

6. *Err on the side of less*—When it comes to words, less is always best! Proverbs 10:19 says, "In the multitude of words sin is not lacking, but he who restrains his lips is wise." Proverbs 17:28 points out that "even a fool is counted wise when he holds his peace." In contemporary language, "Better to be quiet and be thought a fool than to speak and remove all doubt!"

Clearly, when we follow God's two standards of wisdom and kindness, our speech will be beautiful. May God grow us into women of whom it can be said, "She opens her mouth with wisdom, and on her tongue is the law of kindness" (Proverbs 31:26).[10]

An Invitation to Beauty

Now, my faithful, gallant climbing companion, I want you to think again about that fountain in the desert, the one that is a fountain of life. Then think of the hurting, stressed, struggling people who fill your daily world. While they may wear brave smiles, another proverb reveals the truth behind every smile: "The heart knows its own bitterness....Even in laughter the heart is sorrowful, and the end of that mirth is heaviness" (Proverbs 14:10 and 13, KJV).

Won't you join me in making a commitment to refresh

and encourage, to cheer and uplift the hearts of all you encounter with life-giving words, with words that are wise and kind? You can be a fountain of life. Rather than being "one who speaks like the piercings of a sword," yours could be "the tongue of the wise [that] promotes health" (Proverbs 12:18). With God's blessing, His love in your heart, and your careful choice of wise and kind words, you can help heal the downhearted.

And when you fail, dear one, remember this alphabet of wisdom regarding beautiful speech: **A**ccept God's challenge of speaking only wise and kind words, **B**e not discouraged, and **C**ontinue to try! That's how you and I can continue to reach toward God's beautiful standard!

~ 20 ~

A Watchful Eye

HER MANAGEMENT

"She watches over the ways of her household,
and does not eat the bread of idleness."
Proverbs 31:27

So what did you do today?" I can expect this cheerful greeting from my sweet husband every single day when he arrives home from work. Glad to be home and content to make small talk, Jim graciously turns his attention my way. After a challenging day at work, he wants to know about my day. His genuine thoughtfulness always amazes me—but it also makes my heart race because for some reason my mind homes straight in on that little word *do*—"So, what did you *do* today?" Even though Jim is not asking in order to hold me accountable, I'm so tuned in to accountability myself that I automatically answer, "I don't know exactly what I did, but I do know one thing—I never sat down all day long!"

Such vigilance about how wisely and effectively I spend my time has not always been the case for me! But that was before I learned one dynamite lesson from God's beautiful woman, a lesson about time, life, and home management: The woman who is beautiful in God's eyes "watches over the ways of her household, and does not eat the bread of idleness" (Proverbs 31:27). The wisdom from this verse—showing me vividly what I should do and should not do—gave me a double-barreled challenge for a lifetime. First, the positive.

Keeping Watch Over Her Flock

Teaching us even more about the woman who is beautiful in God's eyes, Prince Lemuel's mother says: "She *watches* over the ways of her household" (Proverbs 31:27). We know the Proverbs 31 woman has the finances for servants (verse 15), but here we see that she is actively involved in the hands-on management of her household. No one runs her home for her. It's *her* home, *her* family, *her* household, and she considers its management an area of *her* stewardship.

Using an image familiar to her young son (the boy who would one day be king and "watch over" his people), his mother describes his future wife as a watchman. Charged to be an observant and careful lookout, a watchman guarded and watched over a city or a field. Lemuel had grown up seeing watchmen stationed 24 hours a day on the city walls, watch towers, and hilltops. They were to be on the alert for hostile action and report any kind of suspicious activity to the king.[1] Young Lemuel knew exactly what a watchman was and what a watchman did.

His wise mother, a master manager herself, tells her son to marry the kind of woman who will "watch over" his family and household affairs, a woman with—as the expression goes—eyes in the back of her head! As the one keeping watch, the woman turns her head, looking everywhere so that she doesn't miss a single detail![2] This imagery of the watch-keeper suggests that she stands guard, moving her eyes back and forth to see who is coming and who is going, in order to fulfill her divine assignment as overseer of her precious family and property. She keeps a good watch and oversees everything.

Just how seriously does God's beautiful watch-keeper take her stewardship? The King James Version says, "She [looks] *well* to the ways of her household" (Proverbs 31:27). In other words, she doesn't just glance over things or check the temperature at home (literally and figuratively) only once in a while, but she looks closely, intently studying the situation and overseeing everything that pertains to her home. Alert and energetic, she has her finger on the pulse of her household; nothing escapes her scrutiny and control.[3] You see, her job assignment from God is to maintain a watchful eye, to know all about what's going on under her roof, and to care for the people as well as the place.

Next we see that "she watches over the *ways* of her household" (Proverbs 31:27). She carefully notices the patterns of her home life—the "ways" of her household, the general comings and goings, the habits and activities of the people at home. The Hebrew word for *ways* means literal tracks made by constant use. They're like the foot path that appears through the lawn or the road created by heavy traffic.[4] Our watch-woman is aware of these habits and any changes in habits. Nothing catches her by surprise!

God's beautiful overseer observes all that goes on in her home. She keeps up-to-the-minute on the status of her family members and the general flow of her home. She's aware of everything that goes on within its walls. Just as the watchman for the city reports any suspicious or potentially harmful actions to the king, so God's beautiful woman sounds the alarm when necessary. When a situation goes awry, she sounds the warning to her husband. She remains faithful as his watcher.

Ever faithful, "she watches over the ways of her *household.*" And that household extends beyond the members of her immediate family. Her husband and her children are her greatest concern. They are her sheep; their well-being and activities are her first concern. But, in addition to these sheep and any literal flocks she may have (Proverbs 31:17 and Proverbs 27:23), our beautiful woman also has the flock of her household. As the mistress of her household, she also cares for any extended family members and her servants, watching over them, too, as a shepherd watches over his flock.

Keeping Watch Over Herself

The woman who is beautiful in God's eyes watches over herself as well: "She does not eat the bread of idleness" (Proverbs 31:27). The Hebrew for *eating* suggests a lifestyle of "good living," but God's beautiful woman is *not* engaging in "the good life"! On the contrary, she chooses not to live a leisurely life filled with food and drink.[5] She who vigilantly watches over her household has no place for idleness in her schedule. How could she afford to be idle? How could she even find the time? Busy managing her house and watching over her flock, she has no time to partake of ("eat of") laziness and idleness. This truth could also be flipped: Because she is not idle, she has the time she needs to keep a watchful eye on her home and be sure that it's well-managed!

In Proverbs 31:27 ("She does not eat the bread of idleness"), it's also interesting to note that the Hebrew for "bread" is a word associated with sluggishness. The use of "bread" together with "eat" paints a clear picture: God's beautiful woman has no part in sluggishness of any kind. One translation tells us she is "not content to go through life eating and sleeping."[6] My favorite commentary simply states, "She is never lazy"![7] Now do you understand why I never sit down? Proverbs 31:27 challenges me for a lifetime!

The How-To's of Beauty

First the people—A good principle to remember when it comes to life under your roof is, "The people first, then the place." The precious people who make up your family will always be far more important than the place where you live. After all, the place exists to serve the people. So your beautiful role is to see that the people at home are cared for spiritually, emotionally, and physically. Your job assignment from God requires you to make sure your family members have food and clothing—just as the Proverbs 31 woman did!

In light of that charge, read these haunting words written by wife, mother, grandmother, and great-grandmother Edith Schaeffer: "Neglected mothers and grandmothers may perhaps have been preparing for their own neglect by teaching over and over again that people's sensitive feelings, and people's need of response is never as important as clean houses, schedules, or rules and regulations."[8] When you follow the precept "the people first, then the place," you'll always be focusing your energy in the right place—the place for maximum beauty.

Part of caring for the people is praying for them. As the psalmist says, "Unless the Lord builds the house, they labor in vain who build it; unless the Lord guards the city [or house], the watchman stays awake in vain" (Psalm 127:1). On this side of heaven, you will never know how many discouraged family members have been encouraged by your prayers for them, how many problems have been solved because God granted wisdom given in response to your requests, or how many spiritual battles were won under your roof because you lifted your entreaties beyond your roof to the throne of heaven!

Then the place—With the people at home cared for, you can turn your attention to your "household management." I have on my desk a massive old volume from 1861 entitled *Beeton's Book of Household Management*[9] given to me by a friend living in Scotland. Its 1125 pages detail information on the raising, selecting, killing, dressing, butchering, preserving, and preparing of animals for consumption, how to serve a meal for nineteen, the duties and proper manner of instruction for cooks, maids, coachmen, laundry maids, nurses, etc., who will carry out some of those tasks, and medical and legal information. This manual was definitely intended to assist any woman who desired to watch over and look well to the ways of her household!

I was thinking about what we who are God's beautiful women do to watch over our homes, and I want to share my list which—like yours—is different from Beeton's! Like the Proverbs 31 woman, though, I watch over my house—over the people, the place, the finances, the meals, the "maids," and the clothes. For instance, right now my washing machine (my laundry maid) is spinning away. I've already turned on the sprinklers (my gardener), closed up and cooled down the house (it's August!), delivered a car to be worked on (my coachman assisted), and enjoyed breakfast with my husband (a meal and time of companionship). I've e-mailed both my daughters, still "watching over" them and nurturing relationships from long distance. The house is tidied, the bills are paid, the mail is out in the mailbox, phone calls have been returned, and the day's work is planned. I met with the Lord and He encouraged my heart and strengthened me to handle another fast-paced, demanding day. It's 11:30 AM now, and I've been seeking from my first waking moment today to set my home and family on the right path, the right "way."

When Katherine and Courtney were younger, each day followed the same path except there was also homework for me to watch over and their chores to check up on. I invested time and effort in training Katherine and Courtney so they would one day have the skills they would need to watch over their own homes—skills like housecleaning, cooking, setting the table, taking care of the dog, maintaining the yard, and washing, folding, and ironing clothes. I ingrained certain disciplines like cleanliness, ritualistic toothbrushings, and getting to school on time—and with a sack lunch!

Having already spent six or seven hours watching over my home, now I'll begin my job of writing, with breaks for another meal with Jim tonight, another errand to pick up his car at the end of the day, the final cleanup, and probably another couple of hours of writing before bedtime. But at least I don't have to wring a chicken's neck!

Please pardon me for taking the time and space to list the activities of my days. But I want you to realize—whether you have a job or not—that looking well to the ways of your household and keeping a watchful eye involves many, many things. Any job responsibilities and loyalties at work come after the top priorities of family and home have been fulfilled. I don't write (and I research and write about ten hours a day) until I've looked after the people and the place. For me that takes about eight hours a day! My "job" of writing and teaching can never be a reason to neglect watching over the ways of my household!

And the same is true for you, too. The income from a job can never substitute for your careful watch over family and home. The woman who is beautiful in God's eyes (not necessarily in the eyes of an employer, a supervisor, a boss, the women in the office, or [gulp!] a publisher) makes sure her management at home is beautifully attended to. The joke that reports, "Most homes nowadays seem to be on three shifts—Father is on the night shift, Mother is on the day shift, and the children shift for themselves" must never be true in the beautiful home you are building for God! With a heart set on God's kind of beauty, some good time-management skills, and a plan for your day, you can manage all that life brings your way.

An Invitation to Beauty

I know it may not seem very inviting or sound very exciting, but your home is definitely the place most worthy of your diligent watching. In fact, home is the most important place in the world for you to be spending your time and investing your energy. Why do I say that? Because the work you do in "a little place" like home is eternal work, meaningful work, important work—when you realize that the work you do in your home is your supreme service to God! I invite you to enjoy the beauty of serving in a little place, a little place…like home.

A Little Place

"Where shall I work today, dear Lord?"
And my love flowed warm and free.
He answered and said,

"See that little place?
Tend that place for Me."

I answered and said, "Oh no, not there!
No one would ever see.
No matter how well my work was done,
Not that place for me!"

His voice, when He spoke, was soft and kind,
He answered me tenderly,
"Little one, search that heart of thine,
Are you working for them or ME?
Nazareth was a little place…
so was Galilee."[10]

~ 21 ~

A Cup of Blessing

Her Family

"Her children rise up and call her blessed,
and her husband also, and he praises her."
Proverbs 31:28

As I write this chapter Jim and I are preparing for a trip. We're going to a surprise party for a wonderful couple in their seventies. The party is being given by their sons and daughters. It's not their fiftieth wedding anniversary, it's not a retirement party, and it's not a birthday party either. The invitation simply declares the event to be "a celebration of honor." Isn't that a wonderful idea?

Well, my beautiful friend, this chapter is also a celebration of honor. For twenty chapters you and I have listened in on a mother describing for her son a woman who is beautiful in God's eyes. Together we've drunk in her noble qualities—her diligence, her hard work, her early rising, her careful preparations, her wise management, her enterprising spirit, her encouraging speech, her attentive watch over her loved ones, and her drive to excel for the good of her family. Motivated by love, God's beautiful woman delights in pouring out her life for her family. Hers is a rare kind of beauty indeed (verse 10)!

And now we hear of a celebration in her honor. God's beautiful woman is receiving her highest reward—not from the community or the townspeople or folks at church, at work, or in the neighborhood. Her cup of blessing comes from those who matter most, those who know her best, and those who have received a lifetime of the first fruits of her day-in, day-out love—her family! Let's listen in as her children praise her.

A Blessed Mother

Proverbs 31:28 proclaims, "Her children rise up and call her blessed." We've not seen them or met them, but here, in unison, the offspring of God's beautiful woman "rise up" and sing her praises! I had to chuckle at one interpretation I read: "They rise up in the morning and, finding everything well prepared, the children express their thankfulness to her."[1] Such a display of gratitude is certainly what all moms dream of and train their children toward, but such thankfulness isn't always expressed. Another commentator suggested that rising up means standing up in her presence as a mark of respect (another one of a mother's fantasies!).[2] Still another possibility is that the children rise up as a preparatory movement in order to make an announcement, to give words of tribute in reverential honor of her,[3] much like getting up to make a speech at a special ceremony.

These interpretations may work for you, but more realistically the words *rise up* mean that the Proverbs 31 woman's children grow up and go out to live in a way that brings honor and blessing and credit to her. The children's lives become the living praise of her worth and her work.

My blessed friend, whichever meaning is intended, one thing is clear: The children of our Proverbs 31 woman give her life its highest reward. They bless her. They praise her. The children experience the sweet fruits of her virtues, and she experiences the sweet fruits of their lives and rejoices in them. As I said, they bless her—and she is blessed (which means happy)![4] Their sincere words as well as their very lives bless her. Truly her cup of blessing overflows!

Praying that my children would also "rise up"—not to say "thank you," or stand when I enter a room, or even give a speech, but that they live godly lives—caused me to examine my heart and soul. Those times of prayer also helped me identify some essential elements in the love of a mother who is a blessing to her family. These basics are a matter of the heart—the heart of a mother, *your* heart—and apply to love for children, stepchildren, and grandchildren.

Essential #1: A Mother Cares

A mother shares her love daily with her children through *the gift of the basics*—food, clothing, shelter, and rest. A popular kitchen plaque reads, "Divine services rendered here three times a day!" That's a wonderful perspective on the care we mothers offer our children as we follow in the path of the Proverbs 31 mother: She looks well to her children's ways, spending the majority of each day providing food and clothing for her loved ones. The shelter she offers includes a home warm not only in temperature but in love. Because it goes against her character to be contentious (Proverbs 21:9) or loud (Proverbs 7:11), her home is a shelter where her family can rest and know peace. Daily she extends the cup of physical care for her family.

Motherly care also means pouring out *the gift of time.*

Every minute—indeed every second—we spend with our children matters! Love is spelled T-I-M-E—time, time, and more time; time in terms of minutes and time in terms of years. Indeed, our children call for a lifetime of time! Our very young children need our time—and lots of it! Did you know that 50 percent of a child's character and personality development takes place by age three and 75 percent by age five? Our children need our time when they're older, too. As they learn to reason and become real conversationalists, as they face the challenges of junior high and high school, as they become young adults in the workplace or in college, they need the gift of time from us. And they need our time when they're even older, when they are ready to be our friends. The children of the Proverbs 31 woman—who have become her *friends*—rise up to bless her! Every minute—indeed every second—we spend giving the gift of time to our children is an investment in their character and in their future.

A mother's care doesn't cease when the children are no longer at home. Instead a mother goes to work giving *the gift of long-distance love*. The beautiful Old Testament mother Hannah lavished long-distance love on her little Samuel (1 Samuel 2:19). Despite a distance of a day's journey, Samuel knew he was loved because Hannah (also a weaver) spent every year making him a new coat, which she delivered to him in person at the annual feast in the house of the Lord.

Author Elisabeth Elliot rises up and blesses her mother for letters written and sent over long distances. She exclaims, "How rich we were not to have been able to afford long-distance phone calls! Few families today have the permanent and intimately detailed record which now lies in a box in my attic—the complete set of Mother's letters to her children from 1954 through 1985."[5] When Mrs. Elliot first went away to school, her mother wrote to her twice a week. There was never a week in her life from September 1941 through the mid-1980s when she began to fail mentally that Katharine Howard did not write to her children—all six of them! This mother's letters were the overflow of a mother-heart filled with love, and that love found a way to care across long distances. This outpouring of care took time. Imagine writing a dozen letters a week—and without a word processor! Living out her love, a mother takes care of her children and gives the gift of time.

Essential #2: A Mother Focuses

As God's beautiful mothers, you and I gladly focus all our mothering energies and efforts on one goal: to raise each child to love our Lord. Our assignment from God is to raise a man or a woman who will serve and honor Him. Our focus is not on raising a doctor, a teacher, an engineer, an athlete, or even a minister or a missionary. We'll allow God to decide our child's vocation while we focus instead on raising an individual who has a heart after God. Moses was a shepherd, but his heart belonged to God. David, too, was a shepherd, Paul a tentmaker, and Peter a fisherman, but each had a heart dedicated to God.

What a privilege to join together with God and train up the next generation, the people who will, in turn, train up the generation that comes after them (Proverbs 22:6)! Mother, grandmother, and great-grandmother Edith Schaeffer explains: "We are responsible for 'handing on the flag [of faith]' and for being very careful not to drop it—or to drop out—because of our responsibility to the next generation...To hand down truth to one more generation is one of the central commands of God."[6]

As you work to pass on your faith, I encourage you to pray over your children each night. Consider, for example, the heart-cry of the mother of Dr. Harry Ironside, who was known in the late nineteenth century as the "Boy Preacher of Los Angeles" and who later was pastor of Moody Memorial Church in Chicago and the author of more than 60 books. Each night his mother Sophia poured out this prayer over her son as she tucked him into bed: "Father, save my boy early. Keep him from ever desiring anything else than to live for Thee....O Father, make him willing to be kicked and cuffed, to suffer shame or anything else for Jesus' sake."[7] Mrs. Ironside focused on one thing and one thing only for her child—that he would love God!

Essential #3: A Mother Plans

The beautiful mother of Proverbs 31 planned for progress in her roles (verses 15,27), and you and I need to plan, too. Final outcomes are always in God's hands, but the daily operation of the home is in ours. So let me share with you what I want (and wanted) for my family and how I plan (and planned) for it. Things as grand as these desires of my heart (and I'm sure of your heart, too) simply won't happen without planning for them!

First and foremost, I want the dynamic *presence of the Lord* in my home. This means filling my heart first. It means scheduling some prime time for God's Word and for prayer so that I bear the mark of a woman who is beautiful in God's eyes. For God's presence to be obvious in my home, my homemaking, and my dealings with the family, He must be present in my own heart.

The next thing I wanted as a young mom was to *pass*

on faith in Jesus Christ to my children (grandchildren count here, too). Once again, planning helped. I planned for regular church attendance as well as for daily devotions with my girls. I even, in prayer, planned to speak of the Lord to them and asked God to help me be aware of opportunities to point my daughters to Him. My plans included surrounding Katherine and Courtney with people who shared my faith. Believe it or not, I also had to plan to pray so that I could pray for *them* regularly! I planned bedtime rituals and found Bible books and Bible stories to read to my children. Passing on your faith in Christ to your children is certainly worth some planning.

A *pleasant atmosphere in the home* creates a beautiful background for happy memories. Because I want the warm atmosphere and the good memories it fosters, I plan for it. I plan the meals, including how I'll set the dinner table and make it beautiful. I plan for order in the home, for the housework, for the laundry, and for the upkeep of our clothing so that life is calmer. I plan surprises, too, so that life at home is fun. If all this planning sounds like a lot of effort, remember that no work of art is slapdashed together. Artistry calls for planning and design, and so does the work of art called "Home."

I want *progressing relationships* with my children, so I plan for that. My plans include what words to speak, what questions to ask, what ways to express my love, and what special gifts and deeds of kindness to extend to them. I plan outings, holidays, and Christmas, Easter, and birthday celebrations.

Another kind of planning for relationships is planning for the bits and blocks of time you know you'll have. For instance, when your child runs in one door after school to change clothes and rushes out the other door to get to work or ball practice, when you only have a few minutes, plan for those crucial minutes. When you have only a few hours with your children—the day's been hectic, but you do have mealtime before they go out again—plan for those precious hours (and the meal, too)! Or when you only have your children, stepchildren, or grandchildren for a few days, plan to fill those days with love. You can fill every minute, hour, and day with blessings for your children!

My Katherine and Courtney are married now, but I continue to nurture my relationships with them and their husbands, so (you guessed it!) I plan for it! Writing and e-mailing my daughters, praying for them and their families, giving little gifts that help them in their married lives, helping in the ways needed, visiting them, loving their children, and celebrating holidays—I plan for all these things. And sometimes I even plan not to call or bother them!

The development of one final plan is imperative: You must plan for *persistence*; you must plan to keep on mothering—no matter what! I heard a life-changing (actually a mother-changing!) radio interview with Dr. Richard Mayhue, Dean of The Master's Seminary and a father of grown children. Dr. Mayhue likened parenting to a 100-yard football field that has a life-and-death game being played on it. He pointed out that some parents drive up to the junior high school curb (the 50-yard line), open the car door, drop the kids off, wave good-bye, and say, "Well, we've taught you everything you need to know. Now go and do it!" Then there is the parent who hands the teenager the car keys (and sometimes a car) at age sixteen (the 75-yard line), stands in the driveway, waves good-bye, and yells, "Well, you're on your own now. You can drive, you're old enough to get a job, and you know what you ought to do. Good luck!" Most parents, however, drop their still-moldable child off after high-school graduation (the 95-yard line) and call out to them, "Don't forget to visit us once in a while!"

What Dr. Mayhue stressed was "going the distance" with your child, especially between the 95-yard line and the goal at the 100-yard line, those ages of 18 to 25-ish. He described the brutal blows, the scratching, and the clawing that happen in a real football game as a team struggles to gain every inch of those final five yards. As he wisely pointed out, the final five yards is where your child chooses a career and a mate—the two most important decisions (next to faith in Jesus Christ) they make in their lives!

All of this to say, dear friend and devoted mother, you and I must plan to encourage, assist, advise, and pray for our children, whatever their ages. Our assignment calls for us to lock arms together with them and move forward shoulder to shoulder, inch by inch, all the way to the finish line—no matter what! Our care and guidance can never cease. And, trust me, your children will rise up and bless you for your persistent and prayerful mothering!

Since space is limited, I'm unable to share with you the many other deep convictions I have about what God's Word teaches us about mothering and the many lessons I've learned raising my own children, but I gladly recommend the four chapters in my book *A Woman After God's Own Heart*[8] about "The Heart of a Mother." After all, mothering truly is a matter of the heart—*your* heart!

Essential #4: A Mother Works

Instead of a section on "The How-To's of Beauty," I want to share one more essential that certainly covers some how-to's of mothering: A mother follows God's plan as she does the work of raising her children. You see, love has work to do—hard and self-sacrificing work. In the 19 verses about the Proverbs 31 woman we've looked at so far, I've counted twelve to fifteen obvious and veiled references to her work. We know that she rises while it is still dark and that her lamp does not go out when night falls (verses 15,18). From early in the morning until late at night, she's busy working for her family and doing so because of her great love for them.

Once again hear the heartfelt words of Edith Schaeffer: "Being a mother is worth fighting for, worth calling a career, worth the dignity of hard work."[9] And believe me, being a mother is the hardest work we will ever do! A mother's love is to-the-end, all-the-way work! But consider what your work as a mother can accomplish:

- A mother loves her children.

    Work puts your love into action.
- A mother cares for her children.

    Work gives your loving care expression.
- A mother focuses on making Christ known to her children.

    Work (and especially God's work in their hearts) puts feet on your faith.

As you and I do the hard work of mothering, God blesses our efforts and helps us realize our dreams for our family.

A word now about how we are to do this work. God's Word tells us that we are to work without murmuring or complaining (Philippians 2:14). God's word tells us that we are to work as unto the Lord and not unto men (Colossians 3:23). We are to work willingly and joyfully (Proverbs

31:13). We are to work expecting nothing in return (Luke 6:35). And we are to work—teaching, training, disciplining, caring, planning, giving, praying, and believing—because doing so is a mother's assignment from God!

But What If...?

I can almost hear you thinking, "But what if my children don't follow my spiritual and practical leading? What if they don't live for God? What if they don't follow in the way I've trained them? What if they never say thank you or even seem to notice all I've done for them? What if they don't ever rise up in any kind of honor?"

I've had all these thoughts myself, but I've learned that a mother's energy and efforts must never be motivated by possible rewards. You see, God has determined your role: as a mother, you are to love your children—no matter what (Titus 2:4); you are to teach your children—no matter what (Proverbs 1:8); you are to train your children—no matter what (Proverbs 22:6); you are to discipline your children—no matter what (Proverbs 29:17); and you are to care for your children—no matter what (Proverbs 31:27).

Even when a mother wonders if her efforts will result in the godly children she prays for, she keeps on doing these things. Why? Because in her heart she has faith not in her doing, but in *God*! So a mother heartily does things God's way—no matter what—and then prayerfully leaves the results of her obedience in the hands of her wise, powerful, and good God. It's your job as a mother to follow God's plan. It's God's job to work all things together for His divine purposes (Romans 8:28) and prove what is His good and acceptable and perfect will (Romans 12:2) not only in your child's life, but yours, too! A mother trusts and obeys the God she is serving as she raises her children.

An Invitation to Beauty

Obviously my emotions run deep when it comes to mothering. I hope and pray that my passion provides the push needed to bring out the fighter in you! As Mrs. Schaeffer remarked, "Being a mother is worth fighting for!" When it comes to mothering, there is no place for neutrality, ignorance, aloofness, or a hands-thrown-up-in-the-air, "I give up" attitude! That's why I am trying to call up in you the fierce emotions that can compel the constant care, the ongoing efforts, the never-give-up attitude, and the motivation to give 100 percent-plus! Being a mother—God's kind of mother—touches generations and generations of children.

To close, let me tell you that I wept as I read about the mother of the late Bill Bright, founder of Campus Crusade for Christ. She was described as an "ordinary" woman. Yet as she lay dying at age 93, 109 members of her family, including children, grandchildren, great-grandchildren and great-great-grandchildren, made their way to her bedside to express their love and appreciation. All of them wanted to rise up to call her "blessed."[10] And that, my dear, dear friend, is exactly what I want for myself and for you!

~ 22 ~

A Crowning Chorus

Her Praise

"Her children rise up and call her blessed,
and her husband also, and he praises her:
'Many daughters have done well,
but you excel them all.'"
Proverbs 31:28-29

I was touched by this husband's loving tribute to his faithful wife in the dedication of a book he wrote:

> With deep love and appreciation, I dedicate this book to my beloved partner and wife, Evelyn, who for over four decades has always been by my side to give me love, cooperation, and understanding when others doubted. Through the years she has joined me in mutual devotion and prayer to our Heavenly Father and has helped me keep faith when the vision of others was limited—truly a helpmate given by God.[1]

The words in this dedication reflect the kind of gratitude and appreciation that abides in the heart of the Proverbs 31 woman's husband and sets the stage for this chapter's crowning chorus of praise for the woman who is beautiful in God's eyes.

An Excellent Wife

Not only has the Proverbs 31 woman proved to be a blessed mother, but now we see—not surprisingly—that she's an excellent and appreciated wife, too, who enjoys the sunshine of her husband's approval. In our poem of virtues, the man who has first place in her heart has the last specific word of praise for his beautiful-in-God's-eyes wife.

The finale begins as "her husband also [rises up]" (Proverbs 31:28). This fine woman's children have concluded their commendations, and now the one who matters most speaks. He offers heartfelt words of tribute, recognizing and appreciating all she has done for him. He sings the crowning chorus of praise for the numerous selfless works his beautiful wife has showered him with through the years.

The blessed husband—the great leader of the people and a man of influence who is known in the gates—"praises [his wife]" (Proverbs 31:28)! Proudly and publicly, he lauds the woman who helps bear the burden of his every care; she is his comforter in every distress, his faithful adviser, his best friend, his unceasing joy, and his brightest crown! He who is the companion of her youth (Proverbs 2:17) has shared much of life's journey with her. And here, long after the children have "risen up" and gone out into the world, she continues as his faithful wife, doing him good all the days of her life (verse 12).

An Army of Virtuous Women

In hushed anticipation, we wait as the husband of God's beautiful woman—the person who knows her best—begins his statement of praise: "Many daughters have done well"

(Proverbs 31:29). Knowing what a noble woman is and does (after all, he's married to one!), this wise man recognizes that *many* are noble. Indeed, an entire army of good women ("daughters") exists. Sitting in the gates of the city (verse 23), he knows who the women of strong character are in his town. I'm sure he could list the women who have achieved wealth, who merit the regard of the community, and who live their lives in a worthy manner. Yes, there are many!

And he acknowledges that the "many daughters have done *well*" (Proverbs 31:29). Do you remember our definition of *virtuous* from chapter 1? We discovered that the word virtuous or *excellent* means "power of mind and power of body" and accurately describes an army. Here the husband of the Proverbs 31 woman picks up that military image in the word *well*. Many have done virtuously. Many have done excellently. Many have done valiantly. Many have proven their worth. Many have gained riches and wealth. Many have shown great force and power.

The Best of All!

"But," this proud and grateful husband continues, "you excel them all" (Proverbs 31:29). His precious wife is beautiful not only in God's eyes, but in his eyes, too. His chorus of praise resounds as he declares: "You surpass them all! You transcend them all! You far outdo them all! You are better than all of them!"[2] In other words, he points out that other women "do" worthily, but his beautiful wife "is" worthy. Other women "do" their activities (and do them with excellence), but he praises his wife because of her very character: She "is" excellent![3] Comparing her to the complete army of the other virtuous women in God's army, he confidently claims that she is the noblest of women. Captivated by her excellencies, he exults, "You are the best of all!"[4]

Just a note: The Old Testament Hebrew proclaims, "You ascend over all [of] them."[5] This Hebrew wording suggests that the husband gives his blessing in genuine appreciation of his wife's actual accomplishments and activities—not as an act of graciousness, obligation, or well-meaning politeness. God's beautiful woman truly merits this honest praise because she is indeed the best of all!

A Kaleidoscope of Virtues

Oh, my dear friend, I hope you are not growing weary of this faithful woman who so perfectly exemplifies beauty as God sees it. For 20 verses we've looked at her godly virtues and her sterling character. This great woman is not shallow, nor is her beautiful life built on a thin foundation. Her godly and virtuous beauty permeates her life and her very being, so we can learn much of value from her. Proverbs 20:5 says, "A man [or woman] of understanding will draw [the instruction] out." That's been our purpose throughout this book—to learn all that we can about and from the beauty of the Proverbs 31 woman.

In my mind, she is like a kaleidoscope. As a child, did you ever have a kaleidoscope, a small cardboard tube filled with brightly colored glass or plastic shards? Holding the kaleidoscope up toward the light, you could view the stained-glass patterns fashioned by the shards as the light shined through them. Then, as you turned the kaleidoscope, the many jewel-toned shards changed positions, creating yet another magnificent design of beauty.

Well, my magnificent friend, that's what the woman who is beautiful in God's eyes is like. In Proverbs 31, God allows you and me to view the many rich colors and glorious patterns of her multifaceted life. As we've moved from verse to verse, from virtue to virtue, as we've lifted the character of God's beautiful woman up to the light of His Holy Spirit, He has illumined the brilliance of her virtues. They have burst into an exquisite pattern and then, with a slight change of angle as we've moved to another verse, we've seen yet another splendid display of breathtaking beauty. Proverbs 31 is the study of one woman in all her different roles. Each verse enables us to look at all her virtues, but from a different angle. She is a kaleidoscope of virtues!

Give the Proverbs 31 kaleidoscope a series of twists, and you and I can easily understand why her husband so highly praises his beautiful wife. Marvel at the glory of her multifaceted beauty!

- She adds honor to her husband's name and reputation because she is "a virtuous wife" (verse 10).
- She contributes positively to his financial well-being and manages his money so that "he will have no lack of gain" (verse 11).
- She eases his mind so he can concentrate on the demands of his leadership position: "The heart of her husband safely trusts her....She does him good and not evil all the days of her life" (verses 11 and 12).
- She provides for the needs at home, "[rising] while it is yet night and [providing] food for her household" (verse 15).
- She increases his assets and expands his property: "From her profits [she buys a field] and plants a vineyard" (verse 16).
- She counsels and encourages him with the words she speaks: "She opens her mouth with wisdom and on her tongue is the law of kindness" (verse 26).
- She frees him up from worries at home so that he can

serve his community. She responsibly "watches over the ways of her household" (verse 27).

- She raises his children and, as a result of her fine efforts, "her children rise up and call her blessed" (verse 28).

No wonder that her husband's crowning chorus of praise for this beautiful-in-God's-eyes woman goes on and on through the centuries!

A Beautiful Crown

And here another image catches our eye. The woman praised in this exuberant chorus is herself a beautiful crown for the one speaking forth the praise! As Proverbs 12:4 says, "An excellent wife is the crown of her husband." God's beautiful wife is the crown her husband wears. She is his brightest ornament, and she draws all eyes to him, as one who is eminently honored and blessed.[6] A crown is a mark of dignity, and a virtuous woman—a person of strength and dignity in her own right (verse 25)—brings respectability, credit, and reputation not to herself, but to her husband.[7] Adorning and beautifying *his* life, *she* is an honor to him. She is his crown.

And God's beautiful woman is pleased to be her husband's crown. Shunning the spotlight, she gladly gives her life behind the scenes so that her husband may be noticed and honored. She is glad when he is the center of attention, when he excels, when he is recognized, when he rises to the top. Indeed, she delights in living in his shadow. His promotion is her greatest reward. She desires that her husband be highly respected and esteemed, so she contentedly offers the supreme sacrifice of herself for him.

This image of the crown offers us one more message: This

beautiful crown is a crown of joy. I say that because, in the day of God's beautiful woman, a bridegroom dressed as much like a king as possible for the wedding festivities. If he could afford it, he wore a gold crown. If not, a woven garland of fresh flowers offered him a regal appearance. For that one glorious day, even a peasant seemed a prince as the people paid him the respect called for by the exalted rank which his crown symbolized.[8]

Then, when the wedding day faded away, the festivities were but a memory, and life returned to normal, a man's new wife became his crown. This woman who is beautiful in God's eyes supplies him with the dignity due a king. She has become the symbol of honor for him—a crown to her husband who richly adorns his life and makes his every day a celebration. Thanks to this virtuous woman, the joy of the wedding day has continued throughout his life. This, dear one, is what you and I want to be to our husband—a beautiful crown of dignity and joy for him to wear daily!

But What if...?

Once again, I can hear your heart-cries. You're wondering, "But what if my husband isn't the provider, the husband, the father, the spiritual leader God calls him to be? Why should I bother?" Here's a maxim for both of us: Life's circumstances never negate God's standards. Let me explain what I mean by showing you some beautiful women in God's army who had a difficult marriage.

Hannah—As we learned earlier, Hannah was married to a man with another wife who persecuted and willfully provoked Hannah day after day, year after year (1 Samuel 1). Yet Hannah allowed these difficult circumstances to press her closer to God. As a result, Hannah stands as one of the very few women in Scripture about whom nothing negative is said. Her husband certainly wasn't the leader he should have been, but Hannah did not let her life circumstances negate God's standards for her life or interfere with His desire that she be beautiful in His eyes!

Abigail—You and I also considered the sad life of Abigail (1 Samuel 25). Sentenced to life with a foolish alcoholic husband, Abigail bore down and was the best wife, home manager, and supervisor of the servants she could possibly be. Recognized by them as a virtuous woman, she is the one the servants reported to when her household was in danger. Then, ever virtuous in character, she literally saved the day—and the lives of her husband and his servants, her household and herself.

Esther—Queen Esther, whom I haven't mentioned before in this book, was married to a godless king. Prone to fits of rage and probably an alcoholic, he was a difficult man (see the Book of Esther). Yet Esther (meaning "star") shines forth as another model of a woman who is beautiful in God's eyes. Ten chapters of the Bible are devoted to her humility, courage, and wisdom. She put all her virtues to work to nurture her relationship with her husband and to save the lives of her people, the Jews.

In light of these examples, I urge you to please look beyond your circumstances, *far* beyond your present difficulties, and even beyond your husband. Instead, as you gaze outward, put God's kaleidoscope of virtues up to the light of His bright hope and His shining Word and give it a turn! Behold the beauty He has in mind for you and is maturing in you in the midst of your challenging circumstances. God's grace is sufficient (2 Corinthians 12:9), He is faithful

(1 Corinthians 10:13), and He has His good purposes for your life (Romans 8:28)! One of those purposes is to make you even more beautiful in His eyes, more like His own Son Jesus (Romans 8:29)!

In your situation, however, you may be thinking, "What if my husband never praises me? I do all these things on God's Proverbs 31 'to-do' list and I try so hard, but I still never get even a thank you!" I think you know my answer by now: Just like your role as mother to your children, your energy and efforts as a wife must never be motivated by possible rewards. Again, God has determined your role and Scripture describes it: As wives, you and I are to do what we do "heartily, *as to the Lord* and *not to men*" (Colossians 3:23)—and that "not to men" phrase includes your husband. You are called to give whatever time and effort necessary to be the wife God calls you to be, "hoping for nothing in return" (Luke 6:35). You are called to love and serve and work and watch and get up and stay up and do good all the days of your life (and...and...and...!) because that's what your all-wise, all-loving God asks of you. Your job is to believe in the rightness of His ways and follow through on His plan for beauty, trusting Him for the kind of blessing He chooses to bestow—even if that blessing does not include your husband's praise. Don't let anyone (including your husband) or anything (including a lack of praise) interfere with God's plan for your godly beauty!

Finally, in case you're questioning, "But what if I don't have a husband?" please don't forget that the emphasis throughout this book is on virtues, on godly character, on who you *are*—not on whether or not you are married or have children. God wants all of His women to be beautifully virtuous in His eyes—and that includes *you!*

An Invitation to Beauty

We're standing near the top of the mountain of virtues we began climbing so many chapters ago! But before we take our final step or two, whisper a prayer now and walk with me through this checklist for beauty.

As a woman—Do you put the power of your mind and body to work on behalf of your husband, family, and home? At the same time, is it your deepest purpose to not only *do* worthily, but to *be* a worthy woman, consistently exemplary in character?

As a homemaker—Do you provide for the needs at home? Do you carefully and attentively look over the ways of your household?

As a mother—Are you raising your husband's children to love and serve the Lord, thereby giving your husband peace of mind and strengthening his reputation in the community?

As a wife—Does your behavior give honor to your husband's name and reputation? Do you contribute positively to his financial well-being through careful management of the household finances? Does your husband trust in you and your faithfulness? Do your words encourage and build him up for the demands of life? In your honest opinion, has your husband found a virtuous woman in you, a woman who is beautiful in God's eyes? Pray that he has—and keep pursuing the heights of excellence!

~ 23 ~

A Spirit of Reverence

HER FAITH

> "Charm is deceitful and beauty is vain,
> but a woman who fears the Lord,
> she shall be praised."
> Proverbs 31:30

We've done it! We've made it to the pinnacle of virtue, the goal of the climb we began together in chapter 1—and we have come a long way! Now, finally, *finally*, in this book about beauty, we reach the summit and there discover a verse that actually contains the word "beauty"!

But wait a minute! What this verse says about beauty is not what we might have expected at the start! We've climbed toward the pinnacle of godly beauty only to realize that it is *not* what we've been told all our lives!

Here the message of Proverbs 31 comes into sharp focus, and we see God's truth one more time: This rich, life-changing Old Testament chapter is all about what is beautiful in *God's* eyes—not man's eyes, not the world's eyes, not the media's eyes, not an artist's eyes, but *God's* eyes! As we have acknowledged from the beginning of this primer on beauty, God declares, "My thoughts are not your thoughts, nor are your ways My ways....My ways are higher than your ways, and My thoughts than your thoughts" (Isaiah 55:8-9). And here we have God's specific thoughts on beauty: "Charm is deceitful and beauty is vain, but a woman who fears the Lord, she shall be praised" (Proverbs 31:30).

It has certainly been instructive to sit in on the lessons of young Lemuel as his wise mother has tutored him along through an alphabet of true feminine beauty. At this point of his lessons, he knows the kind of woman he should look for as a partner for life—and you and I know what God's standards for our lives are. Now this mother, who cares oh-so-deeply about her son's future and who knows what is most important in this life, speaks again. Hear what she has to say about exactly what is—and is not—beautiful in a woman.

The Twin Vanities of Charm and Beauty

"Charm is deceitful," Proverbs 31:30 declares. Warning her son (and all who will heed her wisdom), our teacher cries out, "Don't desire what is charming! Don't fall for charm! Charm is deceitful. Charm is fickle. Charm is fleeting. In the end, charm is one of life's illusions, one of life's vanities!" Charm may indeed lure and fascinate, but it can never produce happiness or get the work of life done. Perhaps in the back of this concerned mom's mind was the proverb that condemns "getting treasures by a lying [charming, deceitful] tongue" (Proverbs 21:6).

"And beauty is vain," she adds (Proverbs 31:30). Still sounding the alarm, our teacher continues: "And don't be fooled by looks! Remember that beauty is only skin deep. Beauty is fleeting, fading—nothing but a vapor!" Although everyone appreciates loveliness of form, physical beauty is transitory and temporary. It can also be misleading and even dangerous. And, like its twin sister charm, beauty does not guarantee a happy life. Neither does beauty alone effectively manage the nuts-and-bolts reality of life.

A Love for the Lord

Throughout this book about beauty, you and I have looked closely at the character qualities of the Proverbs 31 woman and at the many activities that fill her busy life. We've looked at her the way we look at a watch, seeing her moving hands and looking for their message to us. But now, dear friend, we are allowed to see what's inside that makes her tick. Where does her love come from? What is the source of her selflessness…her mercy…her remarkable energy? What guides her, giving her purpose and defining her goals? What makes it possible for this wonder-full woman to be such a solid rock? Where does she find the deep motivation to give herself to such noble efforts for a lifetime? What makes her so beautiful in God's eyes?

The answer is right here in Proverbs 31:30, our final step in understanding God's beauty. Key to all that this beautiful-in-God's-eyes woman is and does is *God Himself*! Proverbs 31:30 is very specific: "A woman who fears the Lord, she shall be praised." You see, God's beautiful woman is a woman who loves Him, who "fears the Lord" (Proverbs 31:30)! He finds it beautiful that she takes Him seriously and takes obedience to His Word seriously.

What exactly does it mean to "fear" the Lord? I hear this question often. In simple terms, a woman who fears the Lord is a woman whose spiritual commitment to God is a total commitment.

How can you nurture your commitment to the Lord and

become more beautiful in His eyes? Being beautiful in God's eyes calls for you to focus on your inner character instead of your external appearance. Rather than the clothes you wear, the hairstyle you choose, the car you drive, or the house you decorate, you are to be primarily concerned about living out the holy character that God works in you as you live in His presence. You are to seek the praise of God rather than men. You are to shun the transitory vanities of this world and pursue instead the eternal beauty of the Lord. These—not face and form—are the interests of a woman who fears the Lord. It is your fear of the Lord that sanctifies every other part of your life and shows the internal majesty of God that is at your very core.

What difference does such a deep commitment to the Lord make? Put simply, it influences all that you and I do! Just as the sun radiates its light, so the presence of the Lord shines through in all you do and in the dedication with which you do it, bringing light to all you touch. Just as fountains, springs, and waterfalls are fed by a source, so your joyous, refreshing power and purposes issue forth from your deep-seated commitment to God. When your heart trusts in God, you refresh the people around you with your selfless deeds and dedication. Your supreme love for God energizes your conduct, your character, and your love for others. Your faith in God generates, animates, and adorns the beauty of your moral stature and the usefulness of your life.

The How-To's of Beauty

God's garland of praise is reserved for the woman who believes in God and walks faithfully in His ways. After all, "The fear of the Lord is the beginning of knowledge" (Proverbs 1:7), and we've seen again and again that the woman who is beautiful in God's eyes is wise as well as beautiful in spirit. The good news is that you and I can know her kind—God's kind—of beauty. How?

1. *More love to Thee, O Christ*—In our New Testament day and age, a woman who is beautiful in God's eyes enjoys a personal relationship with God through His Son, Jesus Christ. That's why, over and over again throughout this book, I have pointed to Colossians 3:23—"Whatever you do, do it heartily, *as to the Lord* and not to men." When Jesus Christ rules your heart and life, then all that you do is an act of worship. It is this kind of love for Christ that makes you truly beautiful in God's eyes!

Again, you and I live out our fear of the Lord through our relationship to God's Son, Jesus Christ. Therefore, God's greatest question to you (and mine, too) is "Do you know Jesus Christ as your Savior and Lord?" Your faith in Him is key to being beautiful in God's eyes.

2. *Schedule time with the Lord*—Anyone who is not fully convinced of their need to seek the Lord regularly usually doesn't! I certainly hope that, by this point in our climb, you realize that you need to seek the Lord if you are to do the job to which He has called you.

Speaking of spending time with the Lord, I just looked at my schedule for this week. It includes such exciting appointments as a teeth cleaning at the dentist and the delivery of our drinking water. You and I schedule nonessentials of life like these, so don't you think we should schedule time with the Lord?

Take a look at your own schedule. When are your appointments with the Lord? What additional time with Him can you plan? Your faith is nurtured and strengthened when you spend sweet minutes reading your Bible and hushed in prayer. You've read much in this book about time management, organization, goals, and scheduling. Now use these lessons and skills to ensure that you are spending the life-giving, life-changing, life-beautifying time with God that you need!

As one who names Jesus as Lord, you are privileged to be able to behold the beauty of the Lord (Psalm 27:4) and worship the Lord in the beauty of His holiness (Psalm 29:2). When you do, His beauty becomes your beauty, and your life bears the mark of a woman who fears the Lord.

3. *Embrace God's plan*—A poem of praise for a virtuous woman, Proverbs 31 lays out God's plan for your life and mine. Just to review, God calls you to be a woman of character, a faithful wife (if you're married) and devoted mother, a dedicated home-builder, and a confident woman because of your reverent fear of the Lord. Rather than resist God's perfect design, I invite you to embrace it, to glory in it, to delight in its every aspect, to excel in it, and to experience its beauty. A woman who fears the Lord is a woman who takes seriously God, His Word, and His plan. When you wholeheartedly embrace God's beautiful plan for your life as the Proverbs 31 woman does, you will be clothed—as she is—with strength and dignity, no matter what comes your way.

4. *Do your best*—The woman of Proverbs 31 is strong and physically fit. We don't know what she looked like, but we can be sure that she did her best. We also know that she dressed dramatically in garments of regal purple, but because of her magnificent virtues we can also be sure that she wasn't overly concerned about her appearance. She did, however, bring honor to her husband's name. Clearly, she offers you and me a good guideline: Do what you need to do to be healthy and fit and to bring honor to your family.

How will you know if you are too concerned about your

physical beauty? I'll let two of God's beautiful women of our day share their thoughts in response to that difficult question.

Author Anne Ortlund came to this conclusion: "I noticed that twenty-two verses [of Proverbs 31] describe this woman's kindness, godliness, hard work, loving relationships—and only one verse out of the twenty-two [verse 22] describes how she looked....Seeing this kind of proportion in Proverbs 31...I prayed, 'O Father, I want to give 1/22 of my time to making myself as outwardly beautiful as I can; and I want to give all the rest of my time, 21/22 of my life, to becoming wise, kind, godly, hard-working, and the rest.'"[1]

When another woman I know prayed about nurturing a heart that fears the Lord, she decided to make the commitment of a daily "time tithe." In other words, she sets apart one-tenth of her waking hours for prayer and Bible study.

Figure out for yourself a formula that balances nurturing in God's presence an inner beauty that pleases Him and the demands of your daily life. Always remember that the time, energy, and attention you give to your relationship with the Lord is attention to inner, godly, and *true beauty*!

An Invitation to Beauty

In case you're not sure about how to have a relationship with Jesus Christ, let me invite you to establish one today and so begin living a life of true internal, eternal beauty! You can set foot on the path of growing in godly beauty right now by earnestly praying these words:

> Jesus, I know I am a sinner, but I want to repent of

my sins and turn to follow You. I believe that You died for my sins and rose again victorious over the power of sin and death. I want to accept You as my personal Savior. Come into my life, Lord Jesus, and help me obey You from this day forward.

I'm praying for you right now! True beauty—indeed, all beauty—begins in Jesus Christ!

~ 24 ~

The Harvest of a Lifetime

HER REWARD

"Give her of the fruit of her hands,
and let her own works praise her in the gates."
Proverbs 31:31

A modern-day "proverb" sums up the path of the Christian life: "The way up is down!" Keep this saying in mind as you consider this final verse from Proverbs 31—the verse that closes the Book of Proverbs. I think those five words aptly describe the life of our beautiful lady, the Proverbs 31 woman. For her, the way up was down.

The woman who is beautiful in God's eyes, whose life and work we've been looking at for 22 verses and 24 chapters, has chosen to live her life in the shadows and to bear fruit that grows only in the shade. Hidden at home, she gives her utmost for God's highest glory as a woman who fears the Lord (Proverbs 31:30). Oh, she (like you) does things outside the home as well, but inside the home no task is too meaningless or effort too small to merit her most excellent endeavor. Now we see the rewards that await the one who has long been content to silently serve: A loud and unanimous chorus of praise celebrates the woman who chose the way down.

The Fruit of Her Hands

As young Lemuel's mother ends her lessons, she looks deeply into her son's eyes and gives one more word of instruction: "Give her of the fruit of her hands" (Proverbs 31:31). Just as admirers award conquerors prizes for their feats and prowess, so we too are to give God's beautiful woman her prizes. Paraphrased in today's words, Proverbs 31:31 could read, "Give her credit for her achievements! Give her all that she has earned! Give her all that she has worked for so diligently! Give her the fruit of her hands, the harvest of a lifetime of loving effort! Give her the profit she's earned, the goods she's worked, the reputation she's established, the marriage she's nurtured, the home she's built, the family life she's cultivated, the future she's labored for! Give it all to her!" And, my dear beautiful friend, you and I are called by these final words, too, to give the woman who is beautiful in God's eyes her rewards, a harvest of praise.

And this is indeed a serious call to praise. Too many women are jealous of this woman who is beautiful in God's eyes. They disdain her, even despise her and jeer at her! I've heard her called "mousy," a wall-flower, "just a housewife," a cave woman, and a slave. Some are quick to say, "Look at all her talent! It's such a shame it's wasted at home! Think how far she could rise in the corporate world with her abilities! Poor thing! What a waste!"

This kind of thinking could not be further from the point of the message that God (and His beautiful woman) offers! In fact, as one scholar concludes, "This verse forms a fitting conclusion to what is the most remarkable exposition in the Old Testament on the position of women, exalting... her functions in the home as wife, mother, and mistress, and showing how contentedness and happiness in the domestic circle depend upon the foresight and oversight of this queen of the hearth."[1]

Far from pitying the Proverbs 31 woman, God calls us to praise her, admire her, and follow her—indeed, to become her! You see, as a woman who fears the Lord, *she* shall be praised (Proverbs 31:29)!

Praise in the Gates

Proverbs 31:31 exults, "Let her own works praise her in the gates." These words are an interesting twist to what has come earlier in Proverbs 31. Do you remember looking at the husband of God's beautiful woman and seeing his prominent position in the gates of the city as a lawyer and leader (verse 23)? Well, now we see his wife's position of honor in the gates as well. Others are talking about her in public places. They are praising her for her works—which themselves praise her, too. How lovely and how encouraging to see that where men congregate, where the leaders of the people meet in solemn assembly, her praise is sung and the highest honor ascribed to her!

We've seen her selflessness, her behind-the-scenes work, and her seemingly unnoticed efforts, but here we learn that her deeds are publicly acknowledged and acclaimed. Like her husband, she enjoys a good reputation and a high standing in the community. Although many of her activities are confined to the home, due recognition of the vital contribution she makes to the community is offered publicly in the gates. As one saint marvels, "Much of what...women do is in a supportive role, but imagine what would happen to a building if its support pillars were removed!"[2] Yes, the contributions which the Proverbs 31 woman makes to her husband, her children, her household, her community are necessary and praiseworthy!

But young Lemuel's mother says, "Let her own *works* praise her." Even if all voices were silent, even if no words of praise were spoken, the woman who is beautiful in God's eyes would receive the honor due her: Her very works are a monument to her name. The works of her hands and the fruit of her labor find a voice and proclaim her praise! As our poem declared earlier, "A woman who fears the Lord, she shall be praised" (Proverbs 31:29)—no matter what!

An Invitation to Beauty

O what joy! What glory! What a wonderful harvest of praise! Every voice possible is praising our woman who is so very beautiful in God's eyes! The voice of her children sounds out her praise (verse 28). The voice of her husband issues forth praise (verses 28,29,31—his is one of the voices in the gates!). The voice of God praises her (verse 30—the fear of the Lord results in *His* praise!).[3] The voice of other people praises her (verse 31—all those in the gates). Even the voice of her works praises her (verse 31). I, Elizabeth George, praise our Proverbs 31 friend, too. Indeed I've done so for 24 chapters! The only voice not heard is that of the woman herself. She wisely lives out yet another proverb—"Let another man praise you, and not your own mouth" (Proverbs 27:2).

But there is one more voice I want to hear praising God's beautiful woman—and that is yours! I am most interested in you and your praise because the rich beauty of the Proverbs 31 woman is not appreciated by our culture. Our enemy

Satan and the fallen world in which we live have painted her beauty as something undesirable, unimportant, and even useless. Oh, how very wrong they are! This woman of Proverbs 31, dear friend and follower of God, is true beauty: She lives out all that is beautiful in God's eyes.

So I call you to praise her! Your praise will indicate that you comprehend the splendor of all that is beautiful in God's eyes. And the richest kind of praise you can offer is to follow in her footsteps. Then my heart will rejoice knowing that you, my companion for so long, are well on your way to becoming beautiful in God's eyes!

Won't you bow your head now and offer your voice, too, in praise to God for His beautiful woman? She is indeed one of His beautiful gifts to you. She is here in Proverbs 31 to inspire, instruct, and encourage you when you fail, when you find your vision dimming, or when you sense your priorities shifting. A fresh visit with the woman who is beautiful in God's eyes will renew your vision, restore your strength, and rekindle your love for God and your commitment to His plan for making you and your life beautiful in His eyes!

Notes

CHAPTER 1

1. C. F. Keil & F. Delitzsch, *Commentary on the Old Testament, Vol. 6* (Grand Rapids, MI: William B. Eerdmans Publishing Company, 1975), p. 327.
2. James Strong, *Exhaustive Concordance of the Bible* (Nashville: Abingdon Press, 1973), p. 39.
3. Edith Schaeffer, *Common Sense Christian Living* (Nashville: Thomas Nelson Publishers, 1983), p. 108.

CHAPTER 2

1. Curtis Vaughan, ed., *The Old Testament Books of Poetry from 26 Translations*—The Bible in Basic English (Grand Rapids MI: Zondervan Bible Publishers, 1973), p. 629.
2. Vaughan, *Old Testament Books of Poetry*, The American Standard Version, p. 629.
3. *The Encyclopedia Americana, Vol. 23* (New York: Americana Corporation, 1958), p. 750.
4. Vaughan, *Old Testament Books of Poetry*, New American Standard Bible, p. 630.
5. *The Encyclopedia Americana, Vol. 21*, pp. 454-56.
6. Vaughan, *Old Testament Books of Poetry*, Rotherham, p. 629.
7. *The Encyclopedia Americana, Vol. 7*, pp. 676-77.
8. *Our Daily Bread*, Radio Bible Class Ministries, Grand Rapids, MI, May, 1982.

CHAPTER 3

1. Cheryl Julia Dunn, A *Study of Proverbs 31:10-31*, Master thesis (Biola University, 1993), p. 27.
2. Ibid., p. 27.
3. Ibid., pp. 25-26.
4. Curtis Vaughan, ed., *The Old Testament Books of Poetry from 26 Translations*—The Bible in Basic English (Grand Rapids, MI: Zondervan Bible Publishers, 1973), pp. 629-30.

CHAPTER 4

1. "Building Your Nest Egg," by Deborah Adamson, *Los Angeles Daily News*, April 20, 1997.
2. Cheryl Julia Dunn, A *Study of Proverbs 31:10-31*, Master thesis (Biola University, 1993), p. 25.
3. Barbara Gilder Quint, *Family Circle*, May 29, 1984. (Condensed in *Reader's Digest.*)

CHAPTER 5

1. Merrill F. Unger, *Unger's Bible Dictionary* (Chicago: Moody Press, 1972), p. 313.
2. Cheryl Julia Dunn, A *Study of Proverbs 31:10-31*, Master thesis (Biola University, 1993), p. 31.
3. Robert L. Alden, *Proverbs*, A *Commentary on an Ancient Book of Timeless Advice* (Grand Rapids, MI: Baker Book House, 1990), p. 220.
4. Mrs. Charles E. Cowman, *Streams in the Desert, Volumes 1 and 2* (Grand Rapids, MI: Zondervan Publishing House, original publishing date 1925, reprinted 1965 and 1966 respectively).
5. Ray Beeson and Ranelda Mack Hunsicker, *The Hidden Price of Greatness* (Wheaton, IL: Tyndale House Publishers, Inc., 1991), pp. 97-107.
6. Anne Ortlund, *Building a Great Marriage* (Old Tappan, NJ: Fleming H. Revell Company, 1984), page unknown. (Prayer written by Temple Gairdner, nineteenth-century Scottish missionary and scholar.)

CHAPTER 6

1. James M. Freeman, *Manners and Customs of the Bible* (Plainfield, NJ: Logos International, 1972), p. 198.
2. W. O. E. Oesterley, *The Book of Proverbs* (London: Methuen and Company, Ltd., 1929), p. 284.
3. C. F. Keil and F. Delitzsch, *Commentary on the Old Testament—Vol. 6* (Grand Rapids, MI: William B. Eerdmans Publishing Company, 1975), p. 329.
4. Fred H. Wight, *Manners and Customs of Bible Lands* (Chicago: Moody Press, 1978), p. 83.
5. G. M. Mackie, *Bible Manners and Customs* (Old Tappan, NJ: Fleming H. Revell Company, no date given), p. 59.
6. Cheryl Julia Dunn, A *Study of Proverbs 31:10-31*, Master thesis (Biola University, 1993), p. 38.
7. G. M. Mackie, *Bible Manners and Customs*, p. 667.
8. Ibid.
9. Thomas Kinkade, *Simpler Times* (Eugene, OR: Harvest House Publishers, 1996), p. 69.
10. Edith Schaeffer, *Common Sense Christian Living* (Nashville: Thomas Nelson Publishers, 1983), pp. 88-89.

Chapter 7

1. Curtis Vaughan, ed., *The Old Testament Books of Poetry from 26 Translations*—Lamsa (Grand Rapids, MI: Zondervan Bible Publishers, 1973), p. 630.
2. Gene Getz, *The Measure of a Woman* (Glendale, CA: Regal Books, 1977), p. 125.
3. Elizabeth George, *Loving God with All Your Mind* (Eugene, OR: Harvest House Publishers, 1994).

Chapter 8

1. Curtis Vaughan, ed., *The Old Testament Books of Poetry from 26 Translations*—Lamsa (Grand Rapids, MI: Zondervan Bible Publishers, 1973), p. 630.
2. James M. Freeman, *Manners and Customs of the Bible* (Plainfield, NJ: Logos International, 1972), p. 50.
3. G. M. Mackie, *Bible Manners and Customs* (Old Tappan, NJ: Fleming H. Revell Company, no date given), p. 99.
4. Cheryl Julia Dunn, *A Study of Proverbs 31:10-31*, Master thesis (Biola University, 1993), pp. 52-53.
5. Ibid., pp. 51-53.
6. Ibid., p. 51.
7. Ibid.
8. Ibid., pp. 51-52.
9. Lucinda Secrest McDowell, "This I Carry with Me Always," *Christian Parenting Today*, May/June, 1993, pp. 22-23.
10. Alan Lakein, *How to Get Control of Your Time and Your Life* (New York: Signet Books, 1974), p. 46.
11. Edwin C. Bliss, *Getting Things Done* (New York: Charles Scribner's Sons, 1976), pp. 148-49.

Chapter 9

1. *Webster's New Collegiate Dictionary* (Springfield, MA: G. & C. Merriam Co., Publishers, 1961), p. 954.
2. Robert L. Alden, *Proverbs, A Commentary on an Ancient Book of Timeless Advice* (Grand Rapids, MI: Baker Book House, 1990), p. 220.
3. C. F. Keil and F. Delitzsch, *Commentary on the Old Testament—Vol. VI* (Grand Rapids, MI: William B. Eerdmans Publishing Company, 1975), p. 330.
4. Crawford H. Toy, *A Critical and Exegetical Commentary on the Book of Proverbs* (Edinburgh: T. & T. Clark, 1899), p. 544.
5. Cheryl Julia Dunn, *A Study of Proverbs 31:10-31*, Master thesis (Biola University, 1993), pp. 58-59.

6. *The Living Bible: Paraphrased*, by Kenneth Taylor (Wheaton, IL: Tyndale House Publishers, 1971).
7. Edith Schaeffer, *Hidden Art* (Wheaton, IL: Tyndale House Publishers, 1971).

Chapter 10

1. Crawford H. Toy, *A Critical and Exegetical Commentary on the Book of Proverbs* (Edinburgh: T. & T. Clark, 1899), p. 544.
2. William McKane, *Proverbs, A New Approach* (Philadelphia: The Westminster Press, 1970), p. 668.
3. Cheryl Julia Dunn, *A Study of Proverbs 31:10-31*, Master thesis (Biola University, 1993), p. 64.
4. Ibid.
5. Ibid., pp. 63-65.
6. Curtis Vaughan, ed., *The Old Testament Books of Poetry from 26 Translations*—Knox (Grand Rapids, MI: Zondervan Bible Publishers, 1973), p. 630.
7. Sir Alexander Paterson, *United Evangelical Action*, Fall, 1975, p. 27.
8. "You," by Mac-Sim-Ology.

Chapter 11

1. William McKane, *Proverbs, A New Approach* (Philadelphia: The Westminster Press, 1970), p. 668.
2. Ted W. Engstrom, *The Pursuit of Excellence* (Grand Rapids, MI: Zondervan Publishing House, 1982), p. 36.

Chapter 12

1. C. F. Keil and F. Delitzsch, *Commentary on the Old Testament, Vol. 6* (Grand Rapids, MI: William B. Eerdmans Publishing Company, 1975), p. 332.
2. Sybil Stanton, *The 25 Hour Woman* (Old Tappan, NJ: Fleming H. Revell Company, 1986), p. 169.
3. Anne Ortlund, *The Disciplines of the Beautiful Woman* (Waco, TX: Word, Incorporated, 1977), pp. 66-67.
4. Ted W. Engstrom, *The Pursuit of Excellence* (Grand Rapids, MI: Zondervan Publishing House, 1982), p. 33.
5. Ruth Wagner Miller, "The Time Minder" (*Christian Herald*, 1980), pp. 76-77.
6. "A Woman's Love" by Douglas Malloch.

Chapter 13

1. Cheryl Julia Dunn, *A Study of Proverbs 31:10-31*, Master thesis (Biola University, 1993), p. 36.

2. Barbara Keener Shenk, *The God of Sarah, Rebekah and Rachel* (Scottdale, PA: Herald Press, 1985), p. 127.
3. Dunn, *Study of Proverbs 31:10-31*, p. 85.
4. David Thomas, *Book of Proverbs Expository and Homiletical Commentary* (Grand Rapids, MI: Kregel Publications, 1982), p. 793.
5. Ibid.
6. Edith Schaeffer, *Hidden Art* (Wheaton, IL: Tyndale House Publishers, 1971), pp. 128-32.
7. Stanley High, *Billy Graham* (New York: McGraw Hill, 1956), p. 127.

Chapter 14

1. C. F. Keil and F. Delitzsch, *Commentary on the Old Testament—Vol. 6* (Grand Rapids, MI: William B. Eerdmans Publishing Company, 1975), p. 334.
2. William McKane, *Proverbs, A New Approach* (Philadelphia: The Westminster Press, 1970), p. 669.
3. Keil and Delitzsch, *Commentary on the Old Testament—Vol. 6*, p. 335.
4. Crawford H. Toy, *The Book of Proverbs* (Edinburgh: T. & T. Clark, 1899), p. 545.
5. W. O. E. Oesterley, *The Book of Proverbs* (London: Methuen & Co., Ltd., 1929), p. 285.

Chapter 15

1. Curtis Vaughan, ed., *The Old Testament Books of Poetry from 26 Translations* (Grand Rapids, MI: Zondervan Bible Publishers, 1973), p. 631.
2. Vaughan, *Old Testament Books of Poetry*, The Jerusalem Bible, p. 631.
3. Cheryl Julia Dunn, *A Study of Proverbs 31:10-31*, Master thesis (Biola University, 1993), p. 101.
4. Ibid., p. 102.
5. Robert L. Alden, *Proverbs, A Commentary on an Ancient Book of Timeless Advice* (Grand Rapids, MI: Baker Book House, 1990), p. 221.
6. Linda Dillow, *Creative Counterpart* (Nashville: Thomas Nelson, Inc., Publishers, 1977), p. 23.
7. Denis Waitley, *Seeds of Greatness* (Old Tappan, NJ: Fleming H. Revell Company, 1983), p. 77.

Chapter 16

1. John MacArthur, "God's High Calling for Women," Part 4 (Panorama City, CA: Word of Grace, #GC-54-17, 1986).

2. George Lawson, *Proverbs* (Grand Rapids, MI: Kregel Publications, 1980), p. 883.
3. Donald Hunt, *Pondering the Proverbs* (Joplin, MO: College Press, 1974), p. 432.
4. William J. Peterson, *Martin Luther Had a Wife* (Wheaton, IL: Tyndale House Publishers, Inc., 1983), p. 34.
5. *The Amplified Bible* (Grand Rapids, MI: Zondervan Publishing House, 1970), p. 302.
6. Verna Birkey, *Seminar Workshops for Women* (P.O. Box 3039, Kent, WA 98031), 1979, p. 131.

Chapter 17

1. Cheryl Julia Dunn, *A Study of Proverbs 31:10-31*, Master thesis (Biola University, 1993), p. 125.
2. Elizabeth George, *Loving God with All Your Mind, God's Garden of Grace, A Woman After God's Own Heart* (Eugene, OR: Harvest House Publishers, 1994, 1996, 1997 respectively).
3. Edward H. Griggs.

Chapter 18

1. Curtis Vaughan, ed., *The Old Testament Books of Poetry from 26 Translations*—The American Standard Version (Grand Rapids, MI: Zondervan Bible Publishers, 1973), p. 632.
2. Cheryl Julia Dunn, *A Study of Proverbs 31:10-31*, Master thesis (Biola University, 1993), p. 126
3. Charles Caldwell Ryrie, *The Ryrie Study Bible* (Chicago: Moody Press, 1978), p. 984.
4. Vaughan, *Old Testament Books of Poetry*, The American Standard Version, p. 632.
5. Ray and Anne Ortlund, *The Best Half of Life* (Glendale, CA: Regal Books, 1976), p. 88.
6. Stephen B. Douglass, *Managing Yourself* (San Bernardino, CA: Here's Life Publishers, Inc., 1978). For an expanded treatment of these categories, read Elizabeth George, *Life Management for Busy Women* (Eugene, OR: Harvest House Publishers, 2002).
7. *Great Hymns of the Faith*, "Great Is Thy Faithfulness," by William M. Runyan, 1923.
8. Elizabeth George, *Loving God with All Your Mind* (Eugene, OR: Harvest House Publishers, 1994).
9. Abigail Van Buren, "Dear Abby," *Los Angeles Times*, January 1, 1995.

Chapter 19

1. Curtis Vaughan, ed., *The Old Testament Books of Poetry from 26*

Translations—The American Standard Version (Grand Rapids, MI: Zondervan Bible Publishers, 1973), p. 632.
2. Charles Caldwell Ryrie, *The Ryrie Study Bible* (Chicago: Moody Press, 1978), p. 938.
3. Cheryl Julia Dunn, *A Study of Proverbs 31:10-31*, Master thesis (Biola University, 1993), p. 139.
4. H. D. M. Spence and Joseph S. Exell, eds., *The Pulpit Commentary—Vol. 9* (Grand Rapids, MI: William B. Eerdmans Publishing Company, 1978), p. 601.
5. Dunn, *Study of Proverbs 31:10-31*, p. 139.
6. *Life Application Bible* (Wheaton, IL: Tyndale House Publishers, 1988), p. 449.
7. Elizabeth George, *A Woman After God's Own Heart* (Eugene, OR: Harvest House Publishers, 1997), pp. 38-39.
8. William MacDonald, *Enjoying the Proverbs* (Kansas City, KS: Walterick Publishers, 1982), p. 86.
9. William MacDonald, *Enjoying the Proverbs*, p. 99.
10. Vaughan, *Old Testament Books of Poetry*, The American Standard Version, p. 632.

Chapter 20

1. Merrill C. Tenney, ed., *The Zondervan Pictorial Encyclopedia of the Bible, Vol. 5* (Grand Rapids, MI: Zondervan Publishing House, 1975), pp. 901-02.
2. Cheryl Julia Dunn, *A Study of Proverbs 31:10-31*, Master thesis (Biola University, 1993), p. 144.
3. William McKane, *Proverbs, A New Approach* (Philadelphia: The Westminster Press, 1970), p. 670.
4. Derek Kidner, *The Proverbs* (Downers Grove, IL: InterVarsity Press, 1973), p. 71.
5. Dunn, *Study of Proverbs 31:10-31*, p. 144.
6. Curtis Vaughan, ed., *The Old Testament Books of Poetry from 26 Translations*—Knox (Grand Rapids, MI: Zondervan Bible Publishers, 1973), p. 632.
7. Vaughan, *Old Testament Books of Poetry*, Taylor, p. 632.
8. Edith Schaeffer, *What Is a Family?* (Old Tappan, NJ: Fleming H. Revell Company, 1975), p. 77.
9. Mrs. Isabella Beeton, *Beeton's Book of Household Management* (London: Chancellor Press, 1861).
10. Author unknown.

Chapter 21

1. Abraham Cohen, *Proverbs: Hebrew Text and English Translations with an Introduction and Commentary* (Hindhead, Surrey: The Soncino Press, 1945), p. 214.

2. Ibid.
3. C. F. Keil and F. Delitzsch, *Commentary on the Old Testament—Vol. 6* (Grand Rapids, MI: William B. Eerdmans Publishing Company, 1975), p. 340.
4. W. O. E. Oesterley, *The Book of Proverbs* (London: Methuen and Company, Ltd., 1929), p. 286.
5. Elisabeth Elliot, *The Shaping of a Christian Family* (Nashville: Thomas Nelson Publishers, 1992), p. 201.
6. Edith Schaeffer, *What Is a Family?* (Old Tappan, NJ: Fleming H. Revell Company, 1975), p. 121.
7. E. Schuyler English, *Ordained of the Lord* (Neptune, NJ: Loizeaux Brothers, 1976), p. 35.
8. Elizabeth George, *A Woman After God's Own Heart* (Eugene, OR: Harvest House Publishers, 1997).
9. Schaeffer, *What Is a Family?* p. 92.
10. Vonette Zachary Bright, ed., *The Greatest Lesson I've Ever Learned* (San Bernardino, CA: Here's Life Publishers, Inc., 1991), p. 182.

Chapter 22

1. Robert Gilmour LeTourneau, *Mover of Men and Mountains* (Englewood Cliffs, NJ: Prentice-Hall, 1960).
2. Curtis Vaughan, ed., *The Old Testament Books of Poetry from 26 Translations* (Grand Rapids, MI: Zondervan Bible Publishers, 1973), pp. 632-33.
3. Cheryl Julia Dunn, *A Study of Proverbs 31:10-31*, Master thesis (Biola University, 1993), p. 163.
4. Kenneth Taylor, *The Living Bible* (Wheaton, IL: Tyndale House Publishers, 1971).
5. Ibid.
6. Charles Bridges, rev. by George F. Santa, *A Modern Study in the Book of Proverbs* (Milford, MI: Mott Media, 1978), p. 161.
7. Ralph Wardlaw, *Lectures on the Book of Proverbs—Vol. 3* (Minneapolis, MN: Klock & Klock Christian Publishers, Inc., 1982 reprint), pp. 310-11.
8. Fred H. Wight, *Manners and Customs of Bible Lands* (Chicago: Moody Press, 1953), p. 130.

Chapter 23

1. Anne Ortlund, *The Disciplines of the Beautiful Woman* (Waco, TX: Word Books, 1977), p. 46.

Chapter 24

1. W. O. E. Oesterley, *The Book of Proverbs* (London: Methuen & Company, Ltd., 1929), p. 283.
2. Judy Hubbell, *Messenger*, November 1975, p. 31.
3. Cheryl Julia Dunn, A *Study of Proverbs 31:10-31*, Master thesis (Biola University, 1993), p. 171.

Bibliography

Alden, Robert L. *Proverbs: A Commentary on an Ancient Book of Timeless Advice*. Grand Rapids, MI: Baker Book House, 1983.

Arnot, William. *Studies in Proverbs: Laws from Heaven for Life on Earth*. Grand Rapids, MI: Kregel Publications, 1978.

Dunn, Cheryl Julia. "A Study of Proverbs 31:10-31." Master thesis, Biola University, 1993.

Exell, Joseph S. *Proverbs, The Biblical Illustrator*. Grand Rapids, MI: Baker Book House, 1957.

Hunt, Donald. *Pondering the Proverbs*. Joplin, MO: College Press, 1974.

Ironside, H. A. *Notes on the Book of Proverbs*. New York: Loizeaux Brothers, 1952.

Jamieson, Robert, A. R. Fausset, and David Brown. *Commentary Practical and Explanatory on the Whole Bible*. Grand Rapids, MI: Zondervan Publishing House, 1973.

Karssen, Gien. *The Best of All*. Colorado Springs: NavPress, 1984.

Keil, C.F., and Delitzsch, F. *Commentary on the Old Testament—Vol. 6*. Grand Rapids, MI: William B. Eerdmans Publishing Company, 1975.

Kidner, Derek. *The Proverbs*. The Tyndale Old Testament Commentaries. London: InterVarsity Press, 1973.

Lawson, George. *Proverbs*. Grand Rapids, MI: Kregel Publications, 1980.

MacDonald, William. *Enjoying the Proverbs*. Kansas City, KS: Walterick Publishers, 1965.

McKane, William. *Proverbs: A New Approach*. Philadelphia: The Westminster Press, 1970.

Muffet, Peter. *A Commentary on the Whole Book of Proverbs*. Edinburgh: James Nichol, cir. 1594.

Oesterley, W. O. E. *The Book of Proverbs with Introduction and Notes*. London: Methuen & Co., Ltd., 1929.

Pfeiffer, Charles F. and Everett F. Harrison. *The Wycliffe Bible Commentary*. Chicago: Moody Press, 1973.

Santa, George F. A *Modern Study in the Book of Proverbs: Charles Bridges' Classic Revised for Today's Reader*. Milford, MI: Mott Media, 1978.

Spence, H. D. M. and Joseph S. Exell. *The Pulpit Commentary, Vol. 9, Proverbs, Ecclesiastes, Song of Solomon*. Grand Rapids, MI: William B. Eerdmans Publishing Company, 1978.

Stitzinger, Jim. "Lecture Notes on Proverbs," The Master's Seminary, 1997.

Thomas, David. *Book of Proverbs, Expository and Homiletical Commentary*. Grand Rapids, MI: Kregel Publications, 1982.

Toy, Crawford H. A *Critical and Exegetical Commentary on the Book of Proverbs*, The International Critical Commentary. Edinburgh: T. & T. Clark, 1899.

Wardlaw, Ralph. *Lectures on The Book of Proverbs—Vol. 3*. Minneapolis, MN: Klock & Klock Christian Publishers, Inc., 1982 reprint.

Whybray, R. N. *Proverbs, New Century Bible Commentary*. Grand Rapids, MI: William B. Eerdmans Publishing Company, 1994.

Woodcock, Eldon. *Proverbs, A Topical Study, Bible Study Commentary*. Grand Rapids, MI: Zondervan Publishing House, 1988.

Loving God with All Your Mind

Elizabeth George

HARVEST HOUSE PUBLISHERS
EUGENE, OREGON

Italicized text in Scripture quotations indicates author's emphasis.

Acknowledgment

As always, thank you to my dear husband, Jim George, M.Div., Th.M., for your able assistance, guidance, suggestions, and loving encouragement on this project.

LOVING GOD WITH ALL YOUR MIND

Published by Harvest House Publishers
Eugene, Oregon 97402

Library of Congress Cataloging-in-Publication Data

George, Elizabeth, 1944–
Loving God with all your mind / Elizabeth George.
p. cm.
Includes bibliographical references.
ISBN-13: 978-0-7369-1382-9 (pbk.)
ISBN-10: 0-7369-1382-3 (pbk.)
1. Christian women—Religious life. 2. God—Worship and love. I. Title.
BV4527.G46 2005
248.8'43—dc22 2004018775

To, for, and because of Jim

Contents

Invitation to a Changed Life

Would you like *all* your thoughts to be pleasing to the Lord? Would you like to exchange doubt, discouragement, depression, and fear for energetic faith and joy? Would you like to know what to do and how to handle the next problem that comes your way? Then look to Jesus for the answer. In Matthew 22:37, He tells us to "love the Lord your God with all your heart, with all your soul, and *with all your mind.*" When you do this, you will indeed find your life changed—transformed! You will begin to...

- work on what is real...rather than worry about what is unreal.
- reach forward and press on...rather than remain a prisoner of the past.
- act on what is revealed in Scripture...rather than trust in your emotions.

What I offer in this book are six powerful Scriptures that have brought stability, strength...and sweet peace...into my life and into the lives of others. These Scriptures are guaranteed to be life-changing for you, too—because they come straight from God's Word!

Have you read the original version of *Loving God with All Your Mind?* Are you wondering, "Why this new volume?" The answer in a word is "growth." It's been ten years since this book was first published. During that time, I have grown spiritually. I have grown in my personal application of these six truths through new and different phases and events in my life. I have grown as I've shared these Scriptures in my conferences. And now I want to share this new growth and deeper understanding with you!

Thanks to the graciousness of Harvest House Publishers, what you hold in your hands is an update of what I trust you will find to be a transforming, inspiring, and encouraging book about the power of thinking on God's truth. It is substantially revised and filled with added insights and illustrations. It's language is practical and to the point. And because I understand your busy lifestyle, the chapters are shorter and more manageable. It also includes success stories and victories shared by others.

I also invite you and your Bible-study group to use the companion volume, *Loving God with All Your Mind Growth and Study Guide.* The additional Scriptures and the focus on personal application will further increase your spiritual growth and ignite your desire to love the Lord whole-heartedly.

I give thanks to God for the ministry this book has had so far. And I am praying that *your* life will be truly transformed as you think on these truths about God and look at life's challenges from God's perspective—through His Word. Then He will indeed change your thoughts...and your life! And you will find yourself truly loving God with all your mind.

In His everlasting love,

Elizabeth George

Training Your Thoughts

Finally, brethren,

whatever things are true,

whatever things are noble,

whatever things are just,

whatever things are pure,

whatever things are lovely,

whatever things are of good report,

if there is any virtue and

if there is anything praiseworthy —

— meditate on these things.

PHILIPPIANS 4:8

~ 1 ~

Thinking on the Truth

Whatsoever things are true...
think on these things.

Philippians 4:8 KJV

Because my husband, Jim, is in the ministry, our phone rings a lot. And sure enough, one morning many years ago was no different. As I hurried across the family room to answer another call, I prayed my standard on-the-way-to-answer-the-phone prayer—"God, whoever it is, whatever it is, help me."

That prayer, however, did not prepare me for the startling request this caller made. The woman, a member of our church, explained that she had met with one of the pastors that morning because of her tendency toward depression. At the end of the counseling session, he had given her a homework assignment: "Go home and call Elizabeth George and ask her how she overcame her struggle with depression."

Overcoming Depression

Too shocked to respond, all I could do was ask for the woman's phone number and for some time to think about my answer. As I hung up the phone, a tidal wave of emotions swept over me.

First, I felt concern for this woman. So few Christians face their problems to the point of seeking advice. Even fewer actually show up for a prearranged appointment. Still fewer do what the counselor recommends. And here was a woman who had done it all! And she was asking me for help.

Next came distress. I didn't like hearing that someone was using my name in a counseling session. And I wasn't exactly thrilled to be characterized as someone who battled with depression, even though it was true. Besides, I thought I'd kept up a strong front...but obviously this pastor had seen through my facade. And, praise God, he had noticed some victory and headway!

Then came pain. As you read this book, you'll discover that one key to loving God with all your mind is choosing *not* to dwell on the past or on unpleasant memories. Yet to help this woman, I would need to once again look closely at the painful past. As I made myself remember those darker days, I recalled my morning routine....

Dark days—Every day I woke up in what I selfishly considered less-than-desirable surroundings—a tiny house in the middle of a desert with no air conditioning and no dishwasher. That meant that several times a day I had to stand in sweltering heat at the kitchen sink doing our dishes by hand. (That's enough to depress any woman!)

And there I stood, looking out the window and thinking long and hard while I washed dishes. Amazingly, I could recall almost every negative thing that had ever happened to me in my life! I thought about other days and better times. I relived unkindnesses and mistreatments. I reviewed again and again my failures and disappointments along with my dreams that, by the looks of things, were never going to come true. Soon my thoughts pulled me down so far that tears streamed down my cheeks and into the dishwater.

After the dishes came the housework. As I went from room to room, I felt oppressed and numb. A heavy, dark fog settled in my head. As I made each bed, I wanted to get into it, sink my head into the pillow, pull the covers up over my head, and close my eyes. You see, with my eyes shut, maybe—just maybe!—the fog would go away. Everything would be black, and I wouldn't have to keep groping my way along....

Remarkable change—"Exactly how had my life changed since those days?" I wondered and prayed. What had helped me get past those dark and heavy moods? What had freed me from that almost-immobilizing depression? Was there some key I could pass on, some hope and help I could offer? This dear lady needed to know.

I've learned in the past 20 years that I'm not alone. Others—like you perhaps?—also need help. I now know that...

- Some form of depression affects more than 17.5 million Americans each year.
- Depression can affect anyone, regardless of

background, though major depression strikes women twice as often as men.

- More than 1 in 5 Americans can expect to get some form of depression in their lifetime.[1]

Turning to God's Word

As I mentally journeyed back to those "dark days," I saw how God had worked in my life through three specific practices.

Memorizing God's Word—The first was hiding Scripture in my heart. As a new Christian, I was advised that I should memorize Scripture. And not knowing that I had an option, I dutifully began to memorize passages from God's Word. I wrote Bible verses on index cards and carried them with me in my purse, taped them on mirrors, and laid them on the breakfast table. And, especially important, I placed them on the windowsill over my kitchen sink. I was doing what I knew was right…but I was quite unaware of the great benefits I would reap.

Meditating on God's Word—The second habit I was cultivating was meditating on Scripture. I had learned some methods for reflecting on God's Word in several wonderful books.[2] Furthermore, the Scripture memory course I had enrolled in required meditation exercises for the assigned verses.[3] Again, I knew that I was doing what was right…but I didn't know how helpful meditating on Scripture would actually prove to be.

Applying God's Word—The third…and most challenging!…

practice I was trying to master was obedience—actually doing what God's Word said. I admit, it wasn't always easy to do what God was telling me to do in the verses I was memorizing and meditating on. But I knew that God gave us His Word to show us how to live. And I knew that I needed to *do* what it says, not just *know* what it says (Matthew 7:21).

There was no way in the world to fathom at that time the many ways God would use these three practices to remove the bars of negative thinking that held me prisoner!

Thinking on "These Things"

One morning, as I was standing at my kitchen sink washing dishes (again!), I was looking at the index card that was propped up on the windowsill. The memory verse laboriously written on it was Philippians 4:8. That's a l-o-n-g verse about the eight virtues prescribed by God for a Christian's thought-life. And it had been v-e-r-y hard for me to learn. Anyway, as I reviewed the verse, I counted the eight virtues on my fingers to make sure I didn't leave one out:

> Finally, brethren, whatsoever things are true, whatsoever things are honest, whatsoever things are just, whatsoever things are pure, whatsoever things are lovely, whatsoever things are of good report; if there be any virtue, and if there be any praise, think on these things (KJV).

I had already spent time meditating on Philippians 4:8 as a whole, so I knew it was a guideline for the kinds of thoughts God desired to occupy my mind. But I had never thought about each component separately. And that morning

I decided to take the verse apart while I washed the dishes. Going through an exercise designed for discovering the meaning of Scripture, I said out loud, "Finally, brethren, whatsoever things are true." Then I stopped and asked, "What does *true* mean?" And my answer? "Obviously *true* means truth, the truth of Scripture. And *true* means the truth as opposed to lies. But *true* also means real, because what is true is what is real."

The door of understanding cracked open for me!

Continuing on with the exercise, I asked, "Is there a command to obey?" I recited my way through the entire verse again and landed on God's command at the end of it—*think on these things*. Stated in the positive, God is issuing the command to "let your mind dwell on what is true or real." And stated in the negative, the same command would be "Do not think on things that are not true or real."

Suddenly God's Word seemed to be screaming at me, "Elizabeth, *stop* thinking on things that are not true and real!"

Breaking Through

And there it was! "Whatsoever things are true...think on these things." In just eight words—*eight* words!—out of the fathomless treasure of God's Word, I had my breakthrough. It came when I realized that God did not want me to spend my precious time and equally precious mental energy thinking on things that are not true or real.

As I sought to apply this instruction and obey the command of Philippians 4:8, the darkness over my life began to lift and the light of God's Word flooded into my heart, soul...and mind! Here, in a mere handful of words, God was telling me not to think about anything that wasn't true or real, and I needed to be faithful in putting this truth into practice.

Here's something for us to think about. It's been estimated that 10,000 thoughts pass through the human mind in one day. Obeying God's command to filter our thoughts through His grid of *true* and *real* is no easy task. But, thanks be to God, He helps us accomplish whatever He asks us to do!

Making Progress

Encouraged—and excited!—about my discovery, I started to evaluate my daily thoughts in light of the first few words of Philippians 4:8. I literally had to train my thoughts. I had to make it a point to ask myself, "Am I thinking on the truth—on what is true and real?"

Over the next few weeks, as I continued to ask this question, I made some dramatic progress in changing my thought-life. I also began to realize that God had a solution for my long struggle with depression and worry and fear. For the first time, I understood that His Word offered hope for my moodiness! That solution, and that hope, lay in keeping my thoughts within the biblical boundaries of Philippians 4:8—"Whatsoever things are *true* [or *real*]...think on these things."

These few words helped me take a significant first step toward spiritual mental health. And this scripture continues, to this day, to correct all my unhealthy thinking. And it can do the same for you.

Realizing Strength for Daily Life

Take it from me, blessings abound when you and I think on what is true and real. And one of those blessings is strength for daily life—strength that includes energy, health, and vitality. Let me explain. I'm sure you know how limited you are when you are ill. Well, when you aren't functioning according to what is real, it's like trying to do something when you have a fever or the flu. Even though you force yourself to fulfill your responsibilities, something is missing. Your body's ability and the demands of each task are out of sync! Sure, you go ahead and do your work, but there is little, if any, enthusiasm. And many times your work is half done or done poorly. Why? Because of poor physical health...which means less energy...and even less performance.

The same thing happens in the spiritual realm! Like a virus, your thoughts can drain your energy and cripple your usefulness. But, praise God, the opposite is also true. Your thoughts can be a source of strength. When you think on the powerful truths of Scripture, God uses His Word to change your way of thinking. And one beneficial—and much-needed!—result is that you are strengthened and energized for daily life by thinking on the truth—on what is true and real.

Loving God...Even More

As I think about you as the reader of a book bearing the title *Loving God with All Your Mind,* I am assuming that you already love God. As a believer in Christ, you have already responded to God's love for you. As a truth in the Bible states, "We love Him because He first loved us" (1 John 4:19). Therefore, it is my prayer that as you make your way through this book, each and every truth and step of application will help you love God even more.

So here's a first step: Remember these eight words from God's Word—"Whatsoever things are true…think on these things."

And here's a second step: Every time you hold your thoughts up against God's standards of what is true and what is real…and then *choose* to "think on these things," you are loving God with all your mind. With His help, His Word, and His Spirit, you can triumph over negative emotions, damaging thoughts, and destructive attitudes.

Now, read on to see how thinking on the truth, on what is true and real—will transform your mind…and your life!

~ 2 ~

Thinking the Truth About...God and His Word

Whatever things are true...
meditate on these things.

Philippians 4:8

Dear reader, I pray that a transformation has already begun in your heart and mind...as it did in this woman's life:

> Elizabeth, what ministered to me most from your teaching on "Loving God with All Your Mind" is thinking on what is true and real. As a sufferer of depression, I now think on what is true and real, and trust God and His Word rather than spiraling down into despair and suicidal depression. This is totally new to me!

I'm also praying that you are grasping the importance of training your thoughts to think on what is true and real. For me it was the first step in learning what it means to love

God with all your mind. And here's another step: We must be thinking thoughts about *God* that are true.

Thinking the Truth About God

Through my years of ministry, one scenario has often been repeated. A dear woman will come to me with her problem. Then, after she's poured out her heart, she'll say something like, "God must not care about me. He must not see how I'm being treated. He must not know what's happening to me. If He did, He would do something about it!" And then I can almost predict the next words: "God must not love me."

I never condemn or judge anyone who says these things. That's because I've felt this way, too. And I've said all of those things myself! But I've also learned that whenever you and I feel this way...or begin to think in this way...we must stop and ask, "But what is true and real about *God?*" We can then recall truths from the Bible that confirm God's love for us, His people. Truths such as these...

God cared for the Israelites—One year I set a goal to read through my Bible...and I made it all the way to Exodus, chapter 2! It was there that I witnessed and marked heavily in my Bible how God demonstrated His care for the Israelites. Here's what happened in Exodus 2. After Joseph died, the children of Israel were mistreated by the new pharaoh. Under severe persecution, they felt (as perhaps you have) that God didn't care about them. The Bible, however, reports that this was never the case. Even while the Israelites thought they were unloved and forgotten,

> God *heard* their groaning, and God *remembered*

> His covenant....And God *looked* upon the children of Israel, and God *acknowledged* them (Exodus 2:24-25).

God indeed saw His people, and He took notice of their condition! And, far from forgetting them, God was well aware of His covenant with them. Then God acted on what He heard, saw, and noticed. He told Moses, "I have surely *seen* the oppression of My people...and have *heard* their cry... for I *know* their sorrows....So I have come down to *deliver* them...and I will send you" (3:7-10).

This God-breathed, true account from the Bible reminds us that God sees, hears, and knows all about the sufferings of His people. He also remembers His promises, cares about His people, and acts on their behalf and for their good. You and I must choose to "think on these things"—these comforting, tender, and rock-solid, never-changing truths about God's care and concern for us—rather than focus on our own faulty thoughts or feelings. Regardless of the difficulty and pain of life's circumstances, "these things" are what is true and real about God!

God cared for Hagar—The story of God's concern for Hagar is a favorite of mine. Twice God met this woman in times of great distress. At the first meeting, Hagar was pregnant, alone, and a fugitive. But "the Angel of the LORD found her" and said, "the LORD has *heard* your affliction" (Genesis 16:7,11). After her encounter with God, Hagar referred to Him as "You-Are-*the-God-Who-Sees*" (verse 13). Later, she had a son whom Abram named Ishmael, meaning *"God hears"* (verse 15).[1] Both Hagar and Abram recognized the truth that our God is truly a God who sees and hears...and cares! Hagar personally experienced His care, concern, and provision.

Hagar's second recorded meeting with God occurred 16 years later, and it, too, was initiated by Him. Although time had passed, God still knew, saw, heard, cared, and provided for this single mother. In this scene, Abraham had sent Hagar and her son away. In the blazing, bone-dry desert, the two of them were dying. Yet "God *heard* the voice of the lad" crying and provided the two of them with water as well as encouragement (Genesis 21:9-19).

God cares for you—When I think about the God who heard, saw, knew, and rescued the Israelites and Hagar, my faith in God's caring and concerned nature is strengthened. Then, when I add the truth of 1 Peter 5:7—"He cares for you"—the teaching is clear: God cares about and for His people. And that, dear reader, includes you and me!

Thinking the Truth About God's Word

Another crucial step toward loving God with all our mind is determining to place the Bible's truths above everything we think or feel. For instance, the Bible sets forth the important truth that "if we confess our sins, He is faithful and righteous to forgive us our sins and to cleanse us from all unrighteousness" (1 John 1:9 NASB). Although this statement guarantees that God forgives our sins, I've been guilty of saying, after a time of prayer and confession, "But I don't *feel* forgiven." When I do this, I am allowing my *feelings* to take precedence over the rock-solid, doctrinal truth of the forgiveness of sins available to us through Christ.

On other occasions I say, "But I don't *think* God could really forgive me." With a statement like this, I'm allowing my *thoughts* to take precedence over the Word of God.

My friend, you and I, as believers in Christ, are forgiven, regardless of our feelings and thoughts. That's that! In Christ "we have redemption through His blood, the forgiveness of sins" (Colossians 1:14). To think we are not forgiven is to think a lie, to think something that is untrue. Therefore, when my feelings and thoughts are running counter to what Scripture teaches, I need to stop and ask, "But, Elizabeth, what is true?" The answer is always the same: "The Bible is true, not my feelings or my thoughts." Therefore I choose to "think forgiven."

After I shared the truth of 1 John 1:9 at a Christian women's conference, one woman wrote, "For a long time now, my thoughts have been, 'But I don't feel forgiven' or 'Was I really saved to begin with?' I have confessed my sin over and over, and I hassle with it constantly. Reviewing the principle of thinking on the truth and this scripture is already beginning to correct my thinking."

Thinking the Truth About Ourselves

Another important guideline for our thoughts is we must think on the truth about ourselves. When we view ourselves through the lens of God's Word, we better understand God's love for us and the worth we have in His eyes. For example, Romans 5:8 tells us that "Christ died for us." This truth means that we are of inestimable value, precious in His sight...even when we don't feel or think we are. Such a truth teaches us about our position before God in Christ. Truths like these enable us to experience the power of God instead of suffering from the draining effects of thoughts about ourselves that simply are not true.

A personal story—I admit that I have to fight this battle against thinking negatively—and wrongfully!—about myself almost daily. But I well remember one day when the struggle was tougher than usual. I had accepted a writing assignment that challenged me to venture *way* beyond my comfort zone! However, confident of God's leading, I tackled the job. I worked harder and longer than ever...only to have my writing meet with strong reaction, resistance, and near rejection. I was mortified! I had failed!

Drained physically as well as emotionally, I crawled home to hide and recover. But even there, in the safety and shelter of my home-sweet-home, thoughts like these filled my mind: "Who do you think you are? When are you going to learn that you are nobody! You are nothing! When will you understand that the kind of ministry you were attempting is reserved for others who are better than you?"

As the day went on, my thoughts became even darker. "Why don't you just quit now? Why try? Why care? It was just a dream. And besides, you are a nobody and a nothing!"

I knew the signs all too well. I was sliding down into the dark hole of depression, defeat, discouragement, dismay, and dejection. But I began to fight back! I decided it might help if I got out of the house. So I went for a walk. But walking didn't help this time. With each step up our huge hill, I continued to hear the defeating chorus that had been there all day long.

But then the Holy Spirit broke through my relentless chant and prompted me to ask myself the key question: "But Elizabeth, what is true and real?" And, my friend, the answers from Scripture that God brought to my poor exhausted mind and heart came to my rescue! God reminded me that...

- I am fearfully and wonderfully made, no matter what I or others may think about me (Psalm 139:14),
- He has a grand plan and purpose for my life, no matter how the present may look (2 Timothy 1:9),
- He has given me spiritual gifts that I can use to benefit other believers, no matter how I may be floundering or failing at the moment (1 Corinthians 12:7-11), and
- I am always loved and accepted by God, no matter what I experience or who may reject me (Romans 8:35).

These thoughts are God's unshakable truth! And one by one, I began replacing my untrue thoughts with these *facts*—these *truths* from God's Word about how *He* sees me and about what *He* has accomplished on my behalf. And with each thought, each truth, God gave me His fresh strength and joy.

A personal friend—Another common error in our thinking is dwelling on unmet expectations. My friend Louise suffers from the crippling effects of rheumatoid arthritis and has to constantly guard her expectations for herself. Her unending pain and fatigue can cause her to dwell on what she can't do or on what she thinks she should be accomplishing. However, when this kind of thinking begins, Louise reports, "It comforts me to remember that God is all-knowing and has a plan for me that includes my condition. I find rest as I trust in Him because He is faithful and will do what He promises."

A personal word of encouragement—And for you, dear friend? Be assured that the same is true. When you think on God's Word, on what is true and real about yourself and your circumstances (as Louise does and as I'm learning to do), God uses His truth to break the cycle of destructive thinking that leads to discouragement, despair, doubt, and depression. However real the pain, the hurts, and the disappointments of your life are, you must remember the *greater* reality of God's love, power, and redemption. This brings God's comfort, healing, and hope to your heart and soul.

So...whenever you slip into thinking of yourself as useless, as worthless, as a failure, a hopeless case, or a loser, remember what is true:

- You are a child of God (John 1:12).
- You are His workmanship (Ephesians 2:10).
- You have been bought by the precious blood of Christ (1 Corinthians 6:20; 1 Peter 1:18-19).

Loving God...Even More

Throughout this chapter I've shared from God's Word, from my life, and from the lives of others. But now I'm wondering about you. What untrue thoughts about God do you find yourself entertaining? What truths and teachings in the Bible do you fail to accept and apply to your life as truth? And what debilitating thoughts do you tend to think about yourself...thoughts that don't match up to God's view of you as His child?

Oh, how I want you to understand the importance of training your mind to think on what is true and real! To love God with all your mind! When you do, what happens? You experience the joy and hope of being God's child. And blessings upon blessings, you experience spiritual encouragement, powerful enablement, and fresh energy for handling life as the Holy Spirit uses God's Word in your heart and mind!

That's what happened to the woman who wrote the letter at the beginning of this chapter. Read now how she concluded her triumphant, victorious note:

> I have been a slave to my roller-coaster emotions rather than keeping my eyes on God and trusting Him despite what my emotions are telling me. The Lord has given me so much strength and hope through His Word, despite how I feel. And you know what? When you keep your eyes on God and the Word of God, He gives you a peace in your heart and hope which results in a quiet inner joy.

Dear heart, may the peace of God that surpasses all understanding keep and guard *your* heart and mind through Christ Jesus as you think on what is true and real.

~ 3 ~

Thinking the Truth About...Others

Whatever is true...
think about such things.

Philippians 4:8 NIV

Do you suffer from an overactive mind when it comes to thinking about your relationships? Most people do. And if that's the case for you, Philippians 4:8 can help. That's because your relationships with people also need to be guided by its truth: "Whatsoever things are true [or real]...think on these things" (KJV).

Playing Mind Games

I confess that through the years I've been guilty of playing mind games with people and second-guessing their motives. It's all too easy to wonder about what a person *isn't* saying or try to read between the lines of what he or she *does* say—"He says he loves me, but I don't think he does" or "She said there's nothing wrong, but I'm not so sure."

Isn't it amazing how we can come up with *very* creative explanations for people's actions? For example, "He's been grumpy lately, so he must be angry with me." We can also draw conclusions about why people do what they do—"She left a message on my machine to call her. I must have done something wrong" or "I wonder what she wants from me now." We can even apply this kind of thinking to what people do *not* do—"She hasn't called me in a while. I must have done something to offend her."

Well, there's help and hope for our imaginations *and* for our relationships! Two principles from Scripture can help settle such mind games.

Understanding the Principle of Love

The first principle is based on 1 Corinthians 13, on the apostle Paul's words about love. As he writes to his friends, Paul notes that love "thinks no evil" and "believes all things" (verses 5 and 7). One day I realized that I was violating these two requirements for love whenever I questioned what another person said or did. My habit of second-guessing involved interpreting—and even distorting—the words and actions of others. When I tried to read things into a person's words and actions rather than accepting them at face value, I was essentially making that person a liar.

The solution? I needed to stop my wild, speculative thoughts by asking myself, "But, Elizabeth, what is true and real?" The answer to this question then called me to believe what the other person said.

Putting the Principle of Love to Work

Learning to think no evil about another person and believe what he or she says has helped me make giant strides in my interaction with others. It has helped me eliminate second-guessing and reading between the lines. It has also diminished the misunderstanding and hurt that can come as a result of such untrue thinking. If he says he loves me, I now believe that he loves me. If she says it doesn't matter, I believe that it doesn't matter. If he says nothing is wrong, I believe that nothing is wrong. I think on what is true.

Let me quickly say that this is not always as easy as it sounds! One evening, after a class on this very principle from 1 Corinthians 13, a college student admitted her struggle. She shared, "Even though my friend seems to be avoiding me and not talking to me as much as before, I'm trying not to assume anything. Instead, I'm praying about it and, as 1 Corinthians 13:7 says, believing the best. It's hard, though, because my mind almost automatically wants to assume the worst."

A friend of mine told me about a similar situation. "When spending time with friends, I found myself being too sensitive and taking things they did and said out of context. But I am learning to take things at face value and to distinguish between what is perceived and what is real."

Like both of these growing Christians, you can break the habit of destructive thought patterns that damage relationships. Simply ask yourself, "What is true?" This exercise can help you stop the second-guessing, the analysis, and the introspection that hinder the development of healthy relationships.

Understanding the Principle of a Clear Conscience

In Matthew 18:15, Jesus offers another principle for healthy relationships. He says, "If your brother sins against you, go and tell him his fault between you and him alone."

The primary application of this truth is to simply obey the command and go to any person who sins against us.

But think for a minute about what this command means for you and me when other believers obey it. It means that when we sin against others, they are to come to us in private to talk about it.

I can't begin to describe the freedom this truth has given me! Because of it, I've quit wasting time and energy worrying about what other people think of me or about what I do. I've also stopped wondering what others *might* be thinking...or what I *might* have done wrong. Why? Because if I've done something wrong, they are to come to me and tell me. Until that happens, my guesses are just that. They're guesses... rather than fact, reality, or truth.

As I've stopped analyzing my every move and second-guessing other people's ideas about me, I have experienced more peace and greater openness in my relationships. I no longer fear or dread encounters with people. I've stopped wondering what critical thoughts they might be thinking. And I've begun

> ...looking to God through prayer,
> ...looking to His Word, and
> ...looking to mature Christian mentors

to reveal any wrong attitudes and actions rather than constantly looking for fault in things I've said or done.

Putting the Principle of a Clear Conscience to Work

Hear now the wisdom of Proverbs 28:1: "The wicked flee when no one pursues, but the righteous are bold as a lion."

My paraphrase of this truth is, "If you haven't done anything wrong, don't act like it!" We are to boldly and confidently proceed in our relationships, rather than holding back, wondering what people are thinking about us. And this takes conscious effort, as one student discovered and wrote about in her class paper:

> A certain person was acting differently toward me. Normally I would have probed and speculated a lot, but I decided to act as if everything were okay. The next day she told me that she was dealing with some things and was sorry she had treated me badly. So [her behavior] wasn't because of something I had done after all.

Applying God's Principles to Your Thoughts

What kinds of thoughts do you tend to have about people? I doubt that they are always pure, positive, and prayerful. No one's are! After all, who hasn't slipped into second-guessing, analysis, and suspicion? And who hasn't been plagued by self-doubt or crippled by negative thoughts, insecurity, and worry? Instead of such unhealthy, cynical thinking, applying God's principles to your thoughts—

- ✓ Choose to think on what is true and real.
- ✓ Corral your thoughts and refuse to second-guess or draw conclusions about people's behavior.
- ✓ Count on others to tell you if you have failed in your behavior.

✓ Count on God's Spirit to point out when you have offended someone.

Do you want to nurture love and confidence in your relationships with others? Then changing your thought-life is key! By God's grace and with His help, choose to think no evil about people. Determine to trust what others say and do. Count on others to come to you when you have failed them and count on God to reveal where you have offended them. Thoughts about people that are based on what is true and real will liberate you to generously and joyously love and serve one another. That's what the Christian life is all about!

Tapping into the Power of God's Word

We've covered a lot of ground and addressed many of our everyday problems. But before we step into a new chapter about other issues and concerns that every human must deal with, I want us to return to the basic truth of the power of God's Word to help us in any and all of our life experiences. So let's review...and remember these two facts.

The foundation for a healthy thought-life is God's Word. God has chosen to communicate with us through the Bible. Therefore, His Word is to take priority over everything else we might choose as the basis of our thoughts, actions, and feelings.

The power God extends to us through His Word—and through thinking on His Word—can lift us out of the depths of defeat, discouragement, despair, doubt, dread, and depression and enable us to deal with the challenges that come our way.

With our thoughts based on the Word and Person of God,

we find strength, hope, joy, faith, and peace of heart, soul, and mind. Then, as we encounter the events life brings our way, we will experience victory. Freed from the faulty mental habits that cripple our thought-life, we will be able to move calmly and steadily forward with courage and confidence.

An example of God's power to others—The story Ruth Graham tells about her parents illustrates the power that comes with thinking biblical truths, from thinking on God's Word. Dr. and Mrs. Nelson Bell ministered in China for 20 years during a time in China's history that was characterized by unrest and political and military upheaval. At one point, this faithful couple lay in their dugout shelter, not knowing their fate. The situation appeared to be hopeless, and these missionaries could easily have been overwhelmed by panic and despair. The choice was theirs...and they chose to view their situation through the lens of God's truth. Mrs. Bell reports:

> We were counting over our defenses....Overhead are the overshadowing wings (Psalm 91:4); underneath are the everlasting arms (Deuteronomy 33:27); all around "the angel of the Lord encampeth round about them that fear Him, and delivereth them" (Psalm 34:7); inside, that "peace which passeth all understanding" (Philippians 4:7); also, "Thou wilt keep him in perfect peace, whose mind is stayed on Thee: because He trusteth in Thee" (Isaiah 26:3).[1]

The Bells' focus on God's truth calmed their hearts and strengthened them to endure the challenges they faced.

Loving God...Even More

My dear reading friend, the same assurances and power that sustained Dr. and Mrs. Bell are available to you! You can choose to think thoughts about God and life's situations that are *not* true...or you can choose to love God with all your mind and think the truths stated in Scripture. The next time you feel yourself slipping from confidence to cowardice, from control to emotion, from the strength of spiritual mental health to frailty of spirit, review the resources you have as a child of God. In times of trauma and testing, choose to fill your mind with what is true. Choose to love God.

And when it comes to your thoughts about others again put the power of God's Word to work! Instead of spending your time and mental energy analyzing other people's words and actions or second-guessing what they say and do, think on what is true and real. When you train your thoughts to focus in this way, you experience wonderful peace of mind and heart *and* sound and sincere connections and communications with others. As a result, your relationships become characterized by genuine love, a love for others that finds its source in your desire to love God...even more.

~ 4 ~

Thinking the Truth About . . . the Future

Whatever is true...dwell on these things.

Philippians 4:8 NASB

Whenever I teach or speak, I usually announce that I'm available afterward for any questions. One particular evening, a woman cautiously approached me after our class time. As she began talking, and well before she got to her question, I realized I was hearing someone share her deepest fears.

I had very little eye contact with this lady whose head hung so low. Her gripping fear constricted her breathing, which explained the labored whisper. When she did dare to look up, I saw intense pain in her eyes. Hers was a face robbed of the smile lines God meant her to have. Stress was taking its toll, and my heart ached for this woman in her anguish. God's desire is that she might live "abundantly" (John 10:10), yet fear was robbing her of joy, as it does many of God's people.

Crippling Fear

As I've listened to others—and to my own heart and mind—I've realized that crippling fear comes to us for a variety of reasons. Here's a handful of fears...and I'm sure you can add to the list!

Disasters—In California, where I lived for 30 years, earthquakes cause everyone great concern. Newcomers to the state asked, "How do you know when you're having an earthquake? What does it feel like?"

"Oh, you'll know when it happens," I always said. And they did!

Finances—The prospect of not enough money or a loss of employment generates worry and fear. Add to these anxieties other crippling thoughts such as "I'm afraid we're going to lose our home" and "I'm afraid the economy will never improve," and it's easy to see how fear breeds more fear.

Child-raising—All parents experience fear for their children. First, we worry during pregnancy about a baby's development and safe delivery. After birth, a baby brings money worries and the loss of a more carefree lifestyle. As the baby grows, fears increase as parents worry about accidents, abuse, crime, school environments, pollution, war, and the future of the world. And top on our list is wondering whether our children will come to love Christ and follow Him so they will enjoy eternal life.

Then, when our children are adults, we worry about their choices of marriage partners, the new couple's finances, the possibility of divorce. And when the grandchildren arrive, sure enough, the cycle of fear begins all over again.

Singleness—Many singles fear a lifetime of being alone. I'll never forget a young woman who attended a singles' Bible study in our home. When Amy mentioned that the next meeting would be on her birthday, the group instantly began planning a party for her at the end of our next study. The plans, however, were interrupted when Amy sobbed, "But you don't understand. This is not an occasion to celebrate. I'm going to be 30!" To Amy, her birthday meant another year, another five years, another decade, had passed—and she was still single.

And here's another fact: Even those who are married often fear the singleness of divorce and widowhood.

Aging, illness, and suffering—During his ministry to senior citizens at our former church, Jim regularly heard dear saints express their fears of old age and of needing convalescent care in later years without adequate finances.

And many people—myself included—fear illness and suffering. But I found great hope when I watched my friend Allison, who suffers from multiple sclerosis (MS). Our seminary wives' fellowship group prayed with her through her medical tests and the diagnosis and witnessed Allison's initial struggles. Then, as she began adjusting to a new kind of life, we tried to help out. One evening we wept together as Allison shared a devotional based on James 1:2-4. In that passage, James writes:

> My brethren, count it all joy when you fall into various trials, knowing that the testing of your faith produces patience. But let patience have its perfect work, that you may be perfect and complete, lacking nothing.

Now hear Allison's message! Months before she and her husband came to the seminary, the women in her home church had studied James. Feeling stagnant as a Christian, Allison had read these first verses and prayed, "God, give me an opportunity to grow. Give me the opportunity to apply these truths in my life."

Next came the diagnosis of her disease.

As she faced MS, Allison changed her prayer to, "God, give me joy in my trial." She began a "Journal of Joy" and one entry read, "God, I can have joy and thank You because my illness was not a brain tumor." Seeing how Allison dealt with her illness reminded me that God is with us when we are sick or disease-ridden.

Death and dying—Closely related to the fear of illness is the fear of death. We wonder, "When will I die? How will I die? Will I suffer with dignity?" Too rarely do we have the apostle Paul's perspective on death in our minds. In his letter to the Philippians, Paul explains, "To die is *gain*" (Philippians 1:21). He teaches that to die is simply "to *depart* and *be with Christ*" (1:23) and that to be with Christ "is *far better*" (1:23). As an unknown poet has written, "Better, far better, with Christ to be, living and loved through eternity."

Overcoming Fear

What can we do to overcome our fears? How can we keep fear from robbing today of its joys? What can we do to control this raging and damaging emotion? And how can we stop thinking thoughts that hurt us and hinder our strength? Again, Scripture comes to our rescue. Considering the fact that fear is generally rooted in thoughts about things that are *not real,* we must again remember the admonition of Philippians 4:8—"Whatever things are true [or real]...meditate on these things."

As we've already noted, the first few words of Philippians 4:8 challenge us to think on what is true or real, to function according to facts, not feelings or fantasies. What we think must be...

- true according to what the Bible says,
- true according to the character of God as revealed in the Bible, and
- true according to what people say and do.

As we think on God's Word, He uses it to help us handle what is true and real and to calm our fears about the future, the past, and the present. Here's how.

Thinking About the Future

Do you frequently find yourself asking, "What if...?" That question can generate all kinds of fear about the future. Philippians 4:8, however, teaches that our thoughts should "belong to the nature of reality."[1] This guideline rules out all fearful dwelling on the future. God commands us to think on what is true and real. And it's a fact—events in the future are neither.

Our theme verse—Philippians 4:8—is a challenge to learn not to probe the future with fear-generating questions such as What if I never get married? What if I lose my spouse? What if I get cancer? What if my children rebel? Questions like these can consume our minds and keep us from loving and trusting God.

That was the case with Patty, a woman I met at a church retreat. As I spoke, I spotted Patty's distraught face in the audience. At one of the breaks, she came up to me and explained that she and her husband had wanted a baby for more than ten years. They were thrilled when God blessed them with a baby—but now it was time for the baby's DPT immunization. Having read about the mortality rate linked to DPT shots, this mother was postponing the shot. She voiced her fear to me: "What if my baby dies from that injection?"

Oh, dear friend, whatever your "what if" is, you must remember that "what if" is a guess. If you want to overcome your fears, you cannot think "what if" thoughts. Instead, in obedience to Philippians 4:8, you and I must acknowledge that events in the future are not real. We must eliminate this kind of speculative thinking because thoughts about the future are only guesses.

Furthermore, the future is in God's hands—His loving, capable, merciful, powerful hands! He can enable us to deal with what is real, with what is now. And, the truth is, He will also be with us whatever the future holds. Lo, He is "with you always, even to the end of the age" (Matthew 28:20)! Yes, we need to be prepared for things like earthquakes. And yes, we need to be wise about our finances, our parenting, and our health. But we don't need to waste energy worrying about what is not yet real, about things that may never come to pass.

Asking, "But What Is True and Real?"

We're extremely well-acquainted with fears-on-end, aren't

we? But what does God say about these worries? Consider again, item by item, the list of fears we just looked at. Each one was a "what if" concern. Not one of the events was real. Not one of them had actually happened.

Disasters—Possible calamities (including earthquakes!) exist only in the mind...until they happen!

Finances—Potential money problems aren't today's money problems. Instead of worrying, we need to remember David's testimony in Psalm 37:25: "I have not seen the righteous forsaken, nor his descendants begging bread."

Child-raising—Similarly, a parent's worries about the future are not real. Instead of "forward worrying," we parents are to focus our energy on what we must do *today* because today is real. God asks parents to nurture, train, and discipline their children *today* (Ephesians 6:4)...and then wake up tomorrow and do the same. Being overly concerned about potential parenting problems saps our energy and our joy and interferes with our efforts as parents. God calls us to handle each day, one at a time. *Today* is real, and, beloved, God will enable us to deal with what today holds. That is what's true!

Singleness—This same principle holds for singles like Amy. God doesn't ask single adults to look down through the corridors of time future and imagine that they will be single forever. Again, He calls a single person to address what is real, and what is real is singleness *today*.

Although Amy's desire may be to be married, she—like you and I—can learn much from the wise words of missionary

Jim Elliot. While waiting on God's will regarding marriage, Jim Elliot wrote to his future wife, Elisabeth Howard, "Let not our longing slay the appetite of our living." Commenting on this wisdom decades later, Mrs. Elisabeth Elliot wrote, "We accept and thank God for what is given, not allowing the *not-given* to spoil it."[2] God is adequate.

And what about worrying about singleness through widowhood? Even though widowhood is a possibility, God does not want a married person to ruin today's joy with his or her spouse by entertaining the thought of death. Why worry? God is, always has been, and always will be, sufficient.

Aging, illness, and suffering—God also offers His presence and provision to those who fear old age with the promise that "even to your old age...and even to gray hairs I will carry you!...I will carry, and will deliver you" (Isaiah 46:4). It's a fact...and a promise: God will take care of you and me in our later years.

Illness and suffering? God doesn't want our fear of possible physical suffering to overshadow the reality of our health and usefulness today. If and when we do experience physical trials, God will be with us through them, and we will find, with Paul, that we "can do all things through Christ who strengthens me" (Philippians 4:13). God will strengthen us.

Death and dying—Death is the ultimate reality for everyone, but it is also the ultimate victory for every Christian. The Bible says "to be absent from the body" is "to be present with the Lord" (2 Corinthians 5:8). Fearing death and dying can keep us from living full and productive lives today. But we can surrender that fear to God's promise that He will be with us "through the valley of the shadow of death" (Psalm 23:4). God is and will be present with us.

Did you notice a pattern in these suggestions about how to deal with your "what if" fears? The way to let go of such fears is to acknowledge God's presence, God's power, and God's love. When you and I think "what if..." questions, we fail to acknowledge God. That's when we need to turn to His Word and be reminded of the many promises that God is with us wherever we go (Joshua 1:9).

And remember this, too: Your God is the God of the past, the present, *and* the future! He has promised to guide you throughout your life and receive you to glory afterward (Psalm 73:24). You can shout along with David that "surely goodness and mercy shall follow me all the days of my life; and I will dwell in the house of the LORD forever" (Psalm 23:6).

Noting a Few "Nothings"

I hope you are getting excited! These truths mean we experience peace instead of worry when we choose to believe the Bible's promises that God will superintend every future event. Therefore...

- *Nothing* will ever happen to you that God does not already know about (Psalm 139:1-4).
- *Nothing* will ever happen to you that is a mistake (Psalm 139:4,16).
- *Nothing* will ever happen that you cannot handle by God's power and grace (2 Corinthians 12:9-10).

- *Nothing* will ever happen to you that will not eventually be used by God for some good purpose in your life (Romans 8:28).
- *Nothing* will ever happen to you without God's presence (Matthew 28:20).

Loving God...Even More

Beloved, with promises like these, how can we not but love God? So how can you love God...even more? By remembering that the future is not real. The future exists only in the imagination. Then, when the future arrives...whether in the next minute, hour, or tomorrow...you will—and, by God's grace, you can!—deal with it then, when it is truly present and real. Plan for the future and set goals for yourself, but also be sure to leave them in God's hands. Use your energy to draw close to God in the present and to train your thoughts to think about and deal with things that are true and real...right now!

(P.S. Here's another "nothing" for you as you love God with all your mind: *Nothing* will ever separate you from God's love—Romans 8:38-39!)

~ 5 ~

Thinking the Truth About...the Past and the Present

Fix your thoughts on what is true
and honorable and right.

Philippians 4:8 NLT

One of my passions is reading the biographies of missionaries. These full-of-faith saints teach me much about living a life of faith and endurance. One such person was Adoniram Judson (1788–1850), who has emerged as a personal favorite. This missionary to Burma suffered opposition, failed health, imprisonment, hardship, deprivation, and the death of his wife...and all of this suffering occurred within the first 13 years of his 30-plus years of ministry! Yet this was the man who declared, "The future is as bright as the promises of God."

What a lifestyle! Can't you just relish the power of waking up each day to what is true and real, and staring it in the eye with an attitude of heart and mind that knows that the future is as bright as the promises of God? What a spectacular way to face the future, no matter how trying—thinking on the truths about God and His promises from His Word!

But what about the past? How are you and I to deal with it? And the present? What will help us cope with reality, with the way things really are?

Thinking About the Past

Like our "what if" thoughts about the future, "if only" thoughts about the past can rob us of peace and joy in the present. And the exhortation in Philippians 4:8—to think on "whatever things are true [or real]"—comes to our rescue concerning our thoughts about the past. That's because the past is no more real than the future.

A personal story—I know firsthand how tightly we can be gripped by the habit of looking to events in the past and thinking, "If only I had done that differently....If only I hadn't done that....If only that hadn't happened....If only I had been better informed." Here's just one example of my problems with the past.

For years after I became a Christian, I struggled with the thought, "If only I had become a Christian sooner!" After all, I reasoned, coming to Christ sooner would have given Jim and me God's guidelines for our marriage and for raising our two daughters. The eight years of marriage before I knew Christ were rough ones. And adding two children hadn't helped! However, when Christ entered our hearts and our home and we began to read God's Word, His Spirit opened our eyes and showed us how to live God's way. It was then I realized I had missed out on some precious opportunities and some important years of nurturing my daughters because I was focusing on myself. So my heart cried out, "If only I had become a Christian sooner, I would have been a better wife and mother, I would have had Christ's love to share in our home, I would have known to serve and sacrifice instead of being so selfish! If only…"

Finally the Holy Spirit pointed me to the truth that God was in complete, sovereign control of my salvation and my life! It was as if He asked me, "Elizabeth, who was in charge of your salvation? Who picked the exact day and minute? Who knew from before time began when you would believe in Jesus? Who knew about the two little girls and their needs? Who handpicked you to be their mother? Who used a rocky marriage and an unfulfilling family life to open your eyes to your needs?"

At this point, I was on my knees in adoration of God, the One who controlled my life in the past and controls it in the present and into the future! *He* knew how my life would unfold. *He* knew when I would come to know Him. *He* knew how I would come to serve Him. This is what is true and real and far more important than my "if only" moanings and mournings.

And I'm not alone…

Jenny's story—Jenny, a woman I sat next to at a seminary wives' luncheon, also struggled with "if only" thinking. As the women at the luncheon told how their husbands had come to attend seminary, a common thread in many of the stories was meeting and marrying in college. Jenny, the last one to share, lamented, "I feel left out here today. If only I had gone to college…."

Next on the agenda was my time to teach about (guess what!) thinking on what is real instead of on "if only's." When I finished and sat down, Jenny smiled, leaned over, and whispered, "Thanks so much! I really needed that. I'll never say 'if only' again."

But think about Jenny's situation. What was true and real about it? Was God able to direct Jenny's past and bring her and her husband together even though they both didn't go to college? And could God use Jenny mightily even though she didn't have a college education? I think you know the answer, right? *Of course!* These facts are what was true and real! Jenny's "if only" thinking was unnecessary and untrue. And it was holding her back by fostering feelings of inferiority and regret.

Remembering to Think on What Is True

Note it well: "If only" thinking is counterproductive. How is that? Because it doesn't address what is real. The past is gone. It is beyond repair, beyond restructuring. What is real is what is happening today. And God calls us to deal with what is now, what is true, and what is real.

And, as we've seen in Jenny...and perhaps as you yourself have experienced, "if only" thinking breeds remorse. The backward gaze can produce regret and sorrow because it is impossible to return to the past or change the past. So we must ask, What value is there in rehashing it?

Remembering two exceptions—But also note these exceptions: It is good to remember what we've learned from our mistakes. Those lessons are pearls of wisdom. And it is also good to recall God's marvelous works and gracious faithfulness to us. We should look back and remember how God enabled us in our times of need. Our faith in God is strengthened when we recall how God brought us through our trials, how He taught us on the mountains and in the valleys of life. Psalm 77, often referred to as a "cure for depression,"[1] says we are to meditate on God's goodness in the past whenever the trials of the present seem overwhelming. At such a time, the poet declared, "I will *remember* the works of the LORD; surely I will *remember* Your wonders of old" (verse 11).

So go ahead. Look back at the past...but do so with an eye to appreciate God's faithfulness!

Remembering facts about God—Here's something else to note. When you succumb to "if only" thinking, you fail to acknowledge God's role in your past. You are ignoring the fact that God was there with you. He was with you then... just as He is with you today...and will be with you tomorrow (Psalm 73:23-24).

When you acknowledge God by remembering the facts and evidence of about His care and His character, the wondrous truths about Him help you look back without regret or remorse through eyes of faith.

Looking Back Through Eyes of Faith

Do you know happens when you and I look back at the past without trusting that God was there with us and concerned about us? We sentence ourselves to a life of regret.

Trusting God's guidance—That is what one missionary couple Jim and I met seemed to be doing. When it was time for their oldest child to start school, they enrolled her in a

Christian boarding school. At the end of that first year, the little girl told her parents about her year of loneliness and tears. At that moment, they concluded that they had made a horrible mistake.

My wise Jim listened to their story and then asked, "Did you pray before you decided to send your daughter to boarding school?" Devoted Christians and devoted parents, they had indeed prayed.

Jim then asked, "Did you seek wise counsel before you decided to send her to boarding school?" Again, the answer was a hearty yes.

Gently, Jim asked, "Do you think that after you prayed and sought wise counsel, your decision really could have been a horrible mistake?"

What joy it was for us to watch their faces as, for the first time, this hurting couple looked back at their experience through the eyes of faith! Their "if only" thinking was keeping them from remembering their prayerful, biblical decision-making process. A burden was lifted from the shoulders of our new friends and God's servants! They found real relief as they recalled how they had sought God's guidance each step of the way. As hard as that year must have been on their daughter, they could trust that God had been present with her and that He would use that hard time for her good.

Trusting God's overruling power—Here's something else that's true and real about God. As the God of the past, our heavenly Father does indeed *use* our past. The great truth of Romans 8:28-29 is God's promise that any and all "negative" events in the past will be "overruled" and worked for good to make you more like Christ. By His transforming power,

God will redeem even the worst, the most painful, and the most perplexing aspects of your past.

I've seen God redeem the suffering and the terrible trials in many people's lives, and I'm sure you have, too. In fact, some of the saints I know who graciously and continually extend God's gentleness, peace, and encouragement to others are those who have tasted pain. God, in His goodness and power, has used their experiences to make them more Christ-like, and He is truly glorified in their lives.

Thinking About the Present

And what about the present? Just as we need to follow the exhortation of Philippians 4:8 when thinking about the future ("What if...?") and the past ("If only..."), we need to think on what is true and real in the present. Believe me, I know this is not always easy to do! Too often we are tempted to say, "But this isn't the way it was supposed to be."

A personal story—As a young mother, I chose Proverbs 22:6 as a guiding scripture for raising my children. This admonition says parents are to "train a child in the way he should go, and when he is old he will not depart from it." Holding tightly to this promise, I began to train my children in the way they "should go." A decade later, however, my parenting didn't seem to be working the way I wanted it to. I wasn't reaping the results I had expected. Angry, I said to God, "But this isn't the way it was supposed to be! This isn't the way it went for this family here or that family over there. And this isn't the way it was supposed to be for my family!"

Like a little girl who doesn't get what she wants, I threw a spiritual tantrum. I used my time and energy kicking, screaming, and battling God. Then one day, when I finally took a breath during my rantings to listen, God seemed to say, "But, Elizabeth, this is the way it really is. Now what are you going to do about the way it really is?" I realized I had to quit yelling (so to speak), get up, and go on. And I did.

I was *forced* to face reality. You see, because of my unmet expectations I was postponing any action. Because I didn't like what I saw (which was real!), I was failing to do anything to try to improve the situation. I neglected to deal with the circumstances. Furthermore, I wasn't prepared to because "this wasn't the way it was supposed to be!" And as long as I had that attitude—as long as I didn't accept reality—no progress or solution was possible. As long as I wished for reality to be different, I failed to handle the problem, which was quite real!

Other people struggle, too—I know many women who refuse to face reality when it comes to their marriages. It seems that our fantasies, expectations, and dreams about what marriage will be are usually quite different from the truth. Then, when reality sets in, many women are too stunned and confused to do anything about it. Unhappy, they say to me, "I don't know why I ever married my husband in the first place. I wish I hadn't. This isn't the way it was supposed to be!"

Then, as a friend, I must be the one to say, oh so gently, "But this is the way it really is. Now, what are you going to do about the way it is?" Then the two of us get to work on a solution, a remedy, a plan. You see, once we accept reality—the reality of the condition of our marriage, our family, our job, whatever—we can then use our time and energy to make that reality better.

Loving God...Even More

And now it's your turn. I've shared some of my personal struggles, and I've shared instances from the lives of others. But the most important person reading this book is you.

What does your past hold? What people, events, and circumstances from days gone by have caused you difficulties or brought problems into your life? You love God with all your mind when you acknowledge His sovereignty over every event of your life—past and present, as well as future.

Think about it this way. Whatever has happened to you in days gone by, the Bible teaches us that, as the supreme and sovereign ruler and the One who is omnipresent through time, God knew the events of your life...before the foundation of the world (2 Timothy 1:9). He knew each detail of the path your life would take. He has allowed your life to unfold as it has. He has overseen all that has happened to you. He has been present with you every step and second along the way. And He has been involved in your life as His plan for you has unfolded.

In short, God is the author and the finisher of your faith *and* your life (Hebrews 12:2)! He is the God of not only your future and your present...but also of your past.

Here's an assignment for you: The next time you catch yourself saying or thinking "if only," first, just stop. Ponder the fact of God's sovereignty, knowledge, and presence in any and all past situations. Refuse to allow yourself to get bogged down thinking about something that is no longer real. Instead, thank God for His continual presence with you throughout time and for His promise—and power!—to overrule and redeem the hard times of the past.

And what about the present? About the way things really are for you today? Your assignment here is to accept what is real and acknowledge again that God oversees and has overseen every detail of your life—your singleness, your marriage, your family, your relationships, your job, your every situation and your every circumstance. This knowledge will help you to act on what is true and real today…rather than resent reality and idly wait for fantasies to magically materialize.

Beloved, with a heart full of faith and hope, with God by your side, and by His great grace, you can love Him…even more, no matter what has—or is—happening to you.

~ 6 ~

Taking Every Thought Captive

All that rings true...let this be
the argument of your thoughts.

Philippians 4:8 KNOX BIBLE

If you're like me, right about now you're wondering, "How can I cultivate the kind of thinking that leads to loving God with all my mind?" That was my heart's cry as I began to wrestle with the challenge to think on what is true and real.

Two decades have passed since my breakthrough occurred as a result of tapping into Philippians 4:8. As a result, I can tell you three steps that have helped me and many others develop thought patterns based on God's truth—thought patterns that enable us to love Him even more. Following these steps will definitely move you forward in training your thoughts.

Step 1: Recognizing the Command

Consider again the apostle Paul's final words in Philippians 4:8: "Meditate on these things." Here Paul issues a command to us to think on what is true and real. He is not making a suggestion, and he's not offering a piece of advice that we can take or leave. No, Philippians 4:8 is God's *command* to us to focus our thoughts on the truth of His Word and on the things in life that are real.

So how can we obey this command from Scripture? Here's how I began. Right away it helped me to realize that it is sin to not obey this command. I didn't want to sin, and I'm sure you don't either. So I reasoned, "If the Bible says I should think only on what is true and real, then to think outside of these biblical boundaries is sin."

Wow! I certainly had my "work" (so to speak!) cut out for me. Labeling thoughts that are not based on what is true or real as "sin" was a powerful daily motivator. And the same is still true today. If I want my thoughts to measure up to God's standard of true and real, then I have to accept that my thinking is either based on God's truth or it isn't. My thinking is either right or wrong. It's either acceptable or sinful. I feel that I have to be this rigid if I am to give up of my destructive thought patterns and obey God by thinking on what is true and real.

Are you baffled as to how in the world you are going to be able to obey God's command? Well, take heart, my friend! You have help! God, by and through His grace, is at work helping you (and me!) accomplish all that He calls you to do. Put another way, it is *He* who enables you to love Him with your whole mind.

Step 2: Responding in Obedience

Next, I began asking, "How can I limit my thinking to what is true and real?" Soon I found a clue from Paul himself in 2 Corinthians 10:4-5. Here he writes,

> For the weapons of our warfare are…mighty in God for pulling down strongholds, casting down arguments and every high thing that exalts itself against the knowledge of God, bringing every thought into captivity to the obedience of Christ.

By definition, thoughts that are not true or real are mere "arguments" or, as the New American Standard Bible says, "speculations." They are not truth. They are "high things" raised up against the knowledge of God and the truth of His Word. And such "things" and thoughts have to be brought "into captivity to the obedience of Christ."

As I considered what "bringing every thought into captivity to the obedience of Christ" means, I immediately thought of something from my childhood. While growing up in a tiny Oklahoma town (population 2,000), it was a grand occasion each year when our family attended the local rodeo. And the calf roping was my favorite event.

Here's the scene—The cowboy, ready on his horse, with lasso in hand, waited for a calf to be released from its chute. Then came the chase as the cowboy raced his horse after the bucking, twisting, running animal, lassoed it, brought it in, jumped off his horse, threw the calf down, tied three legs together, stood up, and raised his hands in victory. The timer stopped, and everyone cheered. The cowboy had successfully roped the calf!

It hit me that to handle my thoughts that were not true or real, I needed to be like that cowboy! You see, my inaccurate thoughts about God and His Word—along with my "what if," "if only," and "this isn't the way it was supposed to be" thoughts—were like that calf! They were untamed and rebellious, bucking, jumping, and running wild in my mind.

So, like the cowboy—and with God's strength and help!—I needed to chase after my wrong thoughts, rope them, bring them in, throw them down, and tie them up. That's how I could experience a victory in my thought-life.

Taking our thoughts captive to Christ—to the Word of God, to what is true and real—calls for energy, effort, and a heart commitment to obey God. It is a battle—a battle fought *in* the mind and a battle *for* the mind. And it is a battle fought one thought at a time…for victory over one thought at a time. It is warfare! And the truth of Philippians 4:8 is a weapon we simply must have in our arsenal. Praise God, this is a battle we can fight—and win!—by His grace.

Step 3: Reaping the Benefits

And now for the glorious blessings! What are some of the fantastic benefits you and I enjoy when we obey God's command to think on what is true and real? When we begin "bringing every thought into captivity to the obedience of Christ"? Here's a short list of what we will experience.

- Greater love for God as we think on what He has done for us
- Exceeding joy from pleasing God through obedience
- Positive well-being from living the way God wants us to live
- Improved relationships with others

- Less stress and more peace in our daily lives
- Accelerated spiritual growth and maturity

Energy for God's purposes—But there is one other benefit that every person I know needs and desires, and that is greater energy! Greater spiritual energy, physical energy, mental energy, and emotional energy—greater energy of every kind for handling life's demands, challenges, and opportunities. It's amazing that as we spend less time in melancholy introspection and more time thinking thoughts that are true and real, we have more energy for positive uses and constructive purposes.

I know I experience this multiplication of energy, and I also see it in others. For instance, in my ministry to seminary wives in Southern California, I saw it in the women I met who, new to California, spent their energy thinking about where they used to live, which was no longer true or real. The result? They felt bad, sad, and bitter about where they did live.

Also, many people I meet waste time reminiscing about the good ol' days (which are no longer true and real), and let today (which is true and real) slip right by them. Others are consumed by thoughts of where they wish they were, what they want to have, what could have been, or what they might have done. When we choose this kind of thinking, real life passes by, unused and unenjoyed. My friend, futile thoughts like these drain our precious energy. It is wasted on what is false and what is fantasy. It is spent on all the wrong things—on what are mere memories and speculations!

Strength for today's issues—For a moment, think of your Christian life as a bucket that God wants to fill so that you can enjoy Him and enjoy life. He wants to fill your life with Himself so He can use it to glorify Him, to bless you, and to enrich the lives of others.

Now, how do you fill the bucket with the things of God? Reading the Bible every day is one way. You can also memorize and meditate on Scripture. And you can pray and worship. But you must also realize that every wrong thought you think—thoughts that are not true and real—is like a hole in your spiritual bucket. Every time you think inaccurately about God, about God's Word, and about people, you are draining your bucket. Every time you dwell on "what if" and "if only" and "this isn't the way it was supposed to be" scenarios, you can be sure your energy is leaking out!

My friend, it's a fact: Thinking about things that are untrue and unreal drain your energy, your life, and your strength for dealing with today's issues! Obeying the command of Philippians 4:8, however, helps keep your bucket filled and overflowing! and your energy available to serve God, to take care of your responsibilities, and to move toward accomplishing your dreams.

Loving God...Even More

Do you remember how this book started? With me answering the phone call regarding my struggles with depression. Well, dear friend, that call forced me to recognize how God's Word helped me conquer that horrendous daily problem. And, I have to report, that look back strengthened my commitment to know even more of God's truth and to do exactly what it says!

As I remember the kind of woman I was and the kind of life I lived due to the thoughts that filled my head, I am astonished. Having been a prisoner of dark moods generated by dark thoughts, I know all too well the frightening ability our thoughts have to program our lives. Scripture's analysis is true: "As [a person] thinks in his heart, so he is" (Proverbs 23:7).

As I look back, I am also overwhelmed with gratitude to God for His wisdom. Knowing the struggles His people would have, He provided help for us through the Bible, His written, inspired, profitable, living, powerful, and sharper-than-any-two-edged-sword Word (2 Timothy 3:16; Hebrews 4:12)! As we have seen, when the apostle Paul calls us in Philippians 4:8 to meditate on what is true and real, he is giving us what one commentator labeled a "paragraph on mental health."[1] How thankful I am that God gave me fresh insight into Philippians 4:8 when I needed it so desperately!

Paul gave Philippians 4:8 to help the church at Philippi deal with its problems. And, beloved, this scripture contains truth that also helps you and me develop a healthier thought-life and enjoy the peace of mind, energy, and effectiveness that come when we love God with all our mind.

My prayer for you, dear friend—and for myself—is that we will...

—love God *more* and
—experience *more* of His love
—by knowing *more* of His Word and
—by submitting *more* of our life to His truth.

Winning over Worry

Do not worry about tomorrow, for tomorrow will worry about its own things. Sufficient for the day is its own trouble.

MATTHEW 6:34

~ 7 ~

Focusing on Today

Do not worry about tomorrow,
for tomorrow will worry about
its own things. Sufficient for
the day is its own trouble.

Matthew 6:34

How do the first minutes of your days usually go? Are they anything like mine used to be? Here's a typical scenario from the past, from the days before I learned to think on what is true and real.

Looking at All of Life

The first sound I heard was the blaring alarm clock. Despite the fog of disturbed sleep, I managed to hit the snooze button. I slept deeply through the first nine-minute interval. However, during the next snooze period, my mind moved quickly from barely functioning…to worrying…to a full panic.

"Oh, no!" I moaned. "Another day! Another thousand things to do." And sure enough, the panic had begun. I knew that my bright, fresh day was a gift from God. And, oh how I wanted to say with the psalmist, "This is the day the LORD has made; we will rejoice and be glad in it" (Psalm 118:24). But I just couldn't. I was too overwhelmed by the mountain range of responsibility that comprised my life. My list was long, my schedule was full, and my calendar was booked. Doing all I needed to do that day seemed impossible. And I wasn't even out of bed yet! People, commitments, deadlines, work, housework, errands, needs—my list was endless.

And I'll bet your list and life probably look—and feel!—a lot like mine did. Yes, we know all too well that life is crowded, complex, and challenging. There is always soooo much to do!

Looking at God's Word

But in Matthew 6:34, God's Word comes to our rescue. God gives us His view on the days of our lives and His surefire instructions for handling the "trouble" and trials that come with each one of them. He gives us His truth to think on, believe in, and act on—truth that is true and real, truth that will help us win over worry. Hear now as Jesus speaks to the too-common feeling of being overwhelmed by life. He says to you and to me,

> Do not worry about tomorrow, for tomorrow will worry about its own things. Sufficient for the day is its own trouble.

Looking at Today

With these words of commonsense wisdom, Jesus reduces our responsibilities to those of today...and today only. He forces our focus from the panorama view of the mountain range of all our tomorrows...to the single mountain of today. You see, today is all Christ asks us to cope with. And today is something Christ knows we—with His help—can indeed manage. His words give us hope, and they give us focus. Matthew 6:34 includes Christ's formula for winning over worry. It consists of...

His command—
Do not worry about tomorrow,

His insight—
Tomorrow will worry about its own things, and

His challenge for us today—
Sufficient for the day is its own trouble.

Dear friend, Jesus calls us away from worrying about tomorrow (a major contributor to stress) and to addressing the reality of today. His job assignment for us can be boiled down to three words: "Deal with today!"

The five very practical guidelines presented in the next few chapters have helped me obey Christ's command, adopt His insights, and accept His challenge to focus on today. With that focus, I am more able to love God with all my mind...even as I go about meeting the practical, nuts-and-bolts demands of the day.

As you read through this section on "Winning over Worry," you will see how these same steps will also enable you to meet each day's emotional, physical, and mental demands as well.

Guideline 1: Prepare

Prepare in the evening—If you were going to climb a

mountain early tomorrow morning, I'm sure you would do certain tasks the night before. Well, the same is true for everyone who feels overwhelmed by the demands on them. They do well to follow this same principle of doing certain tasks the night before. For instance...

Look at tomorrow's calendar. What is scheduled? What's happening at work? What's going on in each family member's life?

And by the way, What's planned for dinner? If this is your responsibility, you can prepare as much of tomorrow's evening meal as possible (make the Jell-O, cook the potatoes for potato salad, thaw the chicken pieces, wash and tear the lettuce, chop the vegetables, assemble the casserole). And while you're in the kitchen, go ahead and prepare tomorrow's lunches and set the table for the next meal. Clean up the kitchen and run the dishwasher. Nothing starts a day better than an orderly kitchen.

Before you go to bed, take a few minutes to organize and pick things up, to tidy your space. Again, your neatness and efforts will be a blessing in the morning. Also, lay out clothes for tomorrow so you won't have to think about what to wear in the morning. Before you turn out the lights, put everything you'll need for tomorrow (lunches, briefcases, the dry cleaning, schoolbags, coats, purse, keys, cell phones, mail, packages...you know the list!) by the door. Then, as you go to bed, be sure the alarm is set at a time that ensures that you have enough time to do what needs to be done in the morning...in a calm, orderly manner.

Now, you're half ready to climb that mountain of tomorrow!

Prepare in the morning—The first step we take each new day is crucial because it sets the tone for the day. I've found that getting up when the alarm goes off (versus hitting the snooze button too many times!) puts me in control of my day. (How about you?)

Then, once we're up, we need spiritual input for the day. Jesus knew the value of an early-morning meeting with the Father. In Mark 1:35, we learn that "in the morning, having risen a long while before daylight ['while it was still dark' NASB], He went out and departed to a solitary place; and there He prayed." A little background information makes this feat even more startling. You see, the day before, Jesus had spent His time and energy preaching, casting out demons, and healing many people. Even after sundown, He "healed many who were sick with various diseases, and cast out many demons" (verse 34). Nevertheless, the next morning, after a full and challenging—and successful in human terms—day, Jesus rose early to spend time in prayer so He would be refreshed and refilled for another day of ministry.

However (and I'm sure you can relate!), Jesus' time alone with God was interrupted. Simon Peter and his friends approached Him, saying, "Everyone is looking for You" (verse 37).

Stop just a minute, please. Do you ever feel as if everyone is looking for you? That everyone needs something from you? With people depending on you, you probably have very few moments alone, and even then you know that you're "on call." Our Jesus knows what it's like to have people clamoring after Him for what only He can give. But as one writer points out, although "Christ's life was surrounded by hurricane-like winds and forces...they never deterred Him from His priorities or His sense of mission! He was never unnerved and never responded in a way that was out of line with His character."[1] Jesus remained focused in His work and was loving toward people because He spent time with His Father, "a time of restorative withdrawal...[where] energies are renewed, perspectives refocused, and directions newly defined."[2]

If you're like me, you may find that your most harried days are those days when you have failed to make time to be with Christ. When we "put Christ off, the result is frequently exhaustion (both physical and spiritual), loss of perspective, defensiveness, self-pity, and an absence of joy....We become sapped. With [Christ] we seem tireless by contrast."[3]

Is that your experience? Like Jesus shows us, we must first withdraw from the people who need us so that we will be able to serve them later. When we are faithful to take this all-important step of preparation, we will be more ready to give to others because we will have already received from the Father the guidance, perspective, strength, and grace we need for the day.

Now back to Mark, chapter 1. When the disciples found Jesus and told Him "Everyone is looking for You," Christ confidently said, "Let us go into the next towns, that I may preach there also, because for this purpose I have come forth" (verse 38).

Where did this come from? After all, hadn't Jesus just experienced a tremendously—and miraculously!—"successful" day of ministry there in Capernaum? Shouldn't He remain there and continue to repeat what was obviously working? No. Jesus had obtained fresh orders for His fresh new day in His early morning time with the Father. Furthermore, following the Father's plan took priority over the seemingly urgent needs of the crowds who were looking for Him.

There's a loud lesson here for you and me. We, who so easily fall into the trap of other people's plans for us or give in to "the tyranny of the urgent" without a second thought, can learn from Christ's example. In His quiet time alone with God, before the sun rose, in the stillness of time before daybreak, Jesus focused on the new day. And He let that focus shape His plans for the day. When we don't take time to be alone with God, you and I endanger our relationship with God, our health, and our service to others. In fact, "without large blocks of silence and solitude…we are in danger of losing the very best things that people desire to draw from us."[4]

By contrast, alone with God, during some hushed moments (which are quite different from the hurry and scurry of the rushed activities and busyness of the rest of the day!), we receive from God what people will need us to give to them during the day ahead. Then, by the time everyone is looking for us, by the time the family gets up, the phone rings, or we get into the car, we have God's direction for our day.

Loving God…Even More

What happens when you take time to prepare—spiritually and practically—for each day's mountain climb, when you properly gear up for stepping into the day ahead of you? The list of benefits is long, but here are two you'll notice right away.

Your list of blessings begins with *God's love*. You are more aware of receiving God's love throughout the day when right from the start of each brand-new day your mind is focused on Him and His daily assignment to you. It's *His* day—the day the *Lord* has made. And He has lovingly given the day to you for enjoying Him, glorifying Him, loving Him, and serving Him and the people He chooses to put in your path.

And here's another blessing: *God's perspective*. Taking time alone with God to obtain His perspective on your responsibilities and His ordering of your day's activities will enable you to climb the mountain of today. When you start the day reminded of God's love and focused on His purposes for you, you are better prepared to meet the challenges ahead, including the challenge of loving God through each and every second.

Amazingly, when you make time alone with God your first priority for each day, you begin to live out the command of Matthew 6:33—

Seek first the kingdom of God
and His righteousness.

And then you begin to realize the promise of Matthew 6:33, the promise of God's provision of all that you need...the truth that makes it possible for you to win over worry—

and all these things
shall be added to you.

~ 8 ~

Scaling the Mountain of Today

Do not worry about tomorrow;
for tomorrow will care for itself.
Each day has enough trouble of its own.

Matthew 6:34 NASB

Do you tend to worry about getting through the work, handling the responsibilities, and meeting head-on the challenges that seem to arrive with each new day? Then you, dear friend and reader—and fellow worrier!—should memorize Matthew 6:34. This powerful worry-buster is part of Christ's famous Sermon on the Mount. Kingdom living on earth is His topic, and verse 34 falls into His calling of Christians away from worry about tomorrow—a key cause of tension—and back to the reality of dealing with today. This God-breathed verse is divine help for worrywarts. It is God's truth, shot straight from His heart to yours! To win over worry, you (and all believers) must simply think on this verse and put it to use throughout today...and all the days of your life.

So far we know that to heed Christ's command in Matthew 6:34 to "not worry about tomorrow," we must tend to first things first. We need to follow *Guideline 1* and *prepare* for each new day—practically the night before, and spiritually the morning of (see chapter 7). Then we must move on to...

Guideline 2: Plan Ahead

Like preparing, planning—both long-range and short-range—enables us to follow Christ's instructions for winning over worry. It also makes us more effective during our day.

Long-range planning—Breaking large projects into day-sized bits and pieces is an exercise that keeps us from feeling overwhelmed by our goals and our work. And it also fixes our focus on today. For instance, long-range planning is key to birthday and anniversary celebrations, weddings, reunions, parties, vacations, and business or pleasure trips. Presentations, papers, articles, and dissertations require the same long-range planning that redecorating, adding on to your house, or building a new one demands. We also need to plan ahead for buying or selling a home. And then there's planning for retirement.

I first learned about long-range planning in my own living room where Jim and I were trying to hang new wallpaper. We had the paper and the equipment we needed, but we didn't have a weekend or even a single open day to do the job. Overwhelmed, I stood in the middle of the living room and sobbed, "We'll never get this done. We just don't have time to do this. We'll just get all the stuff out, make a big mess, and then we'll have to put it all away. There's no way to get this done!"

These 30 years later I still remember Jim's next words—"Honey, how do you eat an elephant?" After I whimpered, "I don't know," Jim said, "You eat an elephant one bite at a time. We're going to get the stuff out, we're going to cut the first strip, we're going to put it on the wall, and then we'll put it all away...but we will have taken the first bite." And then we put this "elephant-eating principle" to work. We took the first "bite" and made some progress!

As you can see, long-range planning breaks large projects into small tasks. Such forward thinking enables us to obey Christ's command to not be anxious for tomorrow. Instead of worrying, we can deal with the future by bringing manageable pieces—bites, if you will—into the present day's tasks. This reduces the waste of precious time and energy on worry, fear, panic, or dread of the future. With planning, we are more likely to meet life's challenges head-on and reach our life goals.

Short-term planning—This helps us to meet the day's demands. For me, lists are key. Every morning I make a "to do" list of my work tasks for the day at hand. Included on my daily to-do list are "bites" from my long-range projects, as well as those day-to-day items that are part of keeping a busy life going. The list tells me *what* I need to do. Then, once I complete my list, I schedule *when* I will do each job. Lists and a schedule help me get the work done—the work of today and "its own trouble," and the work of the future that causes me to worry if I'm not doing something (even a small something) about it.

My friend Janelle told me how lists helped her deal with an especially stressful time in her life. She was expecting a baby any time, remodeling her house, and fighting the cleaning problems the construction created. Her solution? Planning! She explained,

> I sat down and wrote out all the projects under three headings—Baby, Remodel, and General Cleaning. I have been able to plan each day by selecting one or two things from each heading to get done that day. This has helped immensely. Instead of one huge to-do list that I know will never get done before the baby arrives, I've been able to put things into manageable bites—and by God's grace, I'm making headway!

Having a plan—a schedule—and Matthew 6:34 to remind you not to be anxious can help you design a productive, enjoyable day that's free of frustration and anxiety and their effects on your life…not to mention, a day characterized by closeness with the Lord!

Guideline 3: Pray

As we prepare and plan, we must also pray, pray, pray! Each day, I try to make the following three transactions a part of my prayers.

First, I *give God everything*. I begin by giving Him myself. British preacher and writer F.B. Meyer had seven rules to live by every day, and Number One on his list was "make a daily, definite, audible consecration of yourself to God. Say it out loud: Lord, today I give myself anew to you."[1] When I give myself to God like this, it reminds me that as His child I belong to Him. And, as a bookmarker in my Bible says,

"God is ready to assume full responsibility for the life wholly yielded to Him."

I also *give God the things in my life*—my home, my possessions, my time, my body, and my mind. This prayerful commitment reminds me again that God has given me everything I have, and I am to care for them and use them in ways that honor and please Him.

I *give God the people in my life*—my husband, my children and their spouses, my grandchildren, and my family members. My love is fierce when it comes to these precious people! But giving them to God calms my thoughts and quiets my worries. He is all-wise, all-powerful, loving, and able to take care of the things *and* the people in our lives.

Peace of mind is available to you, too, when you give God everything—yourself, your things, and the people you care about—as well as the physical, practical, and emotional concerns of your life. All these are His to do with as He likes! This complete commitment to God of all that you are and all that you have is another way you love Him with all your mind—and making this commitment daily is key.

Second, after giving God everything, I *give God my Plan A for the day*. Giving Him my schedule for the day—correction: *His* day!—means laying before Him the projects I want to get done and think I must get done. Committing my plans to God helps me fight against impulsiveness and laziness. It also helps me to follow Him if He leads me in a new direction.

Third (and this is crucial!), I *give God Plan B for the day.* Although I have a plan—Plan A—I want God's will for my life. Therefore I commit my day, my goals, my time, and my energies to Him. I pray to hold my Plan A loosely and to yield to Him during the course of the day. You see, I want my plan to be *His* plan. So, if and when God moves me to do something different—Plan B, *His* plan—I want to be ready, willing, and available.

The perspective that comes with surrendering my agenda to God reduces my frustration. I make Plan A and submit it to God. But when I give Him Plan B, I am acknowledging His right to alter my day. My thinking then goes like this: "Plan A is good…unless God moves me to Plan B. Then 'Plan B is better' because Plan B is God's plan." Knowing God is behind any and every unexpected event helps me accept whatever happens. Besides reducing my frustration level when my plans change, giving God Plan B helps me be more flexible. Writer and pastor Ray Ortlund explains:

> I like to start out the morning covering my whole day by prayer….I take out my appointment book and pray through the hours. I pray for everyone I am scheduled to see….I pray for the unscheduled ones I will bump into. I've found that if I pray over my interruptions and get them squarely under God's sovereign control, they don't irritate me. I realize that they are part of God's plan.[2]

Again, we are to make a plan for the day, pray over that plan, and then proceed to follow that plan. But we must be willing to accept the unexpected as *God's* intervention, to recognize it as *His* plan…and then flex and flow with it!

And here's another benefit of giving God Plan B—it improves my attitude by leaps and bounds! After committing my day to God, I then say, "Okay, God, let's see what's going to happen! Let's see where this day goes!" This positive outlook gives me an attitude of expectancy and acceptance. I actually look forward to seeing God at work in my life...even though His plan usually proves to be quite different from mine!

Thomas Edison supposedly shouted to his son as his laboratories burned and his life's work was going up in flames, "Son, go get your mother quick! She's never seen a fire like this!" When he and his wife looked over the smoldering ruins the next morning, he said, "Just think. All our mistakes have been burned up, and we have a chance to start all over again."[3] (Oh, Lord, may I have this attitude when my plans seem to be going up in smoke! May I be glad for the chance to do what *You* would have me do.)

Jesus commanded us in Matthew 6:34 to focus on today. And prayer helps us to do just that. Through prayer, we can cast all our anxieties and worries upon God (1 Peter 5:7), give Him everything (including Plan A and Plan B for the day), and experience the peace, focus, wisdom, and strength He gives us for managing the mountain of today. After all, He is the one who enables us to meet Christ's challenge to deal with today's trouble—and today's trouble only!

Guideline 4: Proceed

Preparing, planning, and praying move us to the base of the mountain of today. But finally it is time to actually begin the climb. Ancient wisdom reminds us that "a journey of a thousand miles begins with a single step." And, dear climbing friend, that truth can help us tackle the day one step at a time and one task at a time without worry.

When writing about Jesus' command to put off tomorrow's

anxiety until tomorrow, one scholar noted, "If this be done, the greater part of all our anxiety is put aside at once, and for the rest of it, the principle will apply to each hour as well as to each day."[4] In other words, not only do we not need to worry about tomorrow, but we also don't need to worry about the next hour! Why? Because any interruptions and crises are ways God reveals His will for our day. Knowing this frees our concentration and energy to focus on the task at hand. Then, when things change, we'll take the next step and do the next task, again refusing to worry about what lies ahead.

When you prepare, plan, pray, and proceed with a heart that's open to God's plan, you'll find yourself walking with God...with no worries about tomorrow. That's the fruit of obeying the command of Matthew 6:34: *Do not worry about tomorrow*. You can live your day fully. You can experience the joy of the Lord. You can go from task to task, meeting the needs of others. You can do what you must and handle whatever God brings...in His power and without anxiety. And you can wake up tomorrow and do it all over again! As C.S. Lewis wrote, "Relying on God has to begin all over again every day as if nothing yet had been done."[5]

A personal story—Believe it or not, I used to be a runner. And I can't help but think of these steps to winning over worry as being somewhat like my approach to my daily run. Here's the scenario.

I *plan* and *prepare* for my run by first putting on the right clothes and the right shoes (which were laid out the night before). Then I *proceed* out the door. I run to the first major traffic intersection...and then to the next. But as the run gets longer and I get tired, I start targeting the next corner. As I get closer to home, I concentrate on even smaller goals—the next corner, the next trash can on the block, the next driveway, streetlight, or tree. I don't dare look up the huge hill in front of me. I can't! That's too far, too unreachable...but I can take one more step. And I don't dare look all the way home! Again, that's too far...but I can run to the next flower. So, step by step, I complete my run, finally reaching my goal.

Like completing a run, living today begins with preparation, planning, and prayer. But once these things are done, we must then proceed—one step at a time, one task at a time—by focusing our energy on each job as it comes up during the day. This focus helps us to successfully scale the mountain of today and not worry about the mountain of tomorrow. It helps us to live each day to the max!

Guideline 5: Trust God to Provide

There's one more key to winning over worry, and it's a big one—*We must trust God to provide.*

After all of our elaborate preparations and meticulous planning, and after all of our impassioned outpourings in prayer, we must finally proceed. Then, *as* we move forward in faith and obedience to climb the mountain of today, an amazing thing happens. We find that whatever the challenge, task, trial, crisis, or interruption, God provides for us every step of the way! Whatever happens, God provides His wisdom (James 1:5). Whatever happens, God provides His strength (Philippians 4:13; Deuteronomy 33:25; 2 Peter 1:3). Whatever happens, God provides what we need (Philippians 4:19). When we finally move out in faith, we discover that when God commands, He supplies. Where He guides, He provides.

Loving God... Even More

So are you now ready (or more ready) to face your mountain of today? Today will require your full attention and a full-out effort. As Jesus explained, "Sufficient for the day [this day!] is its own trouble." Preparing, planning, praying, and proceeding will enable you to focus on today because these efforts draw you closer to God. And such closeness frees you from the anxiety and worry that keep you from appreciating Him, trusting Him, and loving Him with all your mind.

The five guidelines will also enable you to experience God's provision for you, His beloved child, amid the practical details and demands of daily living. You will experience His provision as He helps you meet the spiritual, mental, physical, and emotional trials of each day.

Dear friend and companion on the climb, proceed ahead! Step out in trust and walk through the days of your life close to the Lord. Not a day will go by without evidence of His care. Not only will you love Him even more, but you will, indeed, win over worry!

~ 9 ~

Living One Day at a Time

Don't worry about tomorrow,
for tomorrow will bring its own worries.
Today's trouble is enough for today.

Matthew 6:34 NLT

When the Persian Gulf War broke out (1990), I had to learn new applications for Matthew 6:34. The fighting in Kuwait forced me to focus on more than the practicalities of putting meals on the table, providing clean clothes for my family, and being ready to teach Bible classes. I had to learn how to focus on today emotionally. I had to learn how to practice the five principles of preparing, planning, praying, proceeding, and then trusting God to provide when it came to the prospect of my husband going to war!

Reviewing a Slice of History

When Jim and I married, he joined the Army Reserves and, as a registered pharmacist, he was assigned to the Medical Service Corps. After 25 years of routine monthly meetings and after Jim finally qualified for army retirement, we were not prepared for what happened.

In September 1990, Operation Desert Shield began to heat up. The first signs warned that something big was about to happen. Soon the initial escalation of military presence was followed by rumors that reserve units would be called up. Then in October, it happened—Operation Desert Shield became Operation Desert Storm, and that meant war! I still remember holding my breath as President George H. Bush addressed the nation on television and spoke the words our family dreaded. He was authorizing the call-up of reservists!

Gearing up for war—Soon actual call-ups began across the country. Yet at his unit meetings, Jim heard, "There's no way our unit is going to be called. They'll never take us." But just in case, his unit began to prepare for the possibility. The reservists were put on a series of practice alerts, and officers called homes to be sure they could reach their personnel. Next, there were emergency drills and night meetings to ensure the commanding officers could expedite a call-up.

One weekend in October, my husband returned from his monthly drill and reported that the leaders had stopped saying "*if* we go" and were now saying "*when* we go." Unit members spent the next monthly meeting packing for war. And that Thanksgiving our family went away for four days together because Jim had been told he should plan to be in Saudi Arabia...that the military wanted all of its troops in place...before the Christmas holiday.

Soon all of the medical units on the West Coast were in Saudi Arabia except Jim's. His would be next. Then 100 reservists from his unit were activated and an additional 100 were put on alert.

Next word came that Jim, as well as the remainder of his unit, were on official alert. That meant that Jim's duffel bag was packed and by the door, and he was to be within four hours of his unit at all times. Jim was issued a gas mask and trained extensively on how to use it. He was instructed to update his insurance forms and his will and to be sure his family files were in order.

Moving one step closer—One morning while Jim was getting ready to go to work, the phone rang. He was being called up for service in the unit office in downtown Los Angeles for two weeks. And Jim's assignment? To process the soldiers leaving for the war. This decision was made when his superiors discovered that Jim was, at that time, a minister. They decided he would be a perfect replacement for the Family Services officer who had been sent to the Persian Gulf. Jim's job was to support the spouses and families of deployed soldiers.

Suddenly every time our phone rang at home, it was a different woman in tears. "I don't know where my husband is" came the cry. "It's been three weeks, and I haven't heard a word." Finances were another common cause for worry—"He's been gone for two months, and I haven't received his paycheck. What are we going to do without any money?"

The duties of the Family Services officer also included leading support-group meetings for family members left behind. At the meetings, Jim updated them on finances and available services, and he offered children as well as spouses help in coping with depression and anxiety. Often I went along with Jim and, as the people shared their worries and concerns, I joined in their tears. I left those meetings thinking, "This is going to be me next month."

My anguished waiting ended on March 6, 1991, when President Bush announced, "The war is over"...one week before Jim was scheduled to go overseas!

Managing Emotions

Needless to say, the months between October and March were an emotional roller coaster ride for me! Every day I struggled with the emotions that came with not knowing what the future held for Jim and me and our girls. Fear, anxiety, uncertainty—I had to cope with these emotions daily. The practical issues of life—managing schedules, a household, work, and family responsibilities—were challenge enough. But harder for me was managing emotions.

For most of us, our family members are our greatest concern. We worry about our spouses and children, about nurturing our marriage and family relationships, about caring for aging parents. Another emotionally charged area is finances as we worry about layoffs, salary cuts, the rising cost of living, growing families, increasing expenses, the loss of retirement benefits, and a sagging economy. What can we do with these realities that drain our emotions?

As we know from the previous chapter, we can apply Matthew 6:34 to dealing with daily responsibilities and the practicalities of everyday life. And here's more good news! We can also use Christ's truth and guidance for managing the emotions of life. The same directives from our Savior apply: "Do not worry about tomorrow, for tomorrow will worry about its own things. Sufficient for the day is its own trouble." During the Persian Gulf War, anxiety was pressing in on me from every direction, and all I had was this command from Christ. And, beloved, I learned that it was all I needed...because it pointed me to Him. In Matthew 6:34, Jesus commands us not to worry about tomorrow and calls us to handle our emotions...one day at a time. So I applied the same five principles—prepare, plan, pray, proceed, and trust God's provision—to my raging emotions.

We prepared—Jim and I cut our budget. We stopped using credit cards and stopped making major purchases. We also checked into possible jobs for me and did some needed home repairs. Jim talked with the seminary about his employment, salary, and job responsibilities. He met with mortgage company officials about our situation and called the college our two daughters attended to check on their tuition payment policy for activated military parents.

We planned—Jim talked to our daughters at length about what might happen and about what his deployment and even his possible death would mean for them. I put my teaching and speaking engagements on hold, and, pulling together as a family, we took that four-day Thanksgiving vacation.

Jim and I also pulled together as a couple. We discussed every option, every step, every phase, even down to my asking Jim, "What do you want me to do if you don't come back?" Bless him, he anchored me by giving clear and specific instructions for the future.

We prayed—Like never before, Jim and I prayed. I also enlisted the help of "The Faithful Five," a group of long-time praying friends. I phoned each of these women and asked them to pray for me every day, and I called them whenever something happened—an alert, an emergency drill, any news from the army.

In addition to my praying, I fasted. God alone could keep my husband from going to war. There was nothing I could do, and there was nothing Jim could do. There was no human way out. So, I began to fast on December 4. On that first day, I decided that I would fast until I knew Jim was not going to the Persian Gulf or, if he did go, until he came back—or died. That was my covenant with God. I also decided to break my fast each day at sundown, a format that followed the Jewish model and least disrupted our family times...and just happened to correspond to the five o'clock close of all army offices! No phone calls ordering my husband to report to duty in Desert Storm would come after five o'clock!

During this time of praying and fasting, God alone knew of four trials, equal in magnitude to the Persian Gulf War, that I would later face. These trials involved the health of one daughter, cancer biopsies for me, a critical financial crisis, and an extremely difficult relationship with another person. In fact, God used this war to force me into a position of total dependence on Him, which enabled me to better handle those other four situations. In the end, prayer and fasting availed as much for those four situations as for Jim and the 63rd Army Command...and the entire U.S. military!

We proceeded—Besides calling us to prepare and plan, Jesus tells us in Matthew 6:34 how to proceed—"Do not worry about tomorrow." As I went about my daily life, I let this verse set boundaries for my thoughts. I was not to speculate on my future because God wasn't asking me to handle my entire life all at once. Instead, His wisdom was telling me to limit my thoughts to today, to what was real right now. Any "what if" imaginings about the future (as we saw in a previous chapter) were not real. Therefore I didn't need to deal with them. But today was real, and I had to deal with it. As Christ points out, "Sufficient for the day [this day!] is its own trouble."

With God's strength and grace, I would be able to function today. I also knew I wouldn't be able to if I gave in to worrying about tomorrow. So I chose to draw near to God and think on His love for me and His promises to care for me. I chose to love Him with all my mind by attempting to keep my thoughts within His prescribed boundary of today and of what was true and real. Choosing to love God with my mind also helped limit my emotions because, as you and I both know, thoughts generate emotions.

Without God's command to limit my thinking, I don't think I could have emotionally handled all that God asked me to bear during and after the Persian Gulf War. But through the teaching of Matthew 6:34, God was telling me not to feel the emotions that would come in the yet-unrevealed future. "Do not worry" spoke directly to my heart. I let today be the boundary for my concerns and emotions, knowing that tomorrow "would worry about its own things." I proceeded with each day as it came, knowing that God was with me.

Every day, however, seemed like an entire lifetime. Emotionally, physically, and spiritually, I was strained to the limit. Each time the phone rang during these long months, it was bad news. It was Jim's unit, or a distraught spouse, or another doctor's report on my daughter's illness, or more test results concerning my physical problem, or an order for another biopsy. In addition, I was living with my husband as if each day was our last and, at the same time, trying to be sensitive to our children's worries, fears, and needs.

My dear reading friend, peace came only as I followed the wisdom of Matthew 6:34. As I proceeded through those six months, I fought to keep my thoughts and feelings focused to one day at a time. (And I often found myself being a lot like Charlie Brown who glumly reports in one *Peanuts* cartoon, "I used to try to take each day as it came, but my philosophy has changed. I'm down to half a day at a time!")

We experienced God's provision—As I planned, prepared, prayed, proceeded, and lived one day at a time, I saw God provide for me each day. The fact that I am writing about this experience 15 years later is a witness to God's provision for me—to His presence with me and to His work in my life—as I proceeded, by His grace, one day at a time. The final entry in my journal from that time of my life remains a real touchstone for me:

> God, You are so good in Your dealings with me and with my family! Thank You for arranging my life so that I need You so greatly. Thank You for the intimate closeness of my walk with You these past months. Thank You for the humility I feel, the lowliness, the dependency, the brokenness, the cleanness. Thank You for opening the floodgates of my heart for so many others—and at the time of my greatest need! Because You have so adequately met my needs, I can give to others in need. I have

needed You and I have sought You, and You have made yourself known to me in new ways. I know that I have grown in faith. It was tested daily, and I now know You better.

Loving God...Even More

Whenever I look back on that challenging time, I am well aware of the lessons I learned about God and about winning over worry. Did He enable me to deal with the circumstances and the stress? Was His grace sufficient? Did spiritual growth occur in my life? Am I a stronger Christian today because of that experience? Do I know more about my God today? Do I know more about waiting, suffering, trusting, and persevering? Is my faith in God greater? Can I better relate to people's pain? Can I be a more effective minister and servant now? Yes—and a thousand more yeses! My trust in God was tested daily, and the only way to pass those tests was to believe in His atrributes, to walk with Him closely, and to love Him more and more...one day at a time.

~ 10 ~

Living Out of God's Grace

Do not worry about tomorrow,
for tomorrow will worry about itself.
Each day has enough trouble of its own.

Matthew 6:34 NIV

As I faced my own daily struggle with emotions during the half-year of the Gulf War, I devoured God's word and prayed without ceasing. I also sought to bring my fearful thoughts captive to the obedience of Christ (2 Corinthians 10:5). In addition, I also read biographies describing God's grace to others who had gone before me in their sufferings.

Learning More About Managing Emotions

It was then I found great guidance and wisdom from the writings of missionary Elisabeth Elliot. Sometimes I thought I was silly to feel so much anxiety about my husband's potential service in a war. No, in the end he didn't go overseas. And no, he didn't die. But I only knew that after the fact, so for many months, fear was a daily reality for me. Elisabeth Elliot helped me understand the intensity of my emotions with her observation that "people who have themselves experienced both grief and fear know how alike those two things are.... They are equally disabling, distracting and destructive."[1]

Elisabeth Elliot indeed knows about fear and grief. When she was serving in the jungles of Ecuador, she and the other missionary wives received word that two bodies had been found at the location where their husbands had gone. What did she think? How did she feel? What did she do?

Thinking on the truth—First, this missionary wife focused her mind on God and the truth in His Word. "It was the first I knew that anything was amiss," she recalls. "A verse God had impressed on my mind when I first arrived in Ecuador came back suddenly and sharply: 'When thou passest through the waters, I will be with thee, and through the rivers, they shall not overflow thee....'"[2] Armed with this promise of God's presence, she then prayed and proceeded to go about her duties. "I went upstairs to continue teaching the Indian girls' literacy class, praying silently, 'Lord, let not the waters overflow.'"[3]

Jim Elliot was one of the men who was killed. And the way his wife faced this crisis helped me to face mine. I wanted to quit. I felt angry. I wanted to fall down in a heap and cry, focus on myself, and forget about everyone else and their needs! But...

Proceeding ahead—I knew that is not how God wants His people to face a crisis. I had to proceed and press on with my duties and responsibilities. I had to go on living life. And as I did so, I experienced the truth of something else Elisabeth Elliot has written: "At such times I have been wonderfully calmed and strengthened by doing some simple duty...like a bed to be made or a kitchen floor to be washed....Sometimes it takes everything you have to get up and do it, but it is surprising how strength comes."[4]

In times of emotional stress, strength *does* come from routine and responsibility. That's another reason why it's important to have a plan for the day. Life must go on! And we must function! Our families need care, and our homes and lives need order. Doing tasks with these goals in mind keeps us from being immobilized by depression and fear. As Elisabeth Elliot points out, "There is wonderful therapy in getting up and doing something. While you are doing, time passes quickly. Time itself will in some measure heal....And in the doing of whatever comes next, we are shown what to do after that."[5]

And where had Mrs. Elliot, a model of Christian maturity for me, learned how to function when catastrophe struck? Jesus Christ had shown her the way. "Our Lord did not halt all activity to brood over what was to come," she writes. "He was not incapacitated by the fear of suffering, though he well knew that fear. To the question, 'What shall I do?' (so often, for us, the cry of despair) he simply answered, 'This,' and did what lay in his path to do at the moment, trusting himself completely into the hands of his Father. This is how he endured the cross."[6]

Following the formula—For nine months of waiting, praying, and fasting—for the war, my daughter's health, my health, our finances, and a painful relationship—I tried to follow Jesus' example, the principles of Matthew 6:34, and the model of Elisabeth Elliot. For nine months, I endeavored to take one day at a time. Nine months is 270 days of living one day at a time, 270 days of not worrying about tomorrow, 270 days of handling the trouble of each day as it came, 270 days of not allowing myself to look ahead or anticipate the worries of 269 tomorrows.

Dear one, for 270 days I had to follow the formula, the five guidelines for winning over worry (see chapters 7 and 8). I had to prepare, plan, and pray. And I had to proceed. I had to live each day as it came. I had to forego my selfish desires to withdraw and give up. And, praise God, as I proceeded ahead, His ever-so-adequate provision and mercy were indeed new every morning!

Managing Affliction

Like emotional stress, physical suffering calls us to follow the principles of Matthew 6:34 and focus on one day at a time. I know people who suffer from incurable diseases, who deal with physical limitations every waking moment, who have nursed loved ones who were dying from cancer, who have children confined to wheelchairs, and who are themselves dying from breast cancer and brain tumors. How do they live when physical suffering is part of their daily reality?

Edith Schaeffer, the wife of theologian and writer Dr. Francis Schaeffer and cofounder with him of the Swiss retreat L'Abri, knows about living with a loved one's physical suffering. When medical tests revealed that Dr. Schaeffer had cancer, he told his wife those "awful words that turned our world upside down."[7]

One thing Edith did after her world was turned upside down was find a biblical perspective on the circumstances she faced. She needed "basic truth and God's Word [to] take the center of thoughts and feelings." She wrote,

> We are always living on the edge of disaster, change, shock, or attack. Peace, and the affluence to enjoy that peace, are always a false separation from the reality of the raging battle....Not only is our understanding blurred of what the Fall actually consists of, but our understanding of the absolute *marvel* of what God has done for us in making victory certain and complete is dimmed![8]

Mrs. Schaeffer knew Scripture's teaching that we will suffer in this world, and she recognized that peace and good times are fleeting on this earth. She also saw confirmed in the Bible the sterility of a life without suffering as well as God's provision for certain victory in suffering.

Preparing—So, armed with spiritual truth, Edith Schaeffer prepared for their time of physical trial. She remembers,

> I felt [it] imperative...to make a home for Fran as soon as possible, if he were to stay [in the United States] for treatment—whether he had six weeks or six months to live!...Why a "home"? I would answer that home is important to a person to help him or her get well, as well as being important for family times together if someone is dying. In either case, beauty

> and familiar surroundings have an effect on the physical, psychological, and even spiritual state.[9]

Planning—Edith Schaeffer also planned. The diagnosis of cancer gave the family some waiting time, and Mrs. Schaeffer learned that "'marking time' is never the way to wait....Creative ideas need to begin to take place in one's imagination....Even in times of shock, waiting can be something more than sitting in abject fear."[10] Planning was one of the ways Mrs. Schaeffer used her waiting time. She explained, "Doing interior decorating inside your head while in a hospital or clinic waiting room is a positive creative activity—as well as a way of planning for demonstrating your love and concern for the person you love."[11]

Praying—During this waiting time, Mrs. Schaeffer also prayed. Every single day, throughout each stage of the cancer, and before, during, and after every doctor's report, Edith Schaeffer prayed. And what did she pray? "Don't let any one of us stop trusting you now, Lord. Please may our love be real for you—solid oak, not a thin veneer. This is the time that counts for your glory; don't let us blow it....Please, Father, give us victory...."[12] She also asked God to give her husband "time and strength to show forth God's strength and power to the next generation."[13]

Proceeding—Having prepared, planned, and prayed, Mrs. Schaeffer proceeded. With three days of cleaning, painting, and assembling an odd assortment of furnishings, she made a home for her beloved husband. She provided opportunities for the family to be together. She thoroughly researched cancer, chemotherapy, vitamins, and diet, and proceeded with the daily challenges of caring for a cancer patient. Mrs. Schaeffer writes, "'One-day-at-a-time' became an important measure to be constantly met.... When you are supposed to die in a short period of time, the dates are more appreciated; the 'and thens' take on a bit of sparkle!"[14]

As Edith Schaeffer moved forward, so did Dr. Schaeffer. Despite his suffering, he continued to minister. He spoke to large gatherings of doctors and local residents and answered their questions about God, life, and death. He "went on in the midst of cancer, trusting the Lord, and continuing to care about other people...[realizing] there is more to life than being 'comfortable' and 'happy'; there is growth going on...."[15]

Tasting God's provision—God provided for the Schaeffers as they proceeded. Even when Dr. Schaeffer felt so dizzy he thought he couldn't speak, Mrs. Schaeffer notes that "strength came in a sufficient quantity....Just enough energy 'was given' to carry on each time. It [wasn't] that Fran felt great. Rather he felt he could ask for the Lord's strength in measure for the needs and that it wasn't time to 'give up' when he could be a help."[16]

During the five years that her husband suffered, Edith Schaeffer focused on today. She took one day at a time and relied on God to be with her. Day-to-day and moment-to-moment, she prepared, planned, prayed, and proceeded with her duties and responsibilities and with a continual outpouring of love. And day-to-day and moment-to-moment, she experienced God's provision for her. She did not give up or quit. She dealt with her emotions when they came, and she never ceased to be a selfless woman, wife, and mother. "Looking back on it," she says, "I don't think I'd do anything differently." Even as she faced enormous emotional and physical challenges, Mrs. Schaeffer lived out of God's grace each and every day.

Loving God...Even More

Now, my friend, where does today find you? What are the circumstances of *your* life? Are your emotions stretched to the limit? Is physical affliction taxing you or a loved one? What fires are purifying your faith in God? Whatever your situation, God calls you to live one day at a time. Again, quoting Jesus, you are not to "worry about tomorrow; for tomorrow will care for itself. Each day has enough trouble of its own" (Matthew 6:34).

Whether your particular challenge is physical, emotional, mental, a combination, or all-of-the-above(!), the strategy of preparing, planning, praying, and proceeding will help you draw close to God, love Him even more, manage life's demands, and win over worry—one day at a time. Then, as you proceed through each day, you will experience God's love in very personal ways as you discover His complete provision. You will witness daily miracles as you find God meeting you in the circumstances of your life and giving you the strength you need...exactly when you need it.

God does indeed enable us to live according to His instruction to focus on today. With Him, you and I can successfully climb the mountain of today, leaving the mountain range of tomorrows to tomorrow. And the peace that comes with knowing that we are following God's guidance day by day, moment by moment, frees us to better love God with all our mind.

Pressing for the Prize

Brethren, I do not count myself
to have apprehended; but one thing I do,
forgetting those things which are behind and
reaching for those things which are ahead,
I press toward the goal for the prize
of the upward call of God in Christ Jesus.

PHILIPPIANS 3:13-14

~ 11 ~

Remembering to Forget

Forgetting those things which are behind...

Philippians 3:13

Although I've never attended one of my high school reunions, I've heard about them! My friends have told me about classmates who still look the way they always did and about others whose personalities haven't changed at all. They also report that others are larger—and/or balder!—and almost unrecognizable. Also, and sadly, some who enjoyed success during their high school years have gone the way of alcoholism, suffered disabilities, and encountered other tragedies.

The past. It makes us who we are. It teaches us lessons about God, about life, and about ourselves. We learn volumes from what lies behind. But our learning must not stop there. We must then take those lessons and move ahead. And this is exactly the truth the apostle Paul teaches in Philippians 3:13-14, another one of my breakthrough passages that I want to share with you now.

After exalting Jesus Christ and exhorting us to be like Him,

Paul tells us how to pursue Christlikeness. Acknowledging that he has not yet arrived in his own pursuit, Paul shares in Philippians 3:13-14 three actions that help him continue his progress toward spiritual maturity. And, my dear friend, these same truths apply to your growth, too. Paul writes,

> *Forgetting* those things which are behind and *reaching* forward to those things which are ahead, I *press* toward the goal for the prize of the upward call of God in Christ Jesus.

Forgetting the Past

The first step toward living a life that pleases Christ—a life that culminates in eternal glory with our Lord—is forgetting what lies behind. The past, as you well know, isn't always easy to forget. Whether it's some previous success that has never been repeated or some failure we haven't let go of, the past can take hold of our minds and our hearts. I know, because thinking too much about past injuries, insults, and sorrows once made sadness and weeping a part of my every day.

As I shared in the first chapter, dwelling on the past—on the kind of disappointments, struggles, and failures we all experience—made me tired and depressed. My backward thoughts became a breeding ground for bitterness. The more I thought about what had happened to me—things like remembering a rejection from a boyfriend, recalling a cruel remark, being passed over after a job interview, or reliving the days and events reflecting on leading up to the death of Jim's father—the deeper I sank into darkness and despair. And none of my backward thinking produced any hope, any answers, or any solutions!

The apostle Paul's words in Philippians 3:13-14, however, came to my rescue. They gave me the guidance I needed for overcoming—by God's grace—the daily negative lifestyle that grew out of my unhealthy dwelling on the past. And like Paul is to me, he can be your teacher and example of forgetting, reaching forward, and pressing on.

Forgetting completely—As we begin looking at Paul's experience with forgetting the past, let me again say that the past is important. It shapes us, it teaches us, and it reminds us of God's faithfulness. Our spiritual growth, however, can be blocked by paying too much attention to the past. How is that?

Dwelling on the past can cause a slackening of pace in our Christian walk. It's easy to look backward and never move forward. As one commentator puts it, "Looking back is sure to end in going back."[1] Christian growth—the process of moving forward—requires looking to the future rather than to the past. In fact, one scholar writes, "The Christian's onward progress is hindered should he dwell on the past full of failures and sins, full of heartaches and discouragements, full of disappointments and thwarted hopes and plans. As long as a Christian has made things right with God and man, he should completely forget the past."[2]

Paul's language in Philippians 3 is strong! Another biblical scholar writes, "When Paul says that he forgets what lies behind, he refers to a type of forgetting which is no mere, passive oblivion. It is active obliteration, so that when any thought of…the past would occur to Paul, he immediately banished it from his mind….It is a constant, deliberate discarding of any thought of [the] past…."[3] Still another scholarly source explains, "Forgetting is stronger in the Greek, [meaning] 'completely forgetting'" and he translates Paul's words, "I in fact am forgetting completely the things that are behind."[4]

Taking Paul's advice—Christians of old took Paul's advice to forget what lies behind much more seriously than we do today. F.B. Meyer, writing in his celebrated devotional commentary at the turn of the century, addressed "the Duty of Forgetting," and called for "no morbid dwelling on the Sinful Past." Meyer appealed to his readers to "learn to forget...and do not dwell upon past sin." He explained, "There may be things in our past of which we are ashamed, which might haunt us, which might cut the sinews of our strength. But if we have handed them over to God in confession and faith, He has put them away and forgotten them." His advice? "Forget them, and...the sin which has...blackened your record, [and] reach forward to realise the beauty of Jesus."[5]

Moving forward in faith—Forgetting what lies behind is not always easy. And note this—the word "forgetting" is in the *present* tense. You see, forgetting is not an act done once and for all. Instead, like Paul, we must *keep on forgetting* those things in the past that hold us back. Paul didn't want to rest on his past accomplishments, and neither should we. And Paul didn't want his past mistakes to keep him from moving on, and neither should we.

So, again and again, I have told myself, "No, Elizabeth, that is past. That is over. That is no longer real. So don't dwell on it! Don't let it hold you back. Forget whatever would keep you from moving forward in faith and in your spiritual growth." As I shared in a previous chapter, I've learned to look to the past only (well, most of the time!) to remember God's role in the problems and pain of yesterday—to recall His gracious provision for me, His presence, His faithfulness, and His compassion.

Looking to the past for lessons God has taught us and forgetting those elements of the past that would stymie our forward progress may sound like a tricky balance to maintain. What more does the apostle Paul teach us about "the art of forgetting" those elements of the past that would block our Christian growth and our progress toward Christlikeness?

Forgetting the Bad

One thing that moves us forward toward healthy spiritual growth is remembering to forget the bad we did before we became Christians. Before he came to know Jesus as Lord and Savior, Paul was Saul, the persecutor of Christians. He was dubbed by one scholar as "the guiding spirit of evil."[6] Paul is described as acting with "brutal cruelty…[as] a wild animal savaging a body."[7] The Bible reports Paul "made havoc of [ravaged] the church, entering every house, and dragging off men and women, committing them to prison" (Acts 8:3).

It's also quite possible that, rather than merely witnessing the stoning of Stephen, Paul was involved in the sentencing and gave his wholehearted approval to the murder (Acts 7:58; 8:1). Then, praise God, on his way to Damascus, with letters in hand from the high priest authorizing him to bind and bring Christian men and women to Jerusalem for trial (Acts 9:1-3), Paul met Jesus Christ! Only his encounter with Christ kept Paul's hands from being bloodied even further.

You and I may not have committed murder, but we probably

did things before we knew Christ that we must forget if we are to grow as Christians. What can you and I do when those past sins come to mind?

First, remember, no fishing allowed!—We need to remind ourselves of the truth of 2 Corinthians 5:17—"If anyone is in Christ, he is a new creation; old things have passed away; behold, all things have become new." If you are a Christian, you—yes, you!—are a new creature. You have been created all over again. What does this mean? It means that old things, including the sin you committed before coming to know Jesus, have passed away and are gone forever! All that you were and all that you did as a non-Christian are gone forever, removed "as far as the east is from the west" (Psalm 103:12). As writer and evangelist Corrie ten Boom loved to say, "When we confess our sins, God casts them into the deepest ocean, gone forever. And even though I cannot find a Scripture for it, I believe God then places a sign out there that says, 'No Fishing Allowed.' "[8]

Dear reader, God's love for you accomplished the forgiveness of your sin, your cleansing, your new birth, and your fresh start. Sure, consequences of your actions may remain, but the sin itself is forgiven! You are covered and cleansed by Christ's precious blood. You can, therefore, go on with your life...without shame and without being held back. And you can show your love for God by refusing to dwell on what He has removed and taken care of. When your past sin comes to mind—and it will—stop fishing! Acknowledge God's forgiveness, thank Him profusely, and move on.

Second, remember to press on!—Besides letting go of those

sins committed before naming Jesus as Lord and Savior, you and I need to let go of the sins we have committed and the bad things that have happened to us since we became Christians. The apostle Paul, for instance, suffered great things for the sake of Christ (Acts 9:16). He experienced beatings, betrayal, hunger, and thirst because of his faith in Jesus Christ (see 2 Corinthians 11:23-27). God also allowed Satan to afflict Paul with "a thorn in the flesh" (2 Corinthians 12:7). Dwelling on these things and asking why they happened would have blocked Paul's spiritual growth and forward movement. Therefore, he needed to forget them...and move on.

Undoubtedly, certain events in life also need to be forgotten if we are to move on and grow in the Lord. These can be acts done to us or by us, acts that have consequences we are forced to deal with as innocent victims, acts we have witnessed. They can be acts like my daughter Katherine witnessed. As a working college student, she saw a tiny boy being physically abused by his father. Thinking quickly, her employer wrote down the man's license plate number and reported him to the police. But what was my Katherine to do with her memory of the abuse? With the sounds she had heard and the anxiety she had felt?

When she told Jim and me about the incident, we agonized with her. And we prayed—for Katherine, for the boy, for the man, and for the police. We also prayed for her to begin the process of forgetting. We encouraged her, through prayer, to leave the situation in God's capable hands and then, again through prayer, to obliterate any thought of what she witnessed. She had to go on.

Here's another example. My friend Laurie called me about her niece Anna. Anna had had an extremely abusive childhood, and her nightmares had begun again. Laurie and I knew Anna also needed to let go of the past and move on. As we talked about how she might help her niece, I mentioned, "And be sure she isn't watching too much news."

Laurie shrieked, "That's it, Elizabeth! When I was at her home, we watched the news together, and now I remember what was on the news that day. No wonder the nightmares started up again!" A news story had brought back the past for Anna when she was trying to move on from it.

Loving God...Even More

My dear friend, God wants Katherine, Anna, and you and me to move on from the suffering of the past. He doesn't want the circumstances and situations of life to weigh us down with guilt, result in bitterness, or cause us to question Him and His goodness. No, such incidents call us to love Him even more!

Whatever suffering you've experienced (from unexplainable losses to someone's thoughtless comment) and whenever it happened (whether 20 years or 2 minutes ago), God's remedy is the same. Don't bog down. Don't let it hinder your love for the Lord. No, follow the counsel of the Lord through Paul instead—Press on! Forget what lies behind. Let it lie behind you. Keep it in the past. Don't let the pain or the questions keep you down.

My dear reading friend, turn your hurting heart upward. Acknowledge that God's ways are not our ways (Isaiah 55:8), that innocents suffer when people sin, that we live in a fallen world. And then press on! Go on with life. In other words, remember to forget!

~ 12 ~

Finding the Gold

Forgetting the past...

Philippians 3:13 NLT

For 20-plus years, I've been learning to apply the truths of God's Word to help me think on what is true and real and to win over worry. And now, as we're considering God's command to be "forgetting those things which are behind" and using our energies instead for pressing for the prize of God's heavenly calling, I want to pass on something that's been most helpful. I don't know where I heard it, but it really stuck with me...and by me. As the saying goes...

> *Learn* from the past,
> *log* the lessons from the past, but
> *leave* the past!

I'm sure you agree that dwelling on the unchangeable past (which is no longer true or real) can sap you of energy and deprive you of much joy. Said more positively, knowing that God is the God of our past, and entrusting it to Him, can free us to enjoy life in the present. It can also free up our energy—spiritual, mental, emotional, and physical—to focus forward on the race at hand and on "the upward call of God in Christ Jesus."

Forgetting the Good

Although it may surprise you, in order to effectively serve the Lord, the apostle Paul needed to leave behind *the good* as well as the bad of his past.

Paul forgot the good—Paul was indeed a bright and shining star! Before he became a Christian, he enjoyed a multitude of privileges as a Roman citizen and as a student of Gamaliel, the great teacher of the law (Acts 22:3). Paul's impeccable Jewish pedigree also meant he enjoyed an enviable position in society (Philippians 3:5-6).

Paul, however, chose to forget his status and the privileges of his position, regarding them as a hindrance to running the race for Christ. In answer to God's call on his life, Paul valued serving God and His eternal truth far more than the fleeting status and privilege the world offered him.

Seven missionaries forgot the good—In more recent times, C.T. Studd, like Paul, forgot the good he had enjoyed before becoming a Christian. Extremely wealthy and Cambridge educated, Studd was one of seven men from that college who ignited the great student missions movement in the nineteenth century.

As this group of men, "The Cambridge Seven," left for China, a news correspondent described them as standing side by side renouncing the careers in which they had already gained no small distinction, putting aside the splendid prizes of earthly ambition, taking leave of the social circles in which they shone with no mean brilliance, and plunging into that warfare whose splendours are seen only by faith, and whose rewards seem so shadowy to the unopened vision of ordinary men.

Later, before leaving on his second trip to China, C.T. Studd "invested in the Bank of Heaven by giving away all of his inheritance" except for 3,400 British pounds, which he presented to his bride before their wedding. She, too, knew about "forgetting those things which are behind." She asked, "Now, Charlie, what did the Lord tell the rich young man to do?" When C.T. answered, "Sell all," she said, "Well, then, we will start clear with the Lord at our wedding." She then gave the 3,400 pounds to General Booth of the Salvation Army.[1]

We must not forget the good—Even God's blessings can keep us from serving the Lord with all of our energy, all of our heart, and all of our self...if we hold on to them, dwell on them, and fail to press on toward spiritual growth and usefulness. The apostle Paul, six missionaries, and Mr. and Mrs. C.T. Studd moved on from the good the world offered to serve the better that God had for them...and so must we.

Forgetting Success

Paul also had to move on from the good that he experienced *after* becoming a follower of Jesus Christ. A brilliant orator, Paul led great numbers of people to salvation. He worked many miracles and healings, and Christ spoke to him three times. Paul saw visions, received revelations, was "caught up to the third heaven...into Paradise and heard inexpressible words" (2 Corinthians 12:2,4). God used Paul mightily to minister to early believers, and today his writings comprise 13 books of the New Testament.

Even ministry accomplishments, when dwelled on too long, can keep us from reaching forward in our journey toward Christlikeness. We cannot make progress when we are resting on our laurels, resting on past successes. Therefore, we must forget the good.

Forget "who you was"—I saw this truth sadly illustrated in a couple who arrived at our church fresh from serving in a fine Christian organization for ten years. They seemed to have been everywhere and done everything for Christ. As a new Christian, I saw what they had and I wanted it...for a while. But during the next decade, I saw them float along on the merits of their former service. They regularly reminded others of their ten-year term with that worthy organization... while doing nothing in the present. Drawing on their past, this couple reminded me of the joke about a man at a Hollywood party who, feeling snubbed, went from guest to guest saying, "But you don't know who I was!"

It's far too easy for us to say, like the man at the party, "But you don't know who I was...back on the East Coast, or in my old church, or where I grew up, or when I was on the mission field, or when I served with this organization. You don't know who I was!" As Dr. John MacArthur explained in a sermon, we are like the star in the sky that died, but we could see it for 30 more years. "Its brilliance," he said, "was from the past, but it was dead in the present."

God doesn't want His people to be like that star! So through Paul, He urges us to "forget 'who you was'! What are you doing now?"

Forget the good ol' days—God wants us to forget our achievements, our accomplishments, and our brilliance so that we will keep achieving and accomplishing for Him in the present. Stopping to remember the good ol' days can too easily lead to dwelling on them and neglecting our ongoing work for the Lord. Good things in the past can keep us from looking and moving and "reaching forward." Paul says, "Forget what lies behind." Whether they happened 20 years ago or yesterday, the wonderful things you have accomplished or experienced are to be forgotten. These things are dead in the present—although we don't always realize that fact.

Pastor Chuck Swindoll wrote this about some time he spent with a group of Christian leaders: "While everyone else much preferred to be on a first-name basis (rather than Reverend or Mister) one man demanded: 'Call *me* doctor.'" Chuck's advice to "Dr. Hotshot" was "get a good education—but get over it. Dig in and pay the price for solid, challenging years in school, and apply your education with all your ability, but *please* spare others from the tiring reminders of how honored they should feel in your presence. Reach the maximum of your potential—but *don't talk about it.*" He then dared his fellow pastors to remove all the diplomas from the walls in their offices and any object that promoted them and their achievements.[2] Such signs of past achievement, back in the good ol' days, mean nothing next to what we are doing for God today.

Don't forget what is yet to be accomplished—Writing about Paul's example and instruction regarding the value of forgetting the past, one scholar comments that "the memory of past successes and attainments may detain us from more splendid triumphs....[Paul did] not please himself by dwelling on...what he had accomplished. No; his thought was what was yet to be accomplished. What was there yet possible to him of Christian experience, of Christian usefulness?"[3] Paul refused to succumb to self-satisfaction. With his gaze focused on the future, Paul knew that "the Christian must forget all that he has done and remember only what he still has to do."[4]

Beloved, thank God for the good of the past, for His blessings, and for the good He has enabled you to do for Him. And thank Him for the good ol' days! But be sure to move on and serve Him in the present.

Three Steps for Forgetting

Forgetting the past is not easy to do. It's not easy to hold lightly the good God has blessed us with and used us to accomplish. And it's not easy to obey God by and not questioning the unexplainable bad that has come our way. The following three steps, however, will help you let go of the past so that you are free to press on and serve Him in the present.

Step 1: Discover the gold—Whatever has happened to you in the past and whatever is happening in your life now, look for the "gold." Look for the hidden blessing, the lesson to be learned, or the character trait being forged. Trust that because God has allowed these experiences, somewhere in them there is gold for you! And while you are looking, remember that gold isn't always easily seen or readily accessible.

How can you discover the gold? During the Gold Rush, miners dipped their pans into the dirt at the bottom of a stream and drew up a plate filled with silt, gravel, and stones.

Patiently and carefully they sifted through the dirt and hoped to find gold shining purely and brilliantly through the refuse they dredged from the riverbed. Many did indeed make their fortunes...but not without a lot of work! And it may take some work on your part to find the good God is working in the bad of your life.

Without dwelling on them, take some time to think back on the "bad things" of your life. (We'll learn more about these "bad things" in a later chapter.) Look for some positive despite the negative. Look for where our merciful and loving God is working redemption in the situations. The good you find may be a lesson learned, deeper knowledge of God, or greater understanding for further service to Him and His people (2 Corinthians 1:4). Find the good—the gold—and let go of the rest! Take it with you and move on!

Step 2: Find forgiveness—Once you discover the gold, you will need to find forgiveness for the bad that resulted from your sin. As we saw in chapter 1, "If we confess our sins, [God] is faithful and just to forgive us our sins and to cleanse us from all unrighteousness" (1 John 1:9). In this truth you find forgiveness. The truth is that you *are* forgiven, and this truth cost Christ His life. Your role is to believe that you are forgiven. Let the truth of God's gracious forgiveness help you let go of the past. After all, as my former pastor asked, "Why should you remember what God has forgotten?" Just *know* that you are forgiven!

Step 3: Forgive others—Finally, having discovered the gold and found God's forgiveness, forgive those who have hurt you. Jesus modeled such forgiveness for us as, hanging on the cross, He prayed, "Father, forgive them, for they do not know what they do" (Luke 23:34). When we fail to forgive others and fail to follow Christ's example, we sentence ourselves to a life of bitterness. We also stop growing in faith, and we compromise our service and witness for Jesus. However, when we—by God's grace—extend forgiveness to those who have hurt us, we can be used mightily by God. For instance...

—Helen Roseveare, a missionary doctor who was brutally raped while serving in the Congo, forgave those who wronged her and returned to the same location for 20 more years of missionary service.[5]

—When Elisabeth Elliot forgave the men who savagely killed her missionary husband, she was able to return and continue her ministry of the gospel of forgiveness.[6]

—Evangelist Corrie ten Boom struggled greatly but found the strength to forgive the German soldier who had been the cruelest to her sister and herself while they were prisoners at Ravensbruck during World War II.[7]

Dr. Helen Roseveare, Elisabeth Elliot, and Corrie ten Boom all found freedom from the past and the freedom to press on and serve when they extended forgiveness to those who had hurt them deeply...and you and I must do the same!

Loving God...Even More

Remembering to forget the past is a shiny key to unlocking the door of days gone by and finding the gold and the freedom from a past that holds back our Christian growth. "Forgetting those things which are behind" is the first stride the apostle Paul took as he ran the race, pressed for the prize, and lived his life for Jesus Christ. So what do you need to let go of from the past? Are you resting on the laurels of past achievements for the Lord? What major accomplishment may be hindering your effort to run the Christian race today? Thank God for using you as He has. Then ask Him to show you where He would have you press on for Him.

Perhaps you are being held to the past by a source of deep pain or an experience that is hard to understand. Ask God to shine His light in your darkness (Psalm 112:4). Ask Him to help you discover the gold of His perfect work in your life. Where it's appropriate, admit any wrong acts or thoughts and ask God's forgiveness. And, when needed, ask God's help in forgiving others.

With the gold gleaned from the past and God's forgiveness both extended and received, you will more fully experience God's freeing and empowering love, an experience that enables us to love Him...even more.

~ 13 ~

Going On and On and On

Reaching forward to those things
which are ahead...

Philippians 3:13

A missionary once labored to teach his tribal people Philippians 3:13-14, where the apostle Paul writes, "Brethren, I do not count myself to have apprehended [spiritual maturity or Christlike perfection]; but one thing I do, forgetting those things which are behind and reaching forward to those things which are ahead, I press toward the goal for the prize of the upward call of God in Christ Jesus." Several days after the lesson, one of the missionary's "students" approached him and asked permission to read the poem he had written about the meaning of Paul's words:

Go on, go on, go on, go on,
Go on, go on, go on.
Go on, go on, go on, go on,
Go on, go on, go on!

And there were seven more identical stanzas to his poem. This man definitely got Paul's message!

To quickly review, Paul learned *Step 1,* the importance of forgetting the elements of the past (both the good and the bad), that would hold back his spiritual growth. And now he shares *Step 2* for growing and serving the Lord—"reaching forward to those things which are ahead."

Like Paul, when we choose to forget the elements of the past that can weigh us down or keep us stuck there, when we leave the good and the bad of the past in God's omnipotent and capable hands, we make a 180-degree turn! No longer do we focus on the past. Instead, we are riveted on what's ahead. Our "no" to the past—to what is behind—is also a "yes" to the present and what is at hand. And, as you'll see now on our walk through what it means to reach forward to what is ahead, this focus on the present is vital.

Where Are You Going?

What characterizes forward-moving, focused Christians? What sets them apart? For starters...

✓ They know where they are going.

✓ They have a sense of God's call on their lives, which gives them sure direction each step of the way and makes decision-making easier.

✓ They understand the purpose of their lives.

✓ They focus on God and God-given goals, which makes it easier to say "no" to what is trivial.

✓ They choose wisely from among their options, which moves them toward life goals.

This brings us back to *energy,* that great secret to success! A forward focus gives us greater energy for reaching our goals...which, as we just noted, are God's goals. Therefore, energy is not wasted on wondering what to do or on wandering aimlessly from option to option. Knowing exactly what to do and what needs to be done also dictates where our energy is spent. A God-confidence blossoms as we gain more certainty about what to do and about God's enabling power to serve wherever He has placed us.

Knowing *where* we are headed and *why* is the kind of focus Paul calls us to in Philippians 3:13-14.

Where Is Your Focus?

When Paul writes about "reaching forward to those things which are ahead," he is likening his life to a race and picturing himself as a runner in the act of racing toward the finish line. His body is bent forward. His eyes are fixed on his goal. Moving along the path God has laid out for him, he leans forward as his feet carry him toward the finish. All of his energy—spiritual, mental, emotional, and physical—is committed to the race he is running, "to those things which are ahead."

This image is quite a contrast to the paintings of an Edwardian lady featured on some note cards I saw in a bookstore one day! With a dreamy half-smile, this woman lounges on a pillowed window seat. With one hand, she holds the book she's reading. With the other, she strokes the cat curled up in her lap. A gentle breeze lifts the gauze curtains to reveal a splendid day outside. Her days of simple leisure hardly reflect the way Christ means for us to live our lives. Instead, like Paul, we are to run a race toward the goal of Christlike maturity and service. Besides keeping our standards high, that prize gives us reason to go on and on and on.

Like me, you may daydream about days of leisure like the greeting card suggests. (Oh, I can taste it…feel it…smell it!) But perhaps, also like me, you realize that life is a race. And like me, you are by God's grace doing your very best to run it for and with Him. If so, here's something that helps. To stay on course, I ask myself the following questions from time to time:

- Am I focusing my efforts toward the prize that awaits at the end, or am I too content watching other people's efforts?
- Am I "training" regularly and "working out" in the daily disciplines of the Christian life?
- Am I properly fueling my body with sleep, nutrition, and exercise for maximum results?

Running the race—living for Christ and growing into His image—requires focus and discipline. And yes, rest and relaxation are important as we respond to God's call on our lives. But we are not to let the desire to rest, relax, and reward ourselves interfere with our efforts for God's kingdom. Like Paul's words encourage us, a runner's focus and mentality can fuel and jet-propel our race toward Christlike perfection.

Focusing on the Present

Here's another message from Paul: A runner who looks backward will lose the race. As we saw in previous chapters,

Paul chose not to allow his past failures and accomplishments to interfere with his present efforts for his Lord. He sought instead to be "reaching forward to those things which are ahead." And that same 180-degree decision to forget the past and focus on present forward movement enables you and me to grow spiritually.

To repeat, leaving the elements of the past in God's hands—elements that would hold us back and drain us of energy—is a crucial first step in the race toward Christlikeness. Forgetting the past frees us from self-condemnation and regret so that we can enjoy God's love for us and love Him in return. As one woman shared with me after she heard this lesson on forgetting what lies behind, "This verse is for anyone who has ever made a mistake. What a splendid wave of comfort washes over me to realize the freedom to not look back over my past failures."

Recognizing God's Purpose for You

Our runner's focus on the present comes when we clearly understand the purpose of our lives. I personally discovered God's purpose for me—His call on my life—in a very special way when a woman handed me a small, flat package wrapped in muted pastels. The card read, "Thank you for your class on prayer," and the package contained a leather-bound, silver-edged book that soon broadened my prayer life.

Unfortunately that tiny prayer volume is now out of print, but here's what changed my life and polished up my purpose. Four questions were posed about our identity in Christ. Puzzled, I paused long enough to scratch my head and then went on. But the questions haunted me until one day I reluctantly tackled the questions—

Who am I?
Where did I come from?
Why am I here?
Where am I going?

The beautiful little book changed my prayers and my prayer life. But, dear friend, answering these four questions changed my life! Before I answered them, I was greatly influenced by other people's ideas about what I should do with my life and what my Christian faith should look like. A "movement" follower and a "program" participant, I allowed other people to determine my purpose. But, praise God, these four questions helped me recognize the purpose of my life and gave me life goals to focus on. Today I know...

- Who I am—I am a Christian woman, wife, mother, and grandmother;
- Where I came from—I was "in [Christ] before the foundation of the world" (Ephesians 1:4);
- Why I am here—I am here to give my life in service to God, my family, and His people;
- Where I am going—by God's amazing grace and love, I am going to heaven!

Please take a few minutes to answer these four questions for yourself. Your answers won't be identical to mine. But they will help you grasp God's great purpose for *your* life. They will give you a sense of direction as you set your goals and plan your activities.

You may be awed like I was by the realization that God has a specific purpose for you. For me, that realization has given me a better sense of mission (I am definitely more focused as a result of glimpsing God's purpose for my life), a clearer understanding of my job assignment (I am to spend myself and be spent in service to Christ and His people), and an urgency as I go about my tasks (knowing that my time on earth is limited, I am frightfully aware of time wasted and time passing). I want to use my time and energy to achieve God's purposes and, along the way, find rest and refreshment in Him. After all, it is He who ultimately makes things happen for the kingdom. I am just thankful that He has chosen to use me in the process!

Loving God...Even More

The apostle Paul was certainly used by God as he responded to the God-given purpose and driving force of his life. He wrote, "I press on, that I may lay hold of that for which Christ Jesus has also laid hold of me" (Philippians 3:12). As one scholar explains, Paul—

> is trying to grasp that for which he has been grasped by Christ....Paul felt that when Christ stopped him on the Damascus Road, He had a vision and a purpose for Paul; and Paul felt that all his life he was bound to press on, lest he fail Jesus and frustrate His dream....Every [believer] is grasped by Christ for some purpose; and, therefore, every [believer] should all his life press on so that he may grasp that purpose for which Christ grasped him.[1]

Do you desire to love God...even more? Then, I beg you, center your entire being in God. Look to Him and do whatever it takes to keep from getting tripped up or stalled by the past. Focus! Reach forward! And press on for that for which you have been grasped by Christ.

~ 14 ~

Focusing Forward... and Sailing On!

Straining toward what is ahead...

Philippians 3:13 NIV

Meet Joseph. He's an amazing man...and an amazing model of someone who had to forget those things that were behind, forgive those who hurt him, fix his gaze upon those things which were before, and go on and on and on. Joseph teaches us valuable lessons on pursuing excellence as we reach forward to serve God...even when circumstances are difficult and painful. His story is preserved for us in Genesis 37–50.

Pursuing Excellence

Sold into slavery in Egypt by envious brothers, Joseph chose to serve God by doing the best he could wherever he was and whatever the circumstances of his life. In Egypt he chose to forget his past in Israel and "go on"...to where he became the best slave and manager of Potiphar's household...until he was unjustly imprisoned.

In prison, Joseph made the same choices, choosing to forget the luxury of Potiphar's palace and "go on"...to where he became the best prisoner in the dungeon, and later, the best manager of the prisoners. When he was finally released from prison, Joseph again decided to forget his dismal past in a dismal dungeon and "go on"...to where he soon became the best in a government position, a priviledged position that enabled him to feed his father, brothers, and their families when they arrived in Egypt in search of food from famine-struck Israel.

Joseph shows us excellence every step of the way... through the good and the bad. Mark this lesson well!

Bearing Fruit in the Land of Your Affliction

Yes, Joseph successfully moved on from the past. But there was one thing he didn't forget—the many instances of God's goodness! In gratitude and remembrance, Joseph named his first son Manasseh, meaning "one who causes to forget," saying "God has made me forget all my trouble and all my father's household" (Genesis 41:51 NASB). Later Joseph named his second son Ephraim, meaning "fruitful," declaring "God has made me fruitful in the land of my affliction" (verse 52 NASB). Moving on from the past, he was able to bear fruit in the present. Joseph bloomed where he was planted, and God blessed him greatly.

Perhaps you, like Joseph (and like me the year our family lived in nine different places while serving as missionaries), find yourself living where you don't want to be. Many times, like Joseph, we are not where we used to be and not where we want to be...and not where we're going to be! And many times, like Joseph, we find ourselves holding positions or having responsibilities we did not choose for ourselves. In times like these, we can follow Joseph's example and...

—forget the past,
—forgive those who have caused us pain,
—focus on the present time and place, and
—follow after excellence

while expecting God to work His goodness and purpose in the circumstances. By determining to be the best we can be wherever we are, you and I can also bloom where we are planted.

So, where has God "planted" you? Are you a missionary in Africa living in a mud hut or a widow roaming through a palatial-but-empty home? Are you in a rural community of 39 people or in a metropolis of millions? Wherever God puts you, He has a purpose. Whatever the situation, it is an opportunity to "go on" and bear fruit for His kingdom. However difficult the circumstances, He will enable you to accomplish something for Him as you look to Him and focus on being useful to Him and to others.

Existing...or Serving?

It's true that difficult and painful circumstances can make it difficult for us to pursue excellence as we serve God. But circumstances that are too comfortable can have the same effect. We can become people who merely *exist* rather than ones who actively *serve* God. Content with where we are, we can fail to press forward toward Christlike maturity.

My husband told me about a woman who lived in her dream home on a lake in middle America, thoroughly enjoying the quiet setting and leisurely pace of country living. Her husband had a once-in-a-lifetime career opportunity that required that they move to Los Angeles. She, however, had no desire to relocate, especially to Los Angeles! So she stayed by her lake...and her husband passed on his golden opportunity.

Don't you wonder if perhaps this woman and wife mistakenly thinks "the prize" is to reside on waterfront property instead of attaining the spiritual maturity that comes with forgetting the past, reaching forward, and pressing ahead toward "the upward call of God in Christ Jesus" (Philippians 3:14)? Leaving her lake meant taking a risk, making a move, and growing her faith through new changes and challenges. In this woman's case, her comfort may actually cause her faith to stop growing and her pursuit of excellence to wane.

Hear Paul's message again! He warns us against resting on past achievements or present comfort. He urges us to purposefully look ahead and to wholeheartedly reach forward. He exhorts us to continue to press on in the race to our very last breath, and to discover a deeper faith in God. For growth to occur, there must be tension in our lives. That healthy, productive tension comes from change. But it can also come from the goals we set that push us to reach and press forward in growth and from our decision to be the best we can be for Him—wherever we are. So set the goals that demand that you grow. And beware of getting too comfortable! Too much comfort invites us to watch the race rather than to energetically participate in it.

Whether we find ourselves in difficult circumstances (like Joseph) or enjoying a life of comfort utterly void of challenge (like "the lady by the lake"), we must resolve to focus on God's purpose for us and press for it...for the prize! We must choose to pursue God's will for us. Strengthened by Him, we must participate fully in the race He calls us to run. Whether we are experiencing pain or pleasure right now, we need Paul's mind-set—"One thing I do: forgetting what lies behind and reaching forward to what lies ahead, I press on toward the goal for the prize of the upward call of God in Christ Jesus" (Philippians 3:13-14 NASB).

Fixing Your Heart and Mind on God

By now I hope you realize the importance of being focused. Focus is essential to running a race because if a runner fails to focus, that runner fails! But focus—whether in an Olympic race or in our Christian walk—does not always come easily.

Here's a race I enter daily. Every day when I sit down to read my Bible, I suddenly—and amazingly!—think of all sorts of things I need to do...not only today, but for the rest of my life! I then have to focus and fight the urge to jump up and move the clothes from the washer to the dryer. Or I think of a person I need to call and instinctively reach for the phone. Again, I have to focus! It is indeed a battle to focus my mind and my heart on reading the Bible and praying. So I go to war.

The conversation I have with myself goes something like this: "No, I'll write that down and do it later. I'm going to read my Bible....No, I'll call her later. I'm going to read my Bible....No, I'll let my answering machine take that call. That's why I have it. I'm going to read my Bible....No, I'm not going to put the clothes in the dryer right now. I'm going to read my Bible....No, I'll write that letter later. I'll load the dishwasher later. I'll make the bed later. I'll call the repairman later. *I'm going to read my Bible!"*

I also imagine myself wearing mental blinders that make it impossible to see all the options available to me. But even more compelling is God's love for me. So I ask *Him* to help me focus on *Him*. I lift before Him my struggle and the concerns and duties that crowd in. I ask for His gracious strength as I seek to fix my heart and mind on Him and Him alone.

Asking God to clear my mind of all that interferes with our time together brings His peace. He enables me to focus on the time at hand, on what is true and real—time with Him—so that I can meet with Him and then go through the day loving Him with all of my freshly filled heart, soul, and mind. True to the promise of Isaiah 26:3—"You will keep him in perfect peace, whose mind is stayed on You"—God does indeed help us fix our hearts and minds on Him.

Keeping a Vigilant, Steady Focus

Throughout our busy days, whatever situations come our way, God will help us keep our focus on Him and on what lies in our path. I remember one morning when I received a telephone call from a woman who was upset with me: "You said this...and then you did that...and I don't think you should have...." I hear critical comments about a lot of things, but this time the attack was personal.

As I was listening to this woman, I also heard the front door open and a familiar "Yahoo!" My daughter Courtney stuck her smiling face around the corner of my office door and waved. She had stopped by to pick up a few papers from her files. Because Courtney lived on her college campus, every moment with her was a blessing.

I explained (I hope graciously) to the caller that my daughter had just stopped by and arranged to finish our talk later. As I hung up the phone, I noticed my heart was racing and my stomach was churning. I felt bewildered, confused, and hurt. I wanted to process all that had been said and deal with the situation...but here, before my very eyes, was my lovely daughter, innocently chattering away as I fixed us a snack. Courtney was here, Courtney was now, and Courtney was real. The phone call was already 30 seconds in the past...and I needed to forget it for the moment, reach forward to what was lying right in my path *now*—a few golden minutes of time with my daughter.

Was I going to let a negative phone call—that was over and done with—ruin my time with my daughter? Although she was an unplanned—and welcomed!—interruption, she was clearly my next assignment from God. Realizing that being with Courtney was God's will for me *now,* I turned my focus forward. I decided to be the best mother I could be at that moment. That meant "forgetting" the call for those few minutes and going on by focusing fully on my daughter. So I riveted my eyes on her and listened intently. I chose to savor the present, precious treasure of time with her.

With God's help, my focus changed from the phone call to my daughter. And, my dear reading friend, such changes in focus are part of the rhythm of life. As the events of our day change and as interruptions arise, our focus must also change. This enables us to put aside unpleasantness or pain so we can experience and enjoy whatever is happening in the present. After all, the demands of the present—the tasks to perform, the duties to fulfill, the responsibilities to handle, the people to minister to—comprise the course on which we run the race toward Christlikeness.

Hearing God's Voice

As you and I run the Christian race, many voices call us to abandon the effort. The world woos us away from following Christ and offers tempting rewards for choosing its way to what it deems "success." We feel pressure to be like people in the neighborhood or at the office, and we aren't always affirmed in our efforts toward excellence. The past would hold us prisoner, chained and bound to darker days and deeds. And the flesh calls us to "have some fun...take it easy...don't worry...take care of it tomorrow!" The world doesn't understand the Christian's race and the glorious prize that awaits. The world doesn't acknowledge the cause of Christ or value the commitment His cause requires.

Despite the din of these various voices, the Christian runner who is looking ahead and reaching forward has ears for only one voice. The runner clearly hears God's strong voice over the weaker but persistent voices of the world that call him to lesser pursuits and duller prizes. Through the pages of Scripture, God's strong voice urges us to "go on, go on, go on, go on" and offers us the encouragement we need as we serve Him.

What kind of encouragement? God's Word calls us to look ahead, to determine our God-given purpose, to "set [our] mind on things above" (Colossians 3:2) and on the goals He gives us, to be the best we can be for Him, to daily fix both heart and mind on God Himself, and to direct our focus forward every minute. God's Word also tells us to "go on." And

God's Word reassures us that He is with us as we run the race, offering guidance and strength each step of the way.

Loving God...Even More

Dear friend, throughout life and throughout the race, discouraging voices will be loud and persuasive. Christopher Columbus experienced such voices on his journey across the Atlantic Ocean. Day after day he sailed without seeing land. And day after day his sailors threatened mutiny. They tried to persuade him to turn back, but Columbus refused to listen. At each day's end, he entered in the ship's log the two words, "Sailed on."

Those are the two words you, too, need to enter into the log of your journey, sometimes even minute by minute! You need to "sail on" as you look ahead and reach forward toward spiritual maturity and the goal of loving God with all your mind. As you focus on God, He will guide your steps, empower your service to Him, and work in you the characteristics of Christ. He will enable you to meet the demands of the present and, as the next chapter explains, to press on toward the prize. And you, fellow pursuer-of-the-prize, must go on, go on, go on, go on!

~ 15 ~

Keep On Keeping On

I press toward the goal for the prize
of the upward call of God
in Christ Jesus.

Philippians 3:14

When my husband was employed by a pharmaceutical company, his manager was known among his sales force for a certain saying. No matter what happened, his words were always the same—"Keep on keeping on." If Jim did well or won the district sales contest, he was told, "Keep on keeping on." If Jim's sales fell or he lost an important account, he was again told, "Keep on keeping on." Whether Jim excelled or failed, neither was to slow his progress. He was to keep on keeping on.

Our Call to Press On

Well, dear reader, in Philippians 3:14, the apostle Paul encourages this same attitude in us toward the journey of life when he writes, "I press toward the goal for the prize of the upward call of God in Christ Jesus." Up to this point in this section about "Pressing for the Prize," Paul has been pointing us toward a scriptural mind-set that is actively forgetting the past—learning from it but letting go of whatever would keep us from growing in our walk of faith. And now, as Paul ends this life-changing and life-directing exhortation, he instructs us to turn our face *toward* Jesus and focus fully on *Him*. As one commentator eloquently observed,

> We must look forward, not backward. Some men stand with their faces to the west, regretting the lost radiance of the setting sun. Others turn their gaze on the east, eager to catch the first streak of dawn. Surely the latter are the wiser. Our faces look forward that we may see the path we are about to tread.[1]

In our race toward becoming like Christ—and loving God with all our mind—we experience God's love more fully when we look to the dawning of each fresh new day. We must therefore answer God's call to press on and invest our energy on progress rather than focusing on the faded events of the past. We must reach forward by forgetting the past, concentrating on the present, and now, as Paul says, to push and press for the future "prize of the upward call of God in Christ Jesus."

How can we keep on keeping on? God gives us an easy formula for sustained growth: By (Step 1) *forgetting* what lies behind (in the past), we next (Step 2) assume a runner's posture of *reaching* forward (in the present), and (Step 3) begin the pursuit by *pressing* "toward the goal for the prize of the upward call of God in Christ Jesus" (which lies in the future—Philippians 3:14). Just as a marathon runner presses on to finish the race, so you and I must settle for nothing less than living every day for Jesus. We must give our utmost for His highest. *Pressing* means running "with utmost effort" and suggests "active and earnest endeavor." We are to "strain every nerve to pursue the ideal,"[2] remembering to draw on God's grace and strength each step of the way.

This pressing on toward the goal is a race we will run for the rest of our lives. And such effort can only be extended toward something significant. That "something significant" is the Savior who died for us. Focusing on Jesus is what enables us to give our wholehearted effort to the race of life. We can only keep on keeping on when we have our eyes on Him, our crucified and risen Lord.

A Grand Purpose

Purpose is paramount! I know I can't do anything, including getting out of bed on time(!), without having a sense of God's purpose for my life. Knowing my purpose—knowing that I am here to give my life in service to God and His people—is a driving motivator that keeps me keeping on in this race toward Christlikeness called life. And this is probably true for you, too. Therefore, it's important to develop goals under this broad aim of serving God with your life.

Here's one way to do this. When my husband conducts goal-setting seminars for men, he asks the men to write at the top of a sheet of paper, "What are my lifetime goals?" Then they are to answer that question by writing without stopping until Jim's timer rings after five minutes. Once they stop writing, they spend a few more minutes fine-tuning their answers. Finally Jim has the participants choose the three goals that are most important and rank them in order from most important to least important.

My story—I remember well the first-ever goal-setting seminar Jim led. It was for the two of us, and it occurred on a Sunday afternoon. We had spent a glorious and uplifting morning at church being taught, stretched, and challenged. Inspired by the worship and full of wishes and dreams, we knew we wanted to love Christ better and serve Him in some greater way. He had saved our souls, blessed our marriage and family, and given our lives purpose. Now what could we do to serve and follow Him more passionately and intently?

This conference-for-two was held in our home. As Jim and I sat facing each other at the dining table, we worked through these simple exercises that would change us forever. The desires of our full hearts spilled out on paper as we penned our responses. Little did we know that something as simple as the question "What are my lifetime goals?" could be the catalyst for grand goals that would energize us to serve our Savior. We were...and still are...willing and enthusiastic about pressing toward those goals that are enabling us now (and have been for 30 years) to reach forward and press on toward fulfilling the purpose of our lives—serving Jesus Christ!

What three goals did I define for myself that day? Here they are:

- To be a supportive and encouraging wife and mother
- To be a woman of God who is growing in knowledge and grace

- To teach the Bible so that women's lives are changed

Since setting these lifetime goals, I have known not only the purpose of my life, but the purpose for each day...and each minute in those days. Although I will never completely reach these goals, they challenge me daily to be the best I can be for God. These goals have kept me on track through the years—both the tough ones and the golden ones—and encouraged me to keep on keeping on.

Your story—Are you, my reading-and-reaching friend, focused on a specific-yet-grand purpose for your life? Can you, like Paul, talk about the "one thing" you do (Philippians 3:13)? It's good to think and dream about what you want to do for Christ, but it's essential to articulate specific lifetime goals that will fuel and further your efforts to fulfill your purpose of serving God. And what will most likely happen? Seeing your goals written out on paper will be sobering as you consider the privilege of working for God's kingdom and that high calling on your daily life. Those goals will also be very motivating as they remind you that you can, by the grace of God, do something eternally significant with your days on this earth.

If you haven't made your God-given purpose of serving Him personal by establishing some guiding goals for your life, please take the next hour to do so. Close the bedroom door, go to a coffee shop on your lunch hour, or clear the breakfast dishes off the kitchen table after everyone leaves. Spend 60 minutes with God, praying and thinking about His goals and purposes for your life. Answer the question, "What are my lifetime goals?" Then select from your list the three goals that are most significant to you as you consider God's causes. Rank them in order of importance.

And the blessed results? You won't be the same after this hour with your Lord. These 60 minutes spent reflecting on His purposes for you will be life-changing! I guarantee that you will discover new dimensions to your life. You'll find new energy for pursuing God's calling as you glimpse what you can be and do for Christ and in Him.

A Concerted Effort

Once you've set goals for your pursuit of serving God, you'll undoubtedly want to do your best and give your all to achieve those goals. You will want to press on and hold nothing back. God's ever-available grace empowers us to persevere and persist in untiring activity. And, praise the Lord, as we depend on God's guidance and His strength we are able to press on. *He* Himself enables us to walk through our days sensitized to His presence and trusting in His perfect timing, to keep moving, keep serving, keep functioning, keep growing, keep giving, and keep pressing on toward our desire to serve Him.

"Wings Like Eagles"

Hear now God's promise of a "secret" source of energy and efforts: "Those who wait on the LORD shall renew their strength; they shall mount up with wings like eagles, they shall run and not be weary, they shall walk and not faint" (Isaiah 40:31). Did you catch it? As we press on, God is there to enable us to serve Him.

Oh, how I hope you have experienced days when mounting up with wings like an eagle and pressing on seem effortless and enjoyable as you soar with God! What a thrill! But perhaps you've also experienced the kind of day that prompted Amy Carmichael, pioneer missionary to India, to pray, "Father, I'm not soaring today. Help me." In her writings, Miss Carmichael pens her heavenly Father's response, "Daughter, soaring is not always flying high above the world. Sometimes one is soaring only two feet above the ground, just enough to keep you from getting tangled in the thorns and crashing against the rocks."[3]

It's true that some days you and I may feel that we're soaring awfully close to the rocks! We may feel too tired to run, and our walk may not be much more than a limp or a stagger. Yet on such days, we are to keep facing forward. (As a chief research scientist of General Motors noted, "The enthusiast fails forward"!)[4]

But even when we weaken, and even when we "fail forward," we are to rest in the Lord and rely on Him. You see, He's in control. And because of this truth, we can keep on keeping on, whatever obstacles and distractions arise. Pressing on is our duty and, as one commentator wisely points out, "We are not blamed if we have not yet reached that crown of goodness. But we are blamed if we are not pressing on to it and rest contented with anything short of it."[5]

Focusing on the Goal

Paul kept pressing on. And one reason he was able to do so was his focus on the goal. You see, the primary aim of his life was to *finish* the race. Have you yet made the decision to press forward for Christ until the end of your life?

I have to admit that when I first became a Christian, I had not made that decision. I daydreamed instead of the world's ideal goal—retirement! I believed that, at a certain time, Jim and I would quit working and together live out the fantasies pictured on the travel brochures and maps I had collected.

My husband, however, had very different ideas! Jim firmly told me, "I'm never going to retire." With that statement, my daydreams vaporized, and I was sobered to recognize God's plan for His people...and for me. I realized that living for Christ means *living* for Him...all the way and to the end. We are called to live for Christ every day, not just until some magical, arbitrary age or income level when we stop serving others and serve only ourselves. No, we are called to press on and to *finish* the race.

Loving God...Even More

Every participant in any race knows that finishing the race is not easy. And the same is true for us as we love God and run the race "for the prize of the upward call of God in Christ Jesus." Sometimes along the way we may have to follow the example of the ice skaters my family and I watched one year during the winter Olympics. We watched the skating competition—but we certainly didn't enjoy it! Instead, holding our breaths and biting our nails, we endured it. During both the women's and men's events, I kept thinking, "If anyone just stays standing, they're going to win the gold medal!" Every single skater fell. But what happened after each fall was, for me, more spectacular than the skating feats. Each skater got up and went on! One skater even fell three times, but got right back up three times, and went on to finish.

The best ice skaters in the world were falling. Every one of them fell—but every one of them got up. During their long years of training, they had learned to always continue to the end. They had learned, among other things, to keep on keeping on. And because they did so, they were indeed winners. In fact, when the skating medals were presented at the Olympics that year, each one was awarded to a competitor who had fallen, gotten up, and finished!

Dear friend, we are to do the same. Our love for God compels us to!

~ 16 ~

Pressing Toward God's Purpose

I press toward the goal for the prize
of the upward call of God
in Christ Jesus.

Philippians 3:14

Retirement. It seems like people's entire lives center around this word...and life goal! And statistics tell us people are retiring earlier and earlier. And sadly, many of them are also retiring from active Christian life and service to God's people. However, fellow runner-of-the-race, this is not in God's plan! As you turn through the pages of Scripture, you won't find one saint who quit. Although many wanted to (do you remember Elijah, Jonah, and David?), not one did. Instead they kept pressing on toward God's purpose for their lives. Consider the following roll call of saints.

People in the Bible Who Focused to the End

Abraham—Throughout his life, Abraham responded to

God's commands to move. He lived in tents, and his nomadic lifestyle represented his search for "the city...whose builder and maker is God" (Hebrews 11:10). And how did Abraham's life end? He died without receiving the fulfillment of God's promises of land, a vast number of descendants, and great blessing (see Genesis 12:1-3 and Hebrews 11:39). Abraham could have quit, but he desired "a better, that is, a *heavenly* country" (Hebrews 11:16). So Abraham pressed on...until he died.

Moses—Aged and weary, Moses kept on (and on and on!) serving the Lord. At one point, he even needed the help of Aaron and Hur to hold his hands up so that God would continue to bless the Israelites' efforts in battle (Exodus 17:8-13). Yes, Moses could have quit...but he didn't. Instead, he got the help he needed to raise his hands heavenward.

Later, because Moses failed to obey God and trust Him for water at Meribah (see Numbers 20:7-13), God did not allow him to cross into the Promised Land he had waited 40 years to enter. Again, Moses could have quit serving God...but he didn't. Instead, he went on and spent the rest of his days teaching the law, preparing the priests, and encouraging Joshua to lead God's people into the land his feet would never touch.

Samuel—The priest Samuel was called by God to be His prophet. But later the people of Israel rejected his leadership and asked him to appoint a king over them so they would be like their neighboring nations (1 Samuel 8:1-5). Most people quit after being rejected, but Samuel didn't. Instead he kept on praying and preaching (12:23), and he spent the rest of his life helping Saul, the man who took his place as the leader of the nation.

David—King David passionately yearned to build a temple to God. But the Lord Almighty said to David, "You shall not build a house for My name, because you have shed much blood on the earth in my sight" (1 Chronicles 22:8). But instead of quitting, David kept pressing on for the Lord. He spent his last days making plans and gathering materials so that his son Solomon could build the temple (1 Chronicles 22:5-19).

Paul—In prison, Paul spent his final days writing letters that would guide the church of Jesus Christ in the future. He did not allow his impending death to shift his focus away from Jesus Christ and His people. Oh no! Paul kept on pressing on to the end of his life by offering encouragement, exhortation, and comfort through his pen.

John—Exiled to the island of Patmos in his old age, the apostle John could have quit. After all, his service for Christ had seemingly earned him only disgrace and dishonor. But John kept on pressing on. In his nineties, he was blessed with "the Revelation of Jesus Christ" (Revelation 1:1). The 22 chapters of the book of Revelation tell what will take place before and when the Lord returns. John served out his purpose as prophet with words that still speak to us today.

Jesus Christ—God's Son knew about the cross, but He pressed on toward it. When it was time, He endured it to the end (Hebrews 12:2). As He hung dying on that cruel instrument of torture to save you and me from our sins, He uttered three simple words—"It is finished" (John 19:30). Jesus, our Savior and our Lord, pressed on to the end.

The list of God's people who pressed on toward God's purposes and served the Lord until the end of their lives goes on and on. At one time or another during the race, each of the men of faith just mentioned had a valid reason to quit. People told them "No!" God told them "No!" to something they wanted. Circumstances seemed to scream "No!" to their personal desires. Yet not one of them quit, resigned, or retired. They knew they hadn't finished the race, that there was more work to be done, that their purpose wasn't fulfilled, and that God had other plans for them and could still use them. They knew that by God's grace they could make a difference for His kingdom right up until the day they left this earth and went to be with Him. They pressed on.

You and I may not be called by God to achieve anything near the magnitude of these men's accomplishments. However, God does view our sphere of service and responsibility as equally important. In my case, God has called me to press on in my service as a wife, a mother, and a teacher in the body of Christ. The examples of David, Paul, and the others encourage me to reach forward daily and press on to the end. These saints had a clear vision of God's purposes for them, which inspired them in their calling (and inspires me in mine) to press on toward the end in service of the Almighty.

People in Our Time Who Focused to the End

Examples that instruct and inspire us to press on are available in our time as well as in the Bible. Two women have especially modeled for me the kind of faith and love for God that keeps us pursuing God's purposes and "the goal for the prize of the upward call of God in Christ Jesus." The first is Corrie ten Boom.

In *The Five Silent Years of Corrie ten Boom,* Corrie's assistant, Pamela Rosewell, writes about Corrie's ministry during the final five years of her life. At age 86, Corrie suffered two debilitating strokes that left her unable to speak and barely able to move. Yet, until her death at age 91, she received visitors and interceded in prayer for others. By doing so, she modeled her trust in God and love for Him to everyone in her presence. Although her ministry moved from public to private, from platform to pallet, from preaching to praying, Corrie ten Boom pressed on to the end.[1]

The other woman whose example has greatly encouraged me is Shirley Price, teacher and creator of the curriculum piece entitled *God's Plan for the Wife and Mother.*[2] She delivered her final messages on Wednesday mornings in late 1974 at First Baptist Church of Van Nuys, California. Although undergoing radiation and chemotherapy for the cancer that would take her life on January 29, 1975, Shirley pressed on and finished those eight sessions that would help countless Christian wives and mothers. I was one of those recipients who later benefitted from her tapes and materials. Focused on her goal of serving Jesus and His people, Shirley pressed on toward God's purpose.

Christians who are focused on "the prize of the upward call of God in Christ Jesus" know that the prize awaits them at the *end* of the race. Although minor rewards come along the way, the highest honor doesn't come until we've run the entire race. So, acting on our love for God, we are to press on and serve Him every day of our lives. Then we will receive the prize as we see face-to-face the Lord who Himself endured to the end.

Running Unencumbered

The writer to the Hebrews knew about running the race and pressing toward God's purposes. He exhorted us to "lay aside every weight, and the sin which so easily ensnares us," and "run with endurance the race that is set before us" (Hebrews 12:1). Running the race is definitely easier when we're not weighted down or encumbered by sin. Here are some questions to help you evaluate your present running condition.

- What habits, thought patterns, or activities are holding you back or slowing you down?
- What goals are keeping your pursuit of God from being the most important activity in your life?
- What messages from the world are drowning out God's call to you?
- What do you need to lay aside so that you can better serve God?

I asked my husband what he's had to lay aside through the years in order to run the race and serve the Lord. Jim laughed and admitted, "Always television and food!" He knows that excess in these two areas is an encumbrance for him. So take an inventory of things that keep you from giving your whole heart to the race God has called you to run. Lay aside the useless, the wasteful, the meaningless, and the unimportant that clutters your life. You'll be freer to serve God with all your being.

A Look in the Mirror

Read again Paul's words in Philippians 3:13-14: "Forgetting those things which are behind and reaching forward to those things which are ahead, I press toward the goal for the prize of the upward call of God in Christ Jesus." These are the words of a man who knows the purpose of his life and who is focused on that goal. Have you, like Paul, determined your purpose in Christ? If so, are you doing your best to serve God and achieve that goal? Are you experiencing His grace as you try? Are you keeping your eyes on Jesus and letting Him inspire you along the way? Are you committed to press on to the end of your life? And are you laying aside whatever entangles you?

We who name Christ our Lord and Savior are called to love Him with all our heart, soul, and mind. This command gives our lives purpose, richness, and a significance that enhances our walk with the Savior. May we seek nothing other than to follow Him to the end, to exhibit His radiance along the way, and to accomplish His purposes for us.

Loving God...Even More

Do you realize that you are now more than halfway through our discussion of loving God with all your mind? So, at this midway point, I want you to consider how God has been at work in your life. Instead of thinking on "if onlys" and "what ifs," are you concentrating on what is true and real—God's love, His provision, His ways—and His timing in your life? Are you addressing the concerns of today, knowing that today is all you can do anything about? Are you trusting in God and leaving your past in His hands, forgetting the good as well as the bad that would keep you from serving Him wholeheartedly? And finally, are you looking ahead, reaching forward, and pressing on toward Christ by serving Him where He has placed you?

If you can answer *yes* to one or more of these questions, please be encouraged! God is transforming you into the image of His Son! As you continue to experience God's transforming love and find yourself loving Him more in return, you will experience a deeper, richer relationship with your Lord. And that relationship is key to a fulfilling life. After all, it is God's love that keeps us focused on the eternal and spiritual aspects of all we do.

In fact, in one of my favorite *Cathy* cartoons, Cathy's mother offers her daughter some advice about focus. As Cathy and her mother shop in the mall, Cathy laments, "Behind me all I see is a trail of relationship blunders." Mother sagely replies, "Don't look back, Cathy."

Next Cathy complains, "Above me all I see are balloons, and when I look down I see that they are attached to strollers full of babies that aren't mine." Again Mother advises, "Don't look up. Don't look down."

Cathy then cries, "Ahead of me all I see is the most romantic day of the year—Valentine's Day—and no man." Mother summarizes, "Don't look back, up, down, or ahead."

With her eyes covered, Cathy says, "Now I can't see anything at all." Mother comes through again, "Trust me, life is less confusing this way."[3]

Like Cathy, we can't follow her mother's advice. We are not to go through life with blinders on. No, we are to have our eyes open and focused on Christ! You see, if we aren't focused on Him, life will indeed be confusing. It is our focus on Jesus, our relationship with Him and our commitment to serving Him...as best we can and as long as we live...that gives significance and purpose to our lives.

But, as we've noted again and again, our efforts to serve God and to live for today, forget the past, and focus fully on the present are not things we are to do on our own. This call to "love God with all your mind" is a call to experience His grace. From Him we receive a new sensitivity to His presence, a better understanding for what He has called us to do, and deeper joy in getting to know Him better as we walk with Him through the minutes of every day.

Now I ask you, how could you help but love—more and more with the dawning of each fresh new day—the One who gives your life purpose? How could you not love the One who enables you to fulfill that purpose, and who promises you the reward of life eternal with Him when you finish running the race?

Counting on God's Goodness

We know that all things
work together for good
to those who love God,
to those who are called
according to His purpose.

ROMANS 8:28

~ 17 ~

Trusting the Lord

We know that all things
work together for good....

Romans 8:28

It was the day of our monthly committee meeting. Eager to plan future events for the women of the church, our leadership group had gathered in the Fireside Room...but something was wrong. Our chairman, who had reminded each of us about the meeting and asked us to please be on time, wasn't there. After waiting for several minutes, we decided to start the meeting without her. Later, as we neared our dismissal time, Bonnie calmly arrived. Smiling broadly, she announced that she had just experienced "another opportunity to trust the Lord."

Then Bonnie shared her "opportunity." Earlier that day, while at the public park, one of her four children had disappeared. Bonnie told us of her initial panic and near-crippling fear. However, in order to think clearly enough to deal with the situation, she had sought to focus on God instead of listening to her raging emotions. Her conversation with herself went like this: "Was God in control? Yes! Did God know where her son was? Of course! Was God able to take care of him? Definitely! Could God help her? Most certainly!"

And what happened? As Bonnie turned her turbulent thoughts to God and considered His presence, His power, His knowledge, and His involvement in her life, she was able to logically and systematically develop a plan of action for finding her son. She also followed the lessons taught in the first three Scripture passages we've looked at. Bonnie thought on what was real, not on any "what ifs" or "if onlys" (Philippians 4:8). She dealt with this assignment from God as it arrived and relied on Him to meet the challenge (Matthew 6:34). And, leaning on God, she focused on the present until the emergency was over (Philippians 3:13-14).

"Another opportunity to trust the Lord" seems to arise almost daily for many of God's children, doesn't it? As Bonnie's experience teaches us, the three passages we've already looked at can help us when such "opportunities" present themselves. And now here's another jewel from Scripture that can help you and me in any and every situation. It's Romans 8:28: "And we know that all things work together for good to those who love God, to those who are called according to His purpose."

Knowing God

When Bonnie told the leadership committee about her experience, I realized that she was able to face her frightening situation because she knew about God and His great love for her and her son. Bonnie knew God and His Word well enough to put her trust in Him. Her knowledge of God gave her hope. And that kind of knowing God determines our view of life and how we approach the challenges—our "opportunities to trust in the Lord"—each day!

As we begin the second half of this book, you'll notice a shift from the practicalities of daily life to an emphasis on God. If we are to live in close relationship with God, and if we are to serve Him and His people as He has called us to, we must, as one pastor observed, "see God as the God of the Bible—supreme, sovereign, and sensitive." He goes on to write,

> The Christian life is kept fine-tuned by biblical theology. We should always interpret experience by truth—we should always filter every pain through the lens of deity. When God is in sharp focus, then life is also undistorted.[1]

An it's true! When God is in sharp focus for us, we are a step closer to loving Him with all our mind. God also uses these biblically sound thoughts to help us respond to the events in our lives calmly, rationally, and with hope because we know Him. In fact, when we acknowledge God's supreme role in our lives and set our minds on Him, He enables us to be filled with hope.

Knowing God the Father

Have you ever met someone with bright eyes and a ready smile, whose positive outlook on life gives out a contagious energy? That person's secret may be knowing that God's great love for him or her means that everything that happens—in the present as well as the past and the future—will be for the good in the hands of our heavenly Father. This kind of Christian is confident that God watches over every aspect of His children's lives. Therefore, every event can be greeted with this knowledge. As a result, an enthusiasm for life is established and rooted in the knowledge of the God who gives us the promise of Romans 8:28.

As we begin now to look at this magnificent promise—and truth!—from the Bible, keep in mind a few background facts. In the book of Romans, the apostle Paul thoroughly and powerfully presents the doctrine of justification by faith. And in chapter 8, Paul affirms the blessed position of those of us who name Jesus as Lord and Savior. By virtue of His death for our sins, we are accepted by God as His children.

Paul then offers believers hope and comfort in their trials as he explains that the very trials that threaten us are actually "overruled" by God.[2] As Paul himself writes, "We know that all things work together for good to those who love God." This truth of Romans 8:28, a verse much loved by many Christians, gives us knowledge of God that bears the fruit of hope in our lives. I especially love the word "know" toward the beginning of this verse. It's a little word that means you and I have some for-real truths we can think on (Philippians 4:8)! What is it we can know?

Knowing God Is at Work

I once met with a woman to talk about some problems in her life that were not going away. As she spoke, her tale turned to her childhood and the extreme poverty and backwardness of her early home. It didn't take me long to see that this dear struggling woman was allowing these past circumstances, as difficult as they were, to affect her present situation…and was blaming God for both.

And this is common. Whenever tough times come our way, we can find ourselves falling into that same trap of thinking that God made a mistake…that He wasn't there when we needed Him. Thoughts like these rob us of our hope.

The Bible, however, describes a God who is perfect in His wisdom, His ways, and His timing. He is a God who is with us always, and a God who loves us. During our tough times, we must turn to these biblical truths about God and let them comfort and assure us of His presence. In our trials and traumas, we must believe the Bible's teaching that God was and is with us always, that He doesn't make mistakes, and that He is always in control.

Through God's inspired Word, He reminds us that He, the Divine Designer, knows what He is doing. He reveals that our history, whatever our experience, is not an error, but is, in fact, a part of His plan. And the result? Reminded that God is in control, we can then face life with hope in Him. And there's more good news! With this truth in mind, we don't need to use up our time and energy trying to reconcile some of the harsher aspects of reality (cancer, airplane crashes, incest, victims of drunk drivers). We can instead—by faith—and by His grace—acknowledge that His ways are not our ways (Isaiah 55:8-9).

So what could the woman I was counseling with do—and what can you and I do—to be more sensitive to God's presence?

Step 1: List the negatives in your life—By negatives I mean the things you don't like about yourself or about your life situation. Your list may include your background, your parents (or lack of them), your siblings, your appearance, your abilities, your personality, your marital status, your children (or lack of them), your finances, and whatever challenges you may currently face.

Step 2: Acknowledge God in the "negatives"—God knew, God allowed, and God permitted. And, as Romans 8:28 states, God overrules and causes all things—including what you perceive to be "negatives"—to work together for your good.

Step 3: Thank God for each "negative"—More specifically, thank Him for His promise to work for your good and for your spiritual growth in everything in your life, even in what you don't like. Remember that God has designed your life (Psalm 139:13-16). He has a plan for your life (2 Timothy 1:9). And He is actively working out His will through the people, events, and circumstances of your life—past, present, and future, positive and negative.

Dear friend, there has never been a mistake, and there never has been or ever will be even a split second when God is not present with you, superintending and being actively involved in your life. Acknowledging that God has planned your life can help free you from bitterness and resentment toward people, events, and circumstances. It also gives you hope! You become a hope-filled Christian when you remember—and grow to know—that God is the author of every moment of your life.

Knowing God Works All Things Together

And what about the unexpected events? The seemingly

coincidental things that happen to you? Those "chance" moments you are an innocent victim? And the times when you are guilty of sin? Because God is God, He is able to weave together every single aspect and event in your life and produce something good of it. Because God is God, He also causes everything in your life "to cooperate to the furtherance and final completion of His high design."[3] Furthermore, because God is God, He is able to overrule all of the evil in your life and cause it to work together for good. Hope comes to our hearts when we know—and remember—that God "works together" all things—the bad, the good…and the mysterious!

You'll love the chapter that follows! It gives us even more glorious assurance about the puzzling details of our lives. We'll grasp even more about this triumphant truth of Romans 8:28—a truth that highlights God's love for us and His awesome almighty power at work in our behalf. But first I want us to consider how to further pursue…

Loving God…Even More

Think about the marvelous truth of Romans 8:28 for a minute. That's what I was doing one day while I was in the kitchen mixing up a chocolate cake…and meditating on this hope-inducing scripture. As I assembled the items needed to make a family favorite, I couldn't help but compare the basic recipe for the chocolate cake I was making to the makeup of common, everyday life:

—Begin with bitter chocolate.

—Stir in some dry, tasteless flour.

—Add several raw eggs and some sour milk.
—Mix these and several more ingredients thoroughly.
—Bake the batter in a hot oven.
—The end result: a lovely chocolate cake.

Now think about your life—the bitter, the dry, the raw, the sour, the mixing, and the heat. Sounds bad, doesn't it? And it feels bad when it's happening! But in God's hands, these things—these unpleasant and uncomfortable and unlovely elements and components of life—will result in something good. That's the promise and the hope of Romans 8:28! In God's hands, the ingredients of our lives will always work out ultimately for our good and, even better, for His eternal purposes.

The next time you are facing the bitterness, the sourness, the agitation, or the heat of life, let this promise encourage you to trust in the Lord and to love Him with all your mind. "Know" that God is in control...and that His end will be "good." "Know" that He will "work together" "all things" for "good." As the saying goes, "If you are taking a beating, cheer up! God is just stirring the batter to bring you a blessing!"

~ 18 ~

Knowing God's Promise

We know that all things
work together for good....

Romans 8:28

How could we sum up the previous chapter and what we've been learning about God from His promise in Romans 8:28? Seven words seem to say it all: "God is in control of all things." That, dear reader, is the truth of Romans 8:28. And there is no fine print to this promise. There are also no disclaimers. All things and every thing—every event, every person, all of the past, all of the present, all of the future—falls under God's jurisdiction.

Knowing God Uses All Things

Are you still wondering, "*All* things"? Well, look one more time at this truth at the top of this page. That's exactly what this God-inspired, God-breathed scripture states. So now we ask, What kinds of "all things" does God work for our good?

All things includes the most pressing problem you currently face—Fill in this blank: "My Number One problem is ______ ______________________________."

Each day I identify the greatest challenge I face and then reaffirm that God has promised to work that very thing for good in my life. My outlook on that problem suddenly changes when I recall God's promise to turn something very bad—the worst thing in my life!—into something good. Reviewing Romans 8:28 points me to God and encourages me to count on His goodness. It gives me dazzling hope for the day ahead, a day that includes my Number One problem.

All things includes good things—Ministry opportunities, a promotion at work, a move to a different city, graduation from college, and a new job are some of the good things that God can use to spark new growth in us. Each of these good things—and any others you might add—carries with it a degree of challenge as you attempt something you've never done before. So, whenever you begin to feel flustered or frustrated by new and challenging circumstances, remember to count on your good, powerful God and His promise to you. He causes the good things in your life to work for good as you learn new skills and grow to greater levels of faithfulness, wisdom, and trust.

For instance, one good thing God uses in the lives of His married couples to cause growth is a baby, a fact I recalled one day as I was making phone calls to invite our church staff wives to a spring luncheon. One of our women had just brought her first baby home from the hospital. As I was dialing Dina's number, I thought back to Jim's and my first days of parenthood—and put the phone down. I decided to give Dina a few more days to adjust to being a mom.

A baby is indeed a miracle, a precious gift from God, and a *very* good thing (Psalm 127:3-5). But every mother will tell you that a baby causes a woman to stretch and grow! For instance, being a parent truly is an assignment from God that He uses to make parents more Christlike through countless opportunities to die to self and dive into nonstop care-giving!

All things includes bad things—The world is full of tragedy, pain, evil, suffering, and heartache. But Romans 8:28 teaches us that God uses even these bad things for our good. That means there can be no completely bad things. What a comfort and hope this is when we face the inexplicable occurrences and tragedies of life!

And unexplainable occurrences and tragedies happen! I know this personally. And I also know it because others have come to me burdened by the death of a child, unemployment, abuse, estranged family members, divorce, a handicapped child, and cancer. And what about an angry phone caller, a friend's snub, a misunderstanding, a canceled vacation? In these instances—and more!—we must remember God's promise!

Hear this explanation regarding Romans 8:28 and such bad things: "Paul is not saying that God prevents His children from experiencing things that can harm them. He is rather attesting that the Lord takes all that He allows to happen to His beloved children, even the worst things, and turns those things ultimately into blessings."[1]

What a wonderful God we have who *would* do this, and what a powerful God we have who *can* do this!

All things includes large things—I certainly heard testimony to this truth one Wednesday night at the weekly college Bible study that used to meet in our home. My husband had helped the young man who was to teach that night on Romans 8:28. When this collegian got up and announced his topic, we saw many stifled yawns of boredom as he read the familiar text out of his Bible. Quickly, however, all of us were drawn into Paul's message as this college student told about the large and bad thing that had happened to him.

We were speechless as our "teacher" described the car accident he had been in, his stay in the hospital, the amputation of his leg, his recovery process, his physical therapy, and the finding and fitting of an artificial leg. He shared openly about his struggles—emotional, physical, and practical—to adjust to a new way of life. The path to an athletic scholarship was closed to him forever, and his plans for the future were undone by that tragic accident. As our friend explained how he had relied on the powerful truth and promise from God in Romans 8:28, that verse was brought to life for us.

How had God used a car accident and the loss of a leg for good in this gentleman's life? First, the young man explained, the hospital stay gave him time to take a spiritual inventory and make fresh commitments to God. During that time on his back, he also listed the many reasons he still had for giving thanks to God. He also shared that relationships with his family were strengthened as they gathered around him during the crisis. And with the death of his athletic dreams, he had made a choice to concentrate on ministry.

Because of the large, bad thing that happened to him, our friend was attending a Christian college, participating as a student body officer majoring in Bible, leading a college

Bible study, and aiming for seminary in preparation for a life of ministry to the God who saved not only his soul, but his life.

All things includes small things—While the bad in our lives may not be on the scale of this younger friend's experience, all of us have had experiences that we label "bad." And, like the small irritation that causes a pearl to grow, even relatively small "bad things" can cause the pearl of greater faith to take shape in our lives as we see God act according to the promise of Romans 8:28. For me, even a small thing like an insult turns me to Romans 8:28 for hope.

One Sunday morning I was starting up the stairs at church. I had gotten up early to read my Bible, pray, and study the lesson I was going to teach in the women's Sunday school class. As I headed toward the classroom, a woman stopped to talk to me...and shared words that hurt me deeply.

Suddenly the benefits of my early-morning Bible study, prayer, and lesson preparation disappeared. The joy of being at church also evaporated. I felt empty and hurt. How could I teach a lesson on God's grace and goodness right now?

I decided to try to do what I've been sharing in this book. First, I had to think about what was real. This woman really had said those hurtful words, but I had to chose not to speculate beyond her words about her motives or about any incident when I might have offended her.

For the moment I also chose to forget the incident. I would deal with it later. Right then, however, I had to focus on the task at hand—on what was real. Between the stairs and the classroom door—about a 45-second walk—I had to shift my sights to the lesson I was to teach and the ladies who were waiting for me. I asked the Lord to calm my thoughts and emotions, to help me forget for the time being, honor my earlier preparation, and to use me to share a helpful message with the class.

And I prayed! "God, You knew from before the foundation of the world that on *this* morning...at *this* time...*this* woman...would say *this* to me." You see, that incident was no surprise to God! No, He knew all about it and had sovereignly permitted it! So I prayed, "Thank You for believing that I am able to handle this. And thank You that You have promised to work this insult for good in my life." I found strength and hope in God's promise to work an insult for my good and my growth.

All things includes people—In the Old Testament, the story of Queen Esther is an intriguing example of how God uses people in our lives. Who were the significant people in the lovely Esther's life? Answer: Her devoted cousin Mordecai, the helpful eunuch Hegai, her temperamental and distant husband, King Ahasuerus, and the evil villain Haman. And how did God work through the people in this queen's life?

Mordecai—An orphaned Jewish girl, Esther was raised by Mordecai.

King Ahasuerus—When King Ahasuerus divorced the queen, he chose Esther to become his new queen.

Hegai—In her difficult situation, God gave Esther favor in Hegai's eyes, and he gave her preferential treatment.

> Haman—God then used Esther's position as queen to deliver His people from the evil plotting of their enemy Haman.

Through the people placed in Esther's life, God provided love, advice, position, and safety for a girl without parents and in a hard situation, while at the same time accomplishing His purposes in history.

Just as God used good and bad—and absent—people for Esther's good and His purposes, He will do the same for you. Whether an individual brings you joy or sorrow, pleasure or pain, comfort or conflict, he or she has come from the hand of God...and He uses every single person for your good and His purposes.

So how do you view your parents, your spouse, your in-laws, your children (whether toddlers or teens), your supervisor, even the angry stranger who yells at you from a passing car? In light of the truth of Romans 8:28, you can view these people—indeed, all people!—as part of all that God is using for good in your life. You can count on the good that will come from *every* relationship, no matter how difficult or painful it is. When it comes to the people in your life, remember, *It's not them, it's Him!* This will free you from resentment, bitterness, and blame.

All things includes all things—

> No matter what our situation, our suffering, our persecution, our sinful failure, our pain, our lack of faith—in those things, as well as in *all* other *things,* our heavenly Father will work to produce our ultimate

> victory and blessing. The corollary of that truth is that nothing can ultimately work against us. Any temporary harm we suffer will be used by God for our benefit (see 2 Corinthians 12:7-10)....*All things* includes circumstances and events that are good and beneficial in themselves as well as those that are in themselves evil and harmful.[2]

As nineteenth-century preacher and teacher D.L. Moody wrote beside Romans 8:28 in the margin of his Bible, "If our circumstances find us in God, we shall find God in all our circumstances."[3]

Knowing God's Promise

Knowing God and trusting in His promise in Romans 8:28—that He causes all things to work together for good—gives us hope. It also eliminates negative responses that block spiritual growth and interfere with daily duties. For instance,

> *Doubt*—You never need to wonder about the events in your life. Why? Because "we know *with an absolute knowledge* that for those who are loving God, all things are working together resulting in good, for those who are called ones according to His purpose."[4]

> *Emotion*—You can respond to good or bad situations alike—with faith and feelings grounded in the knowledge that God is at work in the painful, the tragic, and the disappointing.

> *Bitterness*—You can guard against bitterness

taking root in your heart by believing the truth of the assurance of God's promise.

Negative responses—You will receive strength to persevere rather than succumb to depression, discouragement, despair, defeat, anger, wrath, and frustration.

Manipulation—You will stop trying to take matters into your own hands and trust God instead, having something of a hands-off approach to life.

Loving God...Even More

What honor we give to God when we love Him, when our thoughts about Him and His hand in our lives are true! And what hope and encouragement the truth of Romans 8:28 brings to our aching souls! God has given us a promise. He assures us that He controls all things, and He works all things for our good. This means we can look at each challenge and trial, each disappointment and tragedy life brings as another opportunity to trust the Lord.

My friend, when our hope is in the Lord, we know that everything that happens to us—our most pressing problem, the good things, the bad things, the large things, the small things, indeed *all* things—will be used by God to bless us and make us more like Jesus (verse 29). With David, we can confidently proclaim, "Surely goodness and mercy shall follow me all the days of my life" (Psalm 23:6).

~ 19 ~

Becoming Faith Oriented

We know that all things work together
for good to those who love God,
to those who are called
according to His purpose.

Romans 8:28

The women from our church were crowded into a large conference room for our annual retreat. We were meeting at the headquarters of Campus Crusade for Christ which, at that time, was in Arrowhead Springs, California. Our speaker was Ney Bailey from their staff, and I still remember the story she told that first evening—a story that I read again later in her book *Faith Is Not a Feeling*....

One quiet summer day, Ney was meeting in the Colorado Rocky Mountains with 35 other women leaders from Campus Crusade. Suddenly sirens broke the peaceful stillness and megaphones barked, "Evacuate immediately! Flashflood coming! Evacuate immediately!"

The women immediately got into their cars and left. As

they crossed over a bridge, they realized the urgency of the situation when the raging waters cascading down the mountain washed away the bridge they had just driven over! Continuing on, the women traveled to a fork in the road, got out of their cars, asked for directions, jumped back into the cars, and drove on.

Ney Bailey's car went one way, and another car went a different way. Tragically, the seven women in the other car drowned. Not knowing of her friends' deaths, Ney and her companions huddled together in prayer once their car reached higher ground. With the authority of Scripture undergirding her, she began praying, "Lord, Your Word says, 'In everything give thanks, because this is the will of God in Christ Jesus concerning us.' So while we are in this, we choose with our wills to thank You.

"And, Lord, Your Word says, 'All things'—including this—'work together for good to those who love You'—and we do—'and are called according to Your purpose'—and we are.

"You have also said that heaven and earth will pass away before Your Word passes away. So Your Word is truer than anything we are feeling or experiencing right now."[1]

Praying God's Word

Faith is not a feeling, and Ney lived out that truth in the situation I just described. Despite whatever she was feeling—panic, fear, worry—Ney chose to put her faith in God and the truths of His Word and not in her feelings. As her prayer reveals, she turned to God and clung to the promises found in His Word when her feelings and thoughts might have run wild. Ney Bailey's prayer taught me three lessons I have tried to apply in my own Christian life.

First, *pray "Your Word says..."*—Ney showed me how to pray using the authority of Scripture. I saw right away the value of praying "Your Word says...," of letting God's truths guide my petitions. Now, whenever I counsel a woman who needs help praying about difficult issues, I share Ney's prayer with her and tell her to pray God's Word.

Second, *pray the truth of Romans 8:28*—Ney's prayer taught me how to use the truth of Romans 8:28 concerning my life. Following her model, I now pray, "God, Your Word says 'all things'—including this ____________________ (and I fill in the blank, naming my present problem)—'work together for good.'" The simple exercise of "filling in the blank" forces me to acknowledge God's involvement in my life and reminds me that He is the source of my strength and hope.

Third, *pray to be faith oriented*—This prayer taught me that I can never view my life through the lens of feelings. They are too varied and unstable! No, I must be faith oriented rather than feeling oriented. Faith is not a feeling. Faith looks to God and trusts Him to work out the present difficulty for His purposes and my good. I must look to God and to His Word—and to Romans 8:28!—and I must remember that He will indeed work all things for my good!

As we're continuing to learn, God is in complete control of every aspect of our lives. Furthermore, He promises to work "all things" for our good and His purposes. We can definitely have hope in Him and put our God-given faith in Him.

Trusting God's Good Purpose

In His promise of Romans 8:28, God gives us glorious good news! He reassures us that His purposes for us are good. The words are straightforward—"We know that all things work together for good." This truth assures us that the end result of all that God allows to touch our lives will be good. You see, He is working *all* things (no disclaimers or fine print here!) together for good. When we choose to believe this truth, we can't help but find hope in God as we trust in His good purpose for whatever life holds.

Joseph saw God's good purpose—In this book we have already met Joseph, a person who found hope in God despite the twists and turns his life took (Genesis 37–50). As the favored son of Jacob, Joseph found himself in great disfavor with his brothers. Acting out of hatred and envy, the brothers plotted Joseph's murder. However, at the last moment they sold him into slavery instead.

Joseph ended up in Egypt as a slave to Potiphar, the captain of Pharaoh's bodyguard. Because Joseph was greatly blessed by God, he rose to a powerful position of status within the Egyptian government (Genesis 39:2-3). Then, when famine struck Joseph's homeland, his brothers—the ones who had disrupted his life and brought on unmeasurable pain and torment—suddenly appeared before him in Egypt, asking *him* for food to stay alive!

Now it was decision-making time for Joseph. He had a serious choice to make. He could fill his brothers' grain sacks with life-giving food…or he could have his brothers killed (either directly by an order or indirectly by withholding the grain). As a man of God, Joseph extended grace to his brothers, saying, "As for you, you meant evil against me; but *God meant it for good,* in order to bring it about as it is this day, to save many people alive" (Genesis 50:20).

At this point in time—after being rejected, mistreated, sold into slavery, falsely accused, imprisoned, forgotten, and finally blessed—Joseph saw that God had indeed been at work all along. Joseph, therefore, found no reason to place blame on his brothers...or God(!), or to feel bitter against them...or God! As writer Chuck Swindoll puts it, by choosing to see Jehovah at work, Joseph...

> blazes a new trail through a jungle of mistreatment, false accusations, undeserved punishment, and gross misunderstanding. He exemplifies forgiveness, freedom from bitterness, and an unbelievably positive attitude toward those who had done him harm.[2]

You must trust in God's good purpose—Are you like me? It's soooo easy to let myself get bogged down in the tiny details of my own experience. I tend to spend a lot of time and energy sorting out how I feel about a problem, analyzing my emotions, deciding what I like or don't like about the situation, evaluating the pain on a scale of one to ten, and choosing to worry, blame, rant and rave, or sink into depression. I even try to figure out how I'm going to make the situation better...or get myself out of it!

But I can tell you, this kind of introspection and focus on self hardly leads to hope...or victory...or greater faith. But I'm learning! Now (well, most of the time, anyway), instead of asking, "What does this mean to me?" I'm learning to ask,

"What does this mean to God?" Posing this kind of question points me to God and His perspective. And it will do the same for you.

And let me encourage you! Although trials hurt terribly, you can count on the end being good. Why? Because God Himself is good. In Matthew 7:9-10, Jesus asks, "What man is there among you who, if his son asks for bread, will give him a stone? Or if he asks for a fish, will give him a serpent?" Then, to answer His questions, Christ states this fact about God, the Father: "If you then, being evil, know how to give good gifts to your children, how much more will your Father who is in heaven give good things to those who ask Him!" (Matthew 7:11).

Sometimes what God has given you may look and feel like a stone or a snake. But your heart and mind must believe and trust that your heavenly Father, our good God, is working those things out for your good and according to His good purpose. Look at your life situation. Then look at your powerful and redemptive God and at the promise of Romans 8:28. When you do, you have another decision to make—a decision of faith—to put your trust in God and believe that the end will be good, regardless of how life looks or feels in the present. This is how you love God with all your mind. By faith, decide to trust God for the ultimate purpose He is working in your life.

The promise of Romans 8:28 serves as a lens through which you (and I) can have a godly perspective on your life, from birth to death. Because of the words in this scripture, you can know that your good God is working the miracle of using the bad—*everything*, from the most minor of incidents to the greatest of tragedies—for good. Counting on the fact that the end of all things will be good gives you hope. It also helps you to be faith oriented—not feeling oriented—about your present pain. After all, feelings distort your vision. And today's obstacles often prevent a hopeful and faith-filled view of the end. But by responding to God's love, by loving Him with all your mind and trusting in Him, you will be blessed with hope in His promise that He works in everything to bring about what is good.

Giving God Our Love

Before we finish this chapter about God's glorious goodness and His marvelous, unmerited love for us, we must examine our love for Him. Look again at Romans 8:28. We know that God causes all things to work together for good *"to those who love God...."* The words "to those who love God" are important because the promise of Romans 8:28 is not for everybody. It can be claimed only by those who love God.

How do we show God our love for Him? Christ answered this question in just seven words: "If you love Me, keep My commandments" (John 14:15). Another version of the Bible succinctly says, "If you love me, obey me."[3]

It's obvious that our love for God is measured by our obedience. So take a few minutes—now and regularly—to look at your life and evaluate how closely you are following God. When I do this, I take a pen and paper and run a check of the elements of my entire life. I ask myself, "Is there anything wrong in my relationship with God?" and I write down my answer. I then ask the same question regarding my husband, my children, my parents, my in-laws, my siblings, my home, my spiritual and personal growth, my areas of service to the Lord, and my relationships with other people. I write down whatever comes to my mind and then have a time of prayer. I spend time asking God's forgiveness for where I have been disobedient, unloving, or unfaithful. As 1 John 1:9 tells us, whenever we confess our sins, our good God "is faithful and just to forgive us our sins and to cleanse us from all unrighteousness."

You might want to take some time each day (perhaps during your regular prayer time) to mentally examine the priority areas of your life. Evaluate your relationship with God and with your family members, how things are at home, your spiritual growth, the challenges you face as you serve God, the demands of the workplace, and your involvement with people. Look for areas where you have not obeyed God and His Word. Then purpose to give God greater devotion and obedience...to love Him.

Loving God...Even More

How can you love God...even more? Because we demonstrate our love for God by obeying Him, it helps to begin each day by purposing to follow His ways all day long. My first-thing-in-the-morning prayer is that I will make His choices and do His will with each thought, word, and deed throughout the day. This prayer helps keep me on my toes and keeps me aware of Him as I go about my day meeting people, doing the tasks at hand, and facing any challenges along the way.

And I pray this prayer again whenever the phone rings or

I meet someone I know. I ask God to help me say the right words and do the right thing. For example, if the person who calls is upset, I pray, "Please, God, let me respond in Your way....Help me stay calm....Help me know when to speak and when to only listen....Help me to help."

God works for good all of the things that happen to those who love Him, and we love God by obeying Him. So, dear reader, what is your current level of obedience to the God who loves you and whom you desire to love...even more? How warm is your love for God? Is it red-hot and pure...lukewarm and indifferent...or ice-cold, below freezing? A pure and hot love for God is truly a wellspring of hope in Him!

~ 20 ~

Navigating the Maze of Life

We know that all things work together
for good to those who love God,
to those who are called
according to His purpose.

Romans 8:28

I remember when my life had no purpose. As an average woman with an average marriage, two average preschool daughters, and an average house, I shook my fist at the kitchen ceiling one average and desperate day and cried, "There has to be more to life than this!"

I was hopeless! After all, where could I find hope when I hadn't even found the purpose behind the things I was doing? My lack of purpose caused me to wonder, to doubt, and to rage. But, praise God, He used my search for purpose to help me recognize that I needed Jesus Christ! By following the path He led me on to discover Jesus Christ, and by walking through the circumstances He created, I acted on that need. I became a Christian several months later. And suddenly I saw the purpose of everything in my life because I saw that God had a purpose for me!

Knowing that God has a purpose for my life and for my salvation brings me great joy and hope. But it also brings with it great responsibility. You see, now that I know there is a use and a reason for my life...and days...and minutes, I also know I can no longer live my life according to my own desires, plans, dreams, or whims. I am to live totally for God's purposes. Therefore, I am not to make decisions based on pleasing people. No, I must please God! You see, I exist to serve Him and His people according to the gifts He has given me and in the situations where He places me.

Discovering God's Purpose

Do you ever have what I call doubtful days—days when the dull routine of duty weighs you down? Or days when the curveballs of surprise, disappointment, and tragedy leave you feeling like you're striking out? Well, there's good news for both of us! The constant awareness that God has a purpose for us gives us great hope when the day-to-day practicalities and challenges discourage and bewilder us.

Imagine a maze in an English garden. These intriguing puzzles, created by six- or seven-foot hedges, were used initially to provide people with some entertaining exercise after their meals. The diners would enter the confusing and baffling network of shrubs and try to find their way to the pleasant place in the center of the maze where there was usually a tree, some flowering plants, and a garden seat where they could sit, relax, and visit...before trying to find their way out.

One evening as I looked at pictures of these garden mazes in a coffee-table book at a friend's home, I thought, *Why, this is the way life is!* We follow along the maze of life, randomly making turns and choosing our paths.

Then we come to know Christ as our Lord and Savior. From that point on, we have purpose—to serve God. We're still traversing the maze of life, but now we have direction. God keeps us moving forward as we pray and dedicate our lives to serving Him, becoming more Christlike, and spreading the gospel. As we begin to grow and move along in our Christian life, we come to corners...special moments when God guides our lives into new directions or deeper understandings of His purpose for us. And off we go, following God's will on the new path! Unfortunately, sometimes we stray from God's will or misunderstand His direction and come to dead ends. Then, through further prayer, we take action and seek the Lord for clarification or new guidance... and set off accordingly.

While we're in the maze, we never know who or what we'll encounter. Why, we don't even know exactly where we're going! But we do know that we are to keep moving. And as we continue on according to God's will and His leading, He fulfills His purpose for us. God doesn't ask us to understand the twists and turns, the why's and the how's of life. He asks only that we trust that He is working His purpose in us as we live out our purpose of serving Him.

And now we're right back to the incredible promise of Romans 8:28! We know God has a purpose for us. That's yet another sparkling reason why we can have joy and hope in Him each day...no matter what happens in that day. And knowing that God has a purpose for us makes every day significant.

Finding God's Will

As you know, trying to determine God's will and specific purposes for us is not always easy. The apostle Paul knew this all too well! In Acts 16:6-10, we learn something about how God reveals His will to His people. In this passage, Luke, the writer of Acts, is reporting on Paul's second missionary journey.

> Now when they had gone through Phrygia and the region of Galatia, they were forbidden by the Holy Spirit to preach the word in Asia. After they had come to Mysia, they tried to go into Bithynia, but the Spirit did not permit them. So passing by Mysia, they came down to Troas. And a vision appeared to Paul in the night. A man of Macedonia stood and pleaded with him, saying, "Come over to Macedonia and help us." Now after he had seen the vision, immediately we sought to go to Macedonia, concluding that the Lord had called us to preach the gospel to them.

How were things going on that missions endeavor? The faithful apostle was busy fulfilling God's purpose for his life every single day by proclaiming the gospel. But then look what happened! After preaching in one area of Asia Minor, Paul decided to travel in another direction...but was "*forbidden* by the Holy Spirit to preach the word in Asia"!

So what did Paul do? How did he respond to "a shut door"? Did he stop, quit, turn toward home, and turn in his apostle's badge? Did he have a fit, explode, rant and rave? Did he complain, pout and sulk, sink into a depression? After all, all he was trying to do was obediently and faithfully fulfill his commission and calling to preach the gospel!

No, Paul kept moving. With that direction blocked, Paul simply turned another way, toward Bithynia. However, once again, "the Spirit *did not permit* them." Again, what did Paul do? Did he stop, quit, turn in his apostle's badge...have a fit, explode, rant and rave...complain, pout and sulk, sink into a depression?

No, Paul kept moving. With only one possibility remaining, Paul headed in that direction, toward Troas. And when he did so, "a vision appeared to Paul in the night. A man of Macedonia stood and pleaded with him, saying, 'Come over to Macedonia and help us.'" And Paul and the people traveling with him immediately went to Macedonia to preach the gospel to them.

And the marvelous result? God's purpose? God's plan? The reason for all of the twists and turns, obstacles, and blocked efforts? Paul's response to God's leading in Asia Minor led to the birth of the church at Philippi...in what is now modern Greece!

Discovering God's Purpose...for You!

When you, like Paul, seek to know God's will and to be used for His ultimate purposes, God will guide you, as He did the apostle, through the maze of life. Although Luke does not say in Acts exactly how God "forbade" or refused to "permit" Paul to go in certain directions, the passage does teach us that we can trust God to close doors and block our paths in order to keep us going where He wants us to go.

My friend, our role is to love God and keep moving through life according to His purpose for us. His role is to lead us in the maze so that we can fulfill the specific purposes He calls us to at the same time that He fulfills His purpose in and through us. And God uses people, events, and circumstances, both good and bad, to move us ultimately toward the fulfillment of His will and purpose for our lives.

Exactly what is God's purpose for us, His children? As Paul explains in Romans 8:29, the primary purpose of "all things" in our lives is Christlikeness: "For whom He foreknew, He also predestined to be conformed to the image of His Son." Everything—every person, every event—that touches us is for the purpose of making us like Christ. We can find comfort and hope as we navigate the maze of life when we remember the fact that God will use whatever He permits to happen to us to fulfill His purposes *and* to make us more like Jesus.

Minister and author Alan Redpath writes this about the promise of Romans 8:28 and 29:

> There is nothing—no circumstance, no trouble, no testing—that can ever touch me until, first of all it has gone past God and past Christ, right through to me. If it has come that far, it has come with a *great purpose,* which I may not understand at the moment. But as I *refuse* to become panicky, as I lift up my eyes to him and accept it as coming from the throne of God for some *great purpose of blessing* to my own heart, no sorrow will ever disturb me, no trial will ever disarm me, no circumstance will cause me to fret—for I *shall rest in the joy of what my Lord is*—That is the rest of victory.[1]

The truth of Romans 8:28 should cause us to rest in the

Lord and wait patiently for Him (Psalm 37:7)—for Him to act, for Him to work, for Him to save (if that is His will), for Him to reveal His purposes. Even if we never know why things happen, we can still rest in God, hope in Him, and believe that He is using every aspect of our lives to make us more like Jesus.

One woman in particular shows Christians how to live with hope in God, trusting His goodness...and His purpose. A striking example of faith, this woman loved God and trusted His purposes for her despite tragedy, hardship, and suffering.

God's Songbird

Fanny Crosby, the famous hymn writer, was a woman who believed that God's purposes are good and who clearly heard His calling on her life. You can sense this in her comments about the doctor who caused her blindness: "I have heard that this physician never ceased expressing his regret at the occurrence; and that it was one of the sorrows of his life. But if I could meet him now, I would say, 'Thank you, thank you, over and over again for making me blind.'...Although it may have been a blunder on the physician's part, it was no mistake on God's. I verily believe it was His intention that I should live my days in physical darkness, so as to be better prepared to sing His praises and incite others to do so."[2] Through a doctor's apparent mistake, God gave to the church the wonderful songs of a blind Fanny Crosby who, with her increased spiritual insight, wrote hymns until she died at age 95—hymns that have endured and inspired others to greater faith.

When has someone else's "blunder" or "mistake" touched

your life? Or when has someone's malice severely impacted you? People who have faith in God and hope in Him accept such unexplainable events as "no mistake on God's part." They know that every event involves "His intention" and leads them one step closer to discovering and fulfilling God's purpose. They look to the God they trust and love for strength and let His ability transform their disabilities.

Fanny Crosby found some of her options for life eliminated as she navigated the maze of her life. But, with God's blessing, she also discovered a uniquely personal way—God's will and purpose for her—to serve Him and His people. Fanny Crosby couldn't see, but she could sing and write poems. After a doctor's "mistake," she gave to God what she had—her singing and her writing—and He used her greatly for His kingdom. She became God's songbird.

Loving God...Even More

Like Fanny Crosby, a Christian who experienced tragedy in her life and continued to love God, you can model a strong trust and hope in God despite the events you encounter as you navigate the maze of life. So to start—or continue—down the path of loving God even more, pray and think through these exercises.

First, take an inventory of your life. Chart the path you've walked, and review how God has shown you His will through the years. When did He stop you, turn you, send you back, or direct you in another way? How did God change your direction? Did He "forbid" something? Did He "fail to permit" something? Was there an "accident" or a "mistake" along the way, a tragedy, an unjust slander, an envious person, a failure, a lack, a handicap, an oversight, a deep hurt in your past?

Now look again at the autobiography you have just sketched. Where has God worked bad for good? And where do you see Him making you more like Christ? As you recognize God's unseen involvement along the way, you may now pray the love-filled prayer Ney Bailey taught us: "Lord, Your Word says 'All things—including this (fill in the blank) ___ ______________—work together for good to those who love You'...and I do." You can even thank God for His wisdom and ways, as unsearchable as they may sometimes be.

As you consider your autobiography you'll be able to see that it is in limiting that God reveals the limitlessness of His power and grace and purposes. In God's maze, God's "no" to one thing is "yes" to another. "No" in one direction is a clear indicator of "yes" in a different direction. "No" to certain pursuits only means "yes" to others. With God as your guide in the maze of life, a "no" is never the end. A negative is never permanent.

And even in the darkness that comes when we are unable to see how anything good could possibly come out of the bad, God's promise in Romans 8:28 offers us the light of hope. In fact, Romans 8:28 serves as a rainbow, brilliantly and miraculously arching through the dark clouds and mist that may hang over the maze of life, bringing the hope of God's promise that He, ever faithful to His promise, works all things together for good for those who love Him...and we do!

Living Out God's Plan

For I know the thoughts I think toward you, says the LORD, thoughts of peace and not of evil, to give you a future and a hope.

JEREMIAH 29:11

~ 21 ~

Enduring Difficult Times

"For I know the thoughts that I think toward you," says the LORD....

Jeremiah 29:11

When my friend Judy moved from Missouri to California, she brought her country upbringing with her and began to create a country-style home for her family out West. During the 25 years she has lived in her house, she has worked steadily on her dream of living in a country cottage. In time, when she was satisfied with the inside of her home, Judy went to work on her porch. There you'll find a cozy tea table and chairs surrounded by a wooden bench, a bird cage, several birdhouses, baskets full of plants and old wooden-handled gardening tools. A padded lounge chair, an old wicker rocker, and a low table arranged around a braided rug invite you to relax. Tea on Judy's porch is quite a special treat!

With the porch complete, Judy began working on her

garden. A step off the porch puts you on a walkway that leads you to the left, where wooden rails set off a U-shaped flower bed. There, flowering vines wrap around a trellis, the porch posts, and the rails. Stepping-stones take you to trimmed trees, where bountiful Boston ferns hang from low branches. Flowers have been carefully planted so all the brilliant colors can be seen and enjoyed, and creeping figs happily embrace the aged wooden fence. Judy's garden is a gracious place of peace and beauty.

One evening, as our family visited with Judy and her family, my husband said, "Judy, this is a beautiful garden, but…what happened over there?" Jim was pointing to a rock pile at the border of Judy's garden. Next to the rocks was a woodpile, a tree stump, a dead tree, some gravel, and an assortment of discarded flowerpots. The area spoke of barrenness and neglect.

But Judy said, "Oh, I have a plan!" And glad to have an interested audience, she grabbed a bulging manila file folder. Spilling out of it were newspaper clippings, magazine articles, gardening tips, pictures of other gardens, instructions for choosing year-round plants, and her drawings and sketches. For years, Judy had been collecting ideas and planning her ideal garden, and she was excited about her plan. "Oh, I have a plan!"

God Has a Plan for You

"Oh, I have a plan!" is exactly what God is telling the Israelites in Jeremiah 29:11. To the children of Israel who had been uprooted from their homes and carried away as captives to Babylon—and to you and me as well—God declares, "I know the thoughts that I think toward you…thoughts of peace and not of evil, to give you a future and a hope." As another translation of the Bible puts it, "'I know the plans that I have for you,' declares the LORD, 'plans for welfare and not for calamity to give you a future and a hope'" (NASB).

Although the heartbroken prophet Jeremiah prophesied doom for these stiff-necked people who had turned away from God, he also preached hope to these captives—hope that was based on the promise God made to them as recorded in Jeremiah 29:11. Having announced their sentence of 70 years of bondage in Babylon, Jeremiah then told these displaced Jews how to survive those years.

And here's good news! Jeremiah's words of instruction and "how-to's" can help us, too, when we find ourselves enduring difficult times in places or predicaments we didn't choose for ourselves. To remind yourself of God's message to your heart during hard and difficult times, take to heart—and to memory!—these ABCs.

A—*Acknowledge God's Hand*

According to Jeremiah, we need to first recognize God's hand in whatever has happened. Speaking through Jeremiah, God told the Israelites four times, "*I* have caused you to be carried away from Jerusalem to Babylon...captive" (Jeremiah 29:4,7,14,20). God explained that it wasn't the Babylonians alone who had taken them away from their homeland and into exile. No, God Himself had allowed it. Likewise, whatever circumstances you and I find ourselves in, we need to remember that God has allowed us to be there. We may wonder, "What happened?" and the situation may not be our ideal, but it is in God's hands. Your life is *not* out of control! And nothing has just randomly "happened" to put you where you are.

And the result? We can better endure difficult times when we acknowledge that God is indeed in full control of not only the universe but of our circumstances. Thinking the truth about God and our circumstances can help eliminate insecurity, bewilderment, blaming, and bitterness. We can then enjoy greater peace...*in* our trying situations.

B—Bloom Where You Are Planted

We are to "bloom and grow" where we are planted. What does this mean? We are to go on loving the Lord with our whole being—heart, soul, strength, and mind. And we are to go on fulfilling His purposes for us wherever we find ourselves—no matter how undesirable or unexpected our circumstances. The prophet Jeremiah told the crushed and bewildered people of Israel exactly how to live during their exile. He said (and pay special attention to the verbs), "Build houses and dwell in them; plant gardens and eat their fruit. Take wives and beget sons and daughters; and take wives for your sons and give your daughters to husbands, so that they may bear sons and daughters—that you may be increased there, and not diminished" (Jeremiah 29:5-6).

The priorities of building solid, long-lasting, and ongoing marriages, families, and home lives were to be their focus—not their pain. Captivity for God's people was true and real. God, in essence, said, "You're going to be here a while. This is not temporary. This is not a short-term captivity. So have something to show for it! Focus your energies on something positive—your growth and betterment."

God called the captives to make homes, plant crops, and bear fruit in the land of their affliction. Life was to go on for them. And life is to go on for you and me, too, in our afflictions.

Whatever sorrow or situation we may be facing—when we wonder, *What happened over there?* God wants us to continue building where we are and blooming where we're planted. That's how we endure difficult times.

Jeremiah's "how-to" was this: "Keep on keeping on! Keep on building! Keep on functioning! Keep on planting! Live! Bloom! Grow! Increase! Don't merely sit around being sad or depressed, waiting for things to change or get better. *Make* things better!"

C—*Concentrate on God's Promises*

On the heels of Jeremiah's specific instructions to the Israelites came his pronouncement of God's promise of a return to their homeland:

> After seventy years are completed at Babylon, I will visit you and perform My good word toward you, and cause you to return to this place.... I will bring you back from your captivity; I will gather you from all the nations and from all the places where I have driven you...and I will bring you to the place from which I cause you to be carried away captive (29:10,14).

In the meantime, God comforted His children with these words: "I know the thoughts that I think toward you... thoughts of peace and not of evil, to give you a future and a hope."

Whenever these misplaced people were discouraged, they were to find their hope and strength to endure in *God* and in *His promises*...and so are we. The plans God has for us—plans for welfare and not for calamity, for good and not for evil, to give us a future and a hope—are a source of real confidence and assurance, no matter what challenges, hurts, and questions we face along the way.

Where do you tend to focus your attention when things fall apart, when you wonder, *What happened over there?* No matter what is occurring in your life, concentrate on God's promises. They assure you over and over again of the nature and reality of God and His character. Through them you will never lose sight of the bright hope of your future! You can have glorious hope even when life looks hopeless.

D—Do Something Useful

While you are *in* your difficult times, ever-confident in God's promised outcome for your trials, you can "do something useful." Wherever you are (which is where God has sovereignly placed you!), you can serve God, your family, and His people. Sure, there are a lot of things you don't know about your present condition, but one thing you do know is that God calls us to serve Him and His people (Matthew 20:26-28). So serve away! Roll up your sleeves and serve God and others in the present, even *in* your hard times.

In fact, this is the message Jeremiah delivered to the captive Israelites who are having their first taste of the bitterness of exile. As we've seen, Jeremiah was specific about how the Israelites were to endure their hard years of exile. "The captives in Babylon were to settle down and live as normally as possible under the circumstances (build houses, marry, multiply…and pray)."[1] In other words, the children of Israel were to do something useful. They were to serve God in their marriages, their families, their community, and their businesses. Such effort and usefulness would help ward off depression and discouragement and give each day purpose and fulfillment.

That's our assignment, too. Wherever we are and however good or bad our circumstances are, if we are married, God calls us to serve our spouses. And if we are parents, we are to nurture and love our children (Ephesians 6:4 and Titus 2:4). And each of us—married or single—is also called to serve the body of Christ, His church (1 Corinthians 12:7). Wherever we are and whatever our circumstances, we are to serve God. These roles require energy, self-sacrifice, and strength, but God graciously provides everything we need to do something useful...even in the midst of suffering.

These few lines of poetry express our assignment from God to do something useful...*while* we are in our troubles:

> We cannot see beyond the door,
> We know not what He hath in store...
>
> We can but bow our hearts and pray
> For strength to serve Him day by day.[2]

In our next chapter we'll witness some of God's people who, when they found themselves in hard and difficult places—places they didn't choose and places they didn't want to be in—followed God's plan for enduring difficult times. They...

A cknowledged God's hand,
B loomed where they were planted,
C oncentrated on God's promises, and
D id something useful.

You're in for a treat, as well as a large helping of encouragement!

Loving God...Even More

And now I want to bring our attention back to God. Remembering your gracious God and the promise of His good plan for you and focusing your thoughts on His purposes for your life can establish and anchor you and your emotions. It's also a way to love Him with all your mind. Panic, despair, nervousness, bewilderment, fear—God speaks against emotions like these in His Word. In fact, when the circumstances of life might lead to uncertainty and confusion, the bright promise of Jeremiah 29:11 gives us certainty, clarity, and hope.

My dear friend, God has a plan for your welfare! When you wonder and ask, *But...what happened over there?* He shouts back to you through Jeremiah 29:11, "Oh, I have a plan!" The path of your life may zig and zag, twist and turn, but God has promised you "a future and a hope."

With this promise you don't need to know the future! Instead, you can be content and at peace in knowing, trusting, and loving the Father, whose plans are for good and not evil. All will be well. You can be secure in that fact. It's His promise to you! Therefore, you can endure to the end of your difficult times. And you can build and bear fruit in the meantime.

~ 22 ~

Bearing Fruit During Difficult Times

"For I know the plans that I have
for you," declares the LORD....

Jeremiah 29:11 NASB

When it comes to enduring trials and difficult times, the Bible tells us to "count it all joy" (James 1:2)! In fact, we can even find lists of the benefits to be gained, blessings to be enjoyed, and lessons to be learned in our trials. For instance, James writes that "the testing of your faith produces patience" and to "let patience have its perfect work, that you may be perfect and complete, lacking nothing" (verses 3-4). If you are wondering how in the world this is possible, be sure to remember what we've already learned about enduring difficult times:

- We know that God is the author and the finisher of our lives. Therefore, we know that we can **A**-cknowledge God and His sovereignty in whatever circumstances we are *in* and wherever we are, as difficult and as painful as it may be.

- We know we can, by God's grace, **B**-loom where we are planted and bear fruit—even *much* fruit—in "the land of our affliction," in our situation of sorrow.
- We know we can **C**-oncentrate on God's powerful and reassuring promises *while* we are in our difficult times, and go ahead and plant and increase because we know God will bring all good things to pass.
- We know that we are to **D**-o something useful, wherever we are, no matter how distressing the situation is.

Learning from God's Servants

When we look to the Bible and to believers who have gone before us, we find inspiring examples of people who served God wholeheartedly by doing something useful while they were in difficult times and places.

Joseph—Think again on Joseph's life. He served God as a slave, as a prisoner, and finally as an elevated official in the Egyptian government. He served God as the trusted manager of Potiphar's luxurious palace...as well as from a dark, dank dungeon where he was in irons and his feet were fastened with shackles (Psalm 105:18). Finally released from prison after three years of unjust punishment, Joseph became second in command in Egypt. In this position, his service extended beyond that country's boundaries to the entire known world as he dispensed life-giving grain during a serious famine.

Joseph suffered betrayal by his brothers, separation from

his father and family, condemnation and imprisonment because of a false accusation, and unjust treatment. But Joseph served...no matter where he was...no matter what his situation...no matter who needed his service. He kept "many people alive" (Genesis 50:20) and bettered the lives of countless others. Only in the naming of Joseph's two sons do we sense his sorrow. "Joseph called the name of the firstborn Manasseh: 'For God has made me forget all my toil and all my father's house.' And the name of the second he called Ephraim: 'For God has caused me to be fruitful in the land of my affliction'" (41:51-52).

Paul—The apostle Paul also models ongoing service to God...no matter what or where! Whether he was standing on the heights of Mars Hill debating with the best minds from the highest court of Athens or chained to a single guard in the depths of a dungeon, Paul served his Lord and His causes as a preacher of the gospel. Despite beatings, stonings, death threats, imprisonments, and various other forms of suffering, Paul kept on preaching (2 Corinthians 11:23-33).

How did Paul do it? How did he maintain his energy and zeal? We have already discovered his secret: Paul focused on the object of his love—the Lord Jesus Christ—and kept on keeping on, even through pain. He declared, "Forgetting those things which are behind and reaching forward to those things which are ahead, I press toward the goal for the prize of the upward call of God in Christ Jesus" (Philippians 3:13-14). Paul desired to be useful to his Lord day by day, wherever he was, and whatever his condition.

Madame Guyon—In the eighteenth century, Jeanne Marie Guyon was imprisoned in the Bastille (described by some as the most horrible prison on earth). Madame Guyon spent four of her seven years there in solitary confinement. While serving her sentence, she focused her thoughts on God. It was there she wrote—

A little bird I am,
Shut from the fields of air;
And in my cage I sit and sing
To Him who placed me there;
Well pleased a prisoner to be,
Because, my God, it pleased Thee.[1]

The result of Madame Guyon's time—the fruit she bore while in prison—was her writing. She wrote many books, including a 20-volume commentary on the Bible.[2]

Mrs. Studd—In more recent times, Mrs. C.T. Studd shows us service in every circumstance. She served her missionary husband as his wife and manager. However, as she grew increasingly ill and even as an invalid, Mrs. Studd continued to serve her husband and God's people. "She had to go to her room each night at seven and not come down the next day till lunch time....From her bed and invalid couch she formed Prayer Centres, issued monthly pamphlets by the thousand, wrote often twenty to thirty letters a day, planned and edited the first issues of the *Heart of Africa Mission Magazine*."[3] Mrs. Studd served in sickness as well as in health, bearing fresh fruit in her illness and affliction.

Hudson Taylor—Missions founder Hudson Taylor also served God wherever he was. When illness forced him to leave his ministry in China and return to England, he used this "downtime" to found the China Inland Mission. When he returned to China, he had created a mission organization to support him and had recruited new missionaries to accompany him.[4]

As the man who advocated, "Do small things as if they were great, because of the majesty of Jesus Christ,"[5] Hudson Taylor's "small things" went on to add up to great things as he sought to do something useful…no matter what.

And he suffered! Mr. Taylor suffered physically from illness, was persecuted and attacked in China, had his house set on fire, lost his wife and two children on the mission field in a raging cholera epidemic. Yet he kept on serving, laboring, and praying…and believing "God himself is at the helm, ordering all things after the counsel of his own will. He has a plan and he is carrying it out; he has a throne and that throne rules over all."[6]

Like the examples I've mentioned—and countless others I could list—you and I can and are to serve God…no matter what our circumstances. He calls us to serve Him and, through the prophet Jeremiah's words to suffering captives in Jeremiah 29, God calls us to serve Him even when we're not where we want to be and when life is not easy. Despite their Babylonian exile, the children of Israel were to keep living for God, serving God, and praying to God…and so are we.

As one Bible commentator observes, "Life cannot grind to a halt during troubled times. In an unpleasant or distressing situation, we must adjust and keep moving….When you enter times of trouble or sudden change, pray diligently and move ahead, doing whatever you can rather than giving up because of uncertainty."[7] Put simply, we are to serve God—no matter what. That's a part of His "plan" for us.

Doing God's Will

As followers of Christ, we want to serve Him through the thick and the thin, the good times and the bad, in the best of days and in the difficult times. Our heart's desire is to live out His plan and purpose for us...to bear fruit that glorifies our Lord. But what is His will? And how can we find it so we can do it?

We know that we can search for God's will, pray to discover it, even fast for greater spiritual discernment to perceive God's direction. But here's one aspect of God's will we don't need to look for: His will is for us to serve Him at *all times*, in *all places*, and in *all situations*. And closeness to God gives us greater sensitivity to Him and to what His plans for us are. So to discern God's plan—His will—and to live it out requires that we nurture our relationship to God.

Here are three tried-and-true ways to discover God's will for you and to follow His plan so that you become a masterpiece—*His* masterpiece!

1. *Delight yourself in God*—Consider this truth: *"Delight* yourself also in the LORD; and He shall give you the desires of your heart" (Psalm 37:4). To delight yourself in the Lord means to seek your pleasure in Him, to make Him your true joy,[8] to "indulge thyself in the Lord."[9] When you "delight yourself in the Lord," God, His Word, and His ways become the focus and foundation of your life. He becomes what matters most to you.

And the blessed result? "He shall give you the desires of

your heart." God puts His desires into your heart. His desires will actually become your desires, and your desires will be His. You won't know where one leaves off and the other begins because you will be delighting in Him to the point that you are adopting His thoughts and His ways. His plans are becoming your plans and your plans are becoming His!

2. *Indulge yourself in God's Word*—Have you ever noticed that the more you are with someone, the more you become like that person? Maybe you've noticed that you and your spouse or best friend use the same figures of speech and share many of the same opinions and perspectives on life. Or maybe you've been surprised to see your children reflect your attitudes and mannerisms! That's because the more we are with someone, the more we tend to become like that person.

This same principle holds true when it comes to indulging in God's Word. The more time you spend reading and studying the Bible, the more you resemble God. You will begin to think as God thinks and desire what He desires, which leads to Christlike behavior.

3. *Commit yourself to the Lord*—Psalm 37:5 says, "Commit your way to the LORD, trust also in Him, and He shall bring it to pass." In other words, commit yourself and your activities to the Lord. This involves the complete commitment of your life. A paraphrase of this promise could read, "Trust God to take over your career, home, work, all the circumstances, aims, and ambitions of life, and He will so mould events that your deepest and purest desires shall find unmeasured fulfillment and life will be filled with utter satisfaction."[10] What

a promise! What hope! What a plan God has for us, His children!

Delighting in the Lord, knowing His Word, and committing yourself to the Lord are ways to ensure that your plans and desires for yourself match God's plans.

Loving God...Even More

So now the questions is, How can we love God...even more? How can we tap into His amazing, all-sufficient grace and strength so that we can endure our difficult times and bear His beautiful fruit during them, so that we can become His masterpiece?

Start here: Put God first each day. Delight in Him...first and foremost! Make it a habit not to turn on the television or radio or read the newspaper before you spend some time reading His Word. Delighting yourself in the Lord means choosing Him each day, and that means choosing to make more time for His Word than any other kind of input.

Next, indulge yourself in God's Word. If you're spending five minutes with the Bible and five hours taking in TV programs, beware! Your values, standards, and views on life, marriage, and the world will probably not be God's!

And finally, commit yourself and every aspect of your life to God. When you do, you'll find your thoughts, plans, and activities established and blessed. In prayer, commit each fresh new day to God and dedicate it to Him. That's how you love Him. Then He can direct your thoughts, plans, dreams, and acts for the rest of the day.

Delighting in the Lord, indulging in His Word, and committing ourselves to Him are sure ways we can love God each day. These ways of loving God also enable us to serve Him better because they bring us closer to Him. And serving God—no matter what has happened or is happening—is part of His plan for us.

Dear reading friend, regardless of where you have been placed by God, and regardless of your difficult times, you my friend can acknowledge and worship God, remember His blessed promises, be useful to others, and bloom and bear fruit there. After all, just as my friend Judy was able to say about her garden, "Oh, I have a plan!" God is able to say about your life, "Oh, I have a plan!" What comfort and assurance, what hope and what security there is in the thought that God has a plan for us…a plan that will draw you closer to Him!

~ 23 ~

Becoming God's Masterpiece

"For I know the plans that I have for you," declares the LORD, "plans for welfare and not for calamity to give you a future and a hope."

Jeremiah 29:11 NASB

Learning to Look at God's Good Plan

As we've seen, God's timetable for the Israelites involved 70 years of captivity in Babylon (Jeremiah 29:10). Do you realize that 70 years was a death sentence for those who heard the prophet's words? God was letting them know they would die without ever seeing Jerusalem, their homeland, again. That's why it was urgent for them to plant and build, to focus on the next generation, because God's promise of peace and restoration would be fulfilled through the generations to come.

Imagine learning God's pronouncement that you would never again see your home again. It might be easy to feel that God was turning His back on you, that He no longer loved you, that He was no longer merciful or just. But, my friend, all these would be incorrect thoughts about God. To prevent such wrong thinking, God gave the Israelites—right on the heels of the 70-year sentence—the promise we've been looking at in this section about living out God's plan: "'For I know the thoughts that I think toward you,' says the LORD, 'thoughts of peace and not of evil, to give you a future and a hope'" (Jeremiah 29:11).

How were the sorrowing and suffering children of Israel to endure for 70 years? They would simply have to take God at His word. They would simply have to believe that He would not forget them...or His promise to them. They would have to count on His promise of a better future. For 70 years they would have to place their faith, hope, and trust in these words of assurance spoken to them by God through a prophet.

So far we've seen one reason why the words of Jeremiah offered all the security God's people, then and now, need: God has a plan for us. So, regardless of how your life may look or feel right this minute, take heart! Know that God is busy at work on His good plan for you. Remember, too, that His plan reflects His purposes, His methods, and His timetable...not yours. And never forget that while God is working out His plan in your life, painful as it may be at times, you are becoming His masterpiece!

God's Good Plan Is an Adventure

When my husband said, "Judy, this is a beautiful garden, but what happened over there?" Judy replied, "Oh, I have a plan!" Of course, Judy's plan was for beauty, order, and growth. She would never plan an ugly garden or one that couldn't flourish! Likewise, God would never plan a life for you of ugliness or barrenness, a life where you couldn't flourish in Him.

Let me ask you, Do the circumstances of your life seem overwhelming right now? Then try thinking about God's plan for your life as an adventure. This perspective can change your attitude as you realize that you are in something of "a secret conspiracy" with the Creator of the universe and the Author of your life. And what is the big secret? It's knowing that God has a plan, and His plan will end in good for you. These truths can put an adventuresome spin on the ups and downs, the twists and turns of the path that will eventually take you to God's good plan for you. So let your life be your personal adventure with God! And enjoy it!

Going on an adventure—The attitude that life in the Lord is an adventure certainly helped my friend Lauren and her mother deal with the events of a trip they took to Southern California some years ago. Here's what happened.

This adventuresome mother–daughter team drove down from Seattle to visit Lauren's sister in San Diego before attending a women's retreat at a church in Los Angeles.

While they were in San Diego, the Rodney King verdict was announced and rioting began in Los Angeles. The violence closed down businesses and freeways...and led to the cancellation of the retreat.

When Sunday morning arrived and the city was calm, Lauren decided they would drive several hours north to attend the worship service at a special church. After putting on their dresses and hose, she and her mom headed up the freeway...but somewhere along the way, they missed a freeway exit, and never made it to church.

So they decided to stay overnight with a friend in Los Angeles. When I finally heard they were nearby, I quickly invited them to have brunch with me the next morning... where they showed up wearing old, fading makeup and their Sunday church clothes, the only clothes they'd taken from San Diego! After a wonderful visit together, I walked them out to their car and hugged them goodbye when, as they drove away, I realized I hadn't given Lauren directions to the freeway, which had six freeway on-ramps and not one of them led to San Diego. Oh dear! They would be lost again! (And indeed they were, as I learned weeks later.)

Riding the roller coaster of life—How did they handle this trying trip, this comedy of obstacles and errors? Lauren and her mother actually *laughed* as we talked about it later! Nothing had bothered them. Why? Because they were on an adventure!

Their trip to Los Angeles had been one disaster and disappointment after another. No retreat, no refund, no Sunday-morning worship, no directions, and no clothes or makeup—and lost in L.A. twice! But their trust in God, whose plans are good and not evil, let them approach each event as part of an amazing adventure. They didn't get angry and frustrated because things didn't fit into their schedule or go as planned. They didn't complain, gripe, or get upset. Instead, they focused on the fact that God has a plan for their good. And that focus allowed them to view their obstacles, disappointments, and oversights as an incredible adventure rather than as fuel for frustration.

That's the power of God's promise and the truth in Jeremiah 29:11. Knowing about the end-result God promises invites us to accept the Christian life as an adventure. We can then ride the roller coaster of life, knowing God's plan is for our good.

God's Good Plan Is a Process

One reason many of us fail to enjoy the adventure of the Christian life is because it is a process. We like end results more than we like the process that gets us there. But between today and the good end that God promises, we have to go through a process.

Looking through the eyes of an artist—As the story goes, one day a colossal cube of marble was delivered to Michelangelo's art studio. He walked around it several times, at first surveying it from a step back, then looking at it closely. He touched it with his hands and even pressed his face against the cold block of stone. Suddenly he grabbed a mallet and a chisel and swung mightily. Blow after blow caused small chips of marble as well as large chunks to fly in every direction.

Watching in awe, his apprentice screamed above the noise of shattering stone, "What are you doing? You are ruining a perfect piece of marble!"

With the passion of an artist with a vision, Michelangelo answered, "I see an angel in there, and I've got to get him out!"

Looking through the eyes of the Master Artist—My friend, God looks at you with the same kind of eyes Michelangelo looked at the piece of marble. God sees in you the image of Christ, and He wants to set that beauty free. The "process" is freeing that "angel." In the words of Jeremiah, the process of life involves plans for good and "not of evil, to give you an expected end" (Jeremiah 29:11 KJV).

From time to time, you and I may—like Michelangelo's apprentice—cry out to God in bewilderment and terror, "What are You doing? You are ruining a perfect piece of marble!" Such a cry reveals our failure to understand the Artist, His vision, and the process of His work. God picks up His hammer and chisel and, acting out of His infinite love and wisdom, starts chipping away at the piece of marble that is our life. He carefully knocks off the unimportant, the meaningless, and the excess. His chisel cuts away the flaws and removes all that is ugly. While at times the process may be puzzling and even painful, we can be secure in the knowledge that it is for good, not evil. God wants to make us Christlike and perfect. He wants to make us His masterpiece!

Learning from the old masters—For a perspective on these puzzling and painful times, consider another example from the world of art. To give depth to a painting, Old World artists would first wash their white canvases with black. Only by beginning with that black could they later achieve the contrast, color, dimension, and depth they desired. After all, no painting is a masterpiece that possesses only one color or one intensity.

When the canvas of our life seems to be washed with black, we can remember the promise of Jeremiah 29:11, that the end will be good. We can let God's Word enable us to stand secure in the hope that when God completes His good plans, our lives will have greater depth, more interesting dimensions, and remarkable intensity.

God's Good Plan Is an Opportunity

The adventure of life is often difficult, and God's process in our lives may be quite painful at times. But it helps me to try to profit from every single experience that comes my way, the difficult and painful times as well as those times when life is going smoothly.

In her book *What Is a Family?* Edith Schaeffer advises that we treat adversity as an opportunity. She encourages us to regard hard times as important to our spiritual and personal growth, not merely as something we have to endure. She challenges us to make adversity count for something positive by learning all we can from it. And these words do not come glibly. Mrs. Schaeffer knows pain and adversity. Hear her words—those of a mother whose daughter suffered for two years with rheumatic fever and whose son was born with polio:

> For my own children I always tried to remind them to take the opportunity to get all the information and interesting facts they could, in the midst of their own times in hospitals…! "You may never have this chance again; find out all you can." Not only does it help to alleviate the fears and take minds off pain, but it is an honest fact that one may never have another chance to see certain things and to ask certain questions. "Now is your chance to find out all you can about a…hospital."…"Now is your

> chance to see how a blood transfusion works."... "Now you can read on that bottle what is mixed in the liquid they are about to put into you instead of food."..."See if you can look at the X-ray of that leg. Amazing the way a bone is apart!"[1]

Loving God...Even More

Dear reading friend, neither Edith Schaeffer nor I are encouraging you to downplay or look away from the hard times of life and the pain those times bring. Instead, our message is to look boldly into the face of adversity when it arrives and learn from it. Take it as an opportunity from God to learn something you might not learn otherwise.

Difficult times are opportunities that God promises to use—and is using—for our good. They are also exquisite opportunities to love God more. How? By encouraging you to believe in Him—in His good intentions, in His everlasting love, in His power, and in His promises, especially His promise to bring you to an expected end...to make you a masterpiece!

~ 24 ~

Living Out God's Promise

"For I know the plans that I have for you," declares the LORD, "plans for welfare and not for calamity to give you a future and a hope."

Jeremiah 29:11 NASB

A pastor I know has an unbelievably positive attitude toward life, come what may. In his position as a shepherd to his flock, he has a lot of serious problems to sort through and many heavy-duty counseling sessions to facilitate. And yet he has an incredible confidence in God's process of working in His people's lives through such troubles. So, whenever someone approaches Jerry with a difficult or perplexing problem, he puts a note in a file folder he has labeled "Wait a Week." During that week, Jerry prays over every situation he's filed away. At the end of a week of prayer, he pulls out each paper and prays, "Okay, Lord, what are we going to do?"

What amazes Jim and me the most about this entire procedure is Jerry's attitude! His full counseling schedule means he hears about a lot of heartache, but it in no way affects his personality or his outlook on life. Whenever anyone encounters

Jerry, they are greeted with an exuberant smile, a ton of energy, and the confident statement, "God is still on His throne!" Clearly, Jerry is secure and living out God's promises!

You and I can be just as secure—and joyful!—in God's promises as Jerry is. That's because of what we've been learning. We now know that God has a plan for us that is and will be good. And the assurance that He is still on His throne means that nothing can interfere with God's plans.

Jerry believes and lives out God's promise in Jeremiah 29:11. His example shows us how thinking of God's good plan for our lives as an adventure, a process, and an opportunity can improve our attitude toward life and its trials. Even in problem times, we can be positive in our faith in God's character and His promises.

God's Good Plan: Purging and Pruning

And here's another part of God's good plan: He is faithful to use life's difficulties to purge and prune us of all that does not contribute positively to the masterpiece He is creating. When my husband said, "Judy, this is a beautiful garden, but what happened over there?" he was pointing to an area that was not beautiful at all. He was pointing to the rocks that would have to be carted off, the rotten pieces of fencing that would have to be replaced, the dead tree that would have to be removed, the tree stump that would have to be ground into chips, the sick shrubs that would have to be dug out, and the packed earth that would have to be rototilled before it could sustain any plant life. Everything in that part of the yard was ugly, old, dead, diseased, and useless and would have to be eliminated and destroyed before Judy could complete her beautiful garden. That cleanup was part of her plan.

And God works the same way in our lives. Before His plan can come to full fruition in our lives, He must eliminate all that is old, dead, diseased, and useless in our character.

For instance, when we first meet Sarah in the Old Testament (her story is found in Genesis 11–23), she is impatient, contentious, angry, manipulative, and unbelieving. Her life with Abraham (her husband), Hagar (Abraham's concubine), and Ishmael (Abraham's son by Hagar) is characterized by tension and unfulfillment. But God worked in Sarah's life and used failures, consequences, time, and her unhappiness to bring her to a mature faith in Him. In fact, Sarah is listed in the New Testament (Hebrews 11) as an example of faith.

There's no doubt that a pruning process like Sarah underwent can be painful! But it gives us an opportunity to grow in faith as God works in our lives to eliminate the unattractive and the ineffective and bring about the beauty He has promised.

God's Good Nature

To better enjoy the security God provides, we must understand that He is trustworthy and His nature is good—100 percent good! We must firmly establish in our minds that God can only think and do good. Conversely, God cannot think or do evil. James warns, "Let no one say when he is tempted, 'I am tempted by God'; for *God cannot be tempted by evil, nor does He Himself tempt anyone*" (James 1:13). In fact, God cannot even look upon evil. The prophet Habakkuk declared, "You are of purer eyes than to behold evil, and *cannot look on wickedness*" (Habakkuk 1:13).

Knowing of God's goodness is vital because our thoughts influence our behavior. If, for instance, we believe God can think evil thoughts and do evil deeds, we will never be secure and confident in His love. No, we will suspect that evil and harm are around every corner! But if we regulate our thoughts by the truth that God cannot think or do evil—ever!—we can then proceed through each day of our lives living fully in the promise of God's love and His goodness.

Remembering God's goodness—To help keep my thoughts in line with the truth that God cannot think or do evil, I have a collection of "goodness verses." They guide my thoughts and my prayers whenever I need to remember that I am secure in God. Here are a few to help you start your own list.

> Every good gift and every perfect gift is from above, and comes down from the Father of lights, with whom there is no variation or shadow of turning (James 1:17).

> Oh, taste and see that the LORD is good (Psalm 34:8).

> Oh, that men would give thanks to the LORD for His goodness, and for His wonderful works to the children of men! For He satisfies the longing soul, and fills the hungry soul with goodness (Psalm 107:8-9).

> The LORD is good, a stronghold in the day of trouble; and He knows those who trust in Him (Nahum 1:7).

Verses like these have helped me as well as the women who have asked me for counsel. Gayle is one such woman. She came to me when the circumstances of her life gave her reason to wonder about God and His goodness. So I encouraged her to memorize one of these "goodness verses" each week. Memorizing these words of truth and hope gave her comfort, and I could refer her to them to remind her of God's goodness and her security in Him.

Praying about God's goodness—I also had Gayle write out a prayer using these verses. Then, every time she thought about her situation or had to face the people involved, she could remember her prayer and again remind herself of the truth about God. Whenever she felt anger, sadness, and discouragement, she could turn to her prayer and remember that God is good and that His plan for her is good. And you can do the same! Here's the prayer:

> Father God, I want to thank You for Your sovereign power in my life, that You arrange all circumstances—past, present and future—for good for me because I love You and am called according to Your purposes (Romans 8:28). It gives me great assurance and security in You to know that You know the plans You have for me regarding (*situation, person, problem*) I also can rest in the fact that You want only the best for me, a future and a hope (Jeremiah 29:11). Help me to remember that Your provision is all encompassing.

Writing your own prayer and incorporating your selection of "goodness verses" in it will help you view the challenges and hurts of your life through Scripture's truth. As you draw closer to God in prayer and focus on His goodness, He will bless you with His peace and the assurance of His love.

Looking to the Reward

Have you ever planned a vacation to mark the end of a long project or a special evening out to celebrate the completion of a difficult task? Rewards are powerful motivators because we can endure hard times as long as we know there is something good at the end. We can work hard and sacrifice meals, sleep, and fun when the goal and the reward are worthwhile.

Because God knew that the 70-year exile would be difficult for His people, He gave the Israelites something to look forward to and promised them a "reward" in Jeremiah 29:11: There would be an expected end, a future and a hope, the restoration of peace and prosperity. God did not want "that unexpectant apathy which is the terrible accompaniment of so much worldly sorrow...to be an ingredient in the lot of the Jews."[1] The promise and the "reward" He held out offered them security, hope, and a reason to persevere.

Knowing of God's planned and future reward ministers to me (and you, too) in three different ways.

Rebuke—God's promise rebukes me when I am tempted to doubt Him and question His management of my life. I can almost hear God chiding, "Wait a minute! The plans I have for you are for good and not for evil, and I will indeed bring that good about. I *will* bring you to an expected end."

Although I don't know the specifics of this promised end, I can trust in the fact that He knows.

Comfort—God's promise gives me comfort. He uses Jeremiah 29:11 to calm my emotions. Through the prophet's words, God whispers, "It's okay. You don't have to worry or wonder about anything. I know the plans I have for you, and they are plans for good and not for evil. I'll bring you to the expected end."

God uses this verse to remind me that He has complete knowledge of my life, a plan for me that is for good, and the ability to make that plan happen. This assurance brings me great peace.

Encouragement—Jeremiah 29:11 also offers encouragement. Through the promise in this verse, God encourages me when I am tempted to despair. He prods, "Keep going! Don't give up your hope. And don't worry about the end. The plans I have for you are plans for good and not for evil, to bring you to an expected end."

Through this promise, God reminds me that, no matter how hard or long the journey, I am going to get to the end—where the reward is waiting. And the end is going to be good!

And I've saved the best for last! God's greatest promise for His children is heaven. Heaven is the expected end for all who name Jesus as Lord and Savior. Ultimately, the final future and hope for us who are God's children is heaven, where there will be fullness of joy and pleasures forevermore at His right hand (Psalm 16:11).

Loving God...Even More

Where does life find you today? What difficult times are you enduring? What situation seems to be unbearable? Well, you can be encouraged because God's powerful promise leaves no phase or issue of life uncovered! Jeremiah 29:11 assures us that God's plans, for us personally and for His people in general, are for good, not evil. In God and His sure Word, we find security for any and every situation we'll encounter in life—birth, death, marriage, singleness, widowhood, poverty, persecution, suffering the unknown of a move, or the permanence of being in an unpleasant place.

One morning a pastor's wife called to tell me that her husband was resigning from his church. Margo reported, "Elizabeth, I've been reciting Jeremiah 29:11 all day long! I know God was involved in bringing us here. I know we have learned many lessons and been used in many ways. I also know God has a plan for us and that it's good. He knows where we are going!" In the midst of all that she was feeling due to her life being turned upside down, Margo was using her mind to love God, to reach out to Him, to focus on the truths of Scripture, and to live out God's promise. Margo was dealing with fear, disappointment, worry, anger, confusion, and hurt as she anticipated saying goodbye, being uprooted from her home, and moving in an unknown direction to an unknown place.

Oh, but she is confident in God's perfect plan! And you and I can be, too! The foundations of our daily lives may suddenly collapse, and the security of our income may slip away, but we know about God, His goodness, and His promises. Therefore we can enjoy victory in our thought lives. We can love God with all our minds as we bring each thought into captivity to the truth of Jeremiah 29:11.

Accepting the Unacceptable

Oh, the depth of the riches
both of the wisdom and knowledge of God!
How unsearchable are His judgments and
His ways past finding out!

ROMANS 11:33

~ 25 ~

Responding to Life's Turning Points

Oh, the depth of the riches
both of the wisdom and knowledge of God!
How unsearchable are His judgments
and His ways past finding out!

Romans 11:33 NASB

The sun rose that morning just as it had risen every day of her life. As she ran through her list of chores, there was no hint that today her life would be transformed from the mundane to the mysterious. But something happened that day which changed everything—forever. Seconds after it happened, gone were her hopes of the quiet life she had imagined for herself. Gone were the comfort and safety of a predictable routine. Gone was the peaceful existence she and her family had known, the existence that had led her to expect a simple and unremarkable future.

These words describe a singular day in the life of Mary, the mother of Jesus. The scriptural account for that day simply says, "And having come in, the angel said to her..." (Luke 1:28). "The angel" was Gabriel, sent from God. And what he said to her sent her world reeling. It completely changed her life. Nothing would ever be the same because she had been chosen to be the mother of God's Son. She would bring into the world its Savior, Lord, and King. Nothing could ever be the same for Mary!

Turning Points

Perhaps you can point to a day in your life that changed everything for you, a day after which nothing would ever be the same—a day when dark clouds hid the sun. Such turning points in life can shake us to the core. Such turning points can also send us to God, His Word, and His promises.

Did the pivotal day in your life begin normally? Often our routine is well underway, and nothing out of the ordinary is happening—until the phone rings, the letter arrives, or the appointment unfolds. Whatever the event was for you, it signified a totally changed life. Calling such an event "the turning point," Corrie ten Boom wrote, "The turning point may be announced by the ring of a telephone or a knock on the door."[1] In her own life, "the turning point" was a knock on her door by German soldiers. Her life turned from normal to horrendous as she entered a Nazi concentration camp.

What are we to do at such turning points in life? How can we handle the changes after a life-altering incident and the new kind of life that follows? And what are we to think about the unexplainable and unexpected things that happen to us? How can we accept these mysterious events that clearly spell out God's will for us? How can we accept what seems to be unacceptable?

Accepting God's Will

We can learn from Mary some answers to these questions. The gospel of Luke shows us how, at this major turning point in her life, Mary humbly accepted the news from Gabriel that she would bear God's Son. Mary is noted as a woman of very few words, but this announcement from Gabriel caused her to carefully and thoughtfully pose one question—How? "How can this be, since I am a virgin?" (Luke 1:34 NASB).

Mary's question—a perfectly natural one since she was unmarried and a virgin—received an answer that lay in the supernatural realm: "The Holy Spirit will come upon you, and the power of the Highest will overshadow you; therefore, also, that Holy One who is to be born will be called the Son of God" (verse 35). In other words, the conception would be a miracle! And that was all the explanation Mary got!

Unable to understand what would happen to her, Mary nevertheless consented to God's will for her life. She boldly declared, "Behold the maidservant of the Lord! Let it be to me according to your word" (verse 38).

This simple scenario allows us a glimpse into God's "ways," which Romans 11:33 describes as "past finding out" (NKJV) or "unfathomable" (NASB). Here was a girl, probably a young teenager, going about the daily business of growing up, and one day, by one judgment from God, everything changed. Not only her life, but the entire world changed... forever. God acted and God spoke...and things would never be the same.

When God spoke to Mary through Gabriel and told her that she had been chosen to be the mother of Jesus, her life changed completely. For Mary, God's revealed will meant being pregnant before she was married and being branded a fornicator. God's will meant trouble with her husband-to-be, trouble at home, trouble in Nazareth, and trouble among her children. God's will meant a life of tension as Mary and her baby were hunted down, as she fled from country to country, and as her remarkable Son caused violent reactions in the hearts of the people He met. And for Mary, God's will meant a soul pierced with sorrow (Luke 2:35) as she followed her Son on His path of pain to the cross (John 19:25-27).

Yet when the angel appeared, Mary accepted the news of God's will for her life with the statement, "Let it be to me according to your word."

The Mentality of a Handmaiden

How was Mary able to accept Gabriel's startling announcement? Why was she able to accept this radical turning point in her life?

Clue #1 is found in Mary's reference to herself as "the maidservant of the Lord" or "the handmaid of the Lord" (Luke 1:38 KJV). In the New Testament, a "handmaid" is the same as a bondservant, "whose will was not his own but who rather was committed to another. The slave was obligated to perform his master's will without question or delay."[2] A handmaiden would sit silently and watch for hand signals from her mistress (Psalm 123:2). Through these motions rather than any spoken command, the mistress would communicate her wishes. Her handmaiden, having been trained to watch for these signs, would then obey them—without question or hesitation.[3]

As this cultural background suggests, it is significant that Mary chose to describe herself as a "handmaid." Clearly, she had cultivated the attitude and the mentality of a handmaiden in her fine-tuned attentiveness to her God. She no longer viewed herself as her own or considered herself to have rights. Instead, she was wholly committed to God. Her one purpose in life was to obey her Master's will...quickly, quietly, and without question.

So, that day in Nazareth when God moved His hand and signaled His will, Mary, His devoted handmaiden, noticed. At the flick of God's finger, she responded, "Behold the maidservant of the Lord!" Whatever God wanted, this humble maidservant was willing to do, even though it meant that everything in her life changed—forever. Mary saw herself as God's handmaiden and so accepted His will for her life.

A Knowledge of God

Clue #2 explains why Mary was able to accept Gabriel's startling announcement of God's will for her life. It also explains her ability to accept this radical turning point in her life: Mary had a working knowledge of God. She knew God well enough to trust Him and His love for her. And this knowledge helped her accept His will.

Hear Mary's heart and her words of praise in Luke 1:46-55, the song known as the Magnificat. Her outpouring begins with "my soul magnifies the Lord" (verse 46). And her inspired words of exaltation continue on for nine verses, containing 15 quotations from the Old Testament.[4] Clearly, Mary had "majored on the majors"! She knew about God and His mercy, about His provision and His faithfulness to her forefathers.

As one author has observed, the number of scriptures quoted in the Magnificat show that "Mary knew God, through the books of Moses and the Psalms and the writings of the prophets. She had a deep reverence for the Lord God in her heart because she knew what He had done in the history of her people."[5] Mary knew God well. And knowing God and recognizing His infinite wisdom and knowledge enables us, like Mary, to accept what He has ordained for our lives.

And not only can we accept what God has planned for us, but we can also rejoice, knowing that His plans for us are for good. We can actually look forward with joy to the life and riches God has in store for us!

The Depth of the Riches of God

As we end this chapter, I want us to notice the powerful truths about God that are revealed in Romans 11:33. Four facts about God and His ways are on display in this one verse of Scripture. We'll look more closely at each "fact" in the next few chapters, but here are a few bits of information that make them more understandable.

Learning about the background—In chapters 1–11 of the book of Romans, the apostle Paul pours forth the central truths of Christianity and conveys the great doctrines of grace. And in chapter 11, he deals with many lofty topics like God's righteousness and mercy, the mystery of salvation, and justification by faith. Finally, in verses 33-36 Paul can bear it no longer and bursts into worshipful praise. Standing at the heights of Christianity, he exults over what he sees, and realizes all he does not see:

> Oh, the depth of the riches both of the wisdom and knowledge of God! How unsearchable are His

> judgments and His ways past finding out! "For who has known the mind of the LORD? Or who has become His counselor? Or who has first given to Him and it shall be repaid to him?" For of Him and through Him and to Him are all things, to whom be glory forever. Amen (Romans 11:33-36).

Learning about the language—Look again at the words "depth...unsearchable...past finding out." As I studied various books on Romans to more fully understand Romans 11:33, I had to ask my husband a question. I was using quite a few of his books, and many of them had Greek words scattered throughout them. Now, I don't know Greek, but I could tell there were a number of repeated Greek characters surrounding the nouns *wisdom, knowledge, judgments,* and *ways.* So I took the reference books to Jim, who does know Greek, and he explained the Greek letters in today's vernacular. He said that whenever I saw this particular Greek letter formation, I should think of and add the word "not."

That would make Paul's words read something like this: "Can you trace God's wisdom (...or knowledge...or judgments...or ways)? *Not!* Can you find it? *Not!* Does it have footprints to follow? *Not!* Are there tracks? *Not!* Can you go to the depths of it? *Not!* Can it be exhausted? *Not!* Is there an end to it? *Not!*" In other words, because God's wisdom, knowledge, judgments, and ways lie in the realm of God, can we understand them? *Not!* Therefore the translators of different Bible translations describe the four elements concerning God's manner as un-understandable, unsearchable, inscrutable, inexhaustible, unfathomable, and impossible to grasp. Why? Again, because they lie in the realm of God.

I have to tell you that I experienced something of a breakthrough in understanding...when I realized there would be a myriad of events in life that I would never understand. God works in mysterious ways, which means they are ways that cannot be explained. In the chapters that follow, we'll look more in-depth at the four facts about God that can help us to better accept the unacceptable, to better understand the un-understandable! Such knowledge, along with cultivating the mentality of a bondservant or handmaiden in our relationship with God, can help us to respond to the turning points in life in the way that Mary did—"Behold the maidservant of the Lord! Let it be to me according to your word" (Luke 1:38).

Loving God...Even More

When it comes to loving God with all our mind, we do a better job of it when we, like Mary, pay attention to nurturing the mentality of a servant or a handmaiden. That means praying and desiring and purposing to serve God as He calls us, when He calls us, and where He calls us.

When we can respond to whatever is happening in our lives with Mary's heart-attitude toward God expressed in words like these—"I am the Lord's slave. Let it be as you say"[6]—then we can know that we are loving God with all our mind. We can also, by His grace, consent to God's will and to the unsearchable judgments of our infinitely good and merciful God, even without comprehension.

~ 26 ~

Majoring on the Minors

Oh, the depth of the riches
both of the wisdom
and knowledge of God!

Romans 11:33

I've been extremely blessed to know some incredible Christian women who have modeled faith in God and service to Him. One of these very special women is my Sarah. I first met this amazing woman 25 years ago. She inspires everyone she meets...and I was no exception! Her wisdom, her love for God, and her commitment to memorizing Scripture helped shape my ministry and message.

I vividly remember, for instance, asking her a question: "Sarah, if you were to write a book for women, what would it be about?" Her answer changed my life! She said, "Elizabeth, I don't like many of the books I see when I go into Christian bookstores. There are so few books for women about God. If I were to write a book to share with women what I have learned through the years, I would call it *Forever Father.* Women today have so many problems simply because they don't know God. We are majoring on the minors."

Focusing on God

"Majoring on the minors"—I have literally spent hours thinking about these words! And Sarah's observation and her statement made to me those decades ago changed my philosophy of ministry, my studies, the books I choose to read, the way I use my time, and the ideas I share with others when I teach and write. Her observation also explained to me why she is such a powerful model of faith. Throughout her life, Sarah has majored on knowing God. As a result, she possesses clear vision, a sound mind, and the wisdom to know what really counts in the Christian life.

And what really counts in the Christian life is knowing God. Why? Because that knowledge is foundational if we are to truly love Him, live for Him, and joyfully serve Him. It is, however, much easier to major on the minors than on the person of God. For instance, we tend to center our attention on our problems...rather than on the Person of our all-loving and all-powerful God. We tend to focus on our troubles... and forget to trust our faithful Lord. We tend to look down at the entangling evils of the world around us...and fail to look up at God's heavenly majesty.

And, sadly, efforts today in our churches tend to major on meeting needs, providing support, and facilitating fellowship. Yet many people seem to have more needs than ever, and the old needs are still unmet. We wonder why we have problems we can't handle. What we really need is to know

God, have better knowledge of God, and have more knowledge of God...instead of majoring on the minors.

We, as individuals and in the church, need to be consciously majoring on "the majors," on strengthening ourselves and others in the major areas of Christianity. What are some of "the majors"? God's attributes, the life of Christ, men and women of the Bible, books of the Bible, and our New Testament position in Christ. Emphasis also needs to be placed on the spiritual life, faith, wisdom, prayer, and the Scriptures. As A.W. Tozer writes in his classic book *The Knowledge of the Holy*,

> A right conception of God is basic not only to systematic theology but to practical Christian living as well....I believe there is scarcely an error in doctrine or a failure in applying Christian ethics that cannot be traced finally to imperfect and ignoble thoughts about God.[1]

A.W. Tozer—and my Sarah—calls us to know God, to focus on Him—to major on the majors! And Romans 11:33 is a "major" that teaches us four facts about God.

Acknowledging the Wisdom of God

Oh, the depth of the riches
...of the wisdom...of God!

Where do you get wisdom? If you're like me, you go primarily to the Bible. I try to read from Proverbs each day, and I often follow along in a commentary. Studying the lives of men and women in the Old and New Testament and reading the words of believers who have gone before me also teaches me wisdom.

Then there are Christian mentors and teachers. Through the years these wise people have been great sources of wisdom. Also, I never hesitate to follow the example of Queen Esther. This wise woman never made a significant decision without first asking for counsel. Whenever I have asked for advice from my husband, pastor, peers, friends, and teachers, I've been blessed and guided by God's wisdom.

God, however, doesn't have to study the Bible or read a book. Neither does He need to seek counsel or advice from others. No, God Himself *is* wisdom! And He derives it from no other source. And don't forget how we described the four facts about God found in Romans 11:33, including His wisdom—it is unsearchable, inscrutable, inexhaustible, and unfathomable. It is impossible to understand. Therefore, God's wisdom calls us to faith.

Heeding God's Wisdom as a Parent

Soon after I became a Christian, I had an important decision to make—whether to choose the world's wisdom or God's wisdom when it came to training my children. Previously I had decided that as a parent, I would not physically discipline my children. Instead I would reward, reason with, and convince them to do things my way. But in my daily reading of Proverbs, I was hearing God's instruction to discipline my two preschool daughters. I was also realizing that such discipline might involve the correction of a spanking from time to time. The world was telling me one thing, and God's Word was clearly telling me the opposite. Knowing what God said, I knew I had to obey, so I purchased a little six-inch wooden spoon…just in case!

Sure enough, the day came when I got an opportunity to do things God's way. When my young darlings acted up in a big way and needed to be disciplined, I went into my bedroom and prayed, then picked up the little spoon, explained why I needed to do what I was about to do, and spanked them each with one little pop (which was more like one little pat!).

It couldn't have even hurt, but probably due to shock, both of my girls began to cry. And a "miracle" occurred in our kitchen that day as each little girl hugged one of my legs and cried in unison, "Oh, Mommy, I won't ever do that again!"

Yes, my children cried—and I cried with them—on those rare occasions when I had to use that tiny wooden spoon. But suddenly my girls started following my instructions and listening when I spoke. We began to have a home of peace instead of chaos. As Jim and I offered behavioral guidelines and biblical discipline for our girls, we learned the wisdom of obeying the wisdom of God.

This seemingly small step was major for me because I was doing what I understood God to be telling me through His Word. But I was doing it by faith…because I didn't understand God's wisdom, how it would work, or why it would help. I was, by faith, applying God's wisdom to my life. Without completely understanding how to apply His wise directive to discipline my children, I believed, I trusted, and I obeyed as best I could. As I said, God's unsearchable, inscrutable, inexhaustible, unfathomable, and impossible-to-understand wisdom calls us to faith! On the other side of faith and obedience come the dawning of understanding and some very positive results.

Acknowledging the Knowledge of God

Oh, the depth of the riches
...of the...knowledge...of God!

Closely related to honoring God's wisdom is appreciating His knowledge. And I ask you again, where do you go to get knowledge? If you're like me, you read books, take classes, and watch educational television. We can earn degrees, obtain licenses, and enroll in continuing education courses. We can investigate the various branches of mathematics, physics, chemistry, biology, and the other sciences. We can plumb the mysteries of DNA and genetics and reach beyond the atmosphere to the moon and distant planets. And we can use computers to manage the increasing amount of knowledge available to us in this era of information explosion.

God, however, doesn't need books, computers, encyclopedias, teachers, or classes. No, God Himself is the source of all knowledge! As the Author of all things, God knows all that can be known. And like His wisdom, His knowledge is unsearchable, inscrutable, unfathomable, inexhaustible, and unexplainable. It is impossible to understand. We cannot begin to define God's knowledge. We know, simply and profoundly, that nothing is hidden from Him or incomprehensible to Him.

And what is it that God knows?

Realizing God Knows All About Us

Among all that God knows is His knowledge of your particular situation—and mine, too. God knows our joys and sorrows. He knows our strengths and weaknesses. If we are married, He also knows our spouses' strengths and weaknesses.

If we have children, God knows about each one of them—their temperaments, their needs, and the challenges we face raising them.

If there are no children, God knows that, too, and He knows His purpose in it, as well as our suffering if we desire children. And if we don't have a marriage partner and aren't blessed with the gift of singleness, God knows it, and He knows our pain and how He plans to use our lives for Him. God also knows our finances and our jobs, our problems with our neighbors and our in-laws, our desires to serve Him, and the questions in our hearts.

And, of course, God knows our problems. The difficulties we face are no secret to Him. In fact, He has known about them forever. The challenges we face are known to Him. In fact, He knows—and has known since the beginning of time—exactly how He would use them to draw us closer to Him and to make us more like Christ. God's knowledge extends throughout time and includes our past, our present, and our future.

Knowing that God knows all about the things I've listed—and more!—certainly makes it easier for me to accept whatever comes my way. The fact of God's knowledge also helps me feel His presence with me, especially when life is difficult.

Put simply, God knows all about you and all about me. He knows our hurts, our wants, and our needs. Therefore, He understands us and we are always understood. We can know that He knows all about us and cares deeply about our feelings, our ideas, and our concerns. We can never say to God, "But You don't understand." We can be confident that even when no one else knows or understands, He does!

Loving God...Even More

Knowing more about God's wisdom and knowledge (which we will never fully know and understand!) has caused me to think of them as two bookends. When our family experienced the near-destruction of our home in a killer earthquake while living in Southern California, the violent shaking emptied all of our books off the library shelves. As I stood surveying that room full of rubble, weeping over the ruin of our home, I prayed to God about what I could do to bring even some tiny bit of order to the chaos I was looking at.

It was then I spotted one of our bookends. I picked it up and searched through the books and the debris until I found its mate. Then I placed the matching set of bookends on a shelf and began putting books—any books—between them. By finding the different sets of bookends and placing books between them I did finally bring order to chaos.

And my friend, that's the way it is in your life when you love God and count on His love, when you trust in His wisdom and count on His knowledge. Simply take all of the un-understandable events in your life—the wonderings, the why's, and the bewilderment over the things that happen to you and to others—and file them between God's wisdom and God's knowledge. You don't understand these occurrences...and you never will...because you can't! But God does. And so we rest in Him. Peace and order—and greater love for God—is yours when you place the impossible-to-understand issues and incidents in your life between His infinite wisdom and His all-encompassing knowledge. Oh, the depth of the riches both of the wisdom and knowledge of God!

~ 27 ~

Trusting God in the Dark

How unsearchable are His judgments
and His ways past finding out!

Romans 11:33

Is there anything in your life you struggle to understand? Do you ever wonder why certain things are the way they are? Do you hear yourself questioning something that has or hasn't happened in your life? As we are learning in our walk through Romans 11:33, we must make a conscious effort to accept God's wisdom and knowledge and then live accordingly.

In years gone by, I learned much about God and His wisdom from a young mother who carried a baby full-term knowing for most of the pregnancy that the child would live only a few brief hours due to a genetic defect. I praise God for the triumphant five-page letter this grieving mom wrote to me listing the multitude of lessons God taught her as those months crawled by. She has learned, as hard as it was, to accept God's wisdom in His choice of this purpose for her. She learned to trust Him in the dark. She came to trust in God's knowledge of the situation and of the *whys* of her situation.

As hard as it is and in whatever the situation (everything from disciplining a child to having your baby die in your arms), we must acknowledge, as Paul did, "Oh, the depth of the riches both of the wisdom and knowledge of God!" When we don't understand, like, or agree with the way life has gone, we are to bow before God and once again confess that we cannot understand His wisdom and knowledge. In faith, we are to accept His wisdom, His Word, and His workings, and trust in Him...even in the dark.

Remembering God's Wisdom and Knowledge

For a moment think about what we've been learning about God from Romans 11:33. Think back on my wise Sarah's comment that we have so many problems simply because we don't know God. We've been getting to know God better in the chapters in this section by considering His love, His wisdom, and His knowledge. So I pray that by now your problems look differently when laid before the infinite wisdom and knowledge of your loving God. After all, how big are your problems next to an omnipotent, all-powerful God?

As I suggested in the previous chapter, think of God's wisdom and knowledge as the bookends for your life, holding up all of its incomprehensible happenings and offering a sense of order to God's mysterious working. After all, nothing is ever unknown, nothing is ever overlooked, and nothing is ever a surprise to God. And, as A.W. Tozer reminds us, in all that ever happens to you and me, God in His wisdom is always working toward predestined goals with His flawless precision.[1]

By God's grace, you and I can better accept every event in our lives when we realize that *all* of the details and elements of our lives are in the hands of our infinitely wise God who knows us and loves us as no one else does. This perfect wisdom calls us to faith. Again, Tozer writes, "The testimony of faith is that, no matter how things look in this fallen world, all God's acts are wrought in perfect wisdom."[2]

Although God's ways are often mysterious, by faith we believe in the infinite and holy wisdom behind them. By faith we trust in the wisdom of God that stands behind the events we don't understand. As Oswald Chambers points out, "Trustfulness is based on confidence in God whose ways I do not understand; if I did, there would be no need for trust."[3]

Acknowledging God's Judgments

Hear again the heart of Paul in Romans 11:33. Besides praising God for His wisdom and His knowledge, Paul also praises God for His judgments and His ways. To begin, he exclaims, "How unsearchable are His *judgments*...!" God's judgments have to do with God's decisions and His "rules" and decrees. His judgments reveal His plans for the universe, for the human race, and for you and me individually.

For instance, as parents we make the rule, "Don't play in the street." Does the child fully understand the reasons behind that decree or judgment? No. Does the child need to understand? No. The child simply needs to accept the parents' rule and obey it.

And we, as God's children, need to do the same. It's not necessary for us to understand God's rules, decrees, or judgments.

Furthermore, we aren't expected to always understand them. In fact, like God's wisdom and knowledge, we can't understand all of God's judgments...because they are un-understandable, unsearchable, inscrutable, inexhaustible, unfathomable, and impossible to grasp.

However, it is necessary that we accept those judgments and the events in our lives that result from them...even when we don't understand the reasons behind them. Put simply, our duty is like that of a child—to accept the rules and obey. We don't need to understand why things are the way they are. We only need to follow the rules.

Here's another thought: We can either argue with God or accept His judgments. The choice is ours. And the choice of attitude is ours, too. We can rant and rave, struggle and search, seek revenge and hold grudges, become bitter or bewildered...or we can accept what is happening in our lives as part of God's judgments.

Accepting Without Answers

And that's what the young Mary did. She certainly couldn't understand Gabriel's announcement of God's judgment that she would be the mother of the Messiah. (No one, apart from God, ever has!) She also couldn't understand completely how she would conceive the child. (And no one has ever understood this either!) After all, this plan came from the mind of God.

So Mary had a choice to make. She could either argue with and question God's action...or she could accept His judgment in her life. Either way, the outcome would be the same: She would give birth to the Son of God. She had a choice, however, about her attitude and her conduct. She chose to accept this unsearchable judgment of God even though she didn't understand it. She consented to God's judgment without comprehending the how, the why, or the effects it would have on her life. She asked, "How?" but accepted God's will without receiving any answers. She consented without comprehension, saying, "Behold the maid-servant of the Lord! Let it be to me according to your word" (Luke 1:38).

Like Mary, you and must remember that the events in our lives are the results of God's judgments. We must accept in faith that the events of our lives are accomplishing something in God's plan for us and for His world. He is at work and in control of our universe and our lives, and He has His reasons...which are un-understandable, unsearchable, inscrutable, inexhaustible, unfathomable, and impossible to grasp. The reasons behind His decisions remain in the realm of God, and you and I must rest in the knowledge that they are His domain, not ours. Therefore, we probably won't understand the how's and the why's on this side of heaven.

Acknowledging God's Ways

"How unsearchable are His judgments," Paul exults, "and His *ways* past finding out!" What are God's ways? To begin our understanding, God's ways are the methods by which He carries out His judgments.[4] We must quickly and humbly admit that God's ways—the roads or paths He takes to carry out His judgments and fulfill His purposes—are not usually the way we would do things!

No, we cannot comprehend God's ways. As Paul tells us, they are "past finding out!" The very fact that they are God's ways points to His independence from all human beings and reminds us of the vast difference between Him, the Creator, and us, the created.[5] It is only reasonable, then, that we find God's ways (like His wisdom, knowledge, and judgments) to be un-understandable, unsearchable, inscrutable, inexhaustible, unfathomable, and impossible to grasp—past finding out!

You see, God is in His own unfathomable category. He is not like us and cannot be understood. The prophet Isaiah revealed this truth centuries ago when, speaking on God's behalf, he wrote, "For My thoughts are not your thoughts, nor are your ways My ways....For as the heavens are higher than the earth, so are My ways higher than your ways, and My thoughts than your thoughts" (Isaiah 55:8-9). Speaking on behalf of God, the psalmist offered this rebuke—"You thought that I was altogether like you" (Psalm 50:21).

Paul's rhetorical question in Romans 11:34 further underscores the mystery of God's ways—"For who has known the mind of the LORD?" The only answer is, "No one." As the Living Bible says simply, "How impossible it is for us to understand his decisions and his methods!" (verse 33).

Great freedom and peace is ours when we acknowledge that God is infinitely superior to us in His wisdom, knowledge, judgments, and ways, and when we accept—without understanding—His work in the world and in our lives.

Dear friend, are you beginning to understand why this chapter is entitled "Trusting God in the Dark"? It's because (and I cannot say it enough!) God's judgments and ways, like His wisdom and knowledge, are un-understandable, unsearchable, inscrutable, inexhaustible, unfathomable, and impossible to grasp—past finding out!

So what can we do? We must trust God in the dark! We must trust Him without understanding. Like the psalmist advised in Psalm 46:10, we must simply "be still, and know that I am God." We must "cease striving" (NASB) and, in essence, know that "it is I, God, who is doing this!"

Loving God...Even More

Un-understandable, unsearchable, inscrutable, inexhaustible, unfathomable, and impossible to grasp—past finding out! This God is our God...forever and ever! We will never fully know God or fully recognize or appreciate His deep love for us. But hopefully you are beginning to understand more about Him. And with that understanding, you are more willing to freely yield yourself to His plans, His wisdom, His knowledge, His judgments, and His ways—for you and your life.

Although in your pain you may sometimes ask "Why?" you can fully trust that God loves you and that His plan for you is good. In your deeper understanding, you will also not resist His work in your life. Instead you will know that He closes and opens doors for your good. You will realize that He uses the fires of life to purify your faith, to shape you into Christ's image, and to cause you to love Him...even more.

~ 28 ~

Accepting the Unacceptable

Oh, the depth of the riches both of the wisdom and knowledge of God! How unsearchable are His judgments and His ways past finding out!

Romans 11:33

Acknowledging the truth that God's judgments are unsearchable and His ways mysterious is not merely a theological exercise. Acknowledging that God's ways are not our ways and accepting that truth has made a real difference in my life, and it can in yours, too.

Here's what happened...

A *Problem*

There was a period of time in my life when I experienced "one of those situations" that had me wondering what God was doing in my life. A woman in authority over me seemed to delight in holding me back from growing in the Lord and in keeping me from stretching my wings as I sought to serve Him.

During the eight long years of this painful relationship, I kept asking, "Can't anyone see what is happening here? Don't You see, God? Just look my way! It's so obvious that she's tripping me up as I try to serve You! How can You let this go on time after time?"

Every day for eight years—day after dreary day, year after frustrating year—I spoke daily to God and my husband about this seemingly hopeless and pointless situation. I couldn't stop thinking about it...and I didn't know what to do. My preoccupation seriously affected my spiritual life. For instance, whenever I sat down to have my devotions or whenever I attended a worship service, I found myself thinking about my problem and this problem person! For eight years I limped along in my spiritual growth.

A Scripture

I finally experienced a turning point. The morning began like any other morning. Jim was at work, our girls had been dropped off at school, and I was going through my usual daily routine. When it was time for my morning walk, I grabbed the pack of memory verses I wanted to review and headed out the door.

This particular pack of verses happened to be the first one I had ever memorized. I had been reviewing its 72 verses regularly through the years. But this time, when I came to verse #72—the final verse on my walk—I heard Romans 11:33 differently.

> Oh, the depth of the riches both of the wisdom and knowledge of God! How unsearchable are His judgments and His ways past finding out!

I said this by-now-familiar-scripture to myself as I neared home after my walk through my neighborhood, finally reaching the last sentence. And this time—after many years of knowing this verse—there was a breakthrough in my spirit as God used His Word to get through to my heart in a new way. The message of Romans 11:33 cleansed me! It washed over me! And it washed through me! Many of the unsearchable wonders of this verse opened up for me and gave me freedom from my long struggle with this particular woman.

What happened? Why did that familiar scripture suddenly come alive to me? All I know is that as I said the verse to myself, I found myself emphasizing the facts of...

God's wisdom,
God's knowledge,
His judgments, and
His ways.

There was no "me" in this verse. No, there was only God! And the fact that His wisdom, knowledge, judgments, and ways are unsearchable and "past finding out" was made personal to me. I saw that day that this truth spoke directly to my situation...and suddenly everything was okay.

What joy! What release! I remember stopping right on the sidewalk and saying aloud, "*God* did this! *He* allowed this, *He* planned this, *He* brought this. *He* knows this, and *He* has used it for my good. My situation is a part of *His* wisdom, *His* knowledge, *His* judgments, *His* ways—and those are past finding out!"

Freedom came as I realized right there on the sidewalk of a residential street in the San Fernando Valley that I didn't have to know or understand what was going on. And it was okay to not understand! Furthermore, the situation—which was and always had been in the hands of my loving heavenly Father—would be okay.

An Instrument

God had definitely used Romans 11:33 in my life in other ways before that special morning. But when He spoke to me about the ongoing situation that had been such a burden for so long, I was so glad I had memorized this verse! You see, God's holy Word is an instrument He uses to guide, comfort, correct, rebuke, and teach us.

Dear friend, the passages we commit to memory are like a surgeon's sterilized tools—carefully arranged on instrument trays and ready for his expert use. When there's a problem in our life, God can pick up exactly the verse we need and cut right to our heart. He did so for me during that morning walk, and the surgery He performed on me with His Word set me free.

Now, meet another wonderful woman who taught me about the importance of memorizing Scripture. Each fall while Jim was a student at Talbot Theological Seminary, I drove for an hour in five o'clock freeway traffic to attend the opening session of the wives' fellowship. At those sessions, Dr. Carol Talbot told stunning stories of how God enabled her to serve Him as a missionary, a prisoner of war, and the wife of Louis Talbot.

One fall Mrs. Talbot talked about the impetigo she suffered from when she was a missionary in India. She shared how she underwent nine surgeries during the 17 years she battled this disease, and that battle was almost enough to cause her to give up her missions effort. But there was one thing that kept her from packing her bags and returning home. Every time she wanted to quit, God would bring to her mind a verse she had memorized. She would dismiss it—only to have another one rush in to take its place. She would dismiss that one, too. But again, God would send another one, and another, and another. Because she had memorized too many verses, she said, she was unable to give up her missionary service. In her final analysis, she shared, "God was using my disease to turn me from a pygmy into a giant."

Memorized Scripture can indeed turn us pygmies-in-the-faith into giants! When we love God with our mind and commit His Word to memory, He uses those pieces of Scripture as instruments for our growth in Him. When we store His Word in our mind, God draws from what we know and uses just the truth we need...at just the time we need it...and in just the way we need it!

That, my friend, is what happened to me that morning as I walked and routinely reviewed and recited just one of God's sharp instruments—Romans 11:33.

An Acceptance

But the use of this powerful scripture was in no way done! Through the years, God has used the lessons that Romans 11:33 teaches about Him to help me live out each day for Him with an acceptance of His dealings in my life. This single verse has taught me how to accept the unacceptable. The following principles, drawn from the application of this single verse, give me a lens through which to look at everything that happens to me. I offer them to you as well.

1. *I don't have to understand everything*—What

freedom this acceptance brings! Imagine, no more digging or dogged determination to get to the bottom of an issue.

2. *I don't need to understand everything*—What release this attitude brings! Why? Because it's an attitude that acknowledges that God is in control.

3. *I can't understand everything*—I am finite and limited, but God—who knows all and understands all—is infinite and limitless.

4. *Why ask "Why?"*—The man Job in the Old Testament never asked why when he was suffering. He worshiped instead. Notice very carefully what carried Job through his ordeal. Unlike the stance of the stoic (grin and bear it...or at least, grit your teeth and endure it), Job grabbed on to facts about God. Facts like—God is...

   ...too kind to do anything cruel,

   ...too wise to make a mistake,

   ...too deep to explain Himself.

   Believing these facts about God should erase all why's. We are to stop asking *Why?* and start looking at *Who* stands behind the scene. It is God in His absolute sovereignty! This calls us to worship.

5. *It's O.K.*—When we can say this to God about our unexplainable and seemingly unacceptable situations, we experience the rest of faith and the peace of faith.

6. *Let it go*—Pry your grip off your problem, and let it be gone forever. Oh, the freedom you will experience, even without any change, when you accept the unacceptable.

7. *Let God be God*—And what is He? Un-understandable, unsearchable, inscrutable, inexhaustible, unfathomable, and impossible to grasp.

8. *Let go of your right to know*—Stop demanding answers from God. Cease saying to God, "I'm not getting up from prayer until You tell me or show me why this is happening!"

9. *These are God's judgments*—Whatever has happened to you, it is a part of *God's* judgments…and they are "unsearchable." You will never understand or know why, so you must accept the unacceptable.

10. *These are God's ways*—Again, note the emphasis on *God*. Whatever has happened to you, it has to do with *His* ways, and they are "past finding out!" Again, you will never understand or find out, so you must accept the unacceptable.

11. *No vengeance!*—(And please note, that's spelled n-o, not k-n-o-w!) God is the Author and Creator of your situation. He has a plan and a blueprint for your life that includes your situation and any people involved. God says to you, "Never take your own revenge, beloved, but leave room for the wrath of God, for it is written, 'VENGEANCE, IS MINE, I WILL REPAY, says the Lord'" (Romans 12:19).

12. *It's not them, it's Him!*—One person does not have the power to limit, alter, or change your life. People are only God's instruments, and He uses them to conform you to the image of His dear Son.

For eight years, I wasted time and emotional energy on a situation that was causing me real distress. But it was a situation God knew all about—and had allowed. Those years were rocky and miserable because I didn't understand that the problem was evidence of God's unsearchable wisdom and knowledge, evidence of His unfathomable judgments and ways.

And today? I still don't understand the reasons why my ongoing problem occurred. But guess what? It no longer matters! You see, now I am free! I can accept that God's ways aren't my ways, and I don't need to understand.

And there's more! Finally, because of all God has taught me through Romans 11:33, I am also determined never to waste my time or emotional energy like that again (and, praise Him, I don't think I have!). Instead, I am intent on remembering that God's judgments and ways are not like mine. I want to defer to His wisdom and knowledge. I want to say, along with Mary, "Behold the maidservant of the Lord! Let it be to me according to your word" (Luke 1:38). I want to accept the unacceptable.

Loving God...Even More

What greater way is there to show our love for God than to fully accept His will and His ways in our lives? Than to trust Him fully and completely...even in the dark? Than to accept the unacceptable? And I think you'll agree that this ability to accept His hand in our lives comes more easily when we seek to love Him with all our mind.

It is my prayer that you will want to give God's Word a more prominent place in your thinking by memorizing it, meditating on it, studying it, believing it, and obeying it, thereby drawing closer to the God who loves you and allowing Him to release His power in your life as you serve and follow Him.

A *Prayer of Adoration*

> Oh, the depth of the riches both of Your wisdom and knowledge, O God! How unsearchable are Your judgments and Your ways are past finding out. Your greatness cannot be imagined. You are greater than all language, and no words can express your majesty. You are above all, outside of all, and beyond all I can even imagine. You are without limits. When I speak of You I cannot refer to amount or size or weight, for You are beyond measure. You are not less or more, large or small. You are simply God, the infinite One. A human mind has no capacity to comprehend You. What I can do is praise, adore, and worship You.
>
> —Robert Savage

Still Changing and Growing . . .

Grow in the grace and knowledge
of our Lord and Savior Jesus
Christ. To Him be the glory both
now and forever. Amen.

2 Peter 3:18

Do you ever stop to think about what was happening in your life ten years ago? What was happening then to cause you to grow as a Christian and in your trust in God? What follows is how God used one of those unexplainable, un-understandable events to ensure that I still loved Him and leaned on Him!

"I SURVIVED THE 6.8 NORTHRIDGE EARTHQUAKE!" That's what the Los Angeles sweatshirts heralded. But I don't need that kind of reminder. January 17, 1994, is a morning I will never forget....

Knowing that the week would be busy, I set the alarm to get up early—four in the morning. But this particular day I indulged in 20 extra minutes of rest. I was tempted to sleep in even more because Jim was gone, but I got up and made my way downstairs. I dropped my robe and slippers on a dining room chair and went into the kitchen to fill my teapot and boil water.

The first thing I saw in the kitchen was a stack of newspapers sitting on the counter, ready for the weekly trash pickup later that morning. For some reason, I decided to put them into our recycling bin before I filled the teakettle and got the water boiling. Gathering the papers, I walked toward the entryway door. As I reached for the doorknob, I was suddenly thrown against the wall. I looked up at the entryway light above me, which was swinging wildly...before it suddenly went dark. The electricity was out within a split second of the ground's first jolt.

"It's an earthquake!" Plaster fell on my head, and I was overwhelmed by the terrifying roar and rumble of the earth, sounds of splitting boards, collapsing block walls, shattering glass, falling furniture, and the slam of a tidal wave from the backyard pool against the sliding glass door. "This is the BIG one! I have to get out of this house!" Groping in the dark, I finally felt the doorknob in my hand. Now all I had to do was find and unlock the dead bolt. But finding it made no difference. The quake was twisting and contorting the door. I cried, "God, I can't get out!"

Between the thrusts and rolls of the earth, I managed to open the door. I dropped the newspapers and ran barefoot and in my nightshirt out of the house. At the end of our driveway, I fought to remain standing for the remaining eight horrific seconds of the magnitude 6.8 quake. Neighbors flooded out of their homes, and we stood in clusters, literally holding each other up as the giant aftershocks began rumbling through, attacking our homes as well as our nerves.

For two-and-a-half hours in the early-morning darkness, we huddled under blankets and waited in our cars. Behind us, the black sky burned with a sick orange hue. We found out later that 40 mobile homes two miles across the freeway had burned to the ground. Then we heard—and felt—a new sound. Three booming explosions shook our cars as the gas main on our street ignited. Now the sky in front of us burned with the same awful glow we had seen in the distance.

At last, the sun began to rise. I was shaking from the cold, the unending aftershocks, and the adrenaline racing through my body. I was also dreading going back into our home. I couldn't imagine what the inside must be like. It was then that a verse of Scripture came to mind—"This is the day which the Lord hath made; we will rejoice and be glad in it." But how could I rejoice, Lord? How could I be glad for this?

Two hours and 29 minutes after the initial quake, Jim drove into the driveway, returning from his Army Reserve weekend. We entered the house. It was then that God used each of the six scriptures in this book in new ways in my life.

Making a pathway to the kitchen, we saw that part of the ceiling had fallen in and that all of our cupboards were open. The dishwasher and drawers had also flown open. Broken dishes were in the sink and on the floor, the counters, and the stove. I exclaimed, "Jim, what if I had been in the kitchen? I would have been buried, injured, and cut to slivers! What if I had lighted the burner to boil water for my tea? There could have been a fire, an explosion, and our house could have burned to the ground! What if…?"

And Jim—faithful friend, wonderful husband, godly leader, and reader of the manuscript for this book—said, "Liz, it's time to practice what you preach. Remember Philippians 4:8? 'Whatsoever things are true [or real]…think on these things.' Liz, what is true? What is real? You weren't in the kitchen." This reminder was repeated throughout the next several days as we worked our way through our home.

Finally we forced the door to my office open, and when we did so, we saw that it was the site of the greatest destruction. My office! My sanctuary! When my daughter Katherine saw it, she burst into tears, knowing that I sometimes spent up to 18 hours a day in that room. Then it was her turn. She imagined, "Mom, what if…?" I had already beaten her to that thought. "What if I had been in that room? If I had gotten up at four, I would have been sitting on the couch there with my Bible, prayer book, and tea. And I would have been buried, probably killed by the seven-foot wall unit, loaded with books, bookends, and office equipment, that had shattered as it fell on my couch. What if…?"

Again God's Spirit used Philippians 4:8 to remind me to think on what is true or real and to draw closer to Him. I had not been in my office. I was safe. I was alive. God had protected me. That was true. That was real.

In the aftermath of the quake, I found that all I wanted to do was sit in numb fear, waiting for the next aftershock and watching hour after hour of horrifying but mesmerizing news coverage. But through Matthew 6:34, Christ called me to deal with today and not be anxious about tomorrow… or the next aftershock. So I forced myself to make a list of things to do and to start doing them. I focused on the work at hand, not on the fears of the future.

Beyond these fears for my safety, I worried about the financial implications of the damage to our home, how rebuilding would interrupt daily living, and the setbacks that would result in my already too-busy schedule. My list of fears and worries went on and on. But again and again God offered me relief, peace, and hope through Matthew 6:34, where He called me not to worry.

God was also telling me through Philippians 3:13 and 14 to forget what lies behind and reach for what is ahead. The earthquake was over. I needed to address the tasks at hand and press on. I had to quit looking back.

I also had to resist the temptation to ask, "Why, God? What is going on? What are You doing?" God used Romans 8:28 to offer me daily reassurance that He causes all things to work together for good. Yes, the earthquake was destructive and horrible, and the aftermath continues to be horrible, but already I'm seeing God bring some good out of it. How?

We have grown closer to our neighbors as well as our family members. Katherine and Courtney, ages 23 and 24, thought first of us, as we did of them. We wanted to be together, see each other, spend time with one another, and pray together. Jim's mother's home suffered no damage, and she has taken us in, cooked for us, and provided a haven of peace and order. God is working good out of the bad. I am seeing beauty arise from ashes, experiencing joy despite sorrow, and finding reasons to praise despite the heaviness.

And I'm sure that for years we will be discovering how God is working good from this rubble.

And so many of us are dealing with rubble right now. Just last night I encouraged other women with the promise of Jeremiah 29:11 and its meaning to me during the 11 days since the earthquake. God has used this passage to call me to focus on Him and His promise of future good. He has awakened in me, His child, fresh confidence for handling the far-from-ideal present.

And, finally, God is using the precious truth of Romans 11:33 to teach me new lessons about yielding to His wisdom, trusting Him in the dark (both literal and figurative!), submitting to His judgments, resting in His knowledge of all things, and accepting the mysterious, the unexplainable, the unacceptable. Because earthquakes are in God's domain, I am daily learning more about letting God be God.

Yes, I survived the 6.8 Northridge earthquake! And these last 11 days have been quite an experience. I have spent one night sleeping in the car, one night on the floor, and nine nights on the couch, fully clothed with my shoes on and the door open. For five days I had no makeup and wore the same clothes, and I went six days without a shower. For two days we had no electricity and for ten days no gas, no heat, and no water. For ten days, we carried pool water inside to flush the toilet, and I brushed my teeth outside using a pan of water.

But I have also spent those same 11 days placing my faith and trust in God over and over again—rather than in my shaky thoughts and emotions. During these 11 days, I have found myself loving God with all my mind in new and greater ways. I have also seen Him use the six powerful scriptures presented in this book to remind me of His great love for me. And now I extend to you a fresh invitation to discover the riches of God's love for you and of these wonderful promises that He can use to help you handle whatever comes your way. He has certainly used them in my life!

That was ten years ago, and so much more has happened since then: the deaths of all of Jim's and my parents, the marriages of our two daughters, the arrival of six grandchildren, Jim's military activation to the war in Bosnia, several moves, the launching of a writing and speaking ministry by both Jim and me, not to mention being in Manhattan on September 11, 2001...and, last but not least, weathering Hurricane Jeanne this past weekend while speaking in Florida. With each of these events, I have continued to fall back upon the truths of God's Word and to claim again and again these same six promises from God in the trials and tribulations in my life.

I pray that this book and my earthquake story about the application of these six promises from God were helpful to you. As long as we are alive and walking with the Lord, God's Word assures us that God is in control and that, by His grace, we are still changing, growing ever closer to Him in our daily lives.

Notes

Chapter 1—Thinking on the Truth

1. Colorado Health Net, http://www.coloradohealthnet.org/depression/depression_facts.htm, 3/10/99.
2. Carole Mayhall, *From the Heart of a Woman* (Colorado Springs: Navpress, 1977), pp. 27-31; and Jim Downing, *Meditation: The Bible Tells You How* (Colorado Springs: NavPress, 1981).
3. Lorne Sanny, *Memorize the Word* (Chicago: The Moody Bible Institute of Chicago, 1980), 1-800-621-7105.

Chapter 2—Thinking the Truth About...God and His Word

1. Charles Caldwell Ryrie, *The Ryrie Study Bible* (Chicago: Moody Press, 1978), p. 30.

Chapter 3—Thinking the Truth About...Others

1. John C. Pollock, *A Foreign Devil in China: The Story of Dr. L. Nelson Bell, An American Surgeon in China* (Grand Rapids, MI: Zondervan Publishing House, 1971), p. 183.

Chapter 4—Thinking the Truth About...the Future

1. Charles F. Pfeiffer and Everett F. Harrison, eds., *The Wycliffe Bible Commentary* (Chicago: Moody Press, 1990), p. 1330.
2. Both quotes from Elisabeth Elliot, *Let Me Be a Woman* (Wheaton, IL: Tyndale House Publishers, Inc., 1977), p. 42.

Chapter 5—Thinking the Truth About...the Past and the Present

1. John MacArthur, *The MacArthur Study Bible* (Nashville: Word Bibles, 1996), p. 809.

Chapter 6—Taking Every Thought Captive

1. Charles F. Pfeiffer and Everett F. Harrison, eds., *The Wycliffe Bible Commentary* (Chicago: Moody Press, 1973), p. 1330.

Chapter 7—Focusing on Today

1. Gail MacDonald, *High Call, High Privilege* (Wheaton, IL: Tyndale House Publishers, Inc., 1982), pp. 30-34.
2. Ibid.
3. Ibid.
4. Ibid.

Chapter 8—Scaling the Mountain of Today

1. Ray and Anne Ortlund, *The Best Half of Life* (Waco, TX: Word, 1987), p. 24.
2. Ibid., p. 67.
3. Carole Mayhall, *Lord, Teach Me Wisdom* (Colorado Springs: Navpress, 1979), p. 155.
4. H.D.M. Spence and Joseph S. Exell, eds., *The Pulpit Commentary,* vol. 15 (Grand Rapids: Wm. B. Eerdmans Publishing Company, 1978), p. 239.
5. Albert M. Wells, Jr., *Inspiring Quotations, Contemporary & Classical* (Nashville: Thomas Nelson Publishers, 1988), p. 209.

Chapter 10—Living Out of God's Grace

1. Elisabeth Elliot, *Twelve Baskets of Crumbs* (Nashville: Pilar Books for Abingdon, 1976), p. 18.
2. Elisabeth Elliot, *Through Gates of Splendor* (New York: Harper & Brothers Publishers, 1957), p. 196.
3. Ibid.
4. Elliot, *Twelve Baskets of Crumbs*, p. 18.
5. Ibid., pp. 21-22.
6. Ibid., p. 20.
7. Edith Schaeffer, *The Tapestry* (Waco, TX: Word Books, 1981), pp. 613-38.
8. Ibid.
9. Ibid.
10. Ibid.
11. Ibid.
12. Ibid.
13. Schaeffer, *The Tapestry,* pp. 613-38.
14. Ibid.
15. Ibid.
16. Ibid.

Chapter 11—Remembering to Forget

1. Robert Jamieson, A.R. Fausset, David Brown, *Commentary on the Whole Bible* (Grand Rapids, MI: Zondervan Publishing House, 1973), p. 1310.
2. Kenneth S. Wuest, *Wuest's Word Studies from the Greek New Testament,* vol. 2 (Grand Rapids, MI: Wm. B. Eerdmans Publishing Company, 1973), pp. 97-98.
3. William Hendriksen, *New Testament Commentary—Exposition of Philippians* (Grand Rapids, MI: Baker Book House, 1975), p. 173.
4. Wuest, *Wuest's Word Studies*, vol. 2, pp. 97-98.
5. F.B. Meyer, *Devotional Commentary on Philippians* (Grand Rapids, MI: Kregel Publications, 1979), pp. 183-84.
6. E.M. Blaiklock, *The Acts of the Apostles, An Historical Commentary* (Grand Rapids, MI: Wm. B. Eerdmans Publishing Company, 1976), p. 79.
7. William Barclay, *The Acts of the Apostles,* rev. ed. (Philadelphia: The Westminster Press, 1976), p. 64.
8. Corrie ten Boom, *Tramp for the Lord* (Fort Washington, PA: Christian Literature Crusade and Old Tappan, NJ: Fleming H. Revell Company, 1974), p. 55.

Chapter 12—Finding the Gold

1. Norman Grubb, *C.T. Studd* (Grand Rapids, MI: Zondervan Publishing House, 1946), pp. 50-69.
2. Charles R. Swindoll, *Growing Strong Through the Seasons of Life* (Portland, OR: Multnomah Press, 1983), pp. 315-16.
3. H.D.M. Spence and Joseph S. Exell, eds., *The Pulpit Commentary,* vol. 20 (Grand Rapids, MI: Wm. B. Eerdmans Publishing Company, 1978), pp. 131, 138.
4. William Barclay, *The Letters to the Philippians, Colossians, and Thessalonians,* rev. ed. (Philadelphia: The Westminster Press, 1975), p. 66.
5. Helen Roseveare, *He Gave Us a Valley* (Downers Grove, IL: InterVarsity Press, 1976).
6. Elisabeth Elliot, *Through Gates of Splendor* (New York: Harper & Brothers Publishers, 1957).
7. Corrie ten Boom, *Tramp for the Lord* (Fort Washington, PA: Christian Literature Crusade and Old Tappan, NJ: Fleming H. Revell Company, 1974).

Chapter 13—Going On and On and On

1. William Barclay, *The Letters to the Philippians, Colossians, and Thessalonians,* rev. ed. (Philadelphia: The Westminster Press, 1975), p. 66.

Chapter 15—Keep On Keeping On

1. H.D.M. Spence and Joseph S. Exell, eds., *The Pulpit Commentary,* vol. 20 (Grand Rapids, MI: Wm. B. Eerdmans Publishing Company, 1978), p. 152.
2. Ralph P. Martin, *Tyndale New Testament Commentaries, The Epistle of Paul to the Philippians* (Grand Rapids, MI: Wm. B. Eerdmans Publishing Company, 1976), pp. 152-54.
3. As cited in Carole Mayhall, *Lord of My Rocking Boat* (Colorado Springs: NavPress, 1983), pp. 41-42.
4. As cited in Ray and Anne Ortlund, *The Best Half of Life* (Waco, TX: Word Books, 1987), p. 44.
5. Spence and Exell, eds., *Pulpit Commentary,* vol. 20, pp. 151-52.

Chapter 16—Pressing Toward God's Purpose

1. Pamela Rosewell, *The Five Silent Years of Corrie ten Boom* (Grand Rapids, MI: Zondervan Publishing House, 1986).
2. Shirley Price, *God's Plan for the Wife and Mother* (22422 Kathryn Ave., Torrance, CA 90505, 1976).
3. Cathy Guisewite, *Cathy* comic strip, *L.A. Times,* 1992.

Chapter 17—Trusting the Lord

1. Don Baker, *Pain's Hidden Purpose* (Portland, OR: Multnomah Press, 1983), p. 69.
2. H.D.M. Spence and Joseph S. Exell, eds., *The Pulpit Commentary,* vol. 18 (Grand Rapids, MI: Wm. B. Eerdmans Publishing Company, 1977), p. 212.
3. Robert Jamieson, A.R. Fausset, and David Brown, *Commentary on the Whole Bible* (Grand Rapids, MI: Zondervan Publishing House, 1973), p. 1163.

Chapter 18—Knowing God's Promise

1. John F. MacArthur, *The MacArthur New Testament Commentary, Romans 1-8* (Chicago: Moody Press, 1991), p. 473.
2. Ibid.
3. Dwight L. Moody, *Notes from My Bible and Thoughts from My Library* (Grand Rapids, MI: Baker Book House, 1979), p. 256.

4. Kenneth S. Wuest, *Wuest's Word Studies from the Greek New Testament,* vol. 1 (Grand Rapids, MI: Wm. B. Eerdmans Publishing Company, 1974), p. 143, emphasis added.

Chapter 19—Becoming Faith Oriented

1. Ney Bailey, *Faith Is Not a Feeling* (San Bernardino, CA: Here's Life Publishers, Inc., 1978), pp. 1-5.
2. Charles R. Swindoll, *Joseph: From Pit to Pinnacle,* Bible Study Guide (Fullerton, CA: Insight for Living, 1982), p. i.
3. *Life Application Bible—The Living Bible* (Wheaton, IL: Tyndale House Publishers, Inc., and Youth for Christ/USA, 1988), p. 1587.

Chapter 20—Navigating the Maze of Life

1. Alan Redpath, *Victorious Christian Living* (Old Tappan, NJ: Fleming H. Revell, 1951), p. 166.
2. M.R. DeHaan and Henry G. Bosch, *Bread for Each Day* (Grand Rapids, MI: Zondervan Publishing House, 1962), June 23.

Chapter 21—Enduring Difficult Times

1. Irving L. Jensen, *Everyman's Bible Commentary, Jeremiah* (Chicago: Moody Press, 1966), p. 83.
2. Mrs. Charles E. Cowman, *Streams in the Desert,* vol. 2 (Grand Rapids, MI: Zondervan Publishing House, 1966), p. 368.

Chapter 22—Bearing Fruit During Difficult Times

1. John W. Cowart, *People Whose Faith Got Them into Trouble* (Downers Grove, IL: InterVarsity Press, 1990), pp. 76-77.
2. Ibid., pp. 73, 76.
3. Norman Grubb, *C.T. Studd* (Grand Rapids, MI: Zondervan Publishing House, 1946), p. 161.
4. Cowart, *People Whose Faith Got Them into Trouble,* p. 112.
5. Ibid., pp. 111-12.
6. Ibid., p. 113.
7. *Life Application Bible* (Wheaton, IL: Tyndale House Publishers, 1988), p. 1089.
8. Curtis Vaughan, *The Old Testament Books of Poetry from 26 Translations* (Grand Rapids, MI: Zondervan Bible Publishers, 1973), p. 220.
9. The Septuagint, the Greek translation of the Old Testament.
10. E.M. Blaiklock, *Psalms for Living,* vol. 1 (Philadelphia and New York: A.J. Holman, a division of J.B. Lippincott Co., 1977), p. 94.

Chapter 23—Becoming God's Masterpiece

1. Edith Schaeffer, *What Is a Family?* (Old Tappan, NJ: Fleming H. Revell Company, 1975), pp. 183-84.

Chapter 24—Living Out God's Promise

1. H.D.M. Spence and Joseph S. Exell, eds., *The Pulpit Commentary,* vol. 11 (Grand Rapids, MI: Wm. B. Eerdmans Publishing Company, 1978), p. 587.

Chapter 25—Responding to Life's Turning Points

1. C.C. Carlson, *Corrie ten Boom: Her Life, Her Faith* (Old Tappan, NJ: F.H. Revell Co., 1983), p. 83.
2. Harold D. Foos, *James: Faith in Practice* (Chicago: Moody Correspondence School, 1984), p. 29.
3. James M. Freeman, *Manners and Customs of the Bible* (Plainfield, NJ: Logos International, 1972), p. 231.
4. Charles Caldwell Ryrie, *The Ryrie Study Bible* (Chicago: Moody Press, 1978), p. 1544.
5. Gien Karssen, *Her Name Is Woman* (Colorado Springs: NavPress, 1975), p. 131.
6. Curtis Vaughan, *The New Testament from 26 Translations* (Grand Rapids, MI: Zondervan Publishing House, 1967), p. 215.

Chapter 26—Majoring on the Minors

1. A.W. Tozer, *The Knowledge of the Holy* (New York: Harper & Row Publishers, 1961), p. 10.

Chapter 27—Trusting God in the Dark

1. A.W. Tozer, *The Knowledge of the Holy* (New York: Harper & Row Publishers, 1961), p. 66.
2. Ibid., p. 68.
3. Oswald Chambers, *He Shall Glorify Me* (Fort Washington, PA: Christian Literature Crusade, 1946), p. 52.
4. Robert Jamieson, A.R. Fausset, and David Brown, *Commentary on the Whole Bible* (Grand Rapids, MI: Zondervan Publishing Company, 1977), p. 1173.
5. Charles F. Pfeiffer and Everett F. Harrison, eds., *The Wycliffe Bible Commentary* (Chicago: Moody Press, 1973), p. 1219.

About the Author

Elizabeth George is a bestselling author who has nearly 4 million books in print. She's a popular speaker at Christian women's events. Her passion is to teach the Bible in a way that changes women's lives. For information about Elizabeth's books or speaking ministry, to sign up for her mailings, or to share how God has used this book in your life, please write Elizabeth at:

Elizabeth George
PO Box 2879
Belfair, WA 98528

Toll-free fax/phone:
1-800-542-4611

Website:
www.ElizabethGeorge.com

A Woman After God's Own Heart® Study Series

Bible Studies for Busy Women

God wrote the Bible to change hearts and lives. Every study in this series is written with that in mind—and is especially focused on helping Christian women know how God desires for them to live."

—Elizabeth George

Sharing wisdom gleaned from more than 20 years as a women's Bible study teacher, Elizabeth has prepared insightful lessons that can be completed in 15 to 20 minutes per day. Each lesson includes thought-provoking questions, insights, Bible-study tips, instructions for leading a discussion group and a "heart response" section to make the Bible passage more personal.

HARVEST HOUSE PUBLISHERS
EUGENE, OREGON 97402
www.harvesthousepublishers.com

Powerful Promises for Every Woman

by Elizabeth George

Do you desire greater strength for today and help for all your tomorrows? Discover 12 life-changing promises from God's Word that can carry you through every day and every season of life...promises that truly refresh and encourage, bringing purpose and hope in the midst of life's frantic pace. Even in your seemingly impossible situations, you can know that God's resources are available to you through His promises!

Join Elizabeth George on a powerful journey through Psalm 23 and become a woman whose daily life is energized by God's enabling promises.

For deeper personal or group study—
Powerful Promises for Every Woman
Growth and Study Guide.

A Mom After God's Own Heart

by Elizabeth George

Catch God's Heart for Your Children

You want to raise children who are happy and successful, and who follow after God. But how do you do that in this day of hectic schedules? With biblical wisdom and plenty of encouragement, Elizabeth George offers time-proven ideas and valuable suggestions to help you nurture children of all ages in the Lord. You'll discover…

* Easy-to-implement principles that make parenting enjoyable and effective
* Specific ways you can teach your children that God loves and cares for them
* "Little Choices" you can put into practice immediately to make a big impact
* Special parenting insights and strategies from a Christian dad

Help your children experience God's love, God's blessings, and God's provisions.

For more in-depth and personal or group study—
A Mom After God's Own Heart Growth and Study Guide.

Books by Elizabeth George

- Beautiful in God's Eyes
- Life Management for Busy Women
- Loving God with All Your Mind
- A Mom After God's Own Heart
- Powerful Promises for Every Woman
- The Remarkable Women of the Bible
- Small Changes for a Better Life
- A Wife After God's Own Heart
- A Woman After God's Own Heart®
- A Woman After God's Own Heart® Deluxe Edition
- A Woman After God's Own Heart® Collection
- A Woman's Call to Prayer
- A Woman's High Calling
- A Woman's Walk with God
- A Young Woman After God's Own Heart
- A Young Woman's Call to Prayer
- A Young Woman's Walk with God

Children's Books

- God's Wisdom for Little Girls
- A Little Girl After God's Own Heart

Study Guides

- Beautiful in God's Eyes Growth & Study Guide
- Life Management for Busy Women Growth & Study Guide
- Loving God with All Your Mind Growth & Study Guide
- A Mom After God's Own Heart Growth & Study Guide
- The Remarkable Women of the Bible Growth & Study Guide
- Small Changes for a Better Life Growth & Study Guide
- A Wife After God's Own Heart Growth & Study Guide
- A Woman After God's Own Heart® Growth & Study Guide
- A Woman's Call to Prayer Growth & Study Guide
- A Woman's High Calling Growth & Study Guide
- A Woman's Walk with God Growth & Study Guide

Books by Jim & Elizabeth George

- God Loves His Precious Children
- God's Wisdom for Little Boys

Books by Jim George

- The Bare Bones Bible Handbook
- God's Man of Influence
- A Husband After God's Own Heart
- A Man After God's Own Heart
- The Remarkable Prayers of the Bible
- The Remarkable Prayers of the Bible Growth & Study Guide
- What God Wants to Do for You
- A Young Man After God's Own Heart